William Smith O'Brien
and His Irish Revolutionary Companions
in Penal Exile

WILLIAM SMITH O'BRIEN
and His Irish Revolutionary Companions
in Penal Exile

Blanche M. Touhill

University of Missouri Press
Columbia & London, 1981

Library of Congress Cataloging in Publication Data

Touhill, Blanche M. (Blanche Marie), 1931–
    William Smith O'Brien and his Irish
revolutionary companions in penal exile.
        Bibliography: p. 259
        Includes index.
        1. O'Brien, William Smith, 1803–1864.
    2. Ireland—History—Rising of 1848. 3. Re-
    volutionists—Ireland—Biography. 4. Tasmania
    —Exiles—Biography. I. Title.
DA952.022T68   941.5081′092′4   81–1899
ISBN 0–8262–0339–6   AACR2

All photographs courtesy the
National Library of Ireland, Dublin.

Contents

To Joe

Preface

William Smith O'Brien was a leading Irish political figure in the nineteenth century. He was the acknowledged leader of the 1848 revolution in Ireland. Yet in the twentieth century he is virtually unknown. Part of O'Brien's problem was that prior to 1848 he was overshadowed by Daniel O'Connell. After 1848 he was linked to the failure of the revolution. Yet during his lifetime he was one of the main Irish leaders, and what he thought and what he did affected Ireland, England, and to a lesser extent America and Australia.

While there has been very little written about O'Brien, the sources are many. Most of my research was done at the National Library of Ireland in Dublin where practically all of O'Brien's journals and letters are deposited, as well as the letters of the other Young Irelanders and the *Nation* newspaper. My thanks go unhesitatingly to the Director of the National Library, Mr. Alfred MacLochlainn. His efficiency and kindness to a foreign scholar are deeply appreciated. I also want to express my appreciation to two of O'Brien's direct descendants, the Reverend Aubrey Gwynn, S. J., and Dr. Brendan O'Brien. Both gentlemen relayed family comments about O'Brien and allowed me access to whatever papers were at their disposal. Both Brendan O'Brien and his wife opened their home to me to read the journals and letters still held in their private collection. Mrs. O'Brien assisted me in copying those materials I needed for my research.

I also want to thank the staff at the London Public Record Office, for it was there that I located and used the Colonial Office records as well as one of the Van Diemen's Land newspapers, the *Launceston Examiner*. The British Museum furnished the Palmerston Papers. The Belfast Public Record Office provided John Martin's diary.

In the United States my thanks are extended to the Library of Congress. The Manuscript Division holds the Daniel Webster Papers, and the main reading room contains William Denison's important record of the period published under the title *Varieties of Vice-Regal Life*. My thanks are also extended to the library of the Catholic University of America, which holds Thomas F. Meagher's American newspaper, the *Irish News*, and the New York City Public Library, which holds John Mitchel's *Citizen*.

The librarians of the University of Missouri–St. Louis obtained the additional books and newspapers that I needed primarily by means of interlibrary loan.

I would also like to thank Ms. Fidelma McGuire, who assisted me on two separate occasions when I was researching in the National Library of Ireland. In St. Louis my thanks are extended to Mrs. Carol Norris, who helped me prepare O'Brien's journal for the research effort that was before me.

And finally I would like to thank the University of Missouri for granting me both research monies and a sabbatical leave to write this monograph.

The reader should be aware that nineteenth-century spellings vary. In addition I took two liberties. The first was in regard to Thomas Meagher, who was known throughout his Van Diemen's Land period as O'Meagher. I refer to him by his Irish and later his American name, Meagher. Secondly, I refer to Sir William Denison as Governor Denison when his real title was either Lord Lieutenant or Lieutenant Governor.

B. M. T.
St. Louis, Mo.
April 1981

Introduction

This book is the historical account of seven Irishmen caught up in the Irish revolutionary struggle of 1848, convicted of either urging revolution or taking part in revolution, and sent into penal exile as punishment for that involvement. The historical account deals primarily with their years in exile in the penal colony of Van Diemen's Land. All of the exiles, except William Smith O'Brien, attempted to start a new life in Van Diemen's Land. O'Brien, however, determined to fight the oblivion into which the British officials had sent him and his companions. Slowly the exiles developed a sympathetic public opinion in Van Diemen's Land, Australia, the United States, Ireland, and England favorable to their release. Throughout the period of the exile O'Brien and his companions maintained their devotion to Irish nationalism. That devotion prolonged their exile and shaped their future lives.

The exiles were an interesting group of men both in personality and in background. John Mitchel, Thomas Meagher, and Patrick O'Donoghue were the more controversial members of the group. Mitchel was a radical in politics, as well as a talented and articulate newspaper editor and publisher. He needed a public arena in which to argue and struggle for his radical reforms. His presence in the Irish public arena in 1848 led to his arrest, conviction, and transportation. The lack of such a public arena in Van Diemen's Land made his years in exile appear to him to be years spent in a "trance."

Thomas Meagher did not need a public arena as much as he needed worthwhile projects on which to expend his immense energies. Ireland in the 1840s was filled with such projects, and his father's wealth allowed him the opportunity to make a contribution to the rising tide of Irish nationalism. Meagher was a fine writer, but he was an exceptional speaker, and as Ireland moved toward revolution, Meagher rose to a position of eminence that he held until the revolution collapsed. Meagher was the youngest and most vigorous of the exiles, and even in Van Diemen's Land he sought worthwhile projects on which to expend his energies.

Patrick O'Donoghue's background, taken by itself, would have made him a minor character. Before the revolution, he had been a clerk in a solicitor's office in Dublin. But his personality made him larger than life. He was outspoken and uncontrollable. He was mercurial. He loved his friends and was bitter toward his enemies. He hated England and was swept into revolution by his love of Ireland. In exile O'Donoghue's ability to write would be, simultaneously, his greatest asset and the cause of his ultimate destruction.

Three of the other exiles, John Martin, Kevin O'Doherty, and Terence McManus, were more low-key. Martin was a quiet, retiring individual who was, underneath his mild manner, an ardent reformer and an advocate of repealing the parliamentary union between Ireland and Great Britain. He owned land in Ireland and had a small inheritance that, prior to the revolution, allowed him to travel and to write. His lifelong friendship with John Mitchel led him for a brief period of time to publish a newspaper and hence end up as a transported felon. While in exile Martin continued his friendship with Mitchel and lived with him and his family. That friendship allowed Martin to continue his personal hermitlike ways in the midst of an active family circle.

Kevin O'Doherty was not really a revolutionary in the same sense as his fellow exiles. He was a medical student who worked among the starving poor during the Irish famine. He was so repulsed by the conditions under which he worked that he abandoned his medical studies and began publishing a newspaper expressing his advocacy of Irish self-government. Like Martin, his publishing activities led to his transportation. While in exile, he turned back to his original professional interest, medicine.

Terence McManus was a businessman who believed firmly in Ireland's right to govern herself. As a young man, McManus had moved to Liverpool, England, where he established himself in a mercantile business and met with relative success. As Ireland moved toward revolution, McManus returned to lend his assistance in the forthcoming struggle. When the struggle ended McManus was one of the leaders who fell into the hands of the Irish government. McManus's main attribute was his sociability. Everyone liked him. In addition, McManus was a pragmatist. He took every day as it came and tried to make the most of it. While in exile he turned his attention to making a living and enjoying life.

The recognized leader of the exiles was William Smith O'Brien. He had both the personality and background necessary to make him the leader. O'Brien was a wealthy and intelligent Irish aristocrat who had spent years as a parliamentarian at Westminster. During the 1840s he joined the Loyal National Repeal Association and eventually became the leader of the Young Ireland party. The Young Irelanders were a small group of Irish intellectuals who were inspired by the outbreak of revolution in France in 1848 and demoralized by O'Connell's compromise of the repeal issue and the British ministry's handling of the Irish famine (1845–1848) to take Ireland into revolution in 1848. The revolution failed.

A large part of the responsibility for the failure of the '48 revolution belonged to O'Brien. He misjudged the readiness of the Irish people to go to the barricades. In addition, his views of how the revolution should be fought belonged to a more idealistic age. O'Brien thought revolution could only be successful and lasting if the people were willing to support it. O'Brien relied on the courage, conviction, and self-respect of individual Irishmen to take an active part in the revolution. He hoped to avoid bloodshed by demonstrating the will of the Irish nation. He thought the English would not contest the revolutionary demands for repeal once they recognized that a united Ireland was speaking with one voice. When O'Brien realized the Irish people were not willing to come to the barricades and stand with him in an united front against the English, he brought the revolution to an abrupt end. He wanted to avoid needless bloodshed.

O'Brien's revolutionary leadership was disappointing to many Irishmen because they did not believe it was possible for the Irish people to declare themselves openly for revolution. O'Brien's main critics belonged to an age of realism, not idealism, an age when revolution was conspired and carried out by a small group of determined men and women who spoke for "the people." Those realistic men and women were revolutionaries who would not hesitate to use any means in order to attain their goals. They believed that O'Brien should not have begun the revolution until the plans were complete and once having started it should have continued the fight to the death.

While O'Brien's Irish critics faulted his lack of common sense and his misconceptions of the real attitudes of the Irish people, his English critics announced that he was either insane or a fool. Those English critics were led by the editors of the *London Times*. While the editors announced they could not take O'Brien's leadership of the revolution seriously, they recognized that O'Brien was dedicated to Irish self-government and sincere enough to have his actions reflect his deeds. Such a man was a threat to the maintenance of the Anglo-Irish connection. The British officials came to the same conclusion. While the editors of the *Times* attempted to end O'Brien's threat to union by sentencing him to death by ridicule, the British officials devised their own form of execution. It was arranged that O'Brien would spend the rest of his days in a penal colony as a transported felon. The ministers softened the exile by issuing orders that would allow O'Brien to live as a gentleman, not a convict. Hence O'Brien had been sentenced to "die" from "gentlemanly oblivion." O'Brien's companions were to receive similar treatment.

The importance of the historical account of William Smith O'Brien and his Irish revolutionary companions in penal exile is that O'Brien successfully defeated the attempts of the editors of the *Times* and the British officials to execute him. O'Brien, a direct descendant of Irish kings, believed he had an obligation to serve the Irish people as best he could, wherever he was. As a young man he had attempted to serve the Irish people as a member of parliament. In his middle years he attempted to serve them as member of the Repeal Association and a revolutionary.

In 1849 he carried his obligation to the Irish people with him into exile and looked forward to returning to Ireland in order to continue his role as an Irish leader. O'Brien was anxious to have another opportunity to influence Irish public opinion and thus continue to educate the Irish about the merits of self-government.

Actually, O'Brien proved to be much more of a success as an exile than as a revolutionary. Between 1849 and 1854, O'Brien found himself pitted against a British ministry that had devised an immensely clever policy of "gentlemanly oblivion"; the local government officials in the penal colony, Van Diemen's Land, who considered O'Brien and his companions to be convicts, not gentlemen; and the continued ridicule of the *London Times*. But O'Brien fought back. Several of his personal characteristics helped him in his struggle to obtain a pardon. He had immense pride. He was an unusually stubborn man. He had the intellectual conviction that he was right. He had the emotional dedication to the Irish people that the situation demanded. He had a sense of time and history that gave him the perspective necessary to avoid despair. He understood the English system. O'Brien's major personality weakness, the aloof and somewhat cold mannerisms that he displayed to those he did not know personally, assisted him in exile. In exile, he did not need love, but respect, and his aloofness helped him attain that goal. Slowly, O'Brien found allies among the antitransportation citizenry in Van Diemen's Land and mainland Australia, among Irish Americans and their American political leaders, among his fellow Irishmen, and eventually among members of the British ministry, Westminster, and even the editorial staff of the *London Times*.

In 1854, O'Brien and several of his companions received conditional pardons, and in 1856, those same men received full pardons. But, in addition, O'Brien's image had changed. He was no longer just the leader of the Young Ireland party. He returned from exile as the acknowledged father of the Irish people; and the press of Van Diemen's Land, America, Ireland, and England hailed him as a man of honor who deserved the respect of all. What he accomplished sixteen thousand miles from Ireland was "no mean trick."

CHAPTER 1

Revolution, Conviction, and Transportation

Revolution and Conviction

Between 1842 and 1848 political leaders interested in self-government for Ireland had been working to convince the Irish people to demand the restoration of the Irish Parliament by repeal of the Act of Union, under which Ireland was ruled by the Parliament in England. The Repeal movement was initially led by Daniel O'Connell. Between 1842 and 1846 two groups developed within the repeal organization, Old Ireland and Young Ireland. Slowly the differences between. the two groups became more pronounced. O'Connell's outspoken devotion to the monarch, his abhorrence of the idea of an Irish republic, his seeming willingness to compromise repeal in order to obtain concessions, such as patronage appointments for Irish leaders, as well as good government for Ireland, separated him from the younger men who began to look toward William Smith O'Brien for leadership.

The break came in 1846. In that year O'Connell made the public rejection of physical force a necessary prerequisite to being a member of the Loyal National Repeal Association. However, O'Brien and the Young Irelanders could not compromise their beliefs, and they were forced to secede from the Repeal Association. In 1847 O'Connell died. With his death went "the Irish leader" and the power of the leader's organization, since no heir had been designated. Repeal by peaceful means was no longer a viable lever by which the Irish could obtain concessions from the English. Yet the Young Irelanders were still a force, minor perhaps, but a force. The death and destruction caused by the Great Potato Famine between 1845 and 1848 and the success of the French Revolution in 1848 encouraged many of those younger men to seriously consider revolution as a way of obtaining repeal. There was no doubt that by the spring of 1848 widespread disaffection with English legislative power in Ireland was evident.[1]

Those developments in Ireland were not unknown in England. Many Englishmen were convinced that the Young Irelanders were moving the Irish people toward revolution as the means of obtaining a free Irish Parliament. The immediate question was whether or not the British leaders would be able to enact legislation that would enable them to rid

1

Ireland of those disaffected Irish leaders before the country could be organized and made ready for a revolutionary struggle.

By April 1848, a member of Parliament, Viscount Jocelyn, correctly
concluded that the current treason law was inadequate for the occasion.
In order to be convicted of treason under that law, a man had to commit
an overt act, not merely conspire or contrive to commit one. Viscount
Jocelyn wanted legislation that would allow the British government to
act against individuals who had not yet committed the overt act.[2]

In addition, the sentence imposed by the treason law upon a man
convicted under it was widely considered too harsh for a people as civi-
lized as those of Victorian England. The punishment for high treason
called for the guilty party "to be drawn on a hurdle to the place of execution, to be there hanged by the neck, and afterwards the head to be
struck from the body, and the body itself to be divided into four quarters,
to be disposed of as Her Majesty might think fit."[3] Not only were public
sensibilities in Victorian England moving the people away from those
kinds of proceedings, but there was even a movement toward the aboli-
tion of capital punishment altogether.

Lord Campbell, a former Irish chancellor, was prodded by Viscount
Jocelyn's remarks. He suggested to the parliamentarians at Westminster
that a new statutory offense of treason-felony be enacted by which any
individual who engaged in compassing or designing to wage war against
the monarch could be found to be a felon and punished by transportation
to a penal colony. The treason-felony statute advocated by Lord Campbell also gave government officials power to act against any individual
who promoted treason "by open and advised speaking." The British parliamentarians at Westminster embodied the treason-felony statute in the
crown-and-government-protection bill, which passed in late April.[4]

Four Irish leaders were brought to trial under the treason-felony
statute, and three of them were eventually convicted. All four of the
men were Young Irelanders. The Young Ireland party was a loose collection of a small group of Irishmen, mostly intellectuals, who generally
held several basic principles in common. They believed in "Ireland for
the Irish," wanted the repeal, and were willing to accept a republican
form of government. In 1846 the sanctioning of the use of physical force
to obtain Irish self-government had been more theoretical than practical, but by 1848 the practical value of revolution was acknowledged. Yet,
except for the physical-force commitment, most of the Young Irelanders
were moderates, interested in keeping the political aspects of Irish affairs
separate from the religious aspects, anxious to develop a party that included members from all levels of Irish society, and, while willing to
consider certain economic reforms, they were opposed to upsetting the
right to own private property.

But there were a few radicals among the Young Irelanders. John

Mitchel was one of the extremists. Mitchel was originally from northern Ireland and was the son of a Unitarian clergyman. His father had hoped that he would prepare himself for the ministry, but Michel thought otherwise. After receiving an A.B. degree, the young Mitchell completed an apprenticeship to a solicitor. He then turned to writing. His book entitled *The Life of Aodh or Hugh O'Neill* was well received by Irish nationalists, and Charles Gavan Duffy, the owner of the *Nation* newspaper, which was the organ of the Irish national movement, hired Mitchel to be the editor of his paper. Eventually, Mitchel broke with Duffy, primarily over the editorial policy that the *Nation* was following. Mitchel wanted to use the columns of the *Nation* as a way to instruct its readers on military maneuvers, instructions that Mitchel felt were necessary to prepare the Irish for the forthcoming revolution. In addition, Mitchel urged the Irish not to pay the Poor Rate, as a way of calling attention to Irish land problems and hence of effecting reform.[5] Mitchel's editorial position forced him to leave the *Nation*, and he became editor and proprietor of a Dublin newspaper, the *United Irishman*. With his own paper Mitchel had the freedom to do what he wanted; namely, stir the people up to accept the idea of revolution. The editors of the *London Times* later recalled Mitchel's policy. In the *United Irishman*, "Every Saturday [he] addressed a letter to the Lord-Lieutenant with this heading, 'To the Earl

John Mitchel

of Clarendon, Her Majesty's Executioner-General and Butcher-General of Ireland.' "[6] Mitchel advised the people on how the forthcoming revolution should be fought. He advocated that any means to attain the separation of England and Ireland could be used from direct physical encounters by armed men to indirect guerrilla action. Regarding the guerrilla action he "described how street-fighting should be conducted, how and where the barricades were to be erected, how the women were to be taught to throw vitriol from the windows on the Queen's troops, and to fling broken bottles before the cavalry, how the walls of houses were to be perforated for sharpshooters, and so on."[7] Mitchel did not look to the propertied class of Ireland for voluntary support of his revolutionary ideas. He hoped to get them with him by threats and intimidation, advocating that if they did not support the revolution, "they must fall." He believed the revolution would basically be supported by "the men of no property."[8] Mitchel had another agenda in addition to establishing an Irish republic. He wanted to root out all English institutions in Ireland. As Mitchel detailed later, "I would clear our country of the English, at the price of levelling all that now stands there, at the price of leaving the surviving inhabitants as bare of all social & political orders &c garniture as were the men of Deucalion when they ceased to be stones."[9] Mitchel's political position was representative of the extreme left of the Young Irelanders. Thomas Devin Reilly was Mitchel's closest political ally, and James Finton Lalor had similar views. But most of the remaining Young Irelanders were moderates. The fact that Mitchel never hesitated to express his views made him well known and either sought after or abhorred. In 1848, Mitchel was charged and convicted under the new Treason-Felony Act for writing seditious literature. His trial took place on 26 May 1848, and he was sentenced the next day to fourteen years of transportation. On the evening of 27 May, he found himself on the boat ready to sail to the British penal colony in Bermuda.[10]

Mitchel's conviction in 1848 did not neutralize the disaffection among many of the people in Ireland. On the contrary, the conviction nourished further disaffection as Mitchel became a popular martyr and the personification of the force around which the various disaffected Irish national groups could find common cause. In July 1848, the government again acted to stamp out the seeds of rebellion by arresting, under the auspices of the Treason-Felony Act, three other well-known Irish writers who edited Irish national newspapers. Those men were John Martin of the *Felon*, Kevin Izod O'Doherty of the *Tribune*, and Charles Gavan Duffy of the *Nation*.

Like John Mitchel, John Martin was from the north of Ireland. He had originally entered Trinity College with the expectation of studying medicine, but before he completed the course, his father died leaving to him family responsibilities. In addition, his uncle left him some property.

During the 1830s, Martin busied himself in agricultural activities and travel. His inheritance allowed him to travel extensively both in America and on the Continent. During the 1840s, he joined the repeal movement. Martin had been a dear friend of John Mitchel's for many years. When Mitchel was transported, Martin started the newspaper *Felon* in order to continue Mitchel's work.[11] Martin, however, was quite different from Mitchel. Gavan Duffy compared Martin to the Marquis de Condorcet, writing, "he was a lamb in a passion." Duffy explained that Martin "felt honest wrath at the misgovernment of the country, but it was a wrath which would never explode in action." Martin was not as radical as Mitchel and, in 1848, still held with the doctrine of the late Thomas Davis "that we ought to elevate the whole nation together."[12] Martin had no ill will toward the Irish aristocracy or middle class. He put the blame for the problems of Ireland on the English. He detested English rule in Ireland and advocated violence as a means of getting the English out of Ireland. Only five issues of the *Felon* were published before Martin was arrested and charged under the new Treason-Felony Act with writing seditious literature. He was found guilty and sentenced to ten years of transportation.[13]

During the spring of 1848, Kevin O'Doherty was a medical student in Dublin and had just become engaged to Mary Anne Kelly, well known

John Martin

in Irish literary circles for her nationalistic poetry that was published in the *Nation*. O'Doherty possessed modest financial resources, and, after Mitchel's conviction, he, too, started a newspaper, the *Tribune*. O'Doherty was a young intellectual who was a moderate politically but who had become convinced as a result of his work with the ill and dying during the famine that English legislative rule in Ireland had to cease. He sanctioned revolution as a way of forcing the English out of the country.

As with the *Felon*, the *Tribune* was soon discontinued, and O'Doherty was arrested and charged with writing seditious literature. Two trials failed to bring a conviction, but on the third attempt the government was more successful. O'Doherty was sentenced to ten years of transportation. Mary Anne had no intention of breaking the engagement, telling O'Doherty, "Be patient; I'll wait."[14]

Charles Gavan Duffy was the best known of the three Irish leaders who were arrested in July 1848 and charged under the Treason-Felony Act. In 1842, Duffy had commenced the publication of the *Nation*, and it became an outspoken advocate of Irish nationalism. Initially, Duffy had worked closely with the Repeal Association and its leader, Daniel O'Connell, but O'Connell and Duffy quarreled over numerous problems. Their main differences revolved around Duffy's conviction that O'Connell was too willing to compromise repeal for momentary gains and the fact

Kevin Izod O'Doherty

that Duffy ultimately accepted Ireland's right to revolution. When O'Connell died in 1847, Duffy began to work harder than ever to win the devotion of the Irish people to Young Ireland and the cause of legislative independence. Like O'Doherty and Martin, Duffy expressed the views of the moderate Young Irelanders.

By July 1848, several articles had appeared in the *Nation* justifying violence as a means of obtaining legislative independence. Duffy was promptly arrested, and the *Nation* was temporarily closed. Duffy was never convicted under the Treason-Felony Act, despite five trials, but he was held in prison for more than ten months during the proceedings and received freedom only under bail.[15]

These prosecutions and convictions failed to check the growing wave of discontent and, by the end of July 1848, it was believed in British governmental circles that an Irish rising was being planned for the autumn of 1848. On 21 July, the ministers of the British cabinet decided to utilize direct measures of general restraint; namely, to seek from the British Parliament suspension of the writ of habeas corpus in Ireland until 1 March 1849, and thereafter to cause to be arrested those leaders of the disaffected groups still at large. On 22 July, the British parliamentarians at Westminster moved to suspend the writ as the ministry requested. The members of Parliament evidently shared in the anxieties of the British cabinet.[16]

The suspension of the Habeas Corpus Act forced the hand of the disaffected Irish leaders still at large. The steps taken by Parliament were accompanied by an announcement that membership in a political club was grounds for arrest. The disaffected leaders, therefore, were compelled either to submit to arrest, to leave the country, or to precipitate the rising before they had had time to complete their plans. The dilemma of what to do fell principally upon the most important of the nationalistic leaders in Ireland at that time, William Smith O'Brien.[17]

William Smith O'Brien was not an ordinary revolutionist. He had been a member of the British Parliament for approximately seventeen years, and up until his early forties he was satisfied with British rule in Ireland. O'Brien's background helps to explain his earlier acceptance of British rule and his later commitment to Irish nationalism. O'Brien was a lineal descendant of the eleventh-century Irish king Brian Boru. During the reign of King Henry VIII, the O'Briens surrendered their royal claims and swore allegiance to the Tudors. While the O'Briens did oppose Gen. Henry Irenton, the military leader sent by Oliver Cromwell to subdue Ireland, they eventually accepted Cromwell's rule. O'Brien's father opposed the passage of the Act of Union. By the midnineteenth century, the O'Brien family was firmly attached to the Anglican religion and looked to England not only for political leadership but also for economic and social opportunities.

During the first part of his life, O'Brien followed the family pattern. He was educated in England at Harrow and at Trinity College, Cambridge. He was a member of the Anglican Church. He served his first term in Parliament between 1828 and 1831. He then returned to Parliament in 1835 and remained there until 1848. In his early days as a parliamentarian, he admired Sir Robert Peel, the well-known Tory prime minister. His circle of personal friends among Englishmen was not only a result of his years at school, and his years in Westminster, but also a result of an important marital connection made by his sister, Katherine, who had married into the Malmesbury family.[18] During those early years O'Brien's economic, political, and social future looked bright.

Then in 1843, when O'Brien was forty years old, he turned his back on the Union. He joined the Repeal Association. That was the first decisive step O'Brien took toward nationalism and revolution. By 1843, O'Brien had concluded that only the Irish could legislate for Ireland. He based that decision on a number of observations. Having lived among the English people he concluded that their "spirit . . . is inveterately anti Catholic and that therefore Ireland which is essentially a Catholic Country can never be governed in accordance with the sentiments of the majority of its inhabitants by a Legislature which represents prejudices so adverse to them and to their faith." His years as a parliamentarian at Westminster forced him to ask, "Who has not upon a thousand occasions been compelled to feel that Ireland is governed not with a view to the interest of her own people but with a view of the interest of England?" While at home in Ireland he observed all levels of Irish society, the laborer, artisan, farmer, shopkeeper, professional man, and landlord. He noted that all were "habitually exposed to degradation and ruin." O'Brien concluded that Westminster's concentration on English interests resulted in "continued misrule" in Ireland, and it was thus that he explained the Irish "degradation and ruin" that he saw everywhere.[19]

In seeking a remedy O'Brien began to rely on the "principle of Self-government." In 1843, the repeal movement appeared to O'Brien to be the best way to attain his newly found goals.[20] By joining the Repeal Association, O'Brien was not ready to blindly follow Daniel O'Connell's lead. Like the other Young Irelanders, O'Brien believed in the right of Irishmen to use physical force to protect their rights. Like Duffy, O'Brien was convinced that O'Connell was too willing to compromise repeal.

O'Brien's advocacy of physical force, in principle, did not mean he was ready to start a revolution. He still hoped repeal could be obtained by peaceful means. After the Young Irelanders were forced out of the Repeal Association, they eventually became involved in a new organization similar in goals, but one that would admit advocates of physical force. This organization was called the Irish Confederation.[21] After O'Connell died in 1847, O'Brien and the Young Irelanders attempted to reunite Old Ireland and Young Ireland in a new repeal organization called the League. But many of the Old Irelanders resisted any attempt by Young Ireland to unite the party. Those older men blamed the Young Irelanders "for breaking the heart of the Liberator."[22] Nevertheless, O'Brien continued his efforts to build the League.

But O'Brien suffered from distinct disadvantages when it came to going among the people to build both the Irish Confederation and later the League. O'Brien was never known for possessing a warm open personality that could move and control large groups of people. He was not charismatic. He was not a native Irish speaker. He was not a Catholic. He did not have ties to either the local Catholic clergy or the hierarchy. He was an aristocrat. He was aloof. He was reserved. Years before, Daniel O'Connell had commented on O'Brien's personality weaknesses, concluding that O'Brien was "proud and self-conceited." John Mitchel noted that O'Brien was stubborn to the point of being "intractable."[23]

Yet O'Brien had great strengths. His aristocratic background made him a natural leader, and his knowledge of the British system of government, as well as his personal connections in England, made him valuable to the repeal movement. He made repeal respectable. In addition, he was intelligent, well educated, dedicated to his people's welfare, and prepared to lead. It was widely recognized that he was a man of honor and that once his word was given it was his bond. Finally, it was recognized that he was a moderate and would do what he could to avoid the extreme; particularly the policies of John Mitchel. There was no doubt that he had a following.

In 1847, Peel's Tory government fell. O'Brien hoped the Whigs would react favorably to the Irish demand for repeal, as well as alleviate the suffering caused by the famine that had begun in 1845 and was still raging. During 1847 and 1848, O'Brien became disenchanted with John Russell's measures to relieve the distress of the famine and charged "the British Government with the crime of having willfully allowed our people to perish."[24] His determination to obtain repeal became stronger. Still, he hoped for a peaceful solution.

With the coming of the French Revolution in 1848, O'Brien hoped the liberalizing ideas of the Continent would affect British leaders and lead to the repeal of the Act of Union. He also hoped the liberalizing ideas within Great Britain, such as those articulated by the Chartists, would aid the cause of repeal.[25] O'Brien was wrong. The British leaders moved in a conservative rather than a liberal direction. The passage of the Treason-Felony Act, the arrest and conviction of Mitchel, as well as the arrest of Martin, O'Doherty, and Duffy reflected that conservative swing. Still, O'Brien hesitated to commit himself to the side of revolution; that is, until the suspension of the Habeas Corpus Act. With no constitutional avenue open to obtain redress, O'Brien accepted revolution as the only means by which Ireland could obtain an ameliorization of her condition.[26] At that point he became the leader of the revolution of 1848.

When O'Brien decided to call Ireland to revolution, he thought there was a real chance for success. The famine was just about over, hence "the dependence of Ireland upon foreign Countries for food . . . no longer presented an obstacle to Conflict." O'Brien was also aware that "no class was well affected to the British Government." He believed that the Protestant aristocracy, gentry, and clergy had withheld their support from the repeal movement not because of "attachment to British Rule," but because of fear as to what "should be substituted in its place." Later he wrote, "If these apprehensions could have been allayed by our conduct during the strife I am persuaded that [those Protestants] would willingly have acquiesced in our triumph and have cheerfully Cooperated with us in an endeavour to establish our Institutions upon a National Basis." The middle and lower classes of Protestant Irishmen had already formed their own Protestant Repeal Association, and O'Brien thought they too would acquiesce if the revolutionaries were victorious. O'Brien believed British support in Ireland rested on thirty to forty thousand British soldiers, one-third of whom were Irish. He hoped the mass of Irishmen would stand together against the British troops and thus win the day. O'Brien was also motivated to take to the field because he believed the credibility of the Young Irelanders was at issue. For years the Young Ireland party had talked about "the necessity of preparation for conflict." O'Brien believed "we should have been exposed to ridicule and reproach if we had fled at the moment when all the contingencies which we had contemplated as justifying the use of force were realized."[27] The previous attack on O'Connell by the Young Irelanders for compromising repeal had made their position all the more unyielding. They had always said they would never compromise repeal, and O'Brien believed the moment of truth had come.

The principal problem that faced O'Brien and the small group of men who were determined to precipitate the rising was that their plans and arrangements were far from complete. The revolutionists had no grass-roots organization such as the Repeal Association on which to rely for support. Neither the Irish Confederation nor the League was a flourishing organization. Help was coming from America in the form of money from a group of sympathetic Irish-Americans who began to refer to themselves as the Irish Directory.[28] Meanwhile, the revolutionists in Ireland could only hope to start the rising and trust that the revolution would find root in discontent and spread on the angry fuel of the same discontent. Ireland, however, was recovering from the devastation of the famine, and what effect that devastation would have on the forthcoming revolution was unknown.

O'Brien had hoped to make the town of Kilkenny the springboard of the revolution. From there he would call the people to arms and proclaim the independence of Ireland. O'Brien chose Kilkenny because the city stood on the borders of the three counties most inclined to resort to arms: Tipperary, Wexford, and Waterford. In addition, the nearest railway by which British troops could be sent to challenge the insurgents was separated from the city by a road that could easily be defended.[29]

When O'Brien and his fellow leaders got to Kilkenny they learned that the garrison of British troops stationed there had recently been strengthened, and the leaders were told that it would be necessary to spend a few days mustering men from the nearby rural areas in order to obtain enough men to take the garrison and hence the town. The leaders visited Callan, Carrick, Cashel, Killenaule, Mullinahone, and Ballingarry in an effort to obtain men, but the number of men that joined them varied from day to day and no lasting force could be formed.[30]

The attempt to raise a lasting army engaged the leaders for a week, and, in the end, after a skirmish between the insurgents and the police on 29 July 1848 at Ballingarry, the revolutionary force dissolved. One revolutionist wrote, "The towns bade us try the rural districts; in the rural districts the farmers would not give up their arms, and the labourers had none; the priests opposed us, and the clubs sent about one percent of their number to our aid." The *London Times* reported "the whole affair had broken like a soap bubble."[31]

Once it was clear that the revolution of 1848 had failed, those leaders who could do so left Ireland by whatever means of escape they could find. Richard O'Gorman, John Dillon, Thomas D'Arcy McGee, Thomas Devin Reilly, P. J. Smyth, and Michael Doheny were among those who made their way to safety in America. James Stephens and John O'Mahony fled to France. Four of the principal leaders, however, were not so fortunate. William Smith O'Brien, Thomas F. Meagher, Patrick O'Donoghue, and Terence B. McManus were arrested.

By the time O'Brien was arrested he had already recognized that his chances of escape were rather slight, but he did have time to make a number of very important decisions. O'Brien was a powerful man. He was thoroughly knowledgeable about English attitudes and practices. He knew he could use the power he possessed to obtain a mitigation of the punishment he was bound to receive from being the leader of the revolution. He knew such a mitigation of punishment would require him to apologize for his actions and ask for the queen's mercy. But he had determined not to make such an apology. He had decided to abstain "from soliciting any favour from the British government, or any mitigation of the penalties which [he] incurred." He wrote, "Having done what I considered to be my duty, I could not express contrition."[32]

The government officials in Ireland were unconcerned with O'Brien's attitude toward them. They were intent on stamping out revolution. The four leaders arrested after Ballingarry were charged with committing high treason. Evidently the Irish officials forgot they had the Treason-Felony Act at their disposal. By charging the Irish revolutionaries with high treason, the Irish officials were setting the stage for a torturous execution that British public opinion opposed.

It appears that the editors of the *London Times* realized quite early what had happened. They acknowledged they had a special problem in reporting the happenings of the affair at Ballingarry, since they found the actions of the revolutionaries to be comical and yet fully recognized that "to laugh at a man and hang him also is taking it out both ways."[33] The reality was that the editors of the *Times* understood that there was little chance that British public opinion would ever sanction the execution of the revolutionaries; hence, their goal was set. They would orchestrate the laughter. The battle at Ballingarry became known as a skirmish in Widow McCormack's cabbage patch, and O'Brien as leader of that skirmish was made out to be a fool. The editors put great stress on O'Brien's relationship with Brian Boru, implying that his motives for leading a revolution were self-serving; namely, to become "Smith the First, King of Munster." After studying the battle they noted, "King Charles hid himself in the oak, and King O'Brien in the cabbages." They concluded, "The idea one would receive from it certainly is that Smith O'Brien is of unsound intellect." The editors made fun of O'Brien whenever they could, and when they learned O'Brien had assumed various disguises, especially in the time period immediately after the failure at Ballingarry, they gleefully reported, "Mr O'Brien's dress had undergone almost hourly variations." The editors even reported, "At the barricade of Killenaule he is said to have exchanged caps with a lad in the street."[34]

The *Times* was not alone in ridiculing O'Brien. *Punch* contained an article entitled "An Apology for Smith O'Brien" in which the editors commented on O'Brien's bravery: "The courage of Mr Smith O'Brien in slinking, under the fire of the police at Boniagh common, among the cabbages in Widow McCormack's garden, may be questioned, but it is to be remembered that the hero, if he crept out of the way of the bullets, betrayed no fear of the slugs."[35] There is no doubt that the editors of the *Times* had a great effect on English public opinion for, by the time O'Brien's trial began, the English people were convinced that O'Brien was a self-interested, greedy fool.

Regardless of what was said in the English press, Irish public opinion did not embrace that notion. The Dublin correspondent of the *London Times* found the Irish attitude toward O'Brien to be astounding. He concluded the Irish had no sense of justice. "Reason and common sense are alike forgotten by this impulsive people, because Smith O'Brien is sincere in his conduct, and his ancestors were kings in the land."[36] Even those members of the Irish society who had opposed the revolution of 1848, and who denounced O'Brien for serving as the leader of that revolution, never thought for a moment that his actions were not motivated by sincere and lofty conviction. They usually justified O'Brien's participation in the revolution by saying he had been misled by a group of discontented, evil men.[37]

Meanwhile the trial for high treason had begun. It was not a lengthy affair.[38] Most people expected the revolutionaries to be found guilty, which they were. The real question was how the government would avoid executing them. In the spring of 1849, therefore, the British officials ironically found themselves in the very situation that they had previously been trying to avoid; namely, they had sentenced men to face a grim punishment that public opinion opposed.

A solution surfaced. A writ of error was filed, "first in the Queen's Bench, and afterwards before the House of Lords," but to no avail. Even at that stage O'Brien's friend Richard O'Gorman was hoping for a pardon, realizing such a pardon might be conditional upon the state prisoners having to leave the British Isles. But the government was not contemplating pardon. Nor was the government anxious to create four Irish national martyrs.[39] The British officials decided that the best way out of their dilemma was to extend the mercy of the crown to the prisoners by transporting them for life to a penal colony.

On 5 June 1849, the secretary of state for colonial affairs, Earl Grey, wrote a letter to Sir William Denison, the governor of one of Britain's penal colonies, Van Diemen's Land. In that letter Earl Grey informed Governor Denison of the decision of the British ministry to send the Irish prisoners to Van Diemen's Land. He referred both to O'Brien, Meagher, O'Donoghue, and McManus, taken after the revolution had occurred, and to Martin and O'Doherty, who had been convicted prior to the revolution under the Treason-Felony Act.[40]

Earl Grey also took pains to instruct Governor Denison about the manner of treatment to be accorded such prisoners; namely, that they should be adequately punished for serious crimes against the state, but with consideration of their superior rank in society. Grey was not interested in subjecting the Irish leaders to hard labor and found such procedures to be "scarcely practicable." He believed that for such men "banishment, and the forfeiture of fortune and Station" was an extremely heavy infliction and probably punishment enough. Grey ordered Denison to grant special paroles, called tickets-of-leave, to the Irish prisoners if it was reported that they had behaved themselves during their voyage to Van Diemen's Land and if they promised not to escape. Those tickets-of-leave would give the Irish prisoners certain freedom of movement and activity suitable to men of position. The prisoners were to be assigned to separate districts, each of the districts to be at a distance from the capital, Hobart Town, and they would have to report to the local magistrates at regular intervals. Grey left the other precautions to provide for their security to Governor Denison's discretion. If the Irish prisoners refused to promise that they would not escape, Denison was ordered by Grey to place them in confinement. He also told Denison that any breach of discipline should result in "such punishment as the nature of their fault may appear to render necessary." Under certain circumstances they could be "thrown back among the ordinary offenders."[41]

On 5 June 1849, the governor of Richmond Prison read to O'Brien, Meagher, O'Donoghue, and McManus a letter from Sir Thomas Nicholas Redington, under-secretary for Ireland, announcing that their sentences had been commuted to transportation for life. That news came as a terrible blow to the prisoners, and O'Brien, in particular, considered it to be the worst possible decision. He had been tried and convicted of high treason, and the law demanded that he be executed or pardoned. He bravely considered himself prepared for death, and he would have welcomed a pardon. But he had hoped for a third alternative, much less harsh than transportation. He hoped that the queen would detain him at her pleasure, until she was ready to grant a pardon, but such detention to take place in Ireland.[42]

Prison life in Richmond Prison had certain advantages. Each of the state prisoners had his own room and permission to visit his fellow prisoners. O'Brien occupied rooms in the home of the governor of the prison and had access to two large gardens. He had his regular servant with him to provide for his needs. The wife of the head jailer, Mrs. Marquis, cooked his food, which was provided by his family. O'Brien was allowed to purchase whatever articles he wished. There were no real restrictions on visitors, letters, or newspapers. In fact, the families of all the men visited regularly.[43] Richmond Prison was under the control of the Dublin Corporation, and public opinion in Dublin would not allow the authorities to treat the men in any other way.

Most important, as long as the state prisoners were in Ireland, their friends could effectively work on public sentiment in an attempt to obtain pardons for them. If they were removed sixteen thousand miles from Ireland to Van Diemen's Land, it would not be easy to prevent the decline of emotional support, both among their friends and among the Irish people, which would be so important in official circles.

O'Brien, who was a lawyer, quickly decided to challenge the transportation order as best he could. O'Brien doubted if transportation was legally available to the authorities in connection with a conviction for high treason. On the same day on which Redington's letter was read to him, O'Brien wrote to the sheriff of Dublin, calling on the sheriff not to allow any official to remove him from Richmond Prison except on legal authority. He then wrote his attorney, Sir Colman O'Loghlen, told him about Redington's letter, and directed Sir Colman to obtain a writ of habeas corpus if any attempt were made to transport him. "I emphatically repeat that I do not consent to be transported and if as I am assured is the case the Law does not authorize the Government to transport me I claim the protection of the Law." O'Loghlen agreed with O'Brien's interpretation of the law and notified Redington that if O'Brien was removed from prison, the authorities into whose hands he was delivered would be served with a writ of habeas corpus in order to test the legality of the transportation order.[44]

On 6 June, O'Brien and his fellow prisoners formally protested the transportation order by petition to the House of Commons.[45] They maintained in their petition that the statutes regarding transportation, and commutation to transportation, were different in England than in Ireland, that the Irish statutes allowed transportation only for a felony conviction, and that in Ireland treason was separate and apart from felony. In England treason was a felony and, therefore, a transportation order could not be questioned when an individual had been tried and convicted of treason in an English court. O'Brien considered the transportation order bad for a variety of reasons, but he was also distressed because the decision had the effect of branding him a felon and the revolution of 1848 a felony. Although the House of Commons refused to hear the petition of the state prisoners, the Whig government in power decided that it was "better to remove all shadow of doubt" regarding the transportation of the Irish leaders.[46] Accordingly, a bill was proposed that would allow persons convicted of committing high treason in Ireland to be transported for life.

The friends of O'Brien in the House of Commons made a concerted effort to prevent the bill from becoming law, maintaining that any bill that ordered the state prisoners to be transported was illegal because it was ex post facto legislation. But, regardless of the arguments, the House of Commons voted favorably on the transportation-for-treason bill.[47]

Because of the delays attending the transportation order, the ship that was originally scheduled to take all six of the state prisoners to Van Diemen's Land sailed with only part of the group. Martin and O'Doherty had been convicted under the Treason-Felony Act of 1848, and there had been no question about their punishment. They were taken from Richmond Prison on 15 June and placed aboard the ship *Mount Stewart Elphinston*. They finally set sail on June 28. By the end of June, all questions about the legality of transporting the remaining four state prisoners had been settled, and Earl Grey wrote Governor Denison his final orders in regard to the Irish prisoners.[48]

*   *   *

William Smith O'Brien was a member of a large and influential family. His brother Sir Lucius O'Brien had been working to help him as best he could. By the end of June, Sir Lucius realized the exile was about to begin. He had been in London during the previous weeks where, as a member of Parliament, he had been engaged in the legal battle in Westminster. With that fight over, he crossed to Dublin to visit O'Brien. Lucius told his brother about a statement of the home secretary, Sir George Grey, "to the effect *that no indignity should be offered to* [Smith O'Brien] *on the passage or afterwards.*"[49] That statement was treated as applying to all of the state prisoners. In other words, they would all be treated as "gentlemen." Lucius also thought the state prisoners would be offered tickets-of-leave when they arrived in Van Diemen's Land, and he urged O'Brien to accept such an offer if it were made. O'Brien's wife, Lucy, had also been active in trying to help make her husband's exile as comfortable as possible. She had received a letter from Redington stating that O'Brien could receive money from home while he was in Van Diemen's Land.[50]

While O'Brien's family was making what arrangements it could to make his exile as palatable as possible, O'Brien analyzed his position. He believed that if the English continued their current system of government for Ireland, "it needs no prophetic spirit to foresee that British Power will not long survive" since "power without Beneficence is accursed by God and Man."[51]

Under such circumstances, Irish leadership became extremely important. There was no doubt that in 1849 Ireland was practically leaderless. O'Connell was dead, the Repeal Association was in shambles, neither the Irish Confederation nor the League had ever really had time to get established, and, with the defeat of the Young Irelanders at Ballingarry, the young Irish leaders were either under arrest, had fled the country, or were leading extremely quiet lives in an attempt to avoid notice. It appears that, with those thoughts in mind, O'Brien had determined not to abandon his leadership role. It was later observed that O'Brien's actions while in exile reflected his belief that the revolution, though a failure, lived on in him.[52] There is no doubt that he conducted himself as if his actions were being watched by the Irish people. As an aristocratic gentleman he could do nothing of a dishonorable nature. O'Brien also knew that being sent into exile could mean oblivion for himself and his cause. O'Brien understood how important public opinion could be in demanding his return and eventual pardon. There were those who observed him who maintained that O'Brien knew he would have to gain the public's attention in order to fight oblivion and obtain a pardon and that O'Brien suspected such attention could only be obtained by suffering in some way or another.[53]

It is not difficult to become a national hero after successfully fighting a battle and then dying. That is what Brian Boru did. It is almost impossible to become a hero after leading an unsuccessful revolution, facing a sentence of transportation for life, and becoming the object of public ridicule. Yet O'Brien was not defeated. He determined to do everything he could to maintain his recognized position as an aristocratic Irish leader. Whether or not he would end up as a hero was unknown. The period of his exile was O'Brien's real battleground, not Ballingarry.

*   *   *

At 9:00 A.M. on the morning of 9 July 1849, the prisoners were informed they would begin their journey to Van Diemen's Land at 12:00 noon.[54] The month before, when O'Brien had learned the British government was planning to transport him, he had noted, "One adequate support for the calamities of mortal life exists—one only—an assured belief that the procession of our fate, however sad or disturbed, is ordered by a Being of infinite benevolence and power whose everlasting purposes embrace all accidents converting them to good." On the morning of 9 July, O'Brien, no doubt, once again found consolation by bowing to the will of God. But it was a bow to a God who O'Brien believed would "by his appointed means and in his own appropriate season rescue the Irish nation from the Cruel bondage which it now endures."[55] O'Brien hoped to conduct himself during his exile in such a way as to assist that rescue.

The Transportation of the State Prisoners

On the morning of 9 July 1849, after about a year of legal controversies since the events at Ballingarry, a small group of people gathered in front of Richmond Prison in Dublin in the hope of bidding farewell to the four state prisoners, William Smith O'Brien, Thomas Meagher, Patrick O'Donoghue, and Terence McManus.

While O'Brien was the recognized leader of the group, the most popular was Thomas Francis Meagher. Like his illustrious father, Meagher had unlimited energy. His father was not only a successful merchant who had amassed a fortune, but he was a successful politician serving as mayor of Waterford and as a member of Parliament. Thomas Meagher had devoted his energies principally to the political and literary arenas. He had been an active Young Irelander, and he had a particular talent for speechmaking. Meagher had also written for the Irish newspaper the *Nation*. Meagher was generally respected and well liked by everyone. Even Mitchel acknowledged, "Meagher is eloquent and ardent—brave to act; brave, if need be, to suffer." Mitchel's only concern was "I would that he took the trouble to think for himself."[56] Meagher had met O'Brien while both men were working for O'Connell in the repeal movement. Like O'Brien, Meagher had broken with O'Connell over the right to use physical force to achieve Irish national objectives. It was actually

Meagher's speech "Abhor not the Sword" that precipitated the secession movement in 1846, at which time Young Ireland split with Old Ireland. During the summer of 1848, it was Meagher, in the company of John Dillon, who carried the news to O'Brien that the writ of habeas corpus had been suspended in Ireland and that the government had issued orders for O'Brien's arrest.[57] It was that arrest order that catapulted the Young Ireland party into the arena of revolution and the fields at Ballingarry. O'Brien and Meagher had been through a lot together, and they enjoyed one another's company.

Terence Bellew McManus was the third state prisoner. He had been a boyhood friend of Duffy's and, while not a member of the intellectual elite who contributed prose and poetry to the *Nation*, he was committed to the moderate position of the Young Irelanders. Before participating in the revolution of 1848, McManus had been a prosperous businessman in Liverpool, earning nearly one thousand pounds a year.[58] He lost his fortune as a result of his involvement in the revolution, but he retained enough money to provide modestly for himself. Since McManus was not married, he did not have the worry of providing for a wife or children and, with that liberty, he determined to make the most of his transportation to Van Diemen's Land. He packed a considerable collection of fishing gear along with a treasured backgammon set.

Thomas Francis Meagher

Patrick O'Donoghue was the only one of the four state prisoners who suffered from a lack of funds. He had been a successful solicitor prior to the revolution of 1848, but he had no savings, and because of his revolutionary activities he and his family faced economic disaster. On the morning of 9 July he left Dublin for Van Diemen's Land with only eleven shillings and sixpence in his pocket. While O'Donoghue occasionally lapsed into states of emotional depression, complaining that he had been "deserted" by the Irish people for whom he had sacrificed so much, most of the time his unbounded faith that everything would work out somehow overcame his feelings of despondency. O'Donoghue wrote that the "wretched failure" of the revolution of 1848 had "only one retaining feature—the manliness of its victims—and I will never rob it of that solitary ray of redemption."[59]

The government had informed the prisoners of the actual time of departure three hours before they were to leave Richmond Prison in Dublin. That was time enough for the families of the men to gather in the prison yard to spend a few remaining hours with their loved ones. About noon, the four men were carried off to Kingston Harbor to board the man-of-war the *Swift*, which would transport them to Van Diemen's Land.[60]

Terence Bellew McManus

*   *   *

On the afternoon of the ninth, the commander of the *Swift*, Capt. W. Cornwallis Aldham, made known to the state prisoners the various rules and regulations that would limit their activities while they were on board ship. The Irishmen were to be treated as gentlemen and, while placed under guard, were allowed relative freedom both above deck and below while in their cabins.[61]

The cabin accommodations to which the state prisoners found themselves assigned on board the *Swift* were quite satisfactory. Meagher described the saloon to which they were assigned as a large room about twelve feet square, which was well lighted and well ventilated. The saloon would be used by the prisoners during their waking hours as the common meeting place for eating, reading, talking, and, as Meagher reported, laughing. Along two sides of the saloon were berths that were separated from the main room by a sliding door. Each berth was equipped with two or three lockers, a looking glass, and a washstand, which in turn included a jug, basin, water flask, and soap box. Baths were to be taken by pouring buckets of saltwater over the body, but, occasionally, during calms at sea the prisoners would be able to take a bath in the sea

Patrick Denis O'Donoghue

when the ship was moving slowly, by being lowered on a rope from the stern of the ship.[62]

The prisoners were initially assigned two-thirds of the food allowance given to the sailors, but O'Brien asked the surgeon to see if a grant of full rations could be obtained, and his request was granted. The prisoners also had a marine, by the name of Spriggs, assigned to attend to whatever personal attentions they required.[63]

There is no doubt the Irish prisoners were receiving treatment afforded gentlemen. The normal procedures called for all transported felons to be dressed in a coarse gray outfit and fitted with leg irons before being put on board the transport ship. Flogging was not unusual and could be administered for such minor charges as giving "cheek." Normally, convicts were allowed to come up from below during the day, but they were restricted to only certain areas of the ship.[64]

O'Brien was aware of the special treatment he was receiving, but he was also aware his life had changed. On the morning of 10 July, he noted, after breakfasting "on biscuit and tea without milk—sweetened with brown sugar," that he could not help but "sigh for [a] couple of eggs." He knew he had "long prided" himself on his indifference to luxury, but he now realized, "I shall now have an opportunity of discovering how far this indifference is real or fancied." O'Brien was fearful that he had "acted too much upon the maxim that a wise man will never do for himself what he can get another to do for him." He determined "to wean myself from my former habits and learn also never to ask another to do for me what I can do for myself." Once having made that resolution, he made his bed for the first time in his life and further resolved "except when prevented by sea sickness to continue the practice throughout the voyage."[65]

On their second day aboard ship, 10 July, the prisoners enjoyed the view of the Irish coast passing before them. By evening the Irish coastline was beginning to fade from view. O'Brien thought about his past labors on behalf of his homeland as he watched the sight before him. For years he had struggled to overcome the social and political ills that beset Ireland, and the struggle had given him "incessant pain." Many times he had concluded that the cause was hopeless. "I have felt like one rolling a stone up a hill which is too weighty for his strength and which constantly rebounds so that the work must be recommenced after each successive effort." He asked, "Why should I not consider as a release my future exemption from such toils." But for O'Brien, the ultimate answer could only be that there were a "thousand tendrils which cling round the stem and branches of the tree—Not to speak of the old associations hereditarily inborn, nursed by the side of the lakes, of the rivers, of the castles, of the mountains, of the cliffs of my native isle, cherished also by the wild strains of its old songs and by the traditions of its historic tales—not to speak of these roots and fibres which have imbedded the tree so firmly in its native soil."[66]

Actually, O'Brien believed the project of self-government for Ireland had taken root. Since he had been deprived of the opportunity of working at home to perfect that project, he came to look positively on the effect that his exile could have on that very project.

> If on the contrary the principles for which I have contended are destined to be realized it is possible that our exile may tend to forward that realization more than our stay in Ireland—If the movement in favour of self government has any real foundation in the feelings of the Irish People—if it has not been a gigantic humbug our sufferings will tend to strengthen the aspirations after nationality—to make future compromise impossible— to prove that the Leaders were sincere and deemed Ireland's well being a prize worthy of great sacrifices—and our example will generate an imitation which will one day be crowned with a happier success.[67]

When Ireland would attain the crown of success was unknown. O'Brien realized the likelihood that he would receive a pardon long before Ireland would receive the right to govern herself. He was taking his last look at Ireland as he set out on a sixteen-thousand-mile journey into exile. He thought about his eventual pardon, his possible return to Ireland, and the role he and the members of his family would play in relation to England. He concluded, "I could not exercise any function however subordinate under the crown of England—nor could I ever desire that my children should form part of a community from which I have been excluded. . . . With such sentiments I bid farewell to the soil which gave me birth at the moment at which I catch a last glimpse of its receding shores."[68]

*   *   *

The voyage to Van Diemen's Land was basically uneventful. During the first half of the journey, the *Swift* encountered several storms but, generally speaking, the journey's boredom was broken only by reading, discussion sessions, backgammon contests, or by taking part in some kind of physical exercise while on deck.[69] The prisoners never got used to the lack of fresh water or fresh food. O'Brien, in particular, suffered from the lack of fresh water. Each prisoner had been issued two gallons of wine for the trip that could act as a substitute or as a means of making the water taste better. However, O'Brien had taken a pledge to abstain from anything alcoholic, which caused him great discomfort during the trip.[70]

*   *   *

While the state prisoners proceeded on their journey into exile, Queen Victoria prepared to make her first visit to Ireland. Many of the friends and sympathizers of the state prisoners believed that the queen would use the occasion of her visit to grant pardons to the men.

The queen's reception in Dublin drew a large crowd. The *London Times* took pains to describe the warm manner in which the Irish crowds greeted Victoria: "It is impossible to do justice to the enthusiastic reception of the Queen by her subjects in the Irish capital; we can only express our belief that nothing comparable to it has ever found a place in the chronicles of Dublin." But other newspapers did not evaluate the reception of the queen as did the reporters for the *Times*. A writer for the *New York Nation* took pains to point out that Irishmen went, not to welcome the queen, but to gaze at the "gilded symbol of their degradation," and he characterized Queen Victoria as no more than the patroness in Ireland of the odious national institutions of oppression, "the Prisons, the Workhouses and the Barracks."[71]

Whichever journalistic interpretation was wishful thinking, it is clear that the wishful thinkers, so far as pardons were concerned, were the state prisoners and their friends. True enough, the inhabitants of the town of Six-Mile-Bridge had passed a resolution calling for a petition to the queen for pardon. But the manner in which Irish officialdom handled such popular expressions is typified by the inaction of the repeal mayor of Cork, no doubt an Old Irelander, who did not think the time was right, for he "politely declined to comply with the demands of a requisition calling on him to hold a public meeting to address the Queen on behalf of Mr Smith O'Brien and his associates." But hopes die hard, and, after the queen departed, the rumor of pardon persisted, only slightly reshaped. "It was believed that the exiled Irish state prisoners would soon be pardoned, and that their return might be expected within a year."[72]

*   *   *

Meanwhile the *Swift* proceeded on its voyage and prepared to make its one and only stop in the sixteen-thousand-mile ocean journey. The *Swift* arrived at Capetown, South Africa, on 12 September, but the refueling stop was to be exceptionally brief. The colony was in a state of commotion. Several weeks before, the British government had announced that a new penal colony would be established at Capetown. During the previous May, a group of convicts had been taken from Bermuda, placed on board the vessel *Neptune*, and dispatched to Capetown. John Mitchel was one of those convicts. The Capetown colonists meanwhile had sent a number of petitions to the British government protesting the establishment of a penal colony in their midst and had determined to work together to prevent the landing of any convicts. By the time the *Swift* arrived at Capetown, the *Neptune* was long overdue. Many people in the area concluded that the *Neptune* had been lost at sea and that they had been saved from confronting British officialdom over that issue. But the arrival of the *Swift*, with a passenger list including four state prisoners, caused a near-violent reaction from the citizenry.[73]

The state prisoners were interested in the Capetown situation for a number of reasons. First, John Mitchel was known to be one of the convicts from Bermuda who had been placed on board the *Neptune*. With the ship so long overdue they had to acknowledge that Mitchel might be dead. Personally, O'Brien liked Mitchel and truly lamented the possibility that he had died at sea. But O'Brien had long opposed Mitchel's radical position, particularly Mitchel's sanction of extreme violence as a way to free Ireland from England. On this occasion O'Brien explained what he believed had driven Mitchel to take up such a radical position; namely, "a just and natural indignation which [Mitchel] felt upon witnessing the sufferings and indignities inflicted upon [the Irish people] by the neglect or malignity of those to whose power [the people] have been subject." O'Brien was convinced Mitchel was sincere in his "desire to promote the welfare of his fellow countrymen." For those reasons, as well as his personal friendship with Mitchel, O'Brien could not help but write in his journal regarding Mitchel's probable death, "Poor Mitchel! What a fate! Poor Mrs Mitchel."[74]

The state prisoners were also interested in the attitude of the Capetown colonists toward penal colonies because they knew that for some time the colonists of Van Diemen's Land had been petitioning against the transportation of convicts to their shores. Yet those same colonists had continued to accept the convicts when they were landed. From what the state prisoners could learn, the Capetown colonists were determined to oppose the landing of any prisoners, with all means short of violence, and if the officials went ahead and landed the convicts, the Capetown colonists had devised a plan of passive resistance. They had entered into agreements with each other not to supply any prisoner with goods, hire any prisoner who received a ticket-of-leave, or hire any spouse of a prisoner who might come out to be near his or her loved one. If the colonists at Capetown were successful in blocking the establishment of a penal colony, their example would undoubtedly affect the antitransportation movement in Van Diemen's Land. The state prisoners thought the antitransportation citizenry of Van Diemen's Land might try to use passive resistance as a means of ending transportation there. If transportation came to an end in Van Diemen's Land, the general assumption was that most of the felons would receive conditional pardons. The state prisoners thought it likely that they would be included in that group.[75]

Finally, the state prisoners were interested in the commotion at Capetown because it had an immediate effect on their living conditions on board the *Swift*. Everyone aboard the vessel was looking forward to a period of respite from the sea voyage. The captain was anxious to initiate repair necessitated by damage done to the *Swift* during a recent storm. The state prisoners were looking forward to an opportunity to do their laundry. Everyone on the *Swift* was anxious to receive fresh supplies of food and water. Virtually all of those expectations were frustrated by orders sent out from the British station. Captain Aldham was informed that he would be resupplied the next day and that he should leave Capetown the moment the new supplies were on board. Meanwhile, no one was to leave the *Swift*.[76]

The *Swift* stayed in the harbor overnight, and even though everyone in Capetown knew there could be no communication with the vessel, an acquaintance of O'Brien's rowed out to see if he might catch a glimpse of him. Fortunately, O'Brien was on deck at the time, and, although O'Brien was unaware he had been observed, Ireland learned he had been sighted and that Captain Aldham had been heard to comment favorably about the deportment of the prisoners.[77]

At daybreak on 13 September an ample number of marines and sailors were sent from the British station to assist in preparing the *Swift* for departure. A large tender containing water was brought alongside in order to refill the *Swift*'s tanks. The purser had not been allowed to go ashore to make the necessary food purchases, but food was brought out to the ship. The main food supplies were in the form of a few sheep and a small supply of fresh meat. By one o'clock the work was completed. The *Swift* weighed anchor and stood out to sea with a favorable breeze. By nightfall on the thirteenth the men on board the *Swift* had lost sight of the coast of Africa.[78]

The journey between Capetown, South Africa, and Hobart Town, Van Diemen's Land, directly across, on the southern side of the Indian Ocean, was singularly uneventful, and very long. The days were cold, wet, and dreary. The winds were so fierce at times that the *Swift* was driven further south than had been planned, and icebergs appeared in the "bleak Atlantic." Adding to the discomfort of the cold, the wind, and the rain, came, no doubt, a lonely feeling, since the vessel went six weeks without sighting either land or sail.[79]

By 23 October 1849, after a voyage of more than one hundred days, the *Swift* stood only 380 miles from Van Diemen's Land. The state prisoners had the satisfaction of having traveled nearly sixteen thousand miles on the most friendly terms with the captain and crew of the *Swift*. The prisoners had decided among themselves to write letters expressing their gratitude and appreciation to Captain Aldham. O'Brien wrote to the captain on the twenty-fourth and received a kind reply to his letter from Captain Aldham, who commended all the state prisoners for their gentlemanly bearing.[80]

The trip had not been as unpleasant as it could have been considering the normal difficulties of travel of the day. The prisoners had gotten on eath other's nerves periodically, and at one point O'Donoghue and O'Brien had stopped speaking. But by the end of the journey their differences had been resolved. Actually, the trip had not been such an experience as to imprint any basic changes on the personalities of the prisoners.

Meagher, for example, continued to possess unlimited energies and was looking forward to the adventures waiting for him in Van Diemen's Land. His self-image had not been damaged by the trip but rather enhanced. Meagher's spirit had even allowed him to make his peace with the quality of the rations. When the *Swift* stopped at Capetown, Meagher had written to his family that, while the food was "not composed of the most soft and savoury ingredients," he was not too distressed about it. He wrote, "Besides, a cheerful heart can sweeten all things—can make the best of everything, and bless even darker days than ours with the richest fragrance and the softest sunshine."[81]

O'Donoghue's determined faith in an eventual victory over all his difficulties survived the voyage and was still with him as the *Swift* approached the River Derwent and the harbor at Hobart Town, Van Diemen's Land. Periodically during the journey O'Donoghue had lapsed into a state of despondency when he thought of his wife and child alone in the world with no husband or father to serve as their protector. Yet, at the same time, it was the thought of an eventual reunion with his loved ones that kept him going. He wrote "that fond thoughts of them were all that illuminated the wilderness of gloom which engulfed him."[82]

McManus had started the journey resigned to accept what came and make the most of it. Nothing better illustrates his state of mind than the calm and purposeful way in which he took his fishing tackle and backgammon set along to make the best, as he saw it, of the voyage and his stay in Van Diemen's Land. Even the fact that he failed to catch any fish on the sixteen-thousand-mile journey did not really upset him.[83] McManus was as welcome to the other state prisoners at the end of the journey as he had been at the beginning. He had the special effect of bringing and keeping the group together without the boredom and irritation that should have arisen in such close quarters on so long a journey.

O'Brien started and finished the voyage as the acknowledged leader of the group. It was he who led the reading and discussion sessions aboard the *Swift*. It was he who spoke for the group regarding the inadequacy of the rations. And it was he who most interested the outside world and about whom information was most eagerly sought and given. O'Brien was the natural leader because of his personal qualities and because of his princely connections. But more than that, he carried himself as the people's ideal because he saw himself as the composite of what the Irish people needed in their leader. Accordingly, he reacted to his exile in a manner that he hoped would be reported favorably back to the British Isles and to the Irish people. His refusal to take wine to satisfy his thirst when pure water was unavailable showed that he considered himself called to the high purpose of an ideal. Of all the prisoners, it was he who believed that even in exile he still had a role to play in Irish self-government, regardless of the fact that he was thousands of miles from the scene. For that reason, O'Brien did not intend "to intermeddle with local politics"; his desire to affect politics would be directed only toward Ireland.[84]

On 27 October 1849, the *Swift* entered the River Derwent. The prisoners were surprised by the beauty of the scene. Meagher left a record of what they saw. "To the left were bold cliffs . . . springing up, full two hundred feet and more, above the surface of the water, and bearing on their . . . summits . . . forests of . . . gum-trees. To the right, . . . lay the green lowlands of Tasman's Peninsula, sparkling in the clear, sweet sunshine of that lovely evening." As the ship moved upriver, it passed "a signal-tower, with a red flag floating from it" and then "a farmhouse, with its white walls and green verandah." Next "the fresh, rich fragrance of flowers, and ripening fruits, and waving grass, came floating to us through the blue, bright, air." As the *Swift* moved further up the Derwent, houses became more numerous and were built on a larger scale. As the town came into view, so did Mount Wellington, which stood behind it. Mount Wellington was four thousand feet tall "and wearing a thick circlet of snow upon its head, disclosed itself in all its greatness, grandeur and solemnity."[85]

CHAPTER 2

Van Diemen's Land

Paradise and Hell, the Citizens and the Convicts

The view from the deck of the *Swift*, limited as it was, convinced the Irish exiles that they had come to a very beautiful part of the world. Van Diemen's Land, now called Tasmania, is an island of approximately twenty-five thousand square miles, located about one hundred and fifty miles off the south coast of mainland Australia. The exiles found the climate to be temperate and both the fauna and the flora to be luxuriant and unique. The countryside was lovely to behold, exhibiting gorgeous coastline, rolling hills, splendid mountains, and then, unexpectedly, in the center of the island, a high plateau dotted with alpine lakes.

While nature had done its best to create a paradise, man had done his best to create a hell. Van Diemen's Land had been discovered by the European world in 1642 through the efforts of the Dutch navigator Abel Janszoon Tasman. He had named the island in honor of Gov. Anton Van Diemen, who had been responsible for sending him on his expedition. Capt. James Cook had visited the island in 1777 while on a scientific expedition to the Pacific Ocean. After the American Revolution, the British had needed a place to send their convicted felons who had been sentenced to banishment under the punishment of transportation. America had previously served as a receptacle for transported convicts, but when the British lost the American Revolution in 1783, they were compelled to look elsewhere for a dumping ground. Cook's Pacific expedition in 1777 had uncovered an empty corner of the globe that was suitable for such a purpose, and in 1788 the first penal settlement was established in Sydney, Australia. In 1803, a convict station was opened in Van Diemen's Land, and thereafter the white man started to colonize the island in earnest. The convicts shipped to Van Diemen's Land were accompanied by their military guards and the families of the guards. In addition, a few settlers came into the area. With the introduction of sheep raising, free settlers began to colonize the island in large numbers, so that by the time the Irish state prisoners arrived, there were approximately thirty-seven thousand free citizens and twenty-nine thousand convicts in the colony.[1]

One of the main problems the free citizenry faced was that most of the twenty-nine thousand convicts were not held in confinement. Most of them were at large in the society, presumably holding jobs, but often supporting themselves by criminal activity.

28

*   *   *

Transportation was a unique form of punishment. Its origins can be found in very early English history, and like most other old English political practices, it evolved and changed with the times. Very early in English history the practice developed that a person who had committed a crime against the king "and had fled to sanctuary" could obtain permission from the crown to leave the country, without suffering any further punishment, provided he confessed his guilt and took an oath never to return without first obtaining royal permission. That practice had at the time no expressed foundation in law. Transportation became part of the law during the reign of Elizabeth I, when Parliament passed a statute imposing the penalty of transportation (banishment) against any offenders convicted of being "rogues[,] vagabonds and sturdy beggars." The evident scope of that statute says much about the variety of the types of persons who were transported, from the extremely dangerous to the poor, but it also says much about the apparent importance of the institution to the colonizing effort.[2]

During the reign of Charles II, "it was common to extend the royal mercy to offenders who had been convicted of capital offenses on condition of transportation." Under those circumstances, transportation "was not so much a punishment as a condition of pardon." Transportation took on another feature at this time in addition to mere banishment, that is, it became a type of servitude that provided labor to a master living in the colony to which the felon was banished. The master, however, had no connection with the government. He was merely an individual in need of cheap labor.[3]

During the reign of George I, Parliament passed a statute that allowed persons to be transported other than "rogues[,] vagabonds and sturdy beggars." It was the first time that transportation was "regularly introduced as a punishment." Under that statute the courts were empowered to sentence to transportation an even wider spectrum of offenders for the respective periods of seven years, fourteen years, and life. That law expressly incorporated banishment and servitude. The government continued to play no role in regulating the life of the transported felon.[4]

It was not until the reign of George IV that the transportation statute expressly provided the opportunity for the crown "to extend mercy to any person convicted of a Capital offense upon condition of transportation." It was also the first time that any provision was made for the local British officials to manage the lives of the transported felons in the colonies. Even then, while the powers given to the local British officials in the penal colonies to regulate the lives of the transported felons were broad, they were not without their limitations.[5]

Transportation was a punishment separate and distinct from impris-

onment. An offender sentenced to transportation could not be imprisoned upon arriving in the colony, because he would then be considered
to have been subjected to two punishments. The only time a transported
offender could be imprisoned was when he had been charged, tried, and
convicted for committing a second offense after his arrival in the colony.
So the usual procedure was initially to place the newly arrived transported felon in a probation station where his labor could be used to the
direct benefit of the government.[6] If the felon had been sentenced to a
seven-year term of transportation, he remained in the probation station
for two years, while a fourteen-year term of transportation resulted in a
three-year stay.[7]

After completing the requisite time at the probation station, the
offender would be allowed to become a pass holder, in other words, he
would be allowed to take employment in the regular society and receive
wages. If the felon behaved himself, he would next be granted a ticket-
of-leave, which allowed him not only to obtain employment but also to
own property and, in general, control his own life within the geographic
limits of the colony.[8] At the end of his term of transportation, the ex-
felon was free to leave the colony if he wished. Most of the convicts
received conditional pardons before they had served their full sentence,
allowing them to reside anywhere in the world except the British Isles.

Those were the general rules. But it was not unusual for the local
British officials to issue tickets-of-leave to the transported offenders the
moment they arrived in the penal colony. Labor was in high demand,
and if the settlers needed workers immediately, the terms in the probation station and as a pass holder were obliterated. Often the government
itself hired the "most powerful" newly transported felons as policemen
before they set foot on land.[9]

The fact of the matter was that the free citizenry was surrounded by
criminals. Those convicts in the probation stations were presumably under control. But there were constant complaints from settlers that the
convicts roamed at will, miles from the stations, and took what they
wanted from the homes of the free citizenry. The Jerusalem station had
eight hundred convicts who were allowed "to roam on their parole; to
carry bundles in and out of the barracks unsearched; to disguise their
persons, and to change their dress." The result was that at least some of
the convicts engaged in "daring highway robberies." At St. Mary's Pass
station, the third-class convicts were allowed to roam, as long as they
did not go beyond "hearing of the bell." No check was made, however,
other than the fact the men had to be back at the station at an appointed
hour. Those facts came to light when a "hawker was robbed within about
a mile of the station under very aggravated circumstances, by men in the
dress of probationers." In the vicinity of Oatlands the government had
one overseer responsible for ninety convicts working "in a line of seven

miles extent." Some of those convicts evidently left the line. "A settler, whose flocks had been pillaged, brought back twice in one month the same [probationer robbers]; and again they escaped, threatening vengeance, on the authors of their arrest." Towns, as well as the rural areas, suffered from the lax control of the convicts, since "many hundreds of men were turned out from the penitentiary on Saturday afternoon, and were thus exposed to the temptations of a populous city." A need for the money necessary for a Saturday afternoon's entertainments no doubt stimulated robberies. It probably also caused an increase in prostitution. There were female felons in Van Diemen's Land, and, generally speaking, degradation and ruin among them were widespread.[10]

In addition, escapes from the probation stations were common, and those who made a successful escape often became bushrangers, individuals who lived in the bush but who would periodically come out of hiding and plunder a lonely household or waylay travelers on the road. The victim of the bushranger could not initially tell whether he had fallen into the hands of a depraved felon or merely a robber. Generally speaking, a traveler caught on the road would be tied to a tree and robbed. If the bushranger was depraved, the victim would then be "treated with cruelty." Since the criminals had to live with the idea of "close pursuit" they developed at least one technique to slow down their pursuers. Often the people who had been robbed would be forced "to drink to drunkenness: thus their recollection became confused; they could not follow, and the robbers enjoyed the scene of their helpless intoxication."[11]

But some of the bushrangers were truly brutal. One of the most infamous was a man named Jeffries. He was well known to his fellow convicts because, on his arrival as a transported felon, he had been assigned the job of "scourger," of whipping his fellow convicts who did not work hard enough or fast enough. Jeffries eventually escaped government control and became a bushranger. He invaded the home of a young couple by the name of Tibbs, whom he robbed and then forced into the forest with him. The young mother carried her infant child with her. Jeffries became "disturbed by its cries; perhaps, fearful that the sound might conduct his pursuers." He moved to solve his problem. "He took the child from the arms of its mother and dashed out its brains against a tree!"[12]

Some of the settlers were not only afraid of robbers on the roads and robbers entering their homes, but they were also afraid of their servants, who were often either pass holders, ticket-of-leave holders, or ex-prisoners. At least one settler was seen "counting over the plate which had [recently] been used, and locking it up." That settler probably did suffer from "chronic suspicion."[13]

If all that was not bad enough, the free citizens periodically found themselves pulled into the criminal system. "It was lawful [for the government officials] to arrest any persons suspected of being illegally at large, and to detain them until they 'proved otherwise.'" Mr. Mackay, who was a free citizen, was so arrested at Swan River, "and delivered to [a] . . . hulk, where, loaded with irons of unusual weight, his clothing branded, he was confined with prisoners destined for a penal settlement." Fortunately, by means of a writ of habeas corpus, he obtained his release. He was then rearrested, but once again as a result of assistance from an advocate and the interference of the courts he became a free man.[14] The horrors incurred by Mr. Mackay were also visited on a free female resident of Van Diemen's Land. A young woman who was a native of Van Diemen's Land and a free person had married a man who was a prisoner and who was being taken from Van Diemen's Land to Victoria. The young woman booked passage on the same ship in which her husband was being transported. Suddenly her cabin door was opened. She was charged with being a convict-at-large. She was told that under the circumstances her passage money was forfeited. She was then taken from her cabin, "dragged at night into a boat by constables most of whom were or are prisoners." On landing she was taken to a lockup and stripped naked regardless of "her prayer not to be exposed, as she had lately been confined." "Her feelings [were] insulted." She was treated as a felon until the mistake was discovered.[15]

As a result of those conditions, which the free citizenry called convict pollution, a growing feeling arose during the 1840s on the part of most of the free citizens that their reliance on the labor provided by the transported felons was ultimately destructive to their interests. They believed that the presence of such a large convict element polluted the moral fiber of the society and inclined prospective immigrants, who could provide the necessary and much-needed labor, to settle elsewhere. Leaders had previously sent petitions to the queen asking for an end to transportation and the beginning of representative government. Those petitions were endorsed by a large segment of the Van Diemen's Land population.[16] Accordingly, the desire to end transportation and obtain representative government was daily gaining momentum, and that political climate was the principal indigenous force that was to affect the lot of the Irish exiles.

The lot of the Irish exiles was also to be influenced by the response of the British government in London to the antitransportation and pro–representative-government movements in Van Diemen's Land. The British government formed under Russell sympathized with the demands of the free citizenry, and, during the winter of 1848, the colonial secretary, Earl Grey, had announced that he planned to introduce legislation into the British Parliament at Westminster that would grant representative government to Van Diemen's Land. Grey had previously announced that he intended to bring an end to transportation, but that announcement was not made public in Van Diemen's Land until July 1848. In Van Diemen's Land both of Grey's announcements were originally greeted with great satisfaction, but in the course of time it became painfully clear that, regardless of what was officially announced, transportation would not cease. The convict ships continued to arrive. Grey wanted to end transportation, but he had made his announcement before he had solved several difficult problems, namely where would he direct the flow of convicts that had previously been sent to Van Diemen's Land, and how would he encourage immigration to Van Diemen's Land to provide the free labor necessary to replace that lost from the cessation of convict labor.[17]

Popular reaction in Van Diemen's Land to the government's failure to live up to the promise to end transportation fed fuel to the antitransportation movement. The current governor of Van Diemen's Land, Sir William Denison, favored the practice of transportation. After the British government's failure to end transportation some antitransportation leaders began to suspect that Denison's dispatches had in fact encouraged Grey to discount the significance of the antitransportation movement as a force among the people and that Denison had urged Grey to ignore the protestations of the movement's leaders. Their suspicions had a basis in fact.

Scarcely had Sir William Denison first arrived in Van Diemen's Land in January of 1847 than he reached the conclusion that transportation was not a morally degenerate force and was in fact absolutely necessary for the economic survival of the colony. Denison, a generally able and decisive bureaucrat, was a man quick to form opinions and slow to modify his views under the weight of persuasion. He noted a need for and the benefits of convict labor. He noted with some satisfaction that even the leaders of the antitransportation movement hired convict labor. He sought to portray that situation as displaying a lack of intelligence and a hypocritical inclination and disposition on their behalf. He held two of the leaders in particular abhorrence and later in a private dispatch to Grey referred to them as itinerant agitators. He did not hesitate to vilify the citizenry to Grey as possessing a generally disappointing and self-indulgent character. Denison also expressed his conviction that when representative government was extended to the colony, intelligent administrative leadership, possessing a sense of justice and appointed by himself, would be forced to give way to the leadership of a small group of self-interested wealthy men, who were little more than effective speakers. Denison knew he could not stop Grey from extending representative government to Van Diemen's Land. But Denison urged Grey to rely on him to judge when transportation should end, and he did not hesitate to tell Grey that the moment had not yet come.[18]

At best, Denison was an advocate to Grey for delay in the cessation of transportation. At worst, Denison was a staunch proponent of trans-portation. In the end his inflexible policies were to facilitate the end of transportation and assist the Irish exiles.

The Governor of Van Diemen's Land Carries Out His Orders

On Sunday, 28 October 1849, O'Brien "spent the whole of the day in pacing up and down the deck—enjoying the fineness of the day and the views of the surrounding scenery." The *Swift* stood in Hobart Town harbor, surrounded by small boats, some on errands, some carrying visi-tors, and some of which came out with persons curious to obtain a glimpse of the state prisoners. Sometimes the prisoners on board would see a hat raised, "a handkerchief waved," or hear a voice ask "how the gentlemen were, and when would they come ashore." Meagher construed those expressions to be "evidence of kindly feeling towards us and felt a few warm whispers of the old Irish heart at home were floating through the air." O'Brien also concluded, "We have every reason to believe that there exists towards us here as well as in New South Wales a very kindly feeling of sympathy."[19] O'Brien was right, but there was an unexpected variety of public sympathy awaiting the Irish exiles in the Australian colonies. Generally speaking, it was a sympathy for them as unfortunate individuals and not as revolutionaries.

Most of the Australians were English or Scotch and either did not approve of the rising at Ballingarry or did not give other than passing thought to events so far from their everyday problems. An editorial in the *Hobart Town Courier* probably manifested best the general attitude of most of the inhabitants of Van Diemen's Land toward the Irish state prisoners: "As subjects of the British Crown we must regard their captiv-ity as just—as men we sympathize with their misfortunes." At the same time the intensity of political feeling in the Australian colonies was slowly expanding from that sympathetic tolerance that had motivated the uncontroversial expressions of the *Hobart Town Courier* to a feeling of discontent over the failure of the British authorities to end transpor-tation and extend representative government. It was that discontent, not Irish causes, that motivated the editors of the *Launceston Examiner* to welcome the state prisoners by telling their readers that they believed O'Brien's motives in leading the Irish revolution of 1848 to be both "pure" and "patriotic." The editors thought that O'Brien "erred in judge-ment" and was "deficient in prudence," but he and his associates were not to be considered criminals. They had been sent to Van Diemen's Land to live temporarily in retirement, but they would eventually be pardoned. While in Van Diemen's Land the exiles were urged by the editors to appreciate the fact that they were surrounded by men "sensible of the evils an alien government inflicts." The citizens of Van Diemen's

Land could appreciate "aspirations for freedom" and were willing to "grasp the hand of an honest and high souled man though he erred in his course and fell short of his object."[20]

Governor Denison did not feel at all sympathetic to the state prisoners. Nor was he in agreement with Earl Grey's directive to treat the state prisoners as gentlemen. Governor Denison was prepared to carry out Grey's orders and offer each of the men a ticket-of-leave, but in reality Denison considered the men to be convicts. Grey's orders to treat the men as gentlemen complicated Denison's life, and Lady Denison explained how he felt: "If, indeed, [William] might put them into grey jackets, and send them to wheel barrows on the wharf, or break stones on the roads, like any ordinary convict, it would simplify the matter very considerably." But Governor Denison and his wife both agreed that the gentlemanly treatment ordered by Grey might not last very long. A great deal would depend on how the Irish prisoners behaved, since the orders "are not so precise but that it seems as if they purposely left a good deal to the discretion of the individuals under whom the prisoners are placed."[21] But regardless of Denison's feelings, the clear fact remained that Denison had been ordered to offer tickets-of-leave to the Irish exiles immediately on their arrival, and London preferred for the Irishmen to be officially lost in gentlemanly oblivion.

On Monday, 29 October 1849, between 3:00 and 4:00 P.M., Assistant Comptroller William E. Nairn, and a clerk representing the governor of Van Diemen's Land, came on board the *Swift* to settle the future status of the Irish prisoners. According to Meagher, the meeting took place in the prisoners' saloon with Captain Aldham making the appropriate introductions. Before speaking, Nairn arranged the papers that he carried, "placed them in a line along the table, . . . gently fixed his elbows upon the documents, and join[ed] his hands in a meek and devotional manner."[22] Nairn then told the prisoners that the governor, Sir William Denison, under instructions received from the secretary of state, was authorized to grant special paroles, namely tickets-of-leave, to each of the Irish prisoners, providing the captain could give a good report of their conduct during the voyage, and providing further that they would promise not to attempt to escape from Van Diemen's Land. The regulations appended to those special tickets-of-leave were as follows: "1. Not to proceed out of the district within which your residence has been limited. 2. To report your residence to the Police magistrate and every change of residence which you may desire to make. 3. To report yourself personally to the Police magistrate of the district once a month. 4. Not to be absent from your registered place of residence after 10 o'clock at night. 5. Not to enter any theatre or Billiard Room." In addition, Nairn explained "that each of the State Prisoners was to be placed in a separate district—that they were to hold no communication with each other—

that [the districts] were to be rural inland districts—and that none of the prisoners were to be allowed to reside at Hobart Town." The captain must have given a favorable report of their conduct during the voyage, since Nairn then announced that in order to receive their parole, it only remained for them to promise not to escape.[23]

O'Brien spoke first. He expressed concern with the regulations that would place the state prisoners in rural districts. O'Donoghue's only skill and experience in earning a livelihood had been as a law clerk. To send him to a rural district would deprive him of the means of earning a living and thus "consign him to starvation," therefore, the "offer of comparative liberty" for O'Donoghue was rendered "quite nugatory."[24]

As for himself, O'Brien refused to accept a ticket-of-leave. "Having fully resolved to bind myself by no engagement whatever—a resolution not hastily formed but the result of long deliberation I replied without hesitation that I could not make any pledge that I would not attempt to escape."[25]

McManus followed O'Brien's lead and decided not to enter into any engagement with the government, at least until he knew whether or not he would be located in a district that would afford him an opportunity to make a living as a merchant, the only trade he knew.[26]

Meagher decided to accept the parole "for a limited period—say for three or six months—reserving to himself the power of cancelling it at the end of that period."[27] He reasoned that escape was out of the question. If he accepted the parole, his honor would bind him in the "heaviest irons to the island." If he refused the parole, the authorities would physically bind him. Under those circumstances he wrote, "I thought it much more desirable to accept a small amount of liberty, fettered only by my word of honour, than surrender myself to the confinement of a prison, and the vexatious surveillance of turnkeys and constables." Nairn requested that each of the Irish prisoners put his opinion in writing. After they had complied with his request, he left the ship and carried those opinions to Sir William Denison.[28]

Lady Denison left a record of what both she and her husband thought about the written requests of the Irish prisoners regarding their tickets-of-leave, which Nairn brought to the governor for his consideration. Governor Denison was not completely satisfied with Meagher's insistence on accepting a ticket-of-leave for only six months. Nevertheless, Denison decided to agree to Meagher's conditions since the home government intended Denison to be lenient. Denison thought O'Donoghue's request to be allowed to live in a city was reasonable since it would be necessary for him to get a job in order to support himself. Lady Denison did not leave a record of what her husband thought of the refusal of O'Brien and McManus to accept a ticket-of-leave, but she interpreted their refusal to mean that they would not "do anything which would seem to imply acquiescence in the situation in which they were placed." Denison informed Nairn that O'Brien and McManus would be placed in confinement. O'Brien would be sent to Maria Island and McManus to Salt Water River.[29]

Later that same day, Nairn returned to the *Swift* and informed the prisoners that paroles had been granted to O'Donoghue and Meagher under conditions that suited their individual requirements, but that McManus and O'Brien would be sent to probation stations. Nairn explained that the papers authorizing the arrangements would be delivered to the *Swift* the next day. When it was time for Nairn to depart, he "drew in his lips, economised a smile, slightly bowed, and drawing back his hat as he inclined his head, withdrew."[30]

After Nairn withdrew, the assistant registrar came aboard the *Swift*. His duty was to complete a form describing each prisoner in regard to height, shape of nose, complexion, color of hair and eyes, and other physical marks. The assistant registrar was obviously embarrassed by the duty of having to take such a record of gentlemen who held such a high position in society. He repeatedly murmured, "A delicate, a very delicate business." Meagher reported that when the assistant registrar filled out the required forms describing the prisoners his pen was handled "so softly, that one might have also imagined he wrote upon velvet." With the inspection ended, the registrar apologized for having troubled the men and backed his way out of the room, bowing periodically on his way.[31]

The respect that the assistant registrar afforded the state prisoners was further evidence that even some of the local officials considered the state prisoners to be gentlemen prisoners of war, not convicts. Grey's orders sending four of the state prisoners into exile on the *Swift*, which was a man-of-war, not a convict ship, plus the fact that the men were immediately offered tickets-of-leave, seemed to confirm the conclusion reached by the general populace.

After the assistant registrar departed, O'Brien wrote to his wife and told her that he was not taking a ticket-of-leave. Lucy wanted to join her husband in Van Diemen's Land, but his refusal of the ticket-of-leave made it almost impossible for her to do so. O'Brien asked his wife to wait at least several months before making any decision on the subject. While O'Brien reluctantly opposed Lucy's coming, he made it clear in his letter that he would not forbid her to do so.[32]

O'Brien refused the ticket-of-leave for a number of reasons. He did not want to make any formal arrangements with British officialdom. He did want to take a wait-and-see attitude toward his life as an exile in Van Diemen's Land. He was looking for a way to obtain his release. By refusing the ticket-of-leave he could in honor attempt an escape, if such an opportunity presented itself. If those who observed him were right, he might also find an opportunity for martyrdom and hence a means to end his gentlemanly oblivion. O'Brien was in no hurry to accept a ticket-of-leave. He was in exile, waiting for his release, hoping to return to Ireland.[33] By refusing the ticket-of-leave he asserted his determination from the start to be and remain an Irish leader in exile.

O'Brien's refusal to accept the ticket-of-leave contrasted with the other state prisoners' acceptance of such an arrangement. They were prepared to start life anew. Ireland was important to all the exiles, but they would all, except O'Brien, attempt to build allegiances elsewhere.

The next day, 30 October, the state prisoners did not have much to occupy their time. They knew they would be departing for their new homes on 31 October, but they had not yet received their new assignments. Fortunately, part of the day was spent meeting new friends. The state prisoners were visited by two leaders of the Catholic Church in Van Diemen's Land, the Very Reverend Dr. W. Hall, who was vicar general of the diocese, and the Reverend Mr. Dunne, who was a missionary at Richmond. Both men would in time provide valuable assistance, and Father Dunne in particular became a close friend of O'Brien's. About the same time Dr. Whipple, physician on the *Swift*, introduced O'Brien to the Messrs. Carter, father and son.[34] Mr. Carter, Sr., was an influential leader in Hobart Town who had a number of mercantile stores throughout Van Diemen's Land. While the Carters were known supporters of transportation, Dr. Whipple, no doubt, had thought that O'Brien might find it advantageous to know them, and in the course of time their acquaintance was to prove invaluable.

On the same day, the official papers arrived authorizing the paroles, designating the respective districts in which the Irish exiles were to live, and setting up the arrangements whereby the prisoners would be conveyed to their new places of abode. Lady Denison recorded a last-minute change of plans. O'Brien's "companion in folly, Mr. McManus, repented almost at the last moment" by deciding to accept a ticket-of-leave. The state prisoners learned that on 31 October they were to proceed to their appointed districts. Meagher was to take the 3:30 A.M. coach for Campbell Town; McManus was to proceed a little later on for New Norfolk; and O'Donoghue would proceed to Hobart Town. At 7:00 O'Brien would leave for confinement on Maria Island. Lady Denison unwittingly admitted the government's principal remaining problem by commenting, "So Mr. O'Brien is now the only victim."[35]

Shortly after dark on the evening of the thirtieth, O'Doherty and Martin arrived in Van Diemen's Land. They would also be offered tickets-of-leave under the same conditions as those offered to the others. Both O'Doherty and Martin accepted the tickets-of-leave. O'Doherty was assigned to Oatlands and Martin to Bothwell.[36]

As the state prisoners prepared for their departure from the *Swift* and the *Emma* respectively, Lady Denison penned an interesting comment on the great mistake that the British ministers had made regarding the rebels: "All that can be said in favour of the present system of treatment is, that the English certainly are a generous people, and do not like to tread upon the fallen foe: for which let us give ourselves credit, even though our generosity may be sometimes rather mistaken."[37]

Grey's generosity was cleverly conceived. Unfortunately for the British officials, O'Brien had refused the ticket-of-leave, making the generous policy of "gentlemanly oblivion" not quite complete.

The New Beginning for the Other State Prisoners

Thomas Meagher was the first prisoner to leave the *Swift* on 31 October 1849 to travel to the district to which he had been assigned. The guard boat came for him at 3:00 A.M., and he was on the coach for Campbell Town by 3:30 A.M. He saw very little of Hobart Town as the coach pulled off for its destination, and he arrived in Campbell Town about twelve hours after leaving the *Swift*. The coach delivered him to a hotel where he dined. Meagher then decided to explore the third largest city in Van Diemen's Land. His investigation took only twenty minutes to complete. Campbell Town had one main street, but the street had only one side to it, and there were only about three side streets and an area in which the police had their office, barracks, and jail. If there was an interesting building in Campbell Town, it was the principal hotel. It was operated by an Irish immigrant, Mrs. Kierney, who had hung pictures in her main parlor of some Irish national figures, Brian Boru, Daniel O'Connell, and Father Tom Maguire. Mrs. Kierney believed she had "the most fashionable hotel in the country" and told Meagher that all the important people stopped there, such as the governor, the members of the legislative council, and the bishop. But Meagher was not impressed with Campbell Town. He explained, "Three days having elapsed, I woke up, gave a great yawn, and drove off to Ross."[38]

Ross was much smaller than Campbell Town, but Meagher preferred it. To him Campbell Town had all the characteristics of an "upstart village," a place with "too much glare, dust and gossip." Meagher liked the simplicity of Ross where he could be by himself and feel free enough to live his daily life, apparently without the scrutiny of public comment. Meagher described Ross, in a letter to O'Brien, as the "Elysian of the South Seas." The town not only had forty houses, two hotels, and one of Mr. Carter's stores, but it also had a school for infants. The community's pride in this school was apparently not diminished by the fact that the school building was without windows and a roof. Meagher originally rented rooms from a Mr. and Mrs. Anderson, remembered by him for being devout Wesleyans, but by the end of November he had taken up residence in Hope's Hotel.[39]

Meagher found his days to be exceedingly dull. Although Meagher did form a close friendship at Ross with a Dr. MacNamara, who had originally come from County Clare, in the beginning he spent his days alone, riding and walking, reading and writing, smoking and eating. He explored every corner of the Campbell Town District, an adventure that did not consume a great deal of his time, since the district encompassed an area at the most only thirty-five miles long and fifteen miles wide. While Meagher was physically well and frequently engaged in "loud laughter and skirmishes," he was not happy. The realization that his life had suddenly become purposeless, had become "devoid of all high and ennobling pursuits," affected him greatly. To Meagher, "existence, thus harassed, deadened, drained, ceases to be a blessing—it becomes a penalty." Almost from the moment of his arrival in Van Diemen's Land, Meagher was experiencing "sighs and frets for another destiny, and another world." He soon concluded that there existed little more difference between a prison and a penal district than between a stable and a paddock. "In the one you are tied up by a halter—in the other you have the swing of a tether."[40] From his confinement at Maria Island, O'Brien inquired in one of his letters if Meagher might discover meaning in life by sharing it with a bride. Meagher replied, "As to 'Cupid and his darts'—&c; you are quite wrong if you imagine I have anything to do with the boy in this place." He was quite certain, "I shall never condescend . . . to honour Van Diemen's Land as to make it the scene of my nuptials."[41]

Meagher's unbounding energies required outlets. It was not long before he began writing "volumes for Ireland." He forwarded the fruits of his literary effort in early January 1850, presumably to Duffy.[42] In time Meagher's energies would drive him to discover a means by which he and O'Doherty could regularly meet one another to punctuate their otherwise monotonous lives. Blessed by nature with an exceptionally energetic nature, Meagher's exile became for him a special curse and torment. As his attempts to accommodate himself to his conditions failed, his anxieties multiplied.

*   *   *

Kevin O'Doherty had been assigned to the District of Oatlands, which adjoined the district to which Meagher had been assigned. Living accommodations were provided to O'Doherty through the hospitality of a Mr. Ryan, and O'Doherty was able to continue his medical studies "under the direction of Dr Edward Hall." While in Ireland, O'Doherty had been a medical student and had nearly completed his medical training. When he arrived at Oatlands, he was led to believe that he would be allowed to practice medicine in Van Diemen's Land if he could pass the local medical examination. Accordingly, O'Doherty began to study hard for his qualifying medical examinations. In his spare time he assisted Dr. Hall and Mr. Anstey in their efforts to build a Catholic church in the area. His friends were principally two, a Father W. Bond, who was a young man about his own age and an Irish missionary to Van Diemen's Land, and his fellow state prisoner, Meagher.[43]

The River Blackman constituted the boundary line separating the two districts to which O'Doherty and Meagher had been assigned. The two prisoners had concluded that one-half of the river was property located in the Campbell Town District and the other half in the Oatlands District. Accordingly, the same rule could be applied to the bridge that crossed the River Blackman. The middle pier of the bridge became their meeting place. They resolved to meet every Monday, and on the occasion of their second meeting they christened the place "The Irish Pier." To their weekly meeting O'Doherty and Meagher had the main meal carried over from a nearby inn. On one occasion the river had dried up, and the heat of the day became so intense that the men set up a table under the bridge and dined in the shade.[44]

The meeting place at the River Blackman bridge was soon changed to another location where the penal districts of three state prisoners joined. John Martin wanted to attend the Monday meetings, and he discovered a place, Lake Sorell, where all three of the districts joined. O'Doherty had formed a deep and lasting friendship with John Martin during their long voyage. About this time Martin began to be known as John Knox, probably because he had not attempted to conceal his ardent Protestantism and his inclination to be a reformer in a number of respects. Similarly, O'Doherty began to be known as St. Kevin because, as a Catholic, he had selected St. Thomas à Kempis as his personal spiritual model and openly proclaimed his determination to emulate the saint's patient nature. Those nicknames were adopted by the other exiles and were used with great enthusiasm.

*　　*　　*

Martin had been assigned to the District of Bothwell. When he had first arrived in the town of Bothwell, he had stayed the night in "an inn kept by a person named Whiteway, where the uproar of people drinking here would keep me in a fever." The local magistrate, Captain King, had treated Martin "with perfect courtesy and bonhommie," hardly the treatment normally to be accorded felons by magistrates. The good magistrate told Martin he would recommend a more "eligible lodging," no doubt more suitable to Martin's retiring nature. The reaction of the magistrate to the possible meetings of Martin, O'Doherty, and Meagher betrayed no suspicion or fear of felonious activities. "He laughed good-humouredly when I spoke of the difficulty of discerning the exact boundaries of districts in an expedition [by the state prisoners] to shake hands across the frontier." Martin assured his friends that Magistrate King had no intention of interfering with the meetings of the state prisoners. Captain King in fact suggested several other places where such meetings could conveniently take place.[45]

Regular meetings of the three state prisoners, Meagher, O'Doherty, and Martin, soon became their principal and most promising source of diversion and entertainment. Their respective districts joined where a stream connected Lake Sorell with Lake Crescent. The three men would try to meet every Monday at the junction point, Meagher traveling twenty-four miles, O'Doherty twenty miles, and Martin twenty-five miles. They generally gathered at 11:00 A.M. in a small hut owned by Mr. Cooper. The hut was only fifteen by ten feet and was rather sparsely furnished. Among the items were a bed, a table, two stools and a shelf, two pewter plates, three cups, two knives, and two forks. But Cooper obviously made the men feel welcome. When they arrived, Cooper would begin dinner by "splitting chops, shelling peas, washing onions, and melting himself away in a variety of labours by the log-wood fire." Meanwhile the state prisoners would ramble "along the shores of the lake, talking of old times, singing the old songs, weaving fresh hopes among the old ones that have ceased to bloom." Meagher found welcome relief on those occasions. "They have been summer days, all of them; and through the sunshine have floated the many-coloured memories, the red griefs, the golden hopes of our sad, beautiful old country."[46]

It was not long before other visitors attended the meetings, persons who would not normally have been expected to be found in a circle of felons. Father Bond, Dr. MacNamara, John Connell, the Reverend Thomas Butler, and Mr. Clarke were among those who took part in the festivities. The entertainments were simple but interesting. On at least one occasion Martin recited verses from "The Abbey," Meagher sang "The Bells of Shandon," and O'Doherty read his most recent letter from home. Meagher also was able for the "edification" of the clergy to repeat "word for word the sermon he had heard the previous Sunday."[47] To receive an invitation to the weekly meetings at Lake Sorell was considered by some of the residents of Van Diemen's Land to be quite an honor, and in return the state prisoners were invited to be guests in some of the best homes in Van Diemen's Land, where they were welcome despite their status as prisoners. One of the state prisoners wrote, "Whether those colonists were English, Scotch, Welsh or Irish, they all knew we had no business there, among convicts, and very kindly interposed between us and the extreme vengeance of their home government."[48]

It is significant to note that, at the same time, Governor Denison and his staff, when making their "periodical progresses through the island," were unwelcome in many of the homes that were open to the state prisoners. It was most likely that the unfriendly attitude was due to the controversy over the practice of transportation. Since the state prisoners were not in fact dangerous felons, those prisoners would in time find common ground with those citizens who were opposed to transportation in opposition to the governor. Even some of the magistrates found themselves caught between Denison and strict duty on the one hand and the state prisoners, the settlers who opposed transportation, and their common sense on the other hand. The magistrates who welcomed the Irishmen in their homes soon heard from Denison, who forbade his officials from having any social communication with the Irish prisoners.[49]

* * *

Terence McManus had traveled to the District of New Norfolk after leaving the *Swift*. During his first week in that district he lived in a hotel, but afterward he took up residence in a cottage. McManus wanted to find a job but told O'Doherty, "As to [getting] . . . any remunerative employment you might as well try to catch the moon and make green cheese." McManus managed to live on "about *two pounds per week*." In seeking out friends he "found all the people here Very Civil and altho our Sympathisers are Very few and Very humble still I have met with Civility and hospitality generally." McManus kept himself busy. "From 7 oc [in the] morning til 6 to 9 [at] Night I am out in the back woods with a Double barrell on my shoulder and a fifty mile trip every day between riding and walking is my usual allowance." The exercise had been good for him. He told O'Doherty, "I am now as strong as a . . . horse both in body and stomach."[50] For a man of business, however, such a life did not hold much appeal.

McManus and O'Donoghue met one another at Bridgewater, the common border of the respective districts to which they had been assigned. McManus also found companionship among the few Irish families in the area, and he spent many a "real Irish night" at the home of Bryan Bennett. McManus "asserted that, in altered circumstances, he would spend his days willingly in such surroundings."[51]

McManus kept in contact with O'Doherty by mail. But it was O'Brien whom McManus held in such "affectionate esteem" that, although the older man invited McManus to write to him, McManus found it too painful to do so. Concerning O'Brien, McManus wrote O'Doherty that he had faith "a day will yet arrive that will make all those things straight."[52]

* * *

Patrick O'Donoghue was the only state prisoner to be assigned to Hobart Town. For the first week he lived in a hotel, but later he took lodgings in the house of an English woman named Ludgater. For ten shillings a week he rented a back room that served as "a sleeping room, parlour and drawing room." He had come to Hobart Town to seek employment, with five sovereigns forced on him by O'Brien aboard the *Swift*, and with two more from another friend. Realizing O'Donoghue's predicament, Father John Joseph Therry, Father William J. Dunne, and John Regan offered him the hospitality of their homes. Bishop Robert William Willson also proclaimed his home "to be open to O'Donoghue at all times, and he earnestly pleaded with him by letter, to accept his hospitality at least for a few months." While O'Donoghue dined at the bishop's home on several occasions, he disliked "trenching too much upon generous hospitality." He could not be "the recipient of other men's bounty."[53]

O'Donoghue did not like Hobart Town, and that was part of his problem. "This town, or City as they call it, contains a very base population—a nest of hornets—vipers—snakes worse than the black ones of the Bush." O'Donoghue characterized the entire citizenry as "liars, Drunkards, and scheming hypocrites." He could be more specific when he wanted to be: "The public houses and hotels are filled at 9 o'clock in the morning, they settle down to drink as deliberately as they do at 7 in the evening." He concluded, "I think they do nothing but eating, drinking, whoring and backbiting—and the disease runs through all Classes, from the Merchant and Professional man down to the shoe boy!" Another part of O'Donoghue's problem was his own habit of excessive drinking. It was a problem he recognized, and in an effort to help himself he spent time at the local temperance society. "I have a good deal to do to resist the temptations which my overkind friends here throw in my way—however, I have done so successfully, and will continue to do so." O'Donoghue professed an inconsistency between excessive drinking and the patriotic movement in which he had been involved. "I consider the honour of ourselves and our cause involved in it, therefore it would be traitorism to be culpable in that regard."[54]

O'Donoghue sought a position as a legal clerk in a law office, since he had worked in such an office in Ireland before being transported to Van Diemen's Land. He soon discovered, however, that such positions in the legal profession were "overstocked." He thought of seeking a position as a bookkeeper in a business house, but he was to be disappointed for other reasons. Prospective employers consistently had the impression, through rumors that had preceded O'Donoghue, that he was not under the compulsion to work because O'Brien had reportedly given 150 guineas for his upkeep. In addition, those same prospective employers understood that he might entertain objectives that were politically dangerous. It was rumored that O'Donoghue intended to start a newspaper with Mr. Mone, the printer and publisher of the *Hobart Town Guardian*, or perhaps with the Reverend Mr. Bayley, who published a newspaper of his own. O'Donoghue considered that both rumors "though laughable enough, are calculated to injure me," and as for dangerous political activity, "I look upon an Irish rebel in too respectable a light for that."[55]

After a few weeks of looking for employment to no avail, O'Donoghue apparently changed his mind about the respectability of newspaper publishing and decided to publish a newspaper, the *Irish Exile*. Martin opposed O'Donoghue's plans, and Meagher also joined in opposition, saying that the best course of action for the state prisoners was to stand aloof from the local politics. But while O'Donoghue appreciated "the justness and propriety" of their objections, he believed that the only opportunity "open to him for the realization of an honourable livelihood" lay in the direction of publishing a newspaper.[56]

The prospectus for O'Donoghue's *Irish Exile* was published in December 1849.[57] Lady Denison recorded in her journal the apparent suspicions and convictions of the government officials at Hobart Town, namely, that the authors would be the Irish prisoners and that the paper would advocate violence. Her husband was in the meantime "waiting for quite decisive evidence before he takes any step in consequence," and Governor Denison took care to obtain one of the placards advertising the publication of the *Irish Exile* "in readiness to send it home to Lord Grey, as a specimen of the language they are holding."[58]

*   *   *

On arriving in Van Diemen's Land, Meagher, O'Doherty, Martin, McManus, and O'Donoghue had all attempted to adjust to a life of exile. They had managed to keep in communication with one another and had begun to build new friendships among the free citizens who did view them more as prisoners of war than as convicts. But none of the Irishmen had quite settled down. Those who sought work had not really been successful in their quest, and those who did not have to work had not yet found activities that gave real satisfaction. There was a terrible insecurity to their lives. In addition, Denison's attitude that the men were really convicts and would eventually cross the line of propriety made more difficult an already complex and fluctuating situation.

Maria Island and Confinement for O'Brien

O'Brien left the *Swift* at 7:00 on 31 October 1849. He boarded a special government steamer that was to take him to Maria Island. The steamer sailed under orders to take the prisoner directly from the *Swift* to Maria Island and not to stop at Hobart Town on the way. As the steamer moved out of the harbor shortly after seven, it passed the ship that had brought Kevin O'Doherty and John Martin to Van Diemen's Land the previous night. Luckily, O'Doherty and Martin were on deck and O'Brien was able to exchange salutations with them.[59]

O'Brien enjoyed the trip to Maria Island, but he could not restrain his anxiety about what might await him on his arrival. He found the weather to be excellent and the scenery both beautiful and striking. The ship passed under two headlands, Cape Raoul and Cape Pillar, basaltic rock columns rising from the sea to a height of one thousand feet, "which are rendered remarkable not only by their bold and lofty appearance but also by their columnar formation which is as regular as if it were constructed by the hand of art." No other point of the coast was as outstanding. The forest, which could also be seen from the passing steamer, appeared to have an "interminable continuity" and created an "intense sentiment of loneliness."[60]

While O'Brien journeyed to Maria Island, Captain Aldham of the *Swift* was warning Governor Denison about O'Brien. On 31 October 1849, Sir William and Lady Denison entertained Captain Aldham at dinner, and after discussing general business the conversation turned to O'Brien. Lady Denison later recorded that Aldham believed O'Brien hoped he would be treated with severity while at Maria Island so "that he might have something to make a sensation, and excite commiseration with." The captain was convinced that O'Brien wanted "to be made a martyr of." Lady Denison wrote confidently in reply that O'Brien "will probably, therefore, be extremely disgusted with his situation on Maria Island: no martyrdom, no grievance, and *nobody to hear of it* if he had one!"[61]

By nightfall the steamer carrying O'Brien had let down its anchor off Darlington, the probation station at Maria Island that would serve as his place of confinement. The officials of the probation station, Captain Bailey, the visiting magistrate, and Samuel Lapham, the superintendent of the station, lost no time in coming on board to greet the prisoner and make arrangements for his debarkation. Since they had only very recently received their orders respecting O'Brien, they were unprepared to receive him, and arrangements were promptly made for O'Brien to spend the night on the steamer.[62] But if their orders had been inconveniently tardy, the directions were unequivocal and concise. O'Brien was definitely to be regarded as a prisoner and hence subject to the orders of Superintendent Lapham, but his treatment was to be such as could only be described as "special." Superintendent Lapham was to "personally ascertain that he is present at his Quarters on the night and morning of each day," but he was to be assigned officer's quarters, issued an officer's allowance for fuel and light, and was to receive a hospital ration of food. Lapham was not to subject O'Brien to any "coercive employment," nor to require O'Brien to wear prison garb. Lapham, in consultation with

Bailey, was to determine the area in which O'Brien was to take his exercise and the time when such exercise should be taken. The orders mentioned the fact that there would be no objection if the designated period of exercise was "specified, as between sunrise and sunset."[63]

The next day the officials of the station came to claim O'Brien, since the arrangements ashore had been completed. The special treatment that O'Brien was to receive was evident from the start. He was introduced to a Mr. Miller, who was to be his overseer. Miller had been a soldier, a personal orderly to officers, and, in fact, had been assigned to attend O'Brien, not to oversee him. O'Brien's cottage was small. He told his wife it was "about the size of one of the smallest bathing lodges at Kilkee," and the furniture was of the rudest kind. But O'Brien was satisfied and acknowledged in his diary that he would remain content if he could obtain "as much plain wholesome food as is necessary to support nature and as much furniture as is necessary to prevent me from falling into the habits of one of the Aborigines of this quarter of the world."[64]

O'Brien's social life was to be comparatively active since he was allowed the companionship of the local officials and their families. Several of those officials were Irish, such as Captain Bailey, Superintendent Lapham, and Assistant Superintendent McGauran. Other persons with whom O'Brien formed friendly relationships were a physician, Dr. Smart, and a Catholic priest, Father Odillo Woolfrey. Without any initial hesitation or compunction, the officials "vied with each other in evincing kindness and courteous attention towards O'Brien." O'Brien was allowed to explore the island on 5 November, when he rode with Captain Bailey and some of the other residents to Long Point, another probation station about seven miles from Darlington, where thirty convicts or so had been assigned. On this trip O'Brien learned that the government officials in Hobart Town were planning to close the probation stations on Maria Island, probably within the year.[65]

*   *   *

Confinement of O'Brien, however pleasantly to be endured, was not the means by which the Colonial Office in London had expected to relegate the state prisoners to gentlemanly oblivion. Earl Grey of the Colonial Office had chosen the ticket-of-leave as the means by which the government's purposes could be best effected, a means that was notably free from popular associations with walls and prison paraphernalia and, therefore, a means unlikely to provoke notoriety and sympathy. O'Brien's refusal to accept a ticket-of-leave had forced the government to adopt unwillingly the measure that Grey had sought to avoid. Therefore, Denison's orders for O'Brien's gentlemanly confinement, while likely to forestall public notice temporarily, might not prevent indefinitely an unacceptable increase of public sympathy; furthermore, the initial orders could hardly be expected to incline O'Brien toward accepting the ticket-of-leave desired by Earl Grey.

It appears that Dr. John Stephen Hampton, the comptroller general, who had not been in Hobart Town when the Irish prisoners had arrived,[66] realized the problem. When he returned a new policy was adopted. O'Brien was not "to enter the Quarters of any officer," his exercise area was to be narrowly defined, all of his mail was to be inspected by Dr. Hampton and approved before either being forwarded to him or from him, and the officers were forbidden to speak with him unless it was necessary for the performance of their duties. Those new measures were justified on the basis that they were necessary to prevent an escape.[67] It is possible that Hampton and Denison had another goal in mind. O'Brien was effectively placed in solitary confinement; hence, the chances had greatly increased that, in time, he would be forced into accepting a ticket-of-leave.

On 6 November, Nairn sent to Lapham those additional instructions for O'Brien's confinement. When the new instructions were implemented on 8 November, O'Brien concluded that he had been placed in a certain type of solitary confinement. He knew he did not possess superhuman strength, but he hoped, "If . . . penal infliction stop here I trust that for a season at least, I shall be able to endure it with cheerfulness."[68]

On 13 November, Hampton was at the Darlington Probation Station for the purpose of changing, once again, Denison's instructions for O'Brien's confinement. Governor Denison had purportedly received "various queries . . . from the Officers on the Station, indicative of the embarrassment in which they were placed by the anomalous position of the Prisoner." Using those queries as his apparent justification for changing the current policy toward O'Brien, Denison directed the comptroller general to visit the station "and decide, upon the spot, as to the measures which it would be necessary to take for the proper security of the Prisoner."[69] Hampton was not satisfied that the instructions of 29 October and 6 November were adequate to insure the security of O'Brien. He prescribed another set of instructions, dated 13 November, which were to be observed in addition to those previously issued. Dr. Hampton ordered that O'Brien be moved to another house, that bars of iron be placed on its windows, that a permanent guard be stationed in the house, that O'Brien's presence in his quarters be officially determined every four hours of the day and night, that no one was to speak to him except the visiting magistrate or the superintendent, and then only when it was absolutely necessary in order to discharge their duties. O'Brien was to receive the standard government food allowance for prisoners instead of the previously authorized hospital ration, he was to be allowed a small exercise area immediately outside the house, and he was to be allowed to attend divine services at the probation station church.[70]

As predicted by Captain Aldham, O'Brien hastened to use Hampton's new instructions to gain the attention and sympathy of the public. Ultimately, he hoped that public sympathy would be a useful foundation on which the governing party in England would, at an appropriate time, be able to grant him a pardon. Correspondence, particularly with prominent personages, was to be the principal means by which O'Brien would call attention to himself and thereby lay such a foundation of public sympathy. He first wrote to Archdeacon Marriot of Sydney, a personal friend of O'Brien's brother-in-law, the Reverend Charles Harris. When O'Brien had arrived in Van Diemen's Land, he had received a letter from the archdeacon expressing solicitude for his current situation. O'Brien's first letter of complaint about the stringent regulations that Hampton had recently prescribed was in answer to Archdeacon Marriot's previous letter. The archdeacon received O'Brien's letter with apparent mixed feelings. He regretted to learn of O'Brien's plight, but he believed that O'Brien had erred in not accepting the ticket-of-leave, and he told him that he hoped O'Brien would reconsider his decision. "I cannot help hoping you may think, on reflection, that you formed that purpose, without full information." It was evident from the reply that Archdeacon Marriot would not then be one of the means by which O'Brien's predicament would be publicized or by which O'Brien would otherwise achieve his objectives. O'Brien's second letter of complaint was addressed to Mr. Reeves, a merchant of Hobart Town who, on 1 November, had written to O'Brien introducing himself and saying, "If there is anything I can do or if there is any matter in which I can be of the slightest service I will feel pleased and honoured by the commission." O'Brien thanked him for his offer of assistance and explained that he was being held in solitary confinement and could discern no reason for such treatment.[71] Reeves was not powerful enough to assist O'Brien, so O'Brien's complaint to him had no immediate effect, but Reeves was a prominent man especially sympathetic to the plight of the Irish exiles, and in time he would become a principal agent through whom O'Brien would bring popular opinion to bear on official policy.

On 22 November, O'Brien wrote again for the same purpose, but this time to England. He wrote to Chisholm Anstey, a member of the British Parliament at Westminster, a representative of an Irish constituency, but also a man who had previously lived in Van Diemen's Land and who had family still living there. O'Brien told Anstey that he had refused the ticket-of-leave because he did not want to commit himself before he had had an opportunity to analyze his position. He expressed little expectation of escape, but he thought it "advisable not to fetter myself by an engagement which I should hold binding upon me as a man of honour but which an unscrupulous man would easily find some pretext for evading in case circumstances should hold out a temptation to set it at naught." O'Brien complained to Anstey that Denison was exceeding the strict limits of his duty by imposing unwarranted punishment in the form of solitary confinement. O'Brien expressed his own convictions that Denison's actions were intended to coerce him into accepting a ticket-of-leave and that his friends in Europe "should be made acquainted with the facts."[72]

O'Brien wrote similar letters to influential and sympathetic members of his own family, a family that was well connected with powerful government leaders. Practically speaking, every member of his family disapproved of his revolutionary activities, but family loyalty and affections were strong, and his relatives were determined to do everything they could to obtain his release. O'Brien wrote to his brother, Sir Lucius O'Brien, who was also a member of the British Parliament. After acknowledging that he had not been compelled to wear a prison uniform or perform manual labor, he complained about the harshness of his solitary confinement and its illegality. He argued that solitary confinement was a punishment for misconduct that occurred after a prisoner's arrival, was meted out only after a regular trial, and in any case never exceeded thirty days. He explained that he had already spent four weeks in solitary confinement without any allegations having been made, without having undergone any form of trial, and without any indication of how long he would be so confined. O'Brien acknowledged that neither the British government nor Parliament was likely to be inclined to redress his grievance, but he believed the public should be aware of the facts and that the force of public opinion would eventually obtain for him an amelioration of his condition. O'Brien also addressed similar letters to the brothers William and Charles Monsell.[73] O'Brien was aware that the Monsells were his loyal supporters. Charles Monsell was married to O'Brien's sister Harriet. They, in turn, were personal friends of William Gladstone and his wife. William Gladstone was a leading political figure, and Charles and Harriet repeatedly mentioned the plight of O'Brien to him in an effort to enlist his help in securing a pardon. William Monsell was considered a member of the O'Brien family circle by virtue of his brother's marriage to Harriet, and he never desisted in his attempt to help O'Brien.

Reports of O'Brien's treatment began to appear in the Australian press in late November and early December. The *South Australian Register* editorialized that when the "misguided and exiled patriot" refused the ticket-of-leave "we expected to hear that he would be viewed in the light of a high-minded prisoner of war who contemplated the possibility of escape, and therefore, declined being at large on his parole of honour, and that he would be placed under *surveillance*, but we little dreamed that anything like oppression would be exercised in his case." The *Hobart Town Guardian* also commented on O'Brien's case and referred to the government's "unjust and irresponsible coercion in the case of Smith O'Brien."[74]

Whether those newspaper comments led the local government officials in Hobart Town to check on O'Brien's health is unknown, but on 15 December, Dr. Dawson, the chief of the medical department of Van Diemen's Land, paid O'Brien a visit. O'Brien used the occasion to continue his campaign to gain a sympathetic audience. O'Brien complained to Dr. Dawson about his solitary confinement. O'Brien recorded in his journal that he was not certain whether Dawson would pressure the government to change its policy.[75] Actually Dawson was totally unsympathetic with O'Brien's complaints. Dawson tended to agree with Captain Aldham's opinion that what O'Brien wanted was to excite "great interest and sympathy." Dawson thought that once O'Brien had public sympathy he would turn those expressions to his advantage with the result "that somebody or *bodies* will ask for a ticket of leave for him, thus allowing him to gain the comparative freedom without compromising his own sulky dignity." Dawson was interested in defeating O'Brien's plan. He wanted to exert pressure on O'Brien to request his own ticket-of-leave. Dawson enlisted the support of Dr. Smart. He asked Smart to keep a careful watch on O'Brien's health and when necessary give "any little extra indulgence in the way of diet, &c., that may seem advisable" but "to keep impressing on [O'Brien] that if he requires change, it depends upon himself to get it, by the simple process of asking."[76] Once again O'Brien's attempt to gain the sympathy of someone who would pressure the government to end his solitary confinement had failed.

O'Brien's diet was markedly improved around this time. He was allowed a hospital ration of food rather than a regular convict's ration.[77] It is unknown whether Smart used the relaxation of the regulations governing O'Brien's consumption of food as an opportunity to try and persuade O'Brien to accept a ticket-of-leave.

*   *   *

The coming of the Christmas season was depressing for O'Brien not only because he was in solitary confinement but also because he was a member of a large and loving family whom he missed very much. O'Brien's mother was still very active. He had seven brothers and sisters who were living. He had three brothers, Lucius, Robert, and Henry; three married sisters, Anne Martineau, Harriet Monsell, and Katherine Harris; and a fourth sister, Grace, who never married. His father was dead, as was a fourth brother, Edward. O'Brien and his wife, the former Lucy Gabbett, had seven children. The three older children, Edward

William, Lucy Josephine, and William Joseph, wrote with great regularity, while the four younger children, Donough Robert, Lucius Henry, Charlotte Grace, and Charles Murrough, were too young to correspond. Charles was the most recent addition to the family and had been baptized in Kilmanhain Jail so that his father, who was in prison there, could be present at the ceremony.[78]

O'Brien felt strongly about his family and its relationship to Ireland. Like Lucy, several of his children expressed a desire to come live with him in Van Diemen's Land, but O'Brien opposed any such requests. He wanted his children to have the same feeling toward Ireland that he had, and he was afraid that if any of them came to live with him in exile they would not develop a deep attachment to Ireland. While O'Brien had to admit to his family, "I am afraid it will be a long time before you light up the bonfires on the hills of Cullen which are to welcome my return to Ireland," he believed the day would come when he would return. He had concluded, "I still feel that my destiny and that of my children is inseparably connected with Ireland."[79]

Through an unhappy Christmas Day 1849, O'Brien missed the company of his loving family circle. But although he was unhappy he had not despaired. He still preserved a conviction that his life in Van Diemen's Land served an important purpose: "Still is my belief unshaken that these sufferings are designed to advance some object which my ken cannot scrutinise and under this feeling I accept with cheerful resignation the chastisement and pray that it may conduce if not to my temporal at least to my eternal welfare."[80]

Eighteen forty-nine had not been a good year for O'Brien. He had been transported to Van Diemen's Land against his will. He had been separated from his loving family. He had been placed in solitary confinement and had been unsuccessful in attracting a sympathetic audience to his plight. He was, no doubt, glad to see the year come to an end.

O'Brien Develops a Sympathetic Audience in Van Diemen's Land

O'Brien welcomed the New Year, 1850, with a spirit of determined optimism. But within a few days after making a New Year's resolution to persevere in his decision to refrain from cooperating with the government and to do everything in his power to keep himself from being "buried alive,"[81] O'Brien realized that the conditions under which he had made his initial resolution had changed. By 4 January 1850 he had to admit his health was failing. O'Brien had, for the first time, experienced chest pains that he diagnosed as the beginning of a heart condition. He noted in his journal, "I feel that Dr. Hampton's recipe for extinguishing an Irish patriot is beginning to do its work," and he acknowledged, "The scorpion and the viper can rob men of life as well as the lion—and the sting of a gnat will often irritate the temper more than the severest stroke inflicted by a formidable adversary."[82]

During the first week of January, Dr. Smart, the physician attached to the Darlington Probation Station, also noticed the change in O'Brien's condition, and he informed Superintendent Lapham that O'Brien's health was suffering from his eight weeks of solitary confinement. Lapham was authorized by Governor Denison to relax the regulation that limited O'Brien's physical exercise, as long as the attending physician deemed additional exercise indispensable to the maintenance of the prisoner's health.[83] Lapham adjusted the regulation to such an extent that O'Brien was allowed unlimited exercise during daylight hours as long as he was in the company of his overseer, Miller.

Lapham also "availed himself of a general undefined permission" given a convict superintendent to maintain the health of a prisoner and suspended Dr. Hampton's rule that no one could talk to O'Brien.[84] Lapham informed the officers and members of their families that they should feel free to talk with O'Brien whenever they would meet him while he was taking exercise. In other words, Lapham ended O'Brien's solitary confinement.

On the tenth, accompanied by Miller, O'Brien was allowed to walk around the neighborhood of the station. O'Brien was struck by his physical weakness as he took his first walk after the extended period of solitary confinement. He was convinced "that if I had been shut up for a fortnight longer my constitution would have been irretrievably impaired and it is not improbable that my life or my reason would have been sacrificed." O'Brien implied in his journal that he had previously concluded that Denison had placed him in solitary confinement in order to force him to accept the ticket-of-leave. Now he concluded, "The object of Sir William Denison was to subdue me at any hazard—even though my life should be sacrificed in the attempt."[85]

The seriousness of the situation in which O'Brien found himself moved him to write a detailed letter describing his recent treatment to Sir George Grey, the home secretary. O'Brien also decided to seek legal assistance. He wrote a letter to Robert Pitcairn, a Hobart Town attorney, asking him to represent him and ascertain what his legal rights were in case he decided to challenge "in a court of justice the legality of a species of imprisonment which threatened to be fatal to me." O'Brien did not believe the treatment he was receiving had been ordered by the British ministers in London. O'Brien then asked Pitcairn to answer three specific questions. He wanted to know if either the transportation laws passed by Westminster or the colonial laws passed by the Legislative Council in Van Diemen's Land authorized the government to consign a transported felon to solitary confinement for an indefinite period of time; if he could obtain a writ of habeas corpus that would force Governor

Denison and Dr. Hampton to show under what authority he was kept in solitary confinement; and, finally, whether or not a writ of habeas corpus could be drawn in England or Ireland to discover if his treatment was legal if it was determined that no such writ could be obtained in Van Diemen's Land. Pitcairn answered O'Brien's letter promptly saying that he was a solicitor and could not alone handle a case of that nature. Pitcairn, however, was planning to consult two barristers, J. Gregson and T. Knight, who were experts in the field, and he felt that they could be expected to prepare appropriate legal opinions regarding O'Brien's case. Pitcairn and the two barristers were active leaders in the antitransportation movement.[86]

By the end of February, O'Brien received the legal opinions of Gregson and Knight. Gregson's opinion was forwarded on 19 February. He advised O'Brien not to begin legal action. He did not believe it would be prudent for O'Brien to challenge the Hobart Town officials in the courts.[87] On 26 February, O'Brien received the legal opinion of Knight, who presented some observations and suggestions that inclined O'Brien to expect that legal means might offer him an appropriate avenue for relief from his present predicament. Knight was an outspoken opponent of transportation and as such had made a particularly detailed study of the statutes governing transportation. Knight considered O'Brien's solitary confinement to be illegal. He did not believe the secretary of state would issue such instructions to the governor of Van Diemen's Land. Knight recommended that O'Brien sue for a writ of habeas corpus in Van Diemen's Land and thereby force Governor Denison to disclose the instructions from the secretary of state to the court. Knight told O'Brien, "I cannot for a moment presume that any such order exists." If none did, the courts would issue an order immediately releasing O'Brien from solitary confinement. Knight had some other opinions on the transportation law that he shared with O'Brien. He told O'Brien that the current law contained several obscure passages, which he believed required the secretary of state to designate a specific place of confinement for the transported felon from which the felon could not be released until the expiration of his term. Knight was questioning the release of the felons by means of a pass and a ticket-of-leave.[88] In other words, he was questioning the whole system of transportation as practiced in Van Diemen's Land.

O'Brien decided not to sue for a writ of habeas corpus at that time.[89] No doubt Gregson's recommendation to be prudent had some effect. In addition, O'Brien knew that his current situation was sufficient to maintain his physical and mental health. His letters of complaint to the British Isles might result in orders being issued to Denison to refrain from placing him back in solitary confinement once his health was restored. O'Brien was willing to give the British officials time to issue such orders. If such orders were not forthcoming and he was placed back in solitary confinement he would then consider instructing Knight to sue for a writ of habeas corpus.

Knight's opinion also convinced O'Brien that the antitransportation forces in Van Diemen's Land were serious in their endeavor to end transportation. From what he had heard from the officials and from members of their families on Maria Island, and from the arguments in Knight's opinion, O'Brien believed the British government would end transportation before the storm of protest forced it to do so. He believed that when transportation ceased all of the convicts in Van Diemen's Land would receive conditional pardons, including himself. Knight's opinion gave O'Brien real hope. On 8 March, O'Brien again wrote Chisholm Anstey, this time about the legal opinions he had obtained from Gregson and Knight, and he sent a copy of Knight's opinion to Anstey.[90]

*   *   *

O'Brien's connection with the leaders in the antitransportation movement was extremely important. Since he had been placed in solitary confinement O'Brien had been searching for a sympathetic audience in Van Diemen's Land and Great Britain. Although his initial efforts to locate such an audience in Van Diemen's Land had failed, once O'Brien obtained legal assistance he had connections with three important leaders of the movement, Pitcairn, Gregson, and Knight. O'Brien had accidently located a force that had a mutuality of interest with him. Knight was interested in challenging the transportation law in the Van Diemen's Land courts, and he probably thought his case would be helped by the fact that his client was recognized by the public in Van Diemen's Land as a gentleman. O'Brien was not prepared to sue for a writ of habeas corpus at that time, but Knight could afford to be patient. In addition both O'Brien and the leaders of the antitransportation movement opposed Denison. O'Brien opposed Denison initially because he was struggling against oblivion, and his opposition to Denison grew when he realized his solitary confinement could result in madness, physical collapse, or death. The antitransportationists opposed Denison because they knew his dispatches advocated transportation and they suspected that Denison was defaming them to the British ministers. O'Brien could not have found better advocates. The leaders of the antitransportation movement were, by and large, intelligent men. In addition they had the columns of the *Launceston Examiner* at their disposal. Finally, they were busy building an organization on a grass-roots level. O'Brien knew the importance of martyrdom. The antitransportation leaders also knew its importance. O'Brien's martyrdom was about to be used by those leaders to defame their mutual enemy, Governor Denison. O'Brien had found his sympathetic audience in Van Diemen's Land.

CHAPTER 3

Old Policy and New Plans

Denison Reports to the British Officials in London

The state prisoners had arrived in Van Diemen's Land on 27 October, but it was not until early December that Governor Denison wrote his first dispatch concerning them, and that dispatch he wrote under the compulsion of events. The prospectus for O'Donoghue's *Irish Exile* appeared in early December and was well publicized. Notices of its appearance were carried in the press.[1] It was the publication of O'Donoghue's prospectus coupled with O'Brien's letters of complaint that set off a volley of dispatches during December between Governor Denison and Earl Grey. All of O'Brien's mail was read by Dr. Hampton and, when necessary, Governor Denison before being forwarded to the Colonial Office in London. Denison, therefore, had the opportunity to write detailed explanations for Grey in the dispatches that accompanied O'Brien's letters of complaint.

The purpose of Denison's first dispatch was to prove that the state prisoners were convicts. Denison began his report to Grey by commenting on O'Donoghue's announcement that he planned to publish a newspaper, the *Irish Exile*. Denison believed that all of the state prisoners were involved in the undertaking. His information was that they would all contribute articles for the paper. He had been told that the state prisoners had cleverly devised a plan by which their connection with the paper would be concealed. The original handwritten copy would be placed in the custody of an agent who would take the copy to the printer. As soon as the proofs had been made, the agent would take possession of the original copy again and return it to the writer. Denison told Grey he had disliked granting tickets-of-leave to the state prisoners, but he had obeyed his orders. Now with the publication of the prospectus for the *Irish Exile* he had grounds, he thought, to demonstrate to the ministry that the British leaders had acted too leniently toward the men. Denison believed that the newspaper was an "attempt to sow dissension among the people of this Colony." He felt that the prisoners' objective, "though wild and absurd, is most mischievous." He entertained no doubt that they would fail in their designs, but he believed that their activities proved they had no appreciation of the treatment they had received at the hands of the British ministers and the officials of Van Diemen's Land. He expressed his fear that the state prisoners would continue to cause

56

much inconvenience. He had no doubt that they were inveterate law-breakers.[2]

The purpose of Denison's second dispatch was to demonstrate the seriousness of the error in treating the state prisoners as gentlemen. Denison's report contained the information that the state prisoners were receiving a sympathetic acceptance by many of the citizens of Van Diemen's Land and that O'Brien was currently seeking, by means of letters, a similarly sympathetic audience in the British Isles. Denison was about to demonstrate his bureaucratic abilities by deftly putting the blame for the state prisoners' success at being received sympathetically in Van Diemen's Land and for O'Brien's attempt to reawaken support in Great Britain on Grey and the British ministers.

Denison began his second dispatch by informing Earl Grey that he considered the leniency granted to the state prisoners to be totally without historical precedent, and he supported his opinion with a list of the names of several transported offenders who were men of education, of high social standing, and who were guilty of political offense, yet who "were sent to the Gangs and placed upon the same footing precisely as other convicts." Denison named, for example, two Chartists, John Frost and William Jones, as men who fell into such a category. Denison did not consider it possible to administer the penal stations properly if he was required to classify the convicts on the basis of social rank. He called the attention of Earl Grey to the fact that a difficulty had already arisen as a result of the "anomalous position" in which the state prisoners had been placed. The prisoners had been admitted into the society of the better classes of the community, and even the magistrates were treating them as equals.[3]

After registering his complaint regarding Earl Grey's orders to treat the state prisoners as gentlemen and grant them tickets-of-leave, Denison reported that all of the state prisoners had accepted a ticket-of-leave except O'Brien. Denison did not think highly of O'Brien. He believed O'Brien was self-centered, vain, and obstinate. Denison was shocked when he realized O'Brien viewed himself as a prisoner of war, not as a convicted felon. Denison then warned Grey that O'Brien was writing letters of complaint to friends of his in England. He believed those friends would question Grey about O'Brien's treatment and that some questions would eventually be raised in Parliament and would be the signal for an attack on the government in power. Denison fully realized that Grey needed an explanation from him that could be used to defend such an attack on the government. In the dispatches written in December, therefore, Denison attempted to give Grey the information he needed. He included copies of the regulations issued on 29 October and 6 and 13 November. Denison's position was that O'Brien's mode of treatment was designed to prevent an escape. Denison also told Grey that he hoped O'Brien would "in a short time [see] the folly of his conduct and avail himself of the indulgence of a Ticket of Leave which was offered to him."[4] In a later dispatch, Denison called Grey's attention to O'Brien's letter to Chisholm Anstey, which constituted a type of admission by O'Brien of an intent to escape if the proper circumstances were present. Respecting the severe regulations and limitations about which O'Brien had complained, Denison said that he did not consider the regulations governing O'Brien's confinement to be severe at all. Denison made no mention of the word *solitary*, and he called Grey's attention to the fact that O'Brien had been assigned a two-room house of his own and allowed the use of a garden where he could take exercise. In addition, O'Brien was allowed to have his own books around him, was granted a hospital ration of food, and was not asked to perform manual labor nor wear a prison uniform. As a matter of fact, Denison did not believe greater leniency could have been accorded O'Brien than that which was given, especially when it was remembered that O'Brien could obtain his freedom any time he wished by accepting a ticket-of-leave.[5] Denison no doubt hoped Grey approved of his actions.

By the end of January, Denison was ready to start another group of dispatches to assist Grey in answering any questions that might be asked regarding O'Brien's treatment. The first dispatch in the new group was an attempt by Denison to defend himself against a charge of being responsible for the collapse of O'Brien's health. In a letter to the secretary of state for the Home Department, O'Brien had recounted the details of his ill health and the recent relaxation of the rules that had caused his health to improve. Denison sought to transfer all official responsibility for O'Brien's health to Dr. Smart by taking the position that the doctor did not really require his permission to relax the rules governing O'Brien's diet or area of exercise whenever he conceived such relaxation "to be indispensable for the preservation of [O'Brien's] health."[6]

It was O'Donoghue's actions, not O'Brien's, that triggered the next dispatch. O'Donoghue published the first issue of his *Irish Exile* on 26 January 1850. Denison explained in a dispatch dated 29 January how he had never really believed the paper would be published. He still did not believe it could last. Nevertheless Denison informed Grey that Dr. Hampton had already been in touch with O'Donoghue and clearly warned him he could not comment on government in the columns of the paper. Denison assured Grey that he would keep him fully informed.[7]

The next important dispatch relating to the Irish prisoners was written by Denison on 17 April. On that occasion it was O'Brien's action of seeking legal advice that caused attention. Denison thought very little of Knight's opinion and did not hesitate to say so to Earl Grey. Denison believed Knight's problem was that he had "confounded Penal Settlements, and Places which may be appointed in any part of the British

Dominions for employing Convicts at hard labour." Denison closed his report by stating, "The Prisoner has not taken further steps."[8]

Denison wanted Grey to know that he had everything under control. But he also wanted Grey to understand that the orders the British ministers had issued regarding the state prisoners were causing difficulties. Those orders were responsible for the support that the state prisoners had among the free citizens in Van Diemen's Land and might be responsible for O'Brien receiving support from the general public in the British Isles. Denison realized Grey's policy of gentlemanly oblivion for the state prisoners had failed, and his dispatches were aimed at placing the responsibility for that failure back on Grey.

Reaction in Great Britain

During early April the first detailed reports on the state prisoners began to reach the British Isles. The British ministers received the dispatches of Governor Denison, the family and friends of O'Brien received his letters, and Gavan Duffy, editor of the recently reopened Dublin newspaper the *Nation*, received letters both from the state prisoners and from other acquaintances in Van Diemen's Land. Those reports and letters were used by the recipients as support for their respective positions regarding the treatment of the prisoners and possible pardons for them. Such was the principal purpose for writing those letters and reports, as both the writers and the recipients fully appreciated.

* * *

Between 8 and 17 April, Earl Grey received most of the dispatches written by Governor Denison about the state prisoners during December 1849 and January 1850.[9] Grey dealt swiftly with the report advising him that the state prisoners were about to enter the newspaper business. He informed Denison that if the prisoners abused the indulgence granted to them "by an endeavour to create discontent and disturb Society they should be immediately deprived of their ticket-of-leave." Respecting Denison's general actions in regulating the state prisoners, especially the granting of tickets-of-leave to the five who promised not to escape and the confinement of O'Brien on Maria Island, Grey wrote, "I have to acquaint you that all the steps which you have taken on this occasion meet with the approval of H. M.'s Govt."[10]

More dispatches from Denison were received by Earl Grey during the first week in July. The first dispatch informed Grey that O'Brien's health had indeed suffered a collapse but that the regulations limiting the area and conditions under which O'Brien could take his exercise had been relaxed and O'Brien's health was being restored. The dispatch clearly demonstrated that the local officials were fulfilling their obligations to maintain the health of the prisoner. The second dispatch informed Grey that the *Irish Exile* was being published and that Patrick O'Donoghue was the acknowledged owner. This dispatch convinced Grey that O'Donoghue should be sent to a country district where he would be unable to publish a newspaper, or else Denison should revoke his ticket-of-leave and send him to a probation station.[11]

Denison's dispatch describing O'Brien's attempt to obtain legal assistance from Knight arrived last. Grey sought the advice of Under Secretary Herman Merivale. Merivale agreed with Governor Denison's comments on Knight's legal opinion concerning O'Brien's treatment; namely, that Knight had confounded the "case of a prisoner kept to hard labour in the colonies . . . with that of a prisoner sentenced to ordinary transportation," and therefore Knight's legal opinion had no validity regarding O'Brien.[12]

But Merivale alerted Grey to another problem. Merivale informed Grey that there was a vagueness in the current law governing transportation. The vagueness had been recognized previously. Merivale had no doubt that Denison had acted according to the law in O'Brien's case. But he stated, "It is somewhat hazardous to speculate on the results of an application to the legal tribunals in the present temper of the Colony." Merivale was referring to the rising public discontent in Van Diemen's Land over the continuance of transportation. He concluded, "Vagueness in the law rather strengthens the hands of Government where the courts are strong and independent, but assists those who are at all inclined to give way to the popular feeling of the day."[13]

Reacting to that problem, Earl Grey informed the secretary of state for the Home Office, Sir George Grey, of the latest development in Van Diemen's Land and requested his opinion regarding the problem of the vagueness in the transportation law.[14] Earl Grey was not overly concerned with the fact that O'Brien had obtained a legal opinion, probably because he knew O'Brien had no immediate plans to engage in a court battle. Grey knew his main problem would be handling O'Brien's complaints to influential members of Parliament and that it was only a matter of time before those friends would begin to question the government about the treatment O'Brien was receiving. While his office had promptly forwarded O'Brien's letters of complaint to the appropriate individuals, Grey also allowed Lucius O'Brien, Chisholm Anstey, and William Monsell an opportunity to peruse the sections of Denison's dispatches describing the treatment O'Brien was receiving.[15] Regardless of what course O'Brien's friends were planning to pursue, Grey knew what his own course would be. In brief, Grey had sanctioned Denison's policy and was prepared to defend his own political position.

Anstey was anxious about the health of O'Brien. Some of his

anxiety was relieved when he came across the notice in Denison's dispatches that O'Brien was being treated as "a hospital patient." He interpreted that relaxation of the rules to mean that O'Brien's complaints had "reached the proper quarter [and] had been redressed." But Anstey did not believe his anxiety would ever end until O'Brien accepted a ticket-of-leave. He wrote to O'Brien in an effort to persuade him to accept the offer of the ticket-of-leave. He told O'Brien that he and Lucius understood O'Brien's reasons for refusing the ticket-of-leave: *"You are unwilling to compromise yourself by any submission, because you think that by doing so you compromise your cause."* But Anstey also told O'Brien that he was making a mistake in judgment. "You are not and never were [the] representative [of the revolution of 1848]." Prior to the revolution of 1848, Anstey and O'Brien were both active in the Irish Confederation. Anstey recalled to O'Brien the changes that had occurred in the organization and how Duffy and Mitchel had been able to swing the membership away from the principles on which it was founded; namely, from building a consensus among the Irish people that would be powerful enough to demand repeal, to obtaining repeal by revolutionary tactics. Anstey reminded O'Brien how O'Brien had submitted to the new principles because of his belief in majority rule. Anstey concluded, "Thus you were not the author of the Insurrection—you only joined it." Anstey actually believed that O'Brien had saved lives by joining the insurrection, because he ended the fighting once he saw the revolution had not taken hold among the people. Anstey wanted O'Brien to accept the ticket-of-leave as the first step toward obtaining a pardon, writing, "Your friends *here* have a ground to work upon, if only you will not prevent us, and, by an *useless and a too late* persistence in wearing the aspect of chief criminal obstruct the prerogative."[16]

After receiving O'Brien's letter to him, Sir Lucius O'Brien personally spoke to Lord Grey and Sir George Grey and wrote Sir John Russell about his brother. He then made formal inquiry asking specific questions regarding the conditions under which his brother was to live. Under Secretary Hawes answered Sir Lucius's formal letter, stating that it was impossible to instruct Governor Denison to relax the rules further.[17]

While Sir Lucius was trying to persuade the British officials to help his brother he was also urging other members of the O'Brien family to write to O'Brien and try to persuade him to accept a ticket-of-leave. O'Brien's mother and his sisters, Anne Martineau and Katherine Harris, all sent letters to O'Brien with that purpose in mind.[18]

The details of O'Brien's solitary confinement became known to the general public in mid-April when an article by the editor appeared in the *Dublin Nation* giving a general description of O'Brien's solitary confinement and then turning to the question of why O'Brien refused the ticket-of-leave. The editor's explanation was similar to that of Anstey; namely, that O'Brien considered that an acceptance of the ticket-of-leave, with its conditions, would be a "tacit submission to his enemies" and his "sensitive honour" would not allow such submission.[19]

Next, the *Limerick Chronicle* reported that O'Brien's health was suffering "from this tyrannous oppression, aggravated as it must appear when the Government of a great empire thus concentrates its giant force to crush a solitary unresisting individual." Those editors referred to O'Brien's treatment as "a species of political torture disgraceful to the British name." The editors of the *Dublin Evening Packet* wanted everyone to know that they were opposed to O'Brien's political views but deplored the way he was being treated in Van Diemen's Land. The editors of the *Galway Vindicator* made no political statement for or against the revolution of 1848 but announced their opposition to O'Brien's current treatment. They joined the editors of the *Sligo Champion* and the *Cork Examiner* and called for action. The editors of the *Sligo Champion* asked their fellow Irishmen to speak out against the treatment that O'Brien was receiving, while the editors of the *Cork Examiner* asked the people of Cork to get their mayor to do something about the situation.[20]

With such reports as those appearing in the Irish press, a variety of groups in Ireland began to discuss the subject in their meetings. By the end of June and during July, meetings were being held in Cork, Limerick, Dublin, Ballyhaunis, and Kerry at which expressions of the deepest sympathy for the "exiled patriot" were made in various resolutions. Similar meetings were also being held in London and New York. The groups gathered at Cork and Limerick condemned the treatment accorded O'Brien and sent a petition to the queen on the subject. In Dublin, a large group of gentlemen gathered at the Mechanics Institute to express their sense of the cruel punishment and wanton persecution to which O'Brien had been subject in his penal exile. They discussed measures that would bring the situation to the attention of Parliament.[21]

A group of one thousand met in Tammany Hall in New York to protest the treatment of O'Brien in Van Diemen's Land. In the chair was Horace Greeley. The resolution passed by those in attendance not only expressed sympathy and admiration for O'Brien but also urged all Irishmen to oppose all "those who, unable to bend his brave spirit, are torturing him to death." Michael Doheny, one of the leaders of the revolution of 1848 who had escaped to America, saw no virtue in resolutions. He wanted arms and said, "If you wish to send comfort to Smith O'Brien, tell him there are a hundred thousand Irishmen in America ready to fight the battle of freedom."[22]

Although O'Brien's martyrdom successfully reawakened sympathetic expressions of public opinion regarding his treatment in both Ireland and the United States, the *London Times* was totally unsympathetic and reflected English public opinion when its editors asked, "When will this ill-fated gentleman learn a little common sense? or why endeavour by these childish displays of vanity to damp the sympathy of his friends?"[23]

Later on, the editors of the *Times* wrote a lengthy explanation of why O'Brien refused to enter into any compact with the British officials. They stated that he flattered "himself that the rebellion, though put down in Ireland, still lives in him." Those editors concluded that O'Brien refused the ticket-of-leave because he wanted to be a martyr. They considered his attempts at martyrdom to be the work of a foolish, if not crazy, fanatic, totally lacking in good judgment. They believed O'Brien enjoyed self-torture: "The people of this country will class him with the poor creatures in India who suspend themselves by hooks through their ribs, or clench their fists till their nails come out at the back of their hands, or stand always on one leg, or keep one arm always raised, or practise some other stupid foolery of that sort." The editors called on the queen and the British public to ignore him. They believed that practically all Englishmen considered O'Brien "a mischievous simpleton, who has got considerable less than his desserts."[24]

*   *   *

While the friends and enemies of O'Brien bombarded the public with reasons to extend to him a sympathetic hand or withold all sympathy, O'Brien's friends in Westminster were ready to formally raise the issue of his treatment. On 14 June, Sir Lucius O'Brien rose in the House of Commons to bring the case of his brother before the members. The last communication he had perused was a letter dated 31 January by which he had learned that O'Brien's health had failed to such an extent that his life was in jeopardy. Sir Lucius was aware that the conditions that had brought about the ruin of his brother's health had been relaxed, but he wished to inform the Commons about the seriousness of the situation, maintaining that if his brother died or lost his reason from the abusive treatment he was receiving, a "fatal use" might be made of the situation against the government in Ireland.[25]

Sir Lucius acknowledged that he thought his brother was wrong in not accepting the ticket-of-leave. He recounted that, when O'Brien was still in Ireland before being transported, he had traveled to Dublin and had unsuccessfully attempted to persuade his brother to accept a ticket-of-leave, if offered. He stated that if he would travel to Van Diemen's Land to offer further arguments to his brother to accept the ticket-of-leave, he could expect the trip to be equally as unproductive. Sir Lucius asked whether or not the government would "pursue a person to the death." He stated that O'Brien believed he "was engaged in a good cause." Personally, Sir Lucius "thought him very wrong and injudicious," but he asked, "If a man thought himself right, . . . was it right to pursue him to such an extremity as to cause the loss of his life?" Sir Lucius then "put it to the Government whether they would continue this treatment or not?" He spoke for the friends of O'Brien in Parliament. They all wanted an inquiry made into the treatment O'Brien was receiving.[26]

Sir George Grey, rising in the Commons to answer Sir Lucius, began by stating that every member there sympathized with Sir Lucius and understood his strong feelings, but he observed that if the government could be accused of any charge, it would be of granting O'Brien too many indulgences. Grey saw no need for inquiry, and the majority of the members of the House of Commons evidently agreed with him. The "subject [was] dropped." On 21 June another attempt by the friends of O'Brien met with similar results.[27]

On 1 July, the friends of O'Brien in the House of Commons raised another but related issue. Using the expressions of sympathy that had previously appeared in the Irish press as the foundation of their request, they asked if the government "did not think that the time had come for granting these unfortunate men a free pardon." The main arguments in support of the pardon were that the government would "secure to themselves the gratitude of all classes of the people of Ireland" and that by such action the queen would be assured of an addition "if an addition were possible—to the attachment which already existed in the Irish bosom."[28]

The British ministers had no intention of granting a pardon, and an active discussion followed. During the debate O'Brien was referred to as a convict. That remark brought O'Gorman Mahon to his feet. He resented such a slur on O'Brien's character. Mahon acknowledged the fact that O'Brien had been found guilty of treason, but he reminded those in attendance that no one had lost his life as a result of the 1848 revolution, and he believed lives would have been lost if someone other than O'Brien had been the leader. Mahon believed there was a distinction between a man who sacrificed "himself that he might save others" and a convict who was "thrust out from civilised society as a curse." Once again the pardon issue had found another advocate. But the friends of O'Brien were still too few to effect any change in his condition.[29]

The course of those debates was important to both the government and the friends of O'Brien because both sides had for the first time stated their positions clearly and showed their political strength. The government considered that it had done everything possible for O'Brien by offering him a ticket-of-leave and by seeing to it that he was not placed among the common felons. If as a side effect of that policy O'Brien had been placed in solitary confinement, the officials in England considered the appropriate solution to be reliance on the attending physician to relax the regulations imposed by such a confinement before the prisoner's health and mind were affected.

The friends of O'Brien appreciated the offer of the ticket-of-leave that the government had made to the state prisoners and they appreciated the fact that O'Brien had not been made to live and work with the convicts. But they disagreed that damage caused by solitary confinement could be avoided by relying on the local physician's good judgment. The friends of O'Brien knew that it took almost four months for a letter to come from Australia and a comparable amount of time for the reply to return. Under such conditions, those friends believed that if O'Brien's life was to be kept safe, orders had to be issued almost at once forbidding the penal officials from placing O'Brien back in solitary confinement. O'Brien's friends wanted to take the question of whether or not his health would be damaged out of the hands of a minor official. Their real concern was that O'Brien would become physically incapacitated, deranged, or die before they could obtain a pardon or other relief for him. They wanted the immediate problem solved by having O'Brien treated as he had been treated during the first two weeks of his confinement on Maria Island. The long-range solution to the problem would be for O'Brien to accept a ticket-of-leave, but those who knew him intimately thought the chances of such an acceptance were rather slight; nevertheless they continued to ply him with letters urging him to accept the offer.

Duffy was not pleased with the fight that the Irish members had made in Parliament to help O'Brien. He wrote Meagher that they "seconded us wretchedly." Duffy believed the Irish press led by the *Nation* was responsible for raising "a storm of grief and indignation" among the Irish people over O'Brien's treatment. He hoped orders had been sent out to treat O'Brien properly. "If the most intense indignation on the part of this country will move the Govt. they are moved thoroughly."[30] But Duffy was wrong in hoping that the government had changed its policy toward O'Brien. Earl Grey had approved of Governor Denison's actions toward all the state prisoners. If there were to be any changes for the state prisoners they would be for the worse.

Grey had actually survived the challenge rather well. Although he had been forced to defend the government's treatment of O'Brien, he had been able to prevent any change in that policy. O'Brien was no longer in oblivion, but he was still sixteen thousand miles away from the British Isles. Grey was certain that all of his orders met with the approval of the English people, and even the friends of O'Brien openly admitted that the "strong feeling" in England against the rebellion was still present. But O'Brien was capable of creating a political problem for Grey, even from his far-off confinement in Van Diemen's Land, and O'Brien's friends hoped that when the English feeling against the rising at Ballin-garry subsided, they would be able to help O'Brien receive better treat-ment and eventually a pardon. Their attempt to help him during the summer of 1850 was premature. The wound caused by the revolution of 1848 was still open in England.

Interestingly enough, while the British ministry and Parliament were adamant in their opposition to helping O'Brien directly, those same forces had just completed an effort, begun in the winter of 1848, that would help him indirectly. On 5 August 1850, the royal assent was given to a measure that would establish representative government in South Australia, Victoria, and Van Diemen's Land. New South Wales already had representative government. But under this measure Victoria (Port Phillip), which had been a part of New South Wales, was made a sepa-rate colony and allowed its own legislative council. Under the new mea-sure, the legislative councils would have two-thirds of their members elected by the citizenry and one-third appointed by the governor. In the case of Van Diemen's Land, if the free citizenry really opposed transpor-tation and was able to obtain control of those elected seats, Governor Denison would have difficulty in maintaining transportation.[31] O'Brien believed that the moment transportation ceased, his chances of obtain-ing a pardon would improve.

By the end of the summer of 1850, the foundation of O'Brien's long-range policy had been established. He had forced his way out of oblivion. He had helped to create a sympathetic public opinion in Van Diemen's Land, particularly among the antitransportationists. He had also reawak-ened Irish public opinion on his behalf, reestablished himself among Irish-Americans as a suffering Irish leader deserving of their support, and reconfirmed the friendship that he still had among several dedicated and outspoken advocates of his in Westminster.

O'Brien was not fully aware of his success because he was not al-lowed to read newspapers and because there was approximately a four-month delay in receiving news from the British Isles. But the reality was that his martyrdom had released him from oblivion. In addition, he now had an advocate in Ireland in the form of the *Dublin Nation*. The *London Times* would no longer have the ability to ridicule O'Brien without being challenged.

O'Brien's immediate future, however, was unknown.

Disappointment for the Other State Prisoners

During the Australian summer, fall, and winter months of 1850, when O'Brien was busy working on plans to end his oblivion and both Governor Denison and the British ministers in London were working to dampen the expressions of sympathy that O'Brien had unleashed, the other state prisoners were still attempting to settle into a new life. While those state prisoners had some moments of relaxation and enjoyment, by and large they encountered experiences and adjustments that were disappointing. It almost looked as if it would be impossible for them to ever fit into their new surroundings.

On 4 February, Terence McManus and a friend, Mr. Swift, went out on a shooting expedition. While pursuing their sport, they crossed some ploughed land belonging to a Mr. Gill. R. Jordon, who was a well-known comedian of the Hobart Town theater, but who resided in the New Norfolk area, saw the two hunters crossing Gill's property and told them to leave immediately. McManus informed Jordon that "he would be answerable to Mr Gill for the consequences, and words ensued." [32]

Soon afterward McManus was charged with insolence toward a free citizen, Jordon, and he was summoned to the New Norfolk police office where the trial was set for the eleventh. On that date Jordon appeared and testified against McManus. The case was then adjourned until the fourteenth in order to allow Swift, a free citizen, to testify on behalf of McManus. On the basis of Swift's testimony, McManus was acquitted. [33] McManus escaped the imprisonment to which, had Swift not been with him, he would most summarily have been subjected. The case was significant to the other state prisoners who had accepted tickets-of-leave because it brought home how easily one's comparative liberty could be lost. If McManus had been alone when he "insulted" Jordon, or if Swift had failed to testify on his behalf, McManus would have lost his case and his ticket-of-leave.

Meanwhile, Thomas Meagher, a man of boundless energy and ability, had not yet found meaningful projects on which to spend his time. By early March, he was actively engaged in preparing for a St. Patrick's Day celebration at Lake Sorell. It was to be a grand celebration. Mr. Clarke had forwarded the wine, a large group of friends was gathering, and many of the participants were bringing their guns in order to "fire a grand salute in honour of the day." Meagher had purchased a boat and was anxious that it arrive on time for the big day. He sought out local advice on the best delivery route and the proper mode of transporting the *Speranza* to the lake. [34] However, although such activities might momentarily serve as an outlet for his immense energies, Meagher needed to find more worthwhile projects if his years as an exile were to be at all bearable.

Kevin O'Doherty, during the month of April, completed the studies that he believed were necessary for him to take the local medical examination. But when he made application to the medical board for permission to take the examination, his application was put off supposedly because the board needed verification of his education records. The examiners noted that O'Doherty claimed on his application that he had completed a course of study in Dublin that was equivalent to the one given by the London College of Surgeons. They asked O'Doherty for documentary proof of the completion of such a course. The examiners told him that until he could produce such a document, his application could not be processed. O'Doherty promptly wrote his brother in Ireland requesting him to forward his certificate, but he could not help raise the question "whether this extreme particularity . . . is . . . a . . . hint" that his application would never be received. O'Doherty noted the board was obviously not very particular in certifying the individuals who were taking care of the health needs of the people of Oatlands, for one individual was "a very ignorant old woman" and another was "a self-styled Dr" whom O'Doherty suspected had no qualifications.[35]

Also in April, another Irish state prisoner arrived in Van Diemen's Land. After his conviction in 1848, John Mitchel had been put on board a convict ship and sent west from Ireland to Bermuda. Mitchel suffered from asthma, and the climate in Bermuda aggravated his condition. It was not long before Mitchel's health failed, and in an effort to keep himself alive Mitchel applied for permission to be transferred to the new penal colony in Capetown, South Africa. On 22 April 1849, he was put on board the convict ship *Neptune*, which was under orders to bring the first convicts to the newly designated penal station. The *Neptune* encountered navigational difficulties, and when it did not arrive on schedule at Capetown most people surmised the vessel had gone down at sea.[36]

The *Neptune* finally arrived at its destination in Capetown on 18 September, but the citizenry so vehemently opposed the landing of the convicts that the governor of the colony, Sir Harry Smith, ordered the *Neptune* to remain at anchor in Simon's Bay with the prisoners on board until he could obtain further orders from England. On 13 February 1850 the new orders arrived. The *Neptune* was to proceed to Van Diemen's Land where all of the prisoners, except John Mitchel, would receive conditional pardons "in compensation for the hardships of their long voyage and detention." Ironically, "twelve of the most powerful" convicts would be invited to become constables.[37]

On 7 April 1850, the *Neptune* anchored in the area of Hobart Town, but by that time Mitchel's health had been "shattered." Like the other state prisoners, Mitchel had been treated as a "gentleman" while on board Her Majesty's vessels and had separate quarters from the other convicts. Those separate quarters, however, had the effect of putting him in solitary confinement. He also had received similar treatment while in Bermuda. The result was that Mitchel had been in solitary confinement for ten months in Bermuda and had spent eleven months and seventeen days in solitary on board the *Neptune*. On 8 April, Mitchel was offered a ticket-of-leave, which he accepted, but he added a separate note informing the authorities he was ill "and was utterly unfit to be sent off by myself." The attending physician on board the *Neptune*, Dr. Gibson, verified Mitchel's note with professional comments.[38]

Denison accepted the recommendation of Gibson that Mitchel was too ill to live alone and granted Mitchel permission to live with John Martin. Denison maintained he had received no specific orders regarding Mitchel, so he reported to Earl Grey that he had offered Mitchel a ticket-of-leave on the same conditions offered to the other Irish prisoners, namely, his word of honor that he would not escape.[39]

While Mitchel was preparing to leave the *Neptune*, the citizenry of Hobart Town was drawing up a petition protesting transportation in general and the arrival of the *Neptune* in particular. The petition recalled that previously the colonists had asked the government to stop sending convicts to Van Diemen's Land and on 27 July 1848 the governor had announced that transportation would cease. The antitransportationists wanted to know why that promise was not kept. They wanted to know why the British government bowed to the wishes of the citizenry of Capetown by not landing the convicts there and instead brought the *Neptune* to Van Diemen's Land. The antitransportationists in Van Diemen's Land appealed to the citizenry of Great Britain to help them, stating they had despaired of obtaining relief from the British ministers in London.[40]

The editors of the *Launceston Examiner* had another solution to the problem. They decided that the British officials took no notice of the antitransportation petitions from Van Diemen's Land because Governor Denison had convinced those ministers that the antitransportation movement did not reflect public opinion. Those editors announced their new editorial policy. They planned to do everything they could to convince the British ministers that it was Denison who did not have the support of public opinion. Denison was about to be "excommunicated."[41]

The Reverend John West of Launceston had a third solution, which he announced not long after the arrival of the *Neptune*. He wanted to organize public opinion in the various Australian colonies to demand the cessation of transportation to Van Diemen's Land. The Reverend West, with the aid of the members of the Launceston Association for Promoting the Cessation of Transportation to Van Diemen's Land, began writing letters to the leading men in the other Australian colonies seeking support. The main argument that the Reverend West used was that as long as transportation continued to Van Diemen's Land, the nearby Australian colonies would continue to suffer from convict pollution, because the transported felons from Van Diemen's Land would stream into those nearby areas. The Reverend West referred to the new organization as the Australian League.[42]

On 9 April, Mitchel left the *Neptune*. On landing at Hobart Town, he was met by O'Donoghue and another friend. Mitchel told them that he felt he enjoyed greater freedom in Van Diemen's Land as a holder of a ticket-of-leave than as a free man in Dublin, for "the state of things at home was not to be borne, that we had at least solemnly protested against it, and that at all events we had cleared ourselves of all share in the guilt of it."[43] Mitchel then boarded the coach for Bothwell, and at one of the wayside inns along the route he met McManus. In the short time they spent together, Mitchel attempted to catch up on the news.[44]

By 12 April, Mitchel had arrived at Bothwell. Martin was distressed to see how Mitchel's physical condition had deteriorated. He noted that Mitchel "was wretchedly thin and weak and exhausted in appearance and he could hardly walk a few yards without panting for breath."[45] Within a few days, however, Mitchel began to feel better. Mitchel explained, "And whether it be the elastic and balmy air of these mountain-woods that sends the tide of life coursing somewhat warmer through my veins—or unwonted converse of an old friend that revives the personal identity I had nearly lost—or the mere treading once more upon the firm flowery surface of our bounteous Mother Earth, after two years' tossing on the barren, briny ocean . . . certain it is, I feel a kind of joy."[46]

When Martin saw how rapidly Mitchel was improving he told him about the meetings of the state prisoners at the boundaries of the penal districts, and he suggested that they both might attend the next Monday meeting at the lakes. Martin thought that Mitchel had not then sufficiently regained his physical strength, and so when he wrote Meagher informing him of their plan he commented that they would only come if "the weather be mild." He reminded Meagher of his new role, "I am in the high and responsible office of *nurse tender* and I must do my duty." Martin could not help but admit, however, that Mitchel's mental state was good. "He is in great spirits and as fierce as ten lions, and bullies me outrageously."[47]

The state prisoners hoped that they would be able to meet, with Mitchel present, on 14 April, but the weather was "cold and gloomy." Martin and Mitchel waited until noon in the hope the weather would improve, but it did not. Nevertheless they set out for the rendezvous on a journey that was to prove very difficult for Mitchel. When they set out it was raining, but as they climbed to the plateau where Lake Sorell was located the rain turned to snow. The meeting place that was previously at Cooper's hut had subsequently been moved four miles further on, to a much more hospitable house belonging to Mr. Townshend. By the time Mitchel and Martin arrived in the vicinity of Cooper's hut, Mitchel's strength had virtually given out. When Cooper appeared and offered them the hospitality of his quarters, Mitchel was greatly relieved. While Martin and Mitchel made themselves comfortable, Cooper rode off to Townshend's home to summon Meagher and O'Doherty, who had arrived earlier in the day.[48]

Mitchel described the reunion. "It now began to grow dusk, for we had been four hours and a-half on the way; and the evening was fast growing dark, when we heard the gallop of three horses, and a loud laugh, well known to me." Mitchel and Martin rushed to the door, "and in a minute Meagher and O'Doherty had thrown themselves from their horses; and, as we exchanged greetings—I know not from what impulse, whether from buoyancy of heart, or *bizarre* perversity of feeling—we all *laughed* till the woods rang around; laughed loud and long, and uproariously, till two teal rose, startled from the reeds on the lake-shore, and flew screaming to seek a quieter neighbourhood."[49]

Mitchel did not quite understand the laughter. "I suspect there was something hollow in that laughter, though at the time it was hearty, vociferous, and spontaneous." Actually, Mitchel had to admit, it had not been a joyous meeting, "curses or tears, just then, might have become us better."[50] Meagher had similar thoughts. To begin with, he thought Mitchel was near death and would not have given "ten shillings for the purchase of his life." Meagher wrote, "His appearance—his worn and sunken cheeks, his dull blood-shot eyes, his moist hand, his thick and gasping articulation, his stooped shoulders, his slow and undecided step—everything about him filled me with the saddest apprehension, and despite our merry chat, and songs, and bumpers, a dark shadow seemed to me resting over the little party, and making one face colder and less joyous than the rest."[51]

While the state prisoners were greeting one another, Cooper broiled mutton chops, made the tea, and cut the damper. After dinner, the men talked of Ireland, their life in Van Diemen's Land, and O'Brien. They also talked about the sympathetic factions, made up principally of Irish refugees, that were forming in America, "factions founded principally on the momentous question, who was the greatest man and the most glorious hero, of that most inglorious Irish business of '48; and each [Irish-American] imagines he exalts his own favourite 'martyr' by disparaging and pulling down the rest—as if the enemy's Government had not pulled us all down, and ridden roughshod over us." Mitchel knew, "I have my faction, and Meagher a still stronger one." But Mitchel believed the Irish-Americans would have found the meeting of the exiles at Lake Sorell of value. "If our respective partisans could but have seen—as we discussed this question of our own comparative importance—how bitterly and how mournfully we too smiled at one another across the gum-tree fire in that log-hut amongst the forests of the antipodes, perhaps it might have cooled their partisan zeal."[52]

The men spent several days together, talking and exploring the Lake Sorell area. On the eighteenth they parted. Mitchel enjoyed the scenery on the trip back home to Bothwell and wondered why the country had seemed so desolate to him on the trip to the lake. As he approached Quoin Hill he was able to enjoy a view of the valley of Bothwell. "From this point the view is wide and magnificent—endless forests and mountains; with small bits of clearing here and there, looking like impertinent intrusions upon the primeval solitudes." Mitchel looked upward and saw "two eagles soar majestically above: and from far down in the profound umbrage below, rings the clear bugle note of the white magpie—a bird which, though called magpie by the colonists, is of a species unknown in the northern hemisphere." Mitchel was delighted that he had made the journey. "So ends my first visit to Lake Sorel: and it has pleased me well at any rate to find that my friends are all *unsubdued*." Mitchel was not just pleased, he was very pleased. "The game, I think, is not over yet."[53]

When Mitchel had first arrived at Hobart Town aboard the *Neptune*, he had received a letter from Patrick O'Donoghue in which O'Donoghue enclosed the latest issue of his *Irish Exile*. The letter invited Mitchel to join O'Donoghue in his publishing venture. Mitchel had been surprised to find the authorities allowing O'Donoghue to engage in such an enterprise. Mitchel declined to accept the invitation and, in so doing, adopted the attitude that the other state prisoners had initially taken toward O'Donoghue's newspaper activity, namely, an unwillingness to participate.[54]

When O'Donoghue had first started his newspaper activities, Martin and Meagher had thought the venture neither prudent, considering the difficulties encountered previously in Ireland for the same activity, nor promising, because of the unliklihood of the popular success of such a venture. On 2 April, a newspaper advertisement in the *Sydney Morning Herald* signed by "A Friend to Erin's Exiles" purported that the *Irish Exile* was causing the other state prisoners embarrassment, that the other exiles had attempted to dissuade O'Donoghue from publishing the *Irish Exile* and were so upset with O'Donoghue's recent carrying on that they "blush" when they heard his name, wishing "that *he* had never been amongst them."[55]

As a result of those statements in the *Sydney Morning Herald*, the other state prisoners were "dragged into a rather prominent position, in connection with . . . the *Irish Exile*."[56] But contrary to the assertions of "A Friend to Erin's Exiles," unwillingness to participate in O'Donoghue's venture and even the initial opposition to the paper as expressed by Martin and Meagher did not mean they had a lack of admiration for O'Donoghue. Martin, Mitchel, and Meagher all published statements acknowledging O'Donoghue's devotion to the cause of Irish freedom and the respect that they each felt was due to him for the sacrifices he had made on behalf of that freedom.[57] There was some truth, however, in the statement made by "A Friend to Erin's Exiles." Regardless of the fact that Meagher, Mitchel, and Martin rose to protect O'Donoghue from an outside assailant, inside the group there was a recognition that O'Donoghue was different. The difference between O'Donoghue and the other state prisoners became more pronounced as time went on simply because while O'Donoghue was accepted when he was sober, he was not accepted when he was drunk. As time went on he drank more and more, and the alienation became more distinct.

O'Donoghue had reason to drink. Initially, when he was unable to find a job, he drank as a result of his financial worries. Once he got the *Irish Exile* started, the proceeds were adequate to relieve his financial distress. But the newspaper was a perennial center of controversy and hence a perennial worry. O'Donoghue had merely exchanged one worry for another and one reason to drink for another. For the time being, however, O'Donoghue's lines of communication with his fellow exiles were still good and he was still one of them.

*   *   *

By May, McManus had decided that he would have to leave New Norfolk because he had been unable to find employment there. He informed the government officials at Hobart Town that he intended to resign his ticket-of-leave unless he was permitted to reside in a seaport town where he could carry on a mercantile business. In June 1850, permission was given McManus to take up residence in Launceston, the second largest city in Van Diemen's Land. At Launceston, McManus continued to make friends. He resided at the home of a priest, Dean Bellew. He was able to find employment, and when he received news of his mother's death, another clergyman friend, Father Thomas Butler, offered a mass at St. Joseph's Church for the repose of her soul. The church was filled to overflowing, and "all sections of the community" expressed their sympathy.[58] McManus appeared to be "fitting in" and starting a new life.

During the Australian winter of 1850, Martin and the ailing Mitchel also moved to a more favorable home. When Martin had first arrived in Bothwell in the spring of 1849, he had found lodging in the village itself, and when Mitchel joined him they remained in the same house for several months. Neither man had ever been satisfied with the lodgings, and they began hunting for other accommodations almost from the moment Mitchel arrived in Van Diemen's Land. By the middle of the winter they found what they were looking for, a small cottage about six miles from the village of Bothwell.[59]

During this same period, Mitchel made another important decision. He decided to write his wife and invite her to bring their children and join him in exile in Van Diemen's Land. Mitchel realized that the convict pollution of Van Diemen's Land made it a bad place to bring up children. But he had twelve more years to serve on his sentence, he was settled in a "remote, thinly-peopled and pastoral district," several local families told him they would welcome the arrival of his family into the area, he wanted the opportunity to serve as tutor to his children, and as he stated so aptly, "I do so pine for something resembling a home—something that I could occasionally almost fancy a real home." Mitchel was not certain he had made the right decision. In his diary he wrote, "Pray God, I have done right."[60]

During the same Australian winter Meagher had been so attracted by the lake region that he had begun to talk about building a cottage on a sixty-acre island in Lake Sorell that was owned by his friend Clarke. Meagher's plans became reality. When the cottage was completed, Meagher moved in and only went to town about once a week to restock his provisions.[61]

O'Doherty was also attracted to the lakes and at one point contemplated "building a hut at the extremity of his boundary upon the lake shore." By the middle of August, however, he had abandoned those plans. On 12 August, O'Doherty wrote the assistant comptroller a letter resigning his ticket-of-leave. O'Doherty had been studying medicine under Dr. Edward Hall, but Dr. Hall was transferred to Ross as the government medical superintendent and O'Doherty was unable to follow him. The interruption of his studies and his financial embarrassment were probably the major factors that convinced him to resign his ticket-of-leave. On 15 August, Nairn informed O'Doherty that Governor Denison had accepted his resignation and had issued orders for his assignment to the probation station at Salt Water River where he would work as a dispenser. O'Doherty was to receive one shilling a day plus quarters and rations. He was to proceed immediately to Hobart Town, where he would report to the principal medical officer for further orders before proceeding to the station at Salt Water River.[62]

When Bishop Willson of Hobart Town learned of O'Doherty's action, he promptly wrote to the young man in an effort to dissuade him from going through with his decision. The bishop urged O'Doherty to "quietly come to H. Town" in order that they could discuss the problem.[63] O'Doherty was apparently swayed by Bishop Willson's argument, because he became once again a holder of a ticket-of-leave.[64] Bishop Willson continued his efforts to help O'Doherty. He paid a personal visit to Governor Denison in the hope of obtaining permission for O'Doherty to reside in Hobart Town and was told that if O'Doherty made an application on the basis "of obtaining a situation in Hobart Town . . . which could not be [had] in Oatlands," the application would be received favorably. Not long afterward O'Doherty was granted permission to live in Hobart Town, where he worked with Dr. Crooke for "a nominal salary and 'a share of the profits.'"[65]

*   *   *

By the beginning of the Australian spring of 1850 some of the exiles were beginning to feel more at home in Van Diemen's Land. The initial period of adjustment appeared to be over. McManus had at last found a position that interested him, and O'Doherty, while still denied the right to practice medicine, was about to begin work in a medical field. In addition O'Doherty had found a protector in Bishop Willson, who recognized that the young man was much more of a physician than a revolutionary. Even Martin's life had improved. Mitchel's arrival had thrust upon Martin welcome responsibility.

Meagher, Mitchel, and O'Donoghue were still floundering. Mitchel had put his hopes in the arrival of his wife and children. Meagher had not yet developed even a seemingly workable plan of finding satisfaction in exile. What he needed were worthwhile projects, not seclusion. And O'Donoghue's solution, publishing the *Irish Exile*, would prove to create more problems than it solved.

CHAPTER 4

The Ticket-of-Leave

O'Brien Attempts to Escape

On 7 March 1850, Dr. John Stephen Hampton paid a visit to the Darlington Probation Station and informed Mr. Lapham that O'Brien would be transferred to the Port Arthur Probation Station within the next two weeks. O'Brien was informed of the impending change almost immediately.[1] For some unexplained reason, however, the transfer was delayed for several months. As the Australian winter neared its close, O'Brien was still on Maria Island. Then, unexpectedly, a plan was presented to him that would result in his immediate release.

During the Australian winter an escape plot was devised by persons in Van Diemen's Land sympathetic to O'Brien. The plans were made and sponsored under the leadership of Dr. J. C. McCarthy of Hobart Town. McCarthy had been convinced by his contacts with both Meagher and O'Donoghue that O'Brien's life was endangered by the treatment he was receiving. In addition, Meagher had shown McCarthy a promising but unidentified letter that gave McCarthy the impression "that there would be no hesitation in America to honour any demands for [O'Brien's] escape." The letter convinced McCarthy that he could commit himself financially to the undertaking. O'Donoghue made his contribution to the escape plot by finding a Captain Ellis who was willing to sail the escape vessel into Maria Island and spirit O'Brien away. Ellis had previously delivered supplies to the island and knew the shoreline well. Whether or not the conspirators knew that no prisoner had ever escaped from one of the probation stations on Maria Island was unknown.[2]

O'Brien was not aware of the plot until it was virtually ready to be carried out. He was informed of the plan by the Catholic chaplain on Maria Island, Father Woolfrey, who carried the message from the sympathizers asking if O'Brien was willing to make such an attempt.[3]

O'Brien was motivated to make the escape attempt for several reasons. While his current mode of treatment at the Darlington Probation Station was quite satisfactory, O'Brien thought that once he was transferred to Port Arthur his confinement "would be of a very strict character."[4]

In addition, he knew that if his health failed again, an attempt by him to obtain assistance by means of letters might be difficult. Letters to acquaintances in Van Diemen's Land, if worded indiscreetly, could be stopped by the officials in Hobart Town, and once again there was no guarantee the letters would have any effect. In addition, letters to family and friends in the British Isles seeking assistance might take too long to accomplish the necessary speedy relief, and, as a matter of fact, the letters of complaint that he had written previously to members of his family and friends in the British Isles appeared to have failed to effect any change in his current condition. O'Brien knew his health was restored sufficiently to make the escape attempt. He also knew he was under no engagement not to escape. His honor would not be jeopardized.[5]

Before accepting the offer, O'Brien exacted an important promise from the conspirators. He told them that he could not allow his family to be responsible for the financial expenses incurred in the attempt. During the period prior to, and then immediately after, the revolution of 1848, O'Brien had divested himself of his property in order to prevent the government from seizing it in case he was convicted of committing treason. Two trustees, Sir Lucius O'Brien and Woronzow Greig, assumed the responsibility of handling the property for O'Brien, and it was they who had raised the money for O'Brien's defense during his trial for high treason. The cost of the trial had been high, and O'Brien's sister Grace had relieved the immediate situation by providing a loan. In addition, the trustees had arranged for O'Brien to receive an allowance of two hundred pounds a year on which he was to live during his period of exile. The remaining property was to be used for the support of Lucy and the seven O'Brien children. O'Brien was not willing to ask Lucy to assume any debts on the remaining property that was being used to support her and the children. With that background O'Brien wanted it clearly understood that the financial responsibility belonged to the conspirators and that he would only accept the offer of their assistance with such a condition attached.[6] Ellis carried "proof" to McCarthy that O'Brien and Father Woolfrey had discussed the plan and that O'Brien had agreed to make the escape attempt. McCarthy understood O'Brien's condition, but because of the American letter implying complete financial backing, he expected no difficulties. As a result McCarthy rented the schooner *Victoria*, which could carry O'Brien to California.[7]

The exact date of the escape was not set, but O'Brien was informed that he should be ready any time after 10 August. He was instructed to keep watch for the escape vessel. He was also told about "a secluded spot" where a smaller boat would land to pick him up and carry him to the safety of the *Victoria*, which would be waiting offshore.[8] The waiting was difficult, but on 12 August, O'Brien's opportunity came. O'Brien recalled what happened:

> Accordingly I was on the watch and as my walks were not restricted within any limit I strolled during several successive days along the seashore in the direction from which [the *Victoria*] might be expected to arrive.

Upon several of these occasions I was attended only by my keeper (Mr. Miller) but upon the day in question I was followed by one of the Constables who have lately been in the habit of watching my proceedings more closely than usual. . . . Between one and two o'clock P.M. on [12 August] I observed a vessel in the distance bearing towards the part of the shore on which I was walking. . . . Gradually the vessel approached the shore and I advanced to meet her at the point which she would first reach distant about five miles from Darlington Station. As the wind was very light she came on very slowly. You will easily imagine that during this interval my breast was full of emotion. No one however could have discovered this emotion from my demeanour. I sat down with calmness to eat my lunch after which I took up my book and continued to read to my keeper as had been my usual practice in our rambles. At length we reached the point best suited for embarkation. A shower of rain coming on I took up a position under some trees near the point, occasionally going out so as to make myself visible to those on board the vessel. The wind lulled so much that she was unable to advance but she arrived within less than half a mile of the shore. A boat was then sent from the vessel towards the point. I continued to read to my keeper until the boat approached within two or three hundred yards of the shore. She was rowed by two men and steered by a third. I then strolled down on the rocks to the edge of the sea and when the boat was within about fifty yards of the shore I dashed into the sea. The rocks were less shelving than I expected and I was soon out of my depth but as I can swim this was of little importance. I had gone into the water in order to avoid a struggle with the keeper and I fully expected that I should be pulled up into the boat and carried off without delay. To my great surprise however I found that no hand was reached to me and on looking round I observed that the Constable who had concealed himself until I plunged into the water had rushed out of his hiding place and was presenting a gun at the men in the boat. Without any parley or any effort whatsoever to carry me off the men in the boat at once cried out that they surrendered. . . . At length I got to shore. . . . All hope of escape was now . . . extinct.[9]

Looking back on the escape attempt O'Brien was provoked. The winds had been extremely light and had prevented the *Victoria* from coming closer to shore. The boatmen had lacked resolution, and the constable had demonstrated unusual "promptitude[,] presence of mind and fidelity." If only the winds had been strong, the boatmen resolute, and the constable indifferent, O'Brien thought that he would have made it.[10]

O'Brien was wrong. There was another factor about which he did not know. The government was aware of the plot. Prior to the escape attempt Hampton had informed Lapham that he had recently received information from District Constable Farange that "an arrangement has been entered into by . . . Ellis, Master, to carry off Smith O'Brien." Hampton thought the report to be of dubious value, but he was compelled to admit to himself that Ellis's reputation proved him capable of such a plot. Furthermore, Hampton knew that Ellis had recently been sailing about Maria Island. Hampton accordingly told Lapham to be on his guard and make arrangements "to frustrate any such plan." Hampton's letter was carried by Wicks, a special constable, in the company of another highly recommended convict constable, probably a Mr. Hamerton. Those two men were directed to aid Lapham in preventing any escape and to work in cooperation with the assistant superintendent, McGauran, and the two constables already on the island. Hampton wanted the arrangements that Lapham was to work out to be carried out "quietly."[11] That is exactly what Lapham did.

Interestingly enough, Hampton did not tell even Governor Denison what was happening. On the day of the escape Denison heard that "a report was floating about town that O'Brien had escaped." Denison inquired of Hampton what truth there might be to the report. Hampton informed Denison that O'Brien had made an escape attempt that very morning but had been "frustrated by the courage and presence of mind of a convict constable."[12]

Denison was indeed pleased with himself. O'Brien's escape attempt justified the orders for close confinement. Denison could now quite justifiably take the position "that the precautions taken were not more than necessary for the security of the prisoner." He had received Earl Grey's approval of the way he had been treating O'Brien, but now he believed he would receive public approval. Denison viewed O'Brien's escape attempt as "absurd," noting, "This scheme, like all others in which he has meddled, has been a failure."[13]

One of the first newspapers to carry the story of the escape attempt was the *Launceston Examiner*. The editors had been able to acquire very little information, and what information they had was inaccurate in the extreme. In a single sentence they reported all they knew: "Smith O'Brien had escaped from the colony, on board a Swan Port craft, the *Victoria*." That inaccurate report was picked up by other newspapers in the Australian colonies and was used in altered form with various editorializing added. The editors of the *Melbourne Argus* learned of the escape without regret, "for as no man could well regard Smith O'Brien as in possession of his proper senses, it was painful to witness a madman treated as a condemned criminal."[14]

Shortly afterward, the Van Diemen's Land newspapers were at least accurately informing their readers that the escape attempt had failed, but the details of the attempt were not consistently reported. The *Hobart Town Advertiser* was the first to run the correct account, but then it was recognized as the unofficial newspaper of the government.[15]

Patrick O'Donoghue was not concerned with the details of the escape attempt, because, of course, he was one of the conspirators and knew all about them. After reading the account published in the *Hobart Town Advertiser*, he wrote in his *Irish Exile* that, assuming the account was true, there were enough odd circumstances surrounding the attempt to enable him to conclude that "some foul treachery must have been at work to betray [O'Brien]."[16]

Most people did agree with the statement "Poor O'Brien was betrayed,"[17] but the mystery of the escape was never officially unraveled. After further inquiry, it was discovered that Ellis was a pass holder. He had been sentenced to fourteen years of transportation for piracy, and O'Brien's friends concluded he had traded information about the O'Brien escape plot in exchange for his own freedom. It was generally believed that Ellis had gone to the government and reported the plot at the moment he was hired by McCarthy. The implication was that the government officials had then instructed Ellis to carry out the escape plans so they could set a trap for O'Brien.[18]

The attention of the public was turned to what the government would do with Ellis and Hunt, both of whom had been arrested. Denison told Grey that there was not enough evidence to convict them of trying to aid O'Brien to escape. Denison did know that Father Woolfrey was involved in the attempt, but none of the "conspirators," with the exception of Ellis and Hunt, was in difficulty. Ellis and Hunt were charged, tried, and convicted of acting contrary to a law that forbade anyone to land on Maria Island without the permission of the government. They were fined sixty pounds each and costs, with the *Victoria* declared confiscated until the fines were paid. Since the two men were penniless adventurers, their fines, costs, and lawyers' fees were eventually paid by the "conspirators" who had devised the escape plan in the beginning. Shortly after the trial was over and the fines were paid, Ellis and Hunt gathered the crew of the *Victoria* together, unobtrusively got on board the vessel, and with no apparent motives sailed for unknown ports.[19] The owners of the *Victoria* were not concerned with motives. They wanted the *Victoria* back or compensation for their loss. Those owners held McCarthy responsible, but McCarthy had no money to pay them. In time O'Brien would provide McCarthy with financial assistance, notwithstanding the condition of financial immunity that O'Brien had exacted from the conspirators, but, at the moment, O'Brien was totally unaware of the financial plight of McCarthy.

Meanwhile O'Brien had been confined to his quarters and informed that he would be transferred to Port Arthur shortly. By 20 August, O'Brien was looking forward to the move. While he waited, he thought of how he could best answer a letter he had received from Chisholm Anstey that sought to persuade him to accept a ticket-of-leave. Anstey's letter, however, had another purpose. It purported to absolve O'Brien of the responsibility that the leader of the 1848 revolution would necessarily have had to assume. Anstey reasoned that O'Brien was not "the author" of the insurrection but rather had "only joined it," and that assertion challenged the fundamental principles on which O'Brien had acted, and intended to act, during his period of confinement.[20]

On 20 August, O'Brien answered Anstey's letter and thus publicly discussed for the first time the motives that had taken him into revolution. O'Brien began by thanking Anstey for his letter of 14 April 1850. O'Brien said that on the subject of his personal treatment he had "nothing more to say." O'Brien also relayed the information about his recent escape attempt.[21]

O'Brien then turned to the main question that Anstey had discussed in his letter, namely, O'Brien's role in the revolution of 1848. O'Brien recalled that for approximately twelve years he had sat in Parliament and worked for a united legislature, but in 1843 he had abandoned that principle and become an advocate of repeal. In 1846, he withdrew from the Repeal Association over the question of whether the use of force was valid in a political struggle. Then he had reasoned he could not abdicate the right that every man has from nature to use force to protect himself. In 1848, when the French rose in revolution, sympathy for the cause of the French liberals swept Europe. At the same time the Irish liberals, O'Brien included, determined to use physical force, if necessary, to win repeal of the Act of Union. O'Brien had concluded that Ireland was undergoing a greater loss of life from British mismanagement of the famine than might result from an Irish revolution. When the British suspended the habeas corpus he felt justified to call Ireland to the barricades. O'Brien hoped to conduct the revolution with "spirit" and with as "little injury as possible to life and property." He was anxious to avoid a degeneration of the violence into "a war of the poor against the rich." But O'Brien further proclaimed that if the revolution had succeeded, "I should have acquiesced in the establishment of a Republic as the only form of government which circumstances might have permitted" although O'Brien would "have much preferred . . . the restoration of the ancient Constitution of Ireland—The Queen, Lords, and Commons of Ireland."[22]

O'Brien stated that he had no quarrel with the judgment of the court that he should be executed for his role in the revolution of 1848. He had taken the steps that led him to Ballingarry, first in 1843 when he became a repealer, and next in 1846 when he acknowledged the right of citizens to use physical force in order to protect themselves. O'Brien could not agree with Anstey that he was not responsible for the revolution of 1848; on the contrary, he considered himself to have been its chief conspirator and to have been justified in using physical force in an effort to protect Ireland from England.[23] O'Brien wanted a pardon, and he appreciated Anstey's friendship and efforts to obtain a pardon for him.

But he had no intention of admitting any wrongdoing. He had no intention of denying his leadership role in the 1848 revolution.

O'Brien's letter to Anstey, written so soon after the failure of his escape attempt, demonstrated that his strength had not yet been depleted. He was still pursuing his plan to continue his role as an Irish leader in exile. He was still working on preparing the foundation for his eventual release. He used Anstey's letter as a reason not only to express his appreciation to his friend for his support but also to clearly state his claim to the position of leader of the 1848 revolution. He wanted his friends to understand the events that drew him to the fields at Ballingarry, his justification for the revolution, and the policy he planned to follow in exile. By means of this letter, he sent word to his friends in Westminster that he would never accept a pardon that would require an apology from him for taking Ireland into revolution. Since O'Brien believed his friends in Westminster would persist in their efforts to work for his release, he did not want them to expend their efforts on obtaining a type of pardon that he would feel compelled to refuse.

O'Brien did not know what the future held for him at Port Arthur. He knew his health had returned. He assumed that since he had made an escape attempt the government would no longer extend to him the option of a ticket-of-leave. But he had received no official communiqué on the subject. There was nothing more to do except continue to wait and see.

The Repercussions of the Escape Attempt

On 21 August 1850, O'Brien left his house on Maria Island, boarded a small cutter, and began his journey to his new place of confinement at the Port Arthur Probation Station.[24] This station had been established in approximately 1832. It was built to house a variety of different types of prisoners such as men convicted of committing crimes in the colonies and men whom the secretary of state designated. In addition, any convict who came from the educated classes was sent there, as well as convicts who were charged with serious misconduct while working on the road gangs or as assigned servants.[25]

The purpose behind building the Port Arthur Station was to create a station where "the rigour of discipline might be preserved." The location was ideal. While the area was physically beautiful, it was isolated. The district was "on a peninsula within a peninsula" containing one hundred thousand acres of woodland. A neck of land four hundred and fifty yards wide separated the two peninsulas. Across that neck of land posts were set into the ground to which fierce dogs were chained and on which lamps were placed. Guards were on duty at all times. When it was appropriate, dogs were kept on floating platforms just off the coast where the neck of land joined the two peninsulas.[26] Those dogs would, no doubt, bark and thus give notice to the guards if a prisoner attempted to swim around the line of defense.

The second commandant of the Port Arthur station, Capt. O'Hara Booth, adopted a policy of strict justice and absolute control. Work assignments varied according to the convicts' classifications. The most hardened convicts were assigned the most difficult and severe job, which was both "exhausting and dangerous." That was the work of the carrying gang. Approximately thirty laborers, when worked together "with a massive balk on the shoulders, resembled a huge centipede." Their job was to carry huge weights, sometimes totaling several tons, from one location to another. The ground along which they had to move was not only slippery but also had an incline. The result was that the convicts were "exposed . . . to terrific perils." If prisoners complained of being afraid of falling, or of an inability to lift and carry the assigned burden, they were taken out of the line, "flogged, taken back, and compelled by supernatural effort, to raise the load they had laid down." There were no periods of "momentary relaxation, and the scourge was the chief agent of control."[27]

The other extreme of work assignment was that afforded to the convicts from the educated classes. Although they were made to wear prison uniforms, they were assigned light duties and worked together as a group. However, any sign of disobedience or disorder brought instant punishment and transfer to a more physically demanding work gang.[28]

In its earlier days, Port Arthur's reputation was so horrible that it was believed the crime rate in the colonies went down because criminals knew they could be sent there if convicted. Over a period of several years, however, it was discovered that a term at Port Arthur did not succeed in reforming very many convicts. While serving a sentence the convict reacted mechanically, stayed out of trouble, and thus avoided harsh punishment. The convict gave the appearance of being reformed, but the reality was that he had become debased. Once he had served a term at Port Arthur, the chances were the convict had become a hardened criminal and would spend the rest of his days in and out of confinement.[29]

*   *   *

O'Brien was accompanied on his journey to Port Arthur by Superintendent Lapham and his family. Lapham had just been appointed superintendent of the Port Arthur station. The journey from Maria Island to Port Arthur was a pleasant one. The weather was fine. O'Brien enjoyed the trip principally because the change gave him a sense of exhilaration. At midnight the cutter on which they were sailing passed Cape

Pillar, the natural feature O'Brien had admired so much on his journey from Hobart Town to Maria Island. On the second occasion the scenery did not impress him as much as before, but the view was still striking, being lit on this occasion by the moonlight.[30]

The cutter arrived at Port Arthur at daybreak, and O'Brien was able in the morning light to get a clear picture of his new home. The station was situated in a bay at the end of an arm of the sea that intervened between Cape Pillar and Cape Raoul. Hills rose upward from the lough and were covered with woods. The scene was not only beautiful, but there was also a romantic quality about it. On landing, O'Brien was promptly taken to his new prison. The *Hobart Town Courier* had previously reported that O'Brien was to be housed in a stable. O'Brien never referred to his new place of abode as a former stable, and regardless of its previous use, he considered his new quarters to be superior to his former ones on Maria Island. There was no doubt that he was to be guarded more effectively. Outside the house a platform was being erected on which a military guard would be stationed. Adjacent to the house was a walled-in garden, and inside those walls a military guard paced back and forth.[31]

As was the case at the Maria Island stations, the officers at Port Arthur were largely Irish. Lapham was an Irishman, as was the senior assistant superintendent, Mr. Irvine, and the officer in command of the troops, Major Smiley. Unlike Maria Island, the probation station at Port Arthur was a large and active station. Port Arthur also maintained a depot for fifty convicts destined for confinement at Norfolk Island,[32] an area set aside for the most hardened criminals.

It was not until O'Brien was at Port Arthur for several days that the government sought to bring to an official conclusion the matter of his recent escape attempt. On 23 August, Nairn informed O'Brien that the governor was not prepared to take any special notice of his attempt to escape. However, O'Brien was warned that any future attempt would place him directly "under the current laws and regulations of the convict department" and would result in his being placed with the ordinary convicts and being compelled to work in a gang.[33]

O'Brien was compelled to admit to himself that the government had shown "forbearance." There was little or no difference between how he was personally treated at Port Arthur and how he had been treated at Maria Island while in close confinement. He had expected more severe treatment as a result of his escape attempt, and he even allowed for possible assignment to a work gang as a measure of punishment and closer control. O'Brien recognized that in some ways the life of the convict was preferable to the way he was living. But he also recognized that "considering my previous habits, I should perhaps think otherwise if I were actually treated as such." He concluded that it was better "to bear the ills we have, than fly to others that we know not of." O'Brien did not discount the possibility of there coming another time when solitary confinement would become so unbearable that it might be better for him to make another escape attempt "rather than perish by the slow destruction of all my faculties." He was hoping to retain his health, and he placed his trust in God to see him through his ordeal. [34]

During early September, however, began a series of events that would cause O'Brien to rethink his position. O'Brien had always assumed there would be some repercussions from his escape attempt. When he received formal notice from Nairn that he would not be punished he thought the crisis had passed. In fact, the repercussions did not directly affect him. They mainly affected two men connected to him, Lapham and McCarthy. When O'Brien learned what was happening to those men he began to consider accepting a ticket-of-leave.

On 8 September, O'Brien learned that Lapham had been relieved of his duties. O'Brien was shocked. Although no one had explained to O'Brien why Lapham was fired, he believed Lapham's dismissal was related to him in some way. He concluded that the government thought Lapham had either conspired with him in his escape attempt or allowed conditions to exist that assisted him to escape. [35] O'Brien was correct. Denison had placed the responsibility for O'Brien's attempt to escape where he thought it belonged, namely, on Lapham.

O'Brien decided to try to help Lapham. He wrote his spiritual leader, Dr. Francis Russell Nixon, the Anglican bishop of Tasmania, and solicited his assistance. O'Brien reasoned that if he accepted a ticket-of-leave and left the probation station the government might reconsider its dismissal of Lapham, and he made such an offer in writing. O'Brien then asked Nixon to serve as the mediator between himself and the government officials. [36] Unfortunately, Nixon's schedule prevented him from serving in such a capacity. The bishop assured O'Brien that he too thought highly of Lapham, but he did not have time to see the governor personally regarding the matter since his schedule necessitated a trip to Sydney. Nixon informed O'Brien that he had taken the liberty of forwarding O'Brien's letter to the governor. O'Brien was greatly disappointed. He did not believe that protocol allowed negotiation to take place directly between the governor and a prisoner. He was certain that Nixon's action would not result in the desired effect. [37] O'Brien was right.

Denison referred to the affair as a "modest proposal." He wrote to his mother commenting, "Smith O'Brien has written to say that he will take his ticket of leave like the other state prisoners, if the Government will pardon the Superintendent whose negligence allowed him to make the attempt!" Denison viewed O'Brien's proposal as preposterous. "It would seem that he fancied he was conferring a favour upon the Government by accepting his ticket of leave." Denison had no intention of retaining Lapham, but he was delighted to receive O'Brien's offer because he interpreted it to mean that the end of his problem with O'Brien was near. He concluded, "[O'Brien] is beginning to nibble at the bait, I dare say I shall soon get rid of him."[38]

O'Brien had failed to help Lapham by appealing to friends in Van Diemen's Land. He next turned to his connections in Great Britain. O'Brien wrote his brother Lucius stating that it was Lapham who was responsible for saving his life. In O'Brien's words, Lapham never ceased to treat him as "a gentleman and a Christian." O'Brien hoped Lucius would be able to help Lapham regain his position. But nothing O'Brien said or did made any immediate difference, and, on 19 September, Lapham and his family left Port Arthur.[39]

Meanwhile O'Brien learned about the debts incurred by the conspirators in planning his escape attempt. Initially, O'Brien did not know the total amount of money owed, but he was finally aware that there were serious financial problems. That information plus O'Brien's concern for helping the Laphams led him to further explore the possibility of obtaining a ticket-of-leave. On 21 September, O'Brien wrote the comptroller general inquiring if the government would grant him a ticket-of-leave for a period of a year, with the probability of renewal, and allow him to live at either Hobart Town or Launceston. O'Brien asserted that the necessity of earning a living would require that he live in a town where he could get a job. The government officials refused O'Brien's request to live in Hobart Town or Launceston, and O'Brien decided to refrain from accepting a ticket-of-leave that would place him in a country district where he would be unable to obtain a job.[40]

O'Brien's position was not very enviable. The departure of Lapham was a clear warning to the acting superintendent, Mr. Irvine, that Dr. Hampton wanted his orders governing O'Brien's treatment enforced rigidly. Irvine and O'Brien exchanged approximately two or three brief sentences during any given day. Two officials who might have broken the silence did not. The doctor paid O'Brien a five-minute visit each week during the first four weeks and then never appeared again. Actually, he had received orders not to visit O'Brien unless O'Brien became ill. The Anglican clergyman never appeared. O'Brien carried on as best he could. He spent three or four hours every day working in the garden attached to his house and approximately six to eight hours reading and writing. He hoped his health would not fail.[41]

One of the state prisoners with whom O'Brien was actively corresponding at this time was Patrick O'Donoghue. O'Donoghue had written to inquire how O'Brien was feeling and then proceeded to tell him about his many difficulties as editor of the *Irish Exile*, commenting, "I have experienced martyrdom enough for fifty saints." On 30 September, O'Brien answered O'Donoghue thanking him for his solicitude. O'Brien also commented on O'Donoghue's martyrdom. He told O'Donoghue that an "unavoidable attribute of a journalist [was] to enunciate hostility." He believed that a journalist must of necessity become a partisan and conceive of reasons to support his convictions. It was only natural that collisions of a personal nature would develop. The "Irish Exile" might indeed have learnt prudence if prudence could be taught by adversity—As however I do not feel myself entitled to preach a homily upon this theme I will add no more than that."[42]

On 5 October, O'Brien wrote another short note to O'Donoghue, thanking him for sending him some books. In that note O'Brien mentioned his recent correspondence with the government officials regarding a ticket-of-leave. He stated that if the government had agreed he would have had to accept "many consequences . . . disagreeable to me." O'Donoghue wrote immediately, stating, "It is very gratifying to all who feel anxiety about your health to learn that you have taken into consideration the prudence of accepting a 'ticket of leave.'" O'Donoghue urged O'Brien to come out. He argued from a practical point of view, telling O'Brien he had made an escape attempt and had failed. There was nothing more to be accomplished by continued confinement. All of his family and friends were extremely worried about him, and O'Brien owed them relief from such anxiety.[43] O'Brien did not then have access to newspapers, so he did not know that the public was aware of his inquiries regarding a ticket-of-leave.[44] He was also unaware that his friends, now under the leadership of Patrick O'Donoghue, were preparing a petition asking him to accept a ticket-of-leave.

The Hobart Town Petition

In many ways Denison was right. O'Brien had begun "to nibble at the bait," and the chances were that once he began to consider accepting a ticket-of-leave he would eventually make such a request. The collapse of his health, Grey's obvious endorsement of the treatment that Denison had prescribed, the failure of his escape attempt, the repercussions of that attempt, and finally his belief that neither Acting Superintendent Irvine nor the local physician would keep a careful watch over his health were all reasons he was apparently considering accepting a ticket-of-leave. In addition, O'Brien knew he had accomplished his long-range goal; namely, he was no longer in oblivion. He did not know the extent of the sympathetic statements being made in Van Diemen's Land, America, and Great Britain because he was not allowed to read the newspapers. But the various letters he was receiving told him that he had not been forgotten and that he had been successful in either creating or reawakening a sympathetic following. Dr. Dawson had told Denison that O'Brien would request a ticket-of-leave when a body of sympathetic admirers requested him to do so, and Dawson's analysis of O'Brien was basically correct. Interestingly enough, the sympathetic admirers would be residents of Van Diemen's Land.

During the Australian spring of 1850, public opinion in Van Diemen's Land was decidedly in support of O'Brien against the bureaucratic actions of Governor Denison, Dr. Hampton, and the related governmental forces assisting them. Behind the controversies between O'Brien and the government loomed, of course, the popular dissatisfaction with the practices of transportation in general, but the actions of officialdom toward O'Brien provided the free citizens of Van Diemen's Land with an opportunity to complain loudly and with much justification, all at the expense of the same officials.

The sympathetic expressions of public opinion toward O'Brien appeared initially in the press, and many of those sympathetic expressions were coupled with expressions of general disdain for the local officials. In October, the *Hobart Town Brittania* reported the bad conditions under which O'Brien was living in Port Arthur. It implied that O'Brien's life was in jeopardy. The writer of the report felt confident enough of public support to go so far as to state that the harsh treatment was not the result of oversight, but was deliberate. He noted that the previous superintendent, Lapham, had been dismissed for treating O'Brien leniently. The *Brittania* demanded that an inquiry into Lapham's dismissal be made and the findings reported "without respect to persons."[45] But the main supporter of O'Brien and simultaneously the main defamer of Denison and his associates was the *Launceston Examiner*. It appears that, like Thomas Knight, the editors of the *Launceston Examiner* recognized the commonality of interest between O'Brien and the antitransportationists. Since the arrival of the *Neptune* the editors had been working to defame Denison. Evidently O'Brien's treatment at Port Arthur was seen by those editors as an opportunity to carry out their new policy.

The *Brittania* had charged the government with deliberately abusing O'Brien. The *Launceston Examiner* was emboldened to name the culprits. On 16 October, the *Launceston Examiner* openly identified the first of O'Brien's persecutors, Dr. Hampton, "the late surgeon superintendent of a convict ship." They wrote, "It grates upon the public feelings that a person like Dr. Hampton should be permitted to aggravate the sufferings of [O'Brien,] a high-minded man." The treatment of Dr. Hampton by the editors of the *Launceston Examiner* was actually gentle compared to their treatment of Governor Denison. In the edition published on 26 October, O'Brien was depicted as an intelligent, brave, and honorable gentleman, while Denison was described as being a madman, a liar, a defamer who possessed no moral feeling. The editors acknowledged that Denison was often seen carrying the Bible, and it was assumed that he read it, but the editors knew he did not understand it. "He is an enigma in nature, a monstrosity in politics."[46]

By 2 November, the *Launceston Examiner* was calling on the free citizens of Launceston to express openly their sympathy for O'Brien, expressions that would not only perforce side with a state prisoner against the government but that would also cause the citizens to place themselves in personal opposition to the governor. The editors called on the citizenry to hold a public meeting and petition the crown and the Parliament to end O'Brien's present mode of treatment, which was bound to end in the loss of his life or reason. The editors depicted O'Brien as a man "neither debased in spirit nor corrupted in heart—whose aspirations were and are as high and holy as those of a Russell and a Hampton of olden times."[47]

While the *Launceston Examiner* was calling on the citizens of Van Diemen's Land to petition the monarch to "mitigate the rigour of O'Brien's punishment," Patrick O'Donoghue was putting the final touches on a plan that would secure O'Brien's release from close confinement. During October 1850, O'Donoghue had been one of the leaders of a group that sought to persuade O'Brien to accept a ticket-of-leave. As a result of the group's actions, O'Brien began to receive a series of pleas and petitions urging him to accept a ticket-of-leave, many of them from citizens in Van Diemen's Land who were unknown to O'Brien. In addition, several of the other state prisoners joined in the effort. By fortunate circumstance, the pleas of the O'Brien family that were written the previous spring and summer of 1850 arrived during the same period and added weight to the campaign in Van Diemen's Land.

The letters from McManus, Mitchel, and Martin reflected a variety of views. McManus used a wonderful example from history in his plea to O'Brien. He referred to a period in Roman history: "When Cato the younger stood alone against the combined power of Caesar and Pompey . . . and when banishment from Rome or submission to their tyranny was the only alternative, he was entreated by the most virtuous part of the Citizens, . . . to yield, . . . adding that 'Cato might do without Rome, but Rome not without Cato.'" McManus concluded the story by stating, "[Cato] yielded and was afterwards useful to his country." McManus urged O'Brien to accept a ticket-of-leave and get ready to be useful once again to Ireland. John Mitchel urged O'Brien to accept the ticket-of-leave because he thought O'Brien was the only person who could clear up the bad rumors about the attempted escape. Mitchel told O'Brien that the people were being told only the government's side. Mitchel also explained that, from the other prisoners' standpoint, "We all long greatly to have you away from that infernal place." John Martin also wrote to O'Brien stressing that both the Irish exiles and the public of Van Diemen's Land needed him.[48]

The letters from O'Brien's family urging him to accept the ticket-of-leave were written by his mother, his sisters Ann Martineau and Katherine Harris, and his brother Lucius. O'Brien's mother was a deeply reli-

gious woman and implored her son to fulfill his Christian duty by cooperating with the government. She was referring to the phrase in the
Bible, "Render unto Caesar the things that are Caesar's and to God the
things that are God's." As to her son's previous acts of revolution against
the British government, Mrs. O'Brien considered that her son had
adopted "mistaken notions" about Ireland and that those notions were
the product of a party in Ireland that had led him astray, "a party . . .
who were satisfied to receive what they wanted to get by installments."
She asked him to now take his first installment toward a pardon, a ticket-
of-leave. [49]

O'Brien's sister Anne attempted to explain to him that his refusal
of the ticket-of-leave had been interpreted as an act of defiance and that
he was, therefore, subject to punishment, namely solitary confinement. [50]
His sister Katherine wrote saying she could understand why O'Brien was
shocked by the treatment he had received from the government, since
solitary confinement was not the kind of treatment one gentleman expected from another. Yet she did not think that O'Brien could really
expect anything else. "It seems to me you have no right to expect them
to give you more license because in these matters there are others under
the same punishment." She wrote, "I think you must yourself allow it
would not be a wise thing for the government to have turned you all
[loose] at Hobart Town taking the chance of what you might choose to
do with yourselves." The main thrust of her argument was that O'Brien
had associated with unprincipled men and he could not expect to be
treated differently than his unprincipled associates. [51]

It appears that O'Brien was basically unmoved by the arguments
that his mother and sisters used to convince him to accept the ticket-of-
leave, but he was affected by their obvious concern for his well-being. [52]

Of all the family letters to O'Brien the one from Sir Lucius was
probably the most important, for Lucius quite openly stated that he did
not foresee any change in the government's attitude and thus he could
not help his brother. Lucius told O'Brien never to hesitate in sending to
him any further information that might be of use, but from his vantage
point there was only one person who could save O'Brien from disaster
and that was O'Brien himself. [53] Lucius believed, as did Chisholm Anstey,
that the ticket-of-leave was the first step toward obtaining a pardon.
Until O'Brien accepted the ticket-of-leave, Sir Lucius could do nothing
for him. Once he accepted the ticket-of-leave, he would not only be out
of danger from damaging his health or losing his life but he would also
be on the way toward a pardon.

On 29 October, a public meeting was held in Hobart Town at which
an address to O'Brien was unanimously adopted. The address requested
O'Brien to accept a ticket-of-leave on the same conditions as those that

bound the other state prisoners. The *South Australian Register* reported that the address was subscribed by nine hundred persons "including some of the most wealthy and influential gentlemen in the Island." The *Hobart Town Chronicle* expressed a hope that O'Brien would follow the request of the address "and thereby extricate the Local Government from the painful predicament in which he has placed it." On 5 November, O'Donoghue wrote to O'Brien about that meeting and told him of a petition signed by one thousand citizens of Hobart Town asking him to accept a ticket-of-leave.[54]

On 8 November, Reeves forwarded to O'Brien the address that had been drawn up by the citizens of Hobart Town asking O'Brien to accept a ticket-of-leave. O'Brien noted that the petition was signed "by upwards of 500 persons," not one thousand, but he also noted that it was "written in good taste, earnest and simple."[55] O'Donoghue had written a hasty note calling O'Brien's attention to the high reputation of the men who signed the petition, the first five names on the list being those of magistrates. One of them, Mr. Dunne, was a banker in high standing. All the others were equally men of distinction, "merchants, shopkeepers, traders and other intelligent colonists."[56] At that point O'Brien resolved to comply with the request of the petitioners.

In a letter to his wife, O'Brien explained how he felt:

> Until now I have never felt myself thoroughly beaten by English power—beaten in the Hs. Commons—beaten in the field—beaten in the Courts of Law—beaten before the Lords—beaten in my attempt to escape—beaten in the system of passive resistance which I had proposed to myself to apply by continuing in prison rather than accepting the wretched description of liberty or rather of imprisonment offered by the Govt.—as an equivalent for my parole. Though I exposed myself last year to the risk of premature death by refusing to emancipate myself from solitary confinement according to the terms of Government, I have not had sufficient strength of will or obstinacy of character to resist the united solicitations of nearly all my dearest friends as well as with those of my wife. . . . May God grant this submission of my own opinions . . . may be attended with a blessing.[57]

The truth was that O'Brien accepted the ticket-of-leave because he had no real choice. He knew Denison had no intention of relieving the pressure and that the British officials endorsed Denison's policy. He also knew the conditions under which he was living were sufficient as long as he maintained his health but would be quite insufficient in case his health failed. With Lapham's dismissal he was not certain that either the acting superintendent or the local physician would act swiftly enough if his health began to fail to save him from madness, physical incapacitation, or the grave. Nor could he count on appeals for assistance to friends in Great Britain or Van Diemen's Land. He had made an attempt to escape and had failed. The choice before him was clear-cut. He could accept the ticket-of-leave and await pardon, or he could remain in confinement and take a chance that his health would not desert him while he awaited release.

O'Brien's confinement, however, had not been a total loss. He had successfully undergone "martyrdom" as a means of preventing his exile from becoming the road to oblivion. The public in the British Isles, America, and Van Diemen's Land were all aware of his existence, and there was a growing sympathy for his plight. That growing sympathy could serve as a lever that would push the British ministry into granting the state prisoners a pardon at the appropriate moment.

Although O'Brien had been willing to suffer martyrdom, he recognized that it was a dangerous game and that there would come a time when it could no longer be continued. He did not mind suffering a bit, but ultimately he wanted to be a live and healthy Irish leader, not an incapacitated or dead one. Lucius's letter confirmed his own thinking that the only person who could keep him safe from harm was himself. McManus's letter confirmed his self-image that while O'Brien could do without Ireland, Ireland could not do without O'Brien. The petition from the citizenry of Van Diemen's Land demonstrated that public opinion agreed with the conclusions of Lucius and McManus. The petition soothed his pride. His common sense told him what had to be done. His self-image assured him his life had purpose as an Irish leader.

On 9 November, O'Brien wrote to Reeves thanking him for sending the address. He told Reeves that he had decided to accept the ticket-of-leave, requesting assignment to New Norfolk. In his letter to Reeves, O'Brien enclosed his formal request to the governor of Van Diemen's Land for a ticket-of-leave for a period of six months, and he asked Reeves to deliver his request to the local officials in Hobart Town.[58]

On 12 November, Reeves replied to O'Brien that he had taken his notice of desire of parole to the authorities. Denison wrote to his mother giving his explanation of the affair: "O'Brien is tired out at last, and has taken his ticket-of-leave—having given his parole." Denison did not think highly of the group of petitioners: "A deputation of Irish convicts sent an address to him, asking him to accept the offer of the Government, and as he only wanted a reason for changing his mind, he at once made a merit of assenting to their request." On the twelfth, Nairn wrote to O'Brien informing him that his ticket-of-leave had been granted. In a separate letter Nairn listed the regulations that were to be observed by O'Brien as a holder of a ticket-of-leave, the same regulations that Nairn had read to the state prisoners on their arrival at Hobart Town.[59]

Promptly after receiving official word from Nairn that he had been granted a ticket-of-leave, O'Brien informed Lapham of what had taken place, expressing concern for Lapham and his family and inquiring if he could be of any assistance. On 13 November, O'Brien transmitted a number of letters to the comptroller general so that they could be forwarded, remarking that since he was now a holder of a ticket-of-leave, he assumed his letters would not be opened. O'Brien was correct.[60]

O'Brien's financial problems were somewhat relieved as a result of his acceptance of the ticket-of-leave. Dr. Hampton had ruled previously that O'Brien could not receive the money his family was forwarding to him from Ireland until he accepted the ticket-of-leave. Approximately one hundred pounds had arrived from Ireland, and the money would now be turned over to him.[61]

O'Brien had a mixed reaction to what was happening to him. He recognized that by accepting the ticket-of-leave he was exchanging a "portion of mental independence" for "some participation in the enjoyments of life." One of those enjoyments was the freedom to read the newspapers. He anxiously read the accounts of the meetings in Dublin and Cork protesting the treatment that he had received from Denison and Hampton, commenting, "It is consoling, it is, I confess it, gratifying in the highest degree to my feelings to discover that I am not altogether forgotten by my Countrymen—that they are not altogether insensible to the sufferings which I have undergone for their sake and that by a portion at least of mankind the motives which have animated me to undertake acts which failure has in the eyes of adversaries covered with ridicule and contempt have been duly appreciated."[62]

From the moment Nairn's letter arrived announcing that O'Brien's ticket-of-leave was granted, the officials "unlocked" his prison door and he was allowed to roam at will around the convict station at Port Arthur. The only restriction placed on him was the requirement that he sleep in his own house. As soon as word spread of his release the Roman Catholic priest attached to the station, the Reverend Livermore, hurried over to offer O'Brien "the hospitality of his house" and his companionship.[63]

During his few remaining days at Port Arthur, O'Brien was able to get a closer look at the probation station and to make a series of excursions outside it. As he investigated the station he noticed a remarkable difference between Maria Island and Port Arthur. Port Arthur was a large station handling anywhere from five hundred to fourteen hundred convicts at a time, yet only one hundred acres of ground had been cleared and used for farming. Maria Island held only about one hundred and fifty convicts, yet several hundred acres of ground were under cultivation. The only explanation O'Brien received was that, due to the density of the forest, it would cost too much to clear the land and so the work was never begun. This reply was wholly unsatisfactory to him because he believed that since convict labor cost much less than free labor, if the cost of clearing the land would be figured on that basis, it would pay to clear it. Actually O'Brien thought the convict station at Maria Island superior to that at Port Arthur because the work was more meaningful and thus helped to prepare the convicts for life as free men.[64]

His excursions also gave him another in-depth view of the transportation system. One of those excursions took him to Point Puer, which was formerly a prison station for eight hundred convict boys, whose ages generally were from ten to twenty. The station was closed, the buildings were empty and slowly falling to ruin, and so it was as if O'Brien was visiting a ghost town. Point Puer was only one of the many convict stations on which the British government had expended thousands of pounds while experimenting in an effort to find the best system of convict discipline.[65] It had been established to "reclaim and control" the young prisoners "rather than . . . punish [them]." Prior to the establishment of that station, there was no differentiation made between boys convicted to terms of transportation and men. They were all transported together and received similar treatment. They were placed in the barracks together, and, when disobedient, the boys, like the men, "were tied up to the triangles and punished with the cat." Most of the boy prisoners were in their teens, but there was an account of a seven-year-old boy receiving a sentence of transportation for life. Many judges in the British Isles believed they were doing the young offender a favor by sentencing him to transportation. They believed the young offender would eventually finish the term of work at the probation station and find himself in a country where there was opportunity to develop. A lord mayor of London stated, "Nothing could be kinder than to transport juvenile offenders to a country where their labour would be useful and their prosperity sure."[66] Unfortunately, experience demonstrated that most of the criminals convicted of capital crimes in Van Diemen's Land had spent their boyhoods at Point Puer, and the British government concluded that the scheme was a failure.[67]

*   *   *

On one of his last excursions, O'Brien climbed Mount Arthur, a hill fifteen hundred feet high that gave him a wonderful view of the area. Everywhere O'Brien looked he saw forest. The view did not please him for he could see "nothing that indicates the presence of man or the fertility of nature." O'Brien had to admit that Port Arthur was an area "which has probably witnessed more of human suffering than almost any spot of equal size on the face of the globe during the period of its occupation as a Penal Station." As O'Brien prepared to leave the area, he hoped his "acquaintance with Port Arthur" was at an end.[68]

During his first year in exile, O'Brien had proved to be a more difficult adversary than Denison had anticipated. The British ministers in

London had devised a policy of gentlemanly oblivion to effectively "execute" O'Brien and his companions without making martyrs of them. The struggle that took place between Denison and O'Brien from October 1849 to November 1850 was over the question of whether or not that cleverly devised execution order would be carried out.

As O'Brien and Denison clashed, each man's goals had become readily apparent. Denison wanted O'Brien to request a ticket-of-leave so that he could carry out Earl Grey's directive to treat O'Brien as a gentleman and hence send him into oblivion. O'Brien wanted to delay accepting the ticket-of-leave. He wanted to wait and see what the conditions in the penal colony were really like, to escape if possible, or, if necessary, to suffer martyrdom and hence end his oblivion. By November 1850 it could be said that both men had attained their goals. Martyrdom had merited O'Brien public sympathy, and he was no longer in danger of falling into oblivion. Yet the solitary confinement, ordered by Denison and confirmed by Grey, forced O'Brien to accept the ticket-of-leave. Denison considered that he had won. O'Brien would now be treated as a gentleman. O'Brien must have known it would be difficult to maintain the sympathetic public opinion that had recently been developed. He also must have known he had reached the limit of his ability to suffer direct martyrdom. As O'Brien prepared to leave Port Arthur, he knew his struggle to obtain a pardon was not over, but he did not know what form it would take.

CHAPTER 5

The Three Truants

O'Brien in New Norfolk

At 6:00 A.M. on 18 November 1850 O'Brien left Port Arthur. He boarded a boat that carried him three miles to the terminus of a nearby railway. He then climbed into a small wagon that was set on railroad tracks and powered by the physical exertion of four convicts. O'Brien was startled, noting, "The railway is carried up and down hill and the labour of pushing the waggon up the inclined planes is very severe." The trip was five miles long. O'Brien next boarded a steamer for the final part of his journey to Hobart Town.

The steamer made several stops at the various convict stations along the way, including "'The Cascades', 'Impression Bay', 'The Salt Water River', and 'The Mines.'" "The Cascades" convict station was notorious because the superintendent had been, within the previous six months, "convicted of perpetrating atrocities the recital of which causes the listener to shudder." One of the tortures involved stretching the convicts "against a wall by what is called ringbolting in a position which is described to be not very dissimilar from that of the rack and that they have been gagged by forcing into their throats pieces of wood perforated by a hole for breathing in order to prevent them from uttering cries." Word of those atrocities had been brought to the attention of the Roman Catholic bishop of Van Diemen's Land, Bishop Willson, who caused an investigation, which led to the superintendent being reprimanded by the governor. The reprimand, however, lost virtually all of its preventive effect because, due to pressure exerted from the comptroller general, the superintendent remained in charge of the Cascades station. O'Brien commented that while he suspected Lapham had been dismissed "for the exercise of humanity," the superintendent who had been found to have committed atrocities was actually untouched.[1]

* * *

At 5:00 P.M. on 18 November, O'Brien reached Hobart Town. "Several hundred persons" had gathered at the dock and cheered as O'Brien disembarked. O'Brien was first met by Mr. Reeves, who had acted as chairman of the meeting that had drawn up the address requesting O'Brien to accept a ticket-of-leave, by John Moore, who had acted as secretary of the same meeting, and by Father Therry and Patrick O'Donoghue. Denison was aware of O'Brien's arrival in Hobart Town but merely commented that he "was met by a body of his admirers, and cheered to the inn." O'Brien took lodging at the Freemasons Hotel and soon found himself receiving numerous callers. Several of the leaders of the colony called to express their sympathy and to offer whatever assistance they could. Later in the evening Reeves entertained O'Brien at dinner.[2]

The next day Reeves showed O'Brien around the town. When O'Brien had first arrived in Van Diemen's Land the year before he had marveled from the decks of the *Swift* at the picturesque location of Hobart Town. His tour with Reeves confirmed his original judgment. On Tuesday evening, after O'Brien's tour of Hobart Town, W. Carter called for O'Brien and took him home to meet the other members of his family at dinner. Carter's residence was located at Newtown, three miles from Hobart Town. It had been two years and four months since O'Brien had dined in a private home, and the prisoner appreciated the "kindly feelings" displayed by the Carters. On Wednesday morning O'Brien set out for New Norfolk and upon arriving there was greeted by his old friend and conspirator Father Woolfrey. O'Brien was a true admirer of Father Woolfrey and always enjoyed his company, especially because the priest lacked the "austerity which is sometimes found to result from self-dedication to religious observances."[3]

New Norfolk was in a picturesque valley on the banks of the River Derwent. On every side rose highlands covered with forests, providing pleasing views in almost any direction. O'Brien situated himself in a "very quiet comfortable [hotel] where I have a bedroom and a sitting room and in which I am boarded and lodged at the rate of six pounds per months of four weeks." He early began to follow a routine that allowed him to study in the morning hours, dine at about one or two o'clock in the afternoon, and then explore the neighborhood for the next three or four hours.[4]

O'Brien had not been in New Norfolk very long when he received a letter from Lapham expressing a desire to travel to New Norfolk and visit him. O'Brien was most anxious to receive Lapham and did what he could to make the visit as pleasant as possible.[5] Some of the gentlemen from the surrounding area also dropped by and invited O'Brien to visit them at their homes. O'Brien slowly began to develop friendships with the Barkers of Rose Garland, the Lloyds of Bryn Estyn, and the Fentons of Fenton Forest.[6]

On 3 December, O'Brien began to receive visits from McManus, O'Doherty, O'Donoghue, and Meagher. While they were welcome, they came against O'Brien's better judgment and against the expressed wishes of the government. When O'Brien had accepted the ticket-of-leave, several of the state prisoners had requested permission from the local officials to visit O'Brien at New Norfolk. The officials had refused to grant the requests. O'Brien attempted to discourage the visits once he realized the danger of official reprisals.[7] But during the early part of December, McManus had had urgent commercial business in Hobart Town. He concluded his business in a few hours and then proceeded to New Norfolk. O'Doherty made a similar journey. Their visits with O'Brien were rather uneventful.[8]

O'Donoghue, however, made the journey with Moore, and both men became so intoxicated while on their way that they fell into arguing with one another and actually commenced fighting, causing themselves to be seized by the constables at New Norfolk. O'Donoghue was tried and fined the next day, and O'Brien wrote, "The circumstance occasioned public scandal and was in all respects most disagreeable to my feelings."[9]

Several days later Meagher visited O'Brien in company with a young Irishman, Kean, who was interested in meeting O'Brien. In the midst of their supper meeting the landlord of O'Brien's hotel, Elwin, interrupted the visit to announce that the police were nearing the hotel. Someone had seen Meagher when he had arrived at New Norfolk and had reported his presence to the police. The three men, Meagher, O'Brien, and Kean, continued their supper, but in a short time a waiter interrupted the men and, addressing Kean, stated that "some people below in the hall wanted to see him." Kean went downstairs and was promptly and mistakenly arrested by the police as Thomas Meagher. Kean submitted to the arrest, but he protested against the accusation that he was Meagher. The police ignored his protest and proceeded to take him to the local police office, which was a mile and a quarter from the hotel. Ten minutes after the police departed with Kean, a wealthy Irishman residing in New Norfolk heard of Meagher's predicament and brought one of his finest horses to Elwin's hotel to help Meagher make his escape. Meagher gave "thanks to the speed of a gallant little grey horse, mounted on which I dashed through the police [who were escourting Mr. Kean to jail], and got back to my own boundary before they had time to arrest me." Kean was discharged the moment he was properly identified at the police office in New Norfolk and arrived back home only two hours after Meagher.[10]

Although the affair was closed for Meagher, it was not closed for McManus, O'Doherty, and O'Donoghue. Their presence in New Norfolk had also been noted. On 18 December, McManus was charged in Launceston with misconduct for being absent from his assigned district on 3 December. The trial was held before Police Magistrate Francis Evans who, after hearing McManus's plea of guilty, admonished him for leaving his assigned district without permission, exacted a promise from

McManus that he would not again leave his district without applying for leave, and then let him go.[11] O'Donoghue was charged in New Norfolk on 19 December. He was, however, granted bail and told to return on the following Monday, the twenty-third, for his trial. He received bail and postponement of his trial so that he would have time to be assisted by counsel. O'Doherty was charged in New Norfolk on the twentieth and, although he wished the trial to be held promptly, his trial was set for the same day as O'Donoghue's, Monday the twenty-third. He too was granted bail.[12]

O'Brien was present when O'Doherty was charged by Magistrate Mason. O'Brien did not agree with Mason's opinion that the Irish prisoners had obtained their tickets-of-leave on condition that they would observe the regulations attached to the paroles. He quickly wrote the comptroller general about the "misunderstanding." O'Brien stated his position clearly. "I hold myself bound by my parole to no engagement except that I will not attempt to escape . . . between the 9th Nov 1850 and the 9th May 1851." O'Brien also sent a copy of the letter to Magistrate Mason.[13]

On Monday, O'Doherty stood trial alone. Over the weekend O'Donoghue had returned to Hobart Town, had taken ill, and on the advice of his physicians remained in his bed. The government was aware of his illness and placed a guard on his house to await his recovery. O'Doherty's trial took place before Police Magistrate Mason. At the conclusion of the case, Magistrate Mason stated he was disposed to pronounce a verdict against O'Doherty similar to the one pronounced against McManus. O'Doherty was admonished by the police magistrate and discharged after "promising that he will not again quit the District appointed for his residence without applying to the proper authority for permission."[14]

Magistrate Mason and Magistrate Evans forwarded to Governor Denison reports of the charges against the three Irish prisoners and the records of the trials of two of them. Denison was upset with practically everyone involved in the case. He was upset with Earl Grey for having granted the state prisoners "unusual privileges" placing them in an anomalous position that had caused him problems in dealing with them and had led the free citizens of Van Diemen's Land to treat them sympathetically. He was upset with the magistrates because he believed they had allowed the sympathy that the general public had for the state prisoners to influence their decision, which was a mere admonishment rather than a punishment. He was upset with McManus because he "had twice refused him permission" to leave his assigned district.[15]

But Denison no doubt believed the incident could have a positive effect. He would once again be able to clearly demonstrate to Grey that the British officials had made a mistake in believing the state prisoners were gentlemen. The actions of the three truants were proof that they were inveterate lawbreakers. In addition, Denison had only recently received a dispatch from Grey directing him to send O'Donoghue either to a country district or to a probation station in order to end his publishing career.[16] As a result of O'Donoghue's truancy, Denison had the "cause" that he believed was necessary to revoke a ticket-of-leave. O'Donoghue would have to divest himself of the *Irish Exile* since a felon at a probation station could not own property. In addition, the mail of all convicts at the probation stations was inspected and could be censored, so O'Donoghue would not be able to engage in any editorial or publishing activity.[17] Denison could now carry out Grey's directive and sever O'Donoghue's connection with the *Irish Exile*.

On 24 December, Nairn wrote letters to the truant men officially notifying them that the governor had revoked their tickets-of-leave for having absented themselves from their assigned districts. His letters stated that each of the men was to serve three months at a probation station, McManus at the "Cascades," O'Doherty at "Salt Water River," and O'Donoghue at "Impression Bay." Nairn's letters were delivered by policemen who were under orders to escort their new charges directly to the prisoners' barracks in Hobart Town.[18]

O'Doherty was the first of the three to be taken into custody and to be sent off to a probation station. McManus was arrested at Launceston and then brought to Hobart Town where he was placed in the prisoners' barracks. While he was in the barracks a "local band played Irish airs outside his cell." He was to be sent to the Cascades on 31 December.[19] O'Donoghue was still ill when the police came to take him. He had two broken ribs and complained that he had "really never felt so ill in body and mind." The guard that had been placed on his house when his ill health prevented him from standing trial in New Norfolk was maintained because of the revocation of his ticket-of-leave. The government directed a physician to examine O'Donoghue to determine when he would be able to travel to his newly assigned probation station, and the doctor reported that he would probably be ready to begin his sentence on 8 January.[20]

The day after the men were taken into custody some citizens of Hobart Town drew up two separate petitions to the governor asking for the restoration of the tickets-of-leave for O'Donoghue, O'Doherty, and McManus. The first petition was prepared by the friends of O'Doherty and was sponsored by Bishop Willson and other influential men in Hobart Town. The second petition was on behalf of all three of the exiles and was sponsored by the Very Reverend W. Hall, Father Therry, and other leaders of the community.[21]

The governor quickly refused the petition drawn up on behalf of O'Doherty, O'Donoghue, and McManus. O'Donoghue heard that the government was determined "to make examples of McManus and me!"

But then Governor Denison's secretary, Mr. Clark, "hinted that if the prisoners themselves sent in separate memorials, signed by themselves, expressing regret at what had occurred, and pledging them not to leave their several districts in the future, the Government would forego further punishment." Both McManus and O'Donoghue sent in such memorials, and both were "flatly rejected." O'Donoghue thought the whole memorial business demonstrated how teacherous the government officials could be "in ensnaring and entrapping [McManus and himself] into this admission of error and promise not to repeat it, and then refusing relief." O'Donoghue believed Denison had an ulterior motive. "In my mind it was all done to form the subject matter of a despatch to be read in the House of Commons." Some thought was thereafter given to resorting to the courts to forestall or end the imprisonment of the state prisoners, but O'Donoghue opposed such action. "I have no confidence in them—'Go to law with the Devil, and the Court held in Hell'!"[22]

At that point O'Donoghue realized he could not expect anything to intervene to prevent his being sent to a probation station once his health was restored. Accordingly he turned his attention to the management of his newspaper, the *Irish Exile,* for with the revocation of his ticket-of-leave he lost the right to hold property. On 1 January he told Meagher he was preparing a deed assigning his interest in the newspaper to Mr. M'Laughlin and Mr. O'Donnell. O'Donoghue wanted to keep the newspaper operating at least until the end of the quarter when people normally paid their accounts. With that money O'Donoghue would be able to pay off his outstanding debts.[23]

On Christmas Day, O'Brien wrote his wife, Lucy, a detailed report of what had transpired, and on the basis of those events he strongly urged her not to bring the children and come live with him in Van Diemen's Land, because they might find that all the financial sacrifices that would be necessary, not to speak of the hazards of the voyage, might through some official pettiness be put to naught. Denison's recent actions demonstrated to O'Brien that the governor believed he had the power to revoke the tickets-of-leave of the state prisoners whenever it suited his purpose. O'Brien foresaw what effect such a revocation of his own ticket-of-leave would have on Lucy and the children once they had arrived in Van Diemen's Land. He also foresaw the effect such arbitrary official action would have on him personally. O'Brien told Gavan Duffy that alone he could laugh at the "malevolence which is displayed" by the government. But if his family was with him, "it would break [his] heart."[24]

Meagher also felt acutely the bad luck of his friends that arose out of events in which he had participated. On Christmas Day he wrote to O'Brien and stated that he had only recently heard the news that O'Doherty, McManus, and O'Donoghue had all been taken into custody.

He asked O'Brien whether he thought that O'Brien and himself ought in protest to renounce their tickets-of-leave. Meagher questioned, "Is it honourable or justifiable of us to keep an engagement with a government capable of acting in so coarse, so imperious, and brutal a manner? Do, drop me a line *at once*." Meagher explained to O'Brien that he was hesitating to throw up his ticket-of-leave because he had recently gone to a great deal of effort to establish himself in a cottage on Lake Sorell. If he turned in his ticket-of-leave he would be sent to a probation station and his newly acquired property would be "expose[d] to strangers."[25] Actually Meagher was not anxious to surrender his ticket-of-leave for another reason. He was contemplating marriage. When Dr. Edward Hall and his wife moved from Oatlands to Ross, where Dr. Hall was to serve as the medical superintendent, they took with them to serve as governess to their six children the daughter of Brian Bennett of New Norfolk, Catherine Bennett. Meagher met them all rather accidentally. While walking one day, he went to assist some travelers whose vehicle had broken down. The travelers were the Halls and Catherine en route to Ross. Meagher helped Hall make the repairs and then accompanied the group along part of the route. Coincidentally, Catherine had known of McManus, who, while living in New Norfolk, had spent a great deal of time visiting at the home of her parents. Meagher was evidently charmed by the attractive governess, and he began visiting the Halls regularly.[26] By Christmas 1850 Meagher and Catherine were considering marriage, an announcement not greeted with enthusiasm by all the other state prisoners. Catherine was not of the same social standing as Meagher, and Martin, in particular, was surprised when he heard of the impending event. In a letter to O'Doherty, Martin commented quite openly on the match. He believed the "origin and present condition" of Catherine's family must result in some kind of social degradation, but, worse than that, Martin also believed Meagher was marrying "all merely for want of something to do." Martin was truly alarmed. "And worst of all is that I am unable to discover any grounds of confident hope that any of [Meagher's] sanguine expectations from the marriage project will be realized."[27]

Although Martin's thoughts were included in a letter to O'Doherty and not sent to Meagher, the prospective bridegroom was aware of Martin's attitude. Meagher was beginning to recognize that his forthcoming wedding would not meet with the approval of the "World." But Meagher was also aware that his exile in Van Diemen's Land was affecting him. He told O'Doherty, "I felt, day by day, the impulses, which prompted me to act a generous part at home, withering and dying fast, and felt, with equal pain, despondency, and remorse, a spirit of indifference, inertness, and self-abandonment seizing on my heart." Catherine, no doubt, was the "opportunity" that awakened in him "the proud and generous nature that was sinking, coldly and dismally, into a stupid and sensual stagnation, and that, once more, I feel those sympathies in action, which, in the storm of a nation's deadliest winter, were to me the currents of my soul—the wings on which my intellect was borne aloft, and became, for a time, a light and inspiration to those below." Meagher proudly told O'Doherty, "I am myself again."[28]

Meagher had written O'Brien on 25 December for O'Brien's views on whether they should both resign their tickets-of-leave in protest of the treatment of O'Donoghue, O'Doherty, and McManus. Before the week was out, he received opinions on the matter, but the opinions that helped him make up his mind came not from O'Brien but from McManus, O'Doherty, and O'Donoghue.

McManus wrote from the prisoners' barracks in Hobart Town just prior to being sent to the Cascades Probation Station. He told Meagher, "You'd laugh, my dear fellow, to see me in my grey uniform, with a little bundle already tied up, containing a few pair of socks and a flannel shirt—all other necessaries supplied by the Government." McManus was not looking forward to the "pint of 'skilly'! morning and evening, and mutton broth mid-day." He wasn't certain how he would look at the end of his sentence, three months hence. He advised Meagher, "You have got luckily out of it—keep so, like a dear good fellow."[29] O'Doherty wrote a similar letter. He was serving his three-month sentence at Impression Bay. He entreated Meagher "to keep out of the hands of these men, as you would out of the clutches of the very demon himself." O'Doherty told Meagher, "I am treated as a common convict, obliged to sleep with every species of scoundrel, and to work in a gang from six o'clock in the morning to six o'clock in the evening—being all the while next to starved, as I find it wholly impossible to touch their abominable 'skilly', which is the breakfast and supper offered me." O'Doherty reported that so far he had been able to bear his sufferings, "thanks to my good friend Thomas à Kempis!" But his situation was so terrible that whether or not he could continue to bear up "God only knows!" O'Donoghue gave Meagher similar advice: "You have acted wisely and most discreetly in not resigning your ticket—it would be stark madness." He reasoned, "Better far to have some staunch men outside the walls, than have all hemmed in."[30]

Meagher did not resign his ticket-of-leave, he decided to get married and remain "outside the walls." No doubt he reasoned that if he protested by resigning his ticket-of-leave it would result in oblivion, a loss for all the state prisoners.

*   *   *

O'Donoghue was the last of the three state prisoners to leave the Hobart Town Prisoners' Barracks. On 8 January 1851 he boarded the

Port Arthur steamer, which was to take him to the Salt Water River Probation Station, but he became so ill that he was placed in the hospital at Port Arthur. When O'Donoghue was released from the hospital, he completed his journey and was assigned to a wood-carrying gang at the probation station. That labor was not as rigorous as roadmaking.[31]

None of the three state prisoners in confinement received special treatment, and in a letter written by McManus to O'Brien the remaining four state prisoners received a firsthand account of life in a work gang. McManus was in a work gang that fluctuated in size from twenty-six to forty convicts. The chief work of the gang was felling timber, dragging it to the sand pits, and then carrying the sawed parts to the wharf to await shipment. Every once in a while the gang would load the oceangoing vessels with the sawed wood. McManus referred to that activity as "a pleasant variety." The gang was periodically employed with opening roads through unexplored parts of the bush.[32]

McManus knew his letter would undergo the scrutiny of his convict overseers, so he kept the contents to the simple narrative. But he wanted to assure his friends that he was well, that he was becoming an accomplished "backwoodsman," and that he was looking forward to his release and "the first of April quail shooting day." But, most important of all, he wanted his friends to know a good had come out of his confinement. "The constant occupation too has made my mind much more at ease than it has been for a considerable time, the want of active employment was becoming so unbearable."[33]

*   *   *

On 14 January 1851 Governor Denison informed Earl Grey of the recent truancy of the three Irish prisoners and the fact that the magistrates had merely reprimanded them. He then explained that he had overturned the verdict of the magistrates, revoked the tickets-of-leave, and sent the truants to probation stations. Denison did not hesitate to criticize Earl Grey and the local magistrates for his difficulties with the state prisoners.[34]

Denison recognized that his actions would lead to the charge being made in the House of Commons by the friends of the state prisoners that the three exiles were undergoing "great hardship." But Denison justified his actions by saying, "I have only exercised a power vested in me as . . . Governor, and which has always been found essential to the maintenance of proper order and discipline amongst the Convicts."[35]

Denison gave Grey additional information that would help the ministry. He informed Grey that O'Brien had accepted a ticket-of-leave.[36] O'Brien was at last being treated in the gentlemanly manner that Grey had initially ordered. Denison knew O'Brien was the powerful political figure among the state prisoners, and the fact that he was not one of the truants would ease Grey's problem with Westminster. Denison believed he had everything under control.

The Legal Battle

The trial, conviction, and eventual imprisonment of the three state prisoners, together with all of the events leading up to and following from those official proceedings, were widely and extensively reported in the newspapers of Van Diemen's Land and other regions of Australia.

The campaign to defame Denison and thus help the state prisoners and the antitransportation movement began on 28 December. It appears that the editors of the *Launceston Examiner*, like Denison, were hoping to use the truancy to their advantage. They agreed that the governor could set aside the decision of a magistrate, if the action was to mitigate punishment. But they opposed any idea that the governor could set aside the decision of a magistrate to increase punishment. They expressed the fear that Denison had exceeded the bounds of his authority. The editors were interested in finding for the future "some safeguard against the sudden passion of his excellency."[37]

By 4 January the editors concluded there was only one safeguard; namely, Denison's removal. The editors wrote, "A public appeal will be made to the crown to remove his excellency from a position which he is utterly unqualified to fill." By 11 January the *Launceston Examiner* was emboldened to reexamine Denison's credentials for the post of governor of Van Diemen's Land and compare them to O'Brien's and those of the other state prisoners. The editors concluded that O'Brien's credentials were the best and that the state prisoners who "visited the table" of O'Brien were worthy of that privilege, but Denison did not have the credentials to be properly admitted to O'Brien's house. "O'Brien is as superior to Denison as the occupants of Dante's Paradise to the inhabitants lower down."[38]

All of the newspapers in Van Diemen's Land editorially supported the truant state prisoners except the newspaper widely recognized as the unofficial mouthpiece of the government, the *Hobart Town Advertiser*. It was not long, however, before the press on the mainland also took up their support. The general editorial line was succinctly stated by the *Syndey Morning Herald* when it announced that Denison's decision to cancel the tickets-of-leave of O'Doherty, O'Donoghue, and McManus was "arbitrary and uncalled for."[39]

Previously, Denison had come under public criticism, but the criticism was mainly limited to Van Diemen's Land, for "mistreating" O'Brien. On the occasion of imprisoning the three state prisoners, the criticism was not limited to the borders of Van Diemen's Land but spread to New South Wales and Victoria. Mainland Australia became interested in the truant state prisoners for several reasons. The Reverend John West and his associates had been working during the previous six months to convince the citizens of Victoria and New South Wales that the struggle in Van Diemen's Land to end transportation was also their struggle. Denison could not help but be identified as one of the main stumbling blocks to the cessation of transportation in Van Diemen's Land. When he overruled the magistrates and sent the truants to probation stations his reputation was no doubt already clouded, and it was probably not very difficult to set off a wave of anti-Denison public opinion. But there was another reason Denison's protransportation policy was gaining attention on mainland Australia. As a result of the Royal Assent in August 1850 of the new Constitution, Victoria, South Australia, and Van Diemen's Land had been granted representative government. The free citizens of those areas were aware that within the year they would elect two-thirds of the members of their respective legislative councils. A growing number of those citizens on the mainland recognized that convict pollution in Van Diemen's Land could have a detrimental effect on representative government not only in Van Diemen's Land but also in Victoria, South Australia, and New South Wales. In February 1851 the antitransportation citizens of Victoria joined the antitransportation citizens of Van Diemen's Land in establishing the Australian League, an organization created to influence public opinion in Australia and Great Britain to end transportation. During the next eight months the antitransportation citizenry of New South Wales, South Australia, and New Zealand also joined the Australian League. With such an organized antitransportation public opinion developing, Denison became a particularly prime target to discredit, since he publicly proclaimed his advocacy of the transportation system.[40]

The outcry of the press in Van Diemen's Land and on the mainland against Denison, and in favor of the truant Irish state prisoners, resulted in an agitated atmosphere of public opinion. Public meetings were called to petition the queen to release the three state prisoners, and statements began to be made at those meetings displaying public displeasure with Denison.

One such meeting took place in Sydney during the first week of February. The meeting had been called by the mayor in response to a request signed by 546 individuals. About two thousand persons attended, the mayor presided, and two resolutions were passed unanimously. The first resolution stated that Denison had not only acted "unjustly and arbitrarily but most illegally" in punishing the Irish state prisoners after they had been "admonished and discharged by the local magistrates." The second resolution expressed "indignation" at the governor's conduct. Controversy arose over a proposed third motion to petition the queen to pardon the exiles and recall Governor Denison. Advocates of the state prisoners thought it would be wiser to direct attention to the immediate objective, namely, relieving the distress of the Irishmen. Those individuals won the argument, and the statement demanding the recall of Governor Denison was dropped. Before the meeting broke up "thanks were voted to the Van Diemen's Land Press, with the exception of the Government hack, the Hobart Town *Advertiser*, 'for the able stand they had made against the tyranny of Sir William Denison.' "[41]

A similar meeting was held in West Maitland on 20 February. Once again public interest was so intense that the room quickly filled and many people were compelled to listen from the lobby or from the outside through open windows. Three resolutions, similar to those initially introduced, amended, and passed in Sydney, were unanimously adopted.[42]

Meanwhile two of the three truants were about to undergo a change. The first change affected O'Doherty and had no long-range effects on the other state prisoners. The second change affected McManus and began a series of events that would affect them all. After three weeks of penal discipline, O'Doherty was released. The petition sponsored by Bishop Willson on his behalf had finally met with success.[43]

As for McManus, when he had been taken into custody on 26 December he had retained an attorney, Adye Douglas, to obtain his release by means of a writ of habeas corpus.[44] Douglas evidently, in turn, hired Knight, the attorney whom O'Brien had previously consulted when he had been in solitary confinement, to present the case in court. Thus Knight finally had the opportunity he wanted; namely, to challenge the transportation law by contesting the mode of treatment that Denison was affording one of the state prisoners. On 21 January, Knight started the legal procedures and was, no doubt, surprised to learn that the case would be heard, not by one, but by both Supreme Court justices. The editors of the *Colonial Times* concluded that the announcement implied, from a legal point of view, that Denison appeared to be in difficulty.[45]

The object of the legal controversy, McManus, did not have much confidence that Knight would obtain his release. He was actually concentrating his attention on obtaining a few articles that would make his imprisonment more palatable. On 30 January, McManus addressed a special letter to O'Doherty making several requests and commenting on the legal battle. McManus asked O'Doherty to send him a gallon of rum and some "sheroots." McManus had a private means of receiving those items and he cautioned O'Doherty not to let it be known that they were being purchased for a prisoner. Concerning his application for a writ of habeas corpus McManus commented, "I daresay it will end in nothing."[46]

On 7 February, Knight submitted his arguments before the justices of the Supreme Court for a writ of habeas corpus to remove McManus from the Cascades Probation Station. Once again Knight challenged

Denison's authority to control the convicts as he saw fit. In O'Brien's case Knight had thought Denison lacked the authority to place O'Brien in solitary confinement. In McManus's case he challenged Denison's authority to have the use of McManus's services; to confine McManus at the Cascades Probation Station, by day and by night; and to revoke McManus's ticket-of-leave at his own discretion. Knight was counting on the vagueness of the transportation law, particularly regarding the power that the governor exacted over the convicts, to assist him in obtaining McManus's release. His arguments regarding those challenges rested on what the Irish statutes governing transportation actually said. Finally, Knight also questioned whether Van Diemen's Land had ever been officially designated a penal colony.[47]

As a result of Knight's presentation, the judges ruled there were sufficient grounds for the writ of habeas corpus to be granted. Knight had, in the eyes of the court, made a valid application, so it became incumbent upon the government lawyers to prepare a return to his questions.[48]

The government attorneys immediately set to work collecting all the documents and records related to McManus's trial, conviction, sentence to death, and transportation. Unfortunately, the documents and records were scanty and the return arguments could not be very specific regarding those points. The truth was that the government did not have a document known as the "Certificate of Conviction" for most of the convicts, including McManus. That document was required by law as legal proof of conviction and would have contained all the necessary information. The next major problem confronting the attorneys was that they did not have complete copies of the Irish statutes on transportation. They were able, however, to find sufficient excerpts from those statutes to build a case. The remaining questions raised by Knight did not cause the attorneys much concern.[49]

Denison was upset and wrote Grey outlining the major problems. Denison realized Knight's legal arguments went far beyond helping McManus. He explained that the government lawyers did not have the full text of the Irish statutes on transportation and that as a result the government's case was more difficult to present. Denison pointed out that if Knight could convince the Supreme Court justices of Van Diemen's Land that Denison did not have the power to use McManus's services, McManus would be released. Under those circumstances it would follow that neither did Denison have the right to use the services of other felons convicted in Irish courts. If any or all of the felons so convicted brought a lawsuit demanding to "be at large on their own hands as transported Offenders," they would no doubt win their case.

Denison then spoke of the next issue. If the court ruled that Denison had the power to use McManus's services but did not have the right to confine him "by day and by night" at a probation station in order to have the use of those services, McManus would be released from confinement at the Cascades. Similarly any other Irish convict so confined could sue for his release. As to the certificate of conviction, Denison informed Grey that the authorities in Van Diemen's Land had very few of those documents and if McManus was discharged on the basis that there was no legal proof he was a convicted felon, he could not only obtain his release but he could also sue everyone involved in his detainment at the Cascades Probation Station. And if McManus could, so could every other transported offender for whom there was no certificate of conviction.[50] It was fortunate for Denison and his legal staff that Knight was unaware of the nonexistence or paucity of the various records.

On 14 February, McManus was brought into court dressed in his gray prison uniform in the custody of the superintendent of the Cascades Station, Robert Ballantyne. On his arrival he "was cordially shook by the hand by numerous friends who crowded round him."[51] The solicitor general then read the return to the questions raised by Knight. The solicitor general had found two Irish parliamentary acts governing transportation, one from 1773 and one from 1798. He maintained that those laws did allow the government to confine McManus at the Cascades Probation Station in order to have the use of his services. Next, the solicitor general informed the court that Van Diemen's Land had been designated as a penal colony by an order in council of Queen Victoria on 4 September 1848. Finally, the solicitor general recounted the facts of McManus's arrival in Van Diemen's Land, his grant of a ticket-of-leave, and its subsequent withdrawal. He maintained that to challenge the ability of Governor Denison to withdraw a ticket-of-leave on his own authority was untenable.[52]

According to the legal procedure of the day, Knight was given time to prepare a reply to the return of the government. On 18 February, Knight made his reply. The judges then took several days to study the case.[53]

*   *   *

Previously public opinion had been so sympathetic toward the three truant Irish exiles that Denison believed the magistrates before whom they were tried for leaving their districts without permission had been influenced and let the Irishmen off with a mere reprimand.[54] With public opinion now inflamed as McManus's case went before the Supreme Court, the question was, of course, whether those judges would be influenced by the temper of the times, and if so to what extent.

On 21 February the court announced its decision.[55] Having previ-

ously accepted Knight's application as valid, the court looked quite logi-
cally to the government's return, in which was to be found justification
for the government's detention of McManus. Accordingly, the chief justice began the court's pronouncement by saying that there was an absence of important facts in the government's return relating to Mc-
Manus's conviction and subsequent transportation. The chief justice
announced that because of those defects, "we are of opinion that T. B.
McManus cannot be remanded and that we have no power to detain him
and he is now free to go out of this Court."[56]

Knight had not won the victory he had really sought. But Mc-
Manus's release was interpreted by the *South Australian Register* to be "the
knell of Sir William Denison's arbitrary power" and by the *Irish Exile* to
be the first proof that the independence of Van Diemen's Land "can no
longer be questioned." The editors of the *Launceston Examiner* thought
those interpretations were overstatements. They thought it was not the
independence of Van Diemen's Land that had been proved but the independence of the courts.[57] It was not unlikely that McManus's release
was an attempt by the justices to express their displeasure with Denison's
interference with the decisions of the magistrates.

The government attorneys could hardly believe the decision of the
judges, but they moved quickly to amend the return. They found in
unofficial sources the details they had omitted from the original return.
They then wrote Denison informing him that the way was open to rearrest McManus. The attorneys asked Denison to obtain from the ministers
in London complete copies of the Irish statutes governing transportation
as well as certificates of conviction for all the convicts in Van Diemen's
Land.[58]

Denison lost no time in issuing a rearrest order for McManus. He
also wrote to Grey to assure him that although McManus was currently
at liberty, it would only be a short time before he would be back in
custody. Denison placed the blame for McManus's release squarely on
the British ministers for not providing him with the complete copies of
Irish laws governing transportation and for not forwarding with each
convicted felon the required certificate of conviction. He asked Grey to
forward those items to him as soon as possible. Denison then made a
recommendation that would solve the certificate of conviction problem
not only for Van Diemen's Land but also for any penal colony in the
British Empire. Denison recommended that the government initiate legislation in Parliament that would make the "Assignment List" the legal
proof of conviction rather than the individual certificate of conviction.[59]
The assignment list named every felon on board a convict ship and the
term of transportation to which the felon had been sentenced. McManus
and Knight had certainly caused Denison difficulties, but Denison
viewed those difficulties as a temporary setback. The government had

amended the return, and it would not be long before McManus would be back at a probation station.

*   *   *

There was no doubt that Knight and the editors of the *Launceston Examiner* had assisted O'Brien's long-range goal of establishing a public opinion sympathetic to the plight of the state prisoners. The reality was that at least some of the citizens on the mainland were now sending petitions to the queen requesting her to pardon the state prisoners. It also appears that the efforts of Knight and the editors of the *Launceston Examiner* to challenge Denison's authority helped the antitransportation forces become stronger. Those efforts probably did give the justices of the Supreme Court the opportunity to "announce" their independence from the executive branch of the government.

Denison, however, was not quite ready to call it quits. In his attempt to end the anomalous position of the two inveterate lawbreakers he had gotten embroiled in another controversy; namely, what was the power of the governor over the decisions of the magistrates and over holders of tickets-of-leave. But he was still planning to carry out his original plan regarding McManus. He had issued an arrest order that would return McManus to confinement. Lady Denison was "afraid that [her husband] may be incurring a great responsibility," yet she had to admit that she did "not know what he can do better, for he cannot leave all his prisoners at large in this sort of way."[60] It seemed that McManus's freedom would be short-lived.

McManus Escapes

Upon his release on 21 February by the justices of the Supreme Court, McManus prepared to return to Launceston. First, however, he traveled to the village of Ross to attend, on 22 February, the wedding of Thomas Meagher and Catherine Bennet. McManus had been anxious to demonstrate, by this attendance, his approval of Meagher's decision to marry Catherine. The wedding ceremony was performed by Dr. Willson at the home of Dr. Hall. "Bishop Willson counselled a dense silence concerning the identity of the mysterious visitor, and gave [McManus] his blessing as he set out for Launceston."[61] On his return to Launceston, the press noted that McManus was "worn out in bodily strength, enfeebled in mind, and his energies heretofore so quick—heretofore so vigourous [were] bowed down and deadened by the weight of the tremendous punishment with which he had been so cruelly visited." For the first day or two some of the citizens celebrated his deliverance, and, "that over, he sank on his bed in a state of high fever."[62]

Shortly after McManus's return to Launceston, statements began to appear in the press that Governor Denison had decided to issue new orders for his arrest and return to the Cascades. Those statements were, of course, true.[63]

At 10:00 A.M. on 26 February, Mr. Douglas, superintendent of the hiring depot at Launceston, went to the home of George Deas, where McManus was staying, to deliver a communication from the government officials in Hobart Town to McManus. Superintendent Douglas had not opened and read the communication. The superintendent was told McManus was not at home, and when he returned at 1:00 P.M. and again at 2:00 P.M. he was told the same thing. At that point, however, he took it upon himself to open the communication and thereby discovered that it contained an order for McManus to report to the hiring depot at Launceston. Promptly the superintendent called in the chief constable and instructed him to apprehend McManus and bring him before the visiting magistrate in order to force his obedience to the communication. While the chief constable was searching for McManus, McManus was visiting the local jail and the home of the Roman Catholic priests. On the evening of the twenty-sixth, the superintendent came again to the home of Deas and on that occasion was told McManus was at home but was ill. A private physician, Dr. Grant, was in attendance and certified that McManus was too ill to be removed. The superintendent immediately informed the chief constable of what was happening. McManus had applied to Dr. Grant for medical assistance during the afternoon of the twenty-sixth. After examining him and noting how excited he was, Dr. Grant "had found it necessary to bleed him copiously, and adopt other treatment." During part of the night McManus had been delirious.[64]

By the twenty-seventh, the chief magistrate, W. Gunn, was concerned. He requested Dr. C. Gavin Casey, who was a government surgeon assigned to Her Majesty's General Hospital in Launceston, to examine McManus and determine whether the prisoner could be taken into custody. After talking with Dr. Grant and making his examination, Dr. Casey concluded McManus was too ill to be moved. The two surgeons wrote, "We hereby certify that T. B. McManus is labouring under severe indisposition for which he is at present under medical treatment; and that he cannot with safety leave his bed."[65]

When Denison read the certificate, he found it to be "very vague." On the twenty-eighth, he ordered the certificate to be forwarded to the chief medical officer, Dr. W. Dawson, who at the time was in the vicinity of Launceston. Denison ordered Dr. Dawson "to report on the sickness of McManus and whether he could not be removed into Hospital, if in such a state as to require Hospital treatment."[66] On the same day, Dr. Casey and Dr. Grant made another visit to the sick man's room. They found he had suffered illusions the night before and was still "much excited, fevered, and requiring medicine." Both surgeons agreed it would be dangerous to remove him from his bed and as a result once again certified "that he cannot be removed without hazard."[67]

Before leaving McManus on 28 February, Dr. Casey and Dr. Grant obtained the prisoner's "distinct and solemn promise that he would not, whilst under our . . . charge, make any attempt to escape, or act in any way tending to compromise us." They also informed him of the hour they would return on Saturday for their next visit.[68]

At the appointed hour on Saturday, the two surgeons arrived at the door of McManus's residence. They "were peremptorily refused admission." A search warrant was obtained by one of the local officials, and, when the official entered the home of George Deas and did not find McManus, warrants were forwarded throughout the island for his arrest.[69] McManus was not apprehended. He had indeed escaped.

Actually McManus had begun his flight to freedom on 26 February. When the rumors reached Launceston that McManus was to be rearrested, his friends decided the time had come for the young man to make his escape. There was no question of breaking his parole. Denison had revoked McManus's original ticket-of-leave on 24 December 1850 when he ordered McManus sent to a probation station for three months. When the Supreme Court freed McManus under the writ of habeas corpus, no new ticket-of-leave had been issued and no promise given by McManus that he would refrain from escaping. On 26 February, McManus went into hiding at Dean Butler's house, and preparations were made to get him out of the country. A gentleman of the area, John Galvin, who bore a remarkable resemblance to McManus, took his place. Galvin had sought medical assistance from Dr. Grant and had taken to the sickbed in the home of Mr. Deas. "He had been asked no questions concerning himself and had volunteered no information."[70] It was Galvin who had promised that he would not escape. Meanwhile, with the aid of his friends, McManus was provided with ample funds and surrounded by men who were willing to hazard their lives in order to protect his life. With that help he made his way to George Town and reportedly boarded the *Elizabeth Thompson*, which was headed for the Sandwich Islands and California.[71]

* * *

Several of the newspapers openly took a sympathetic view of the escape. The editors of the *Cornwall Chronicle* summed up their thoughts by asking, "Can [McManus] be looked upon as an absconder anxious to evade the just punishment due to him? or, rather, may he not be said 'to have been hunted out of the place by an inhuman tyrant!'" The editors of the *Launceston Examiner* agreed with the editors of the *Cornwall Chronicle*. They commented, "The authorities have been thrown into a state of consternation by the escape of Mr McManus, but no other person is surprised: it was the natural fruit of their own vicious policy." The *Hobart Town Advertiser* did not agree. It charged breach of faith.[72]

*   *   *

The only one of the three state prisoners who was still in confinement was O'Donoghue. By the end of February, his friends were preparing to help him by initiating legal action. O'Donoghue, however, refused their offer and announced he was prepared to complete his sentence.[73]

*   *   *

Denison made his final report to Earl Grey on the whole McManus affair on 22 March. In that report he discussed the major problem between himself and the state prisoners; namely, that he regarded the Irish prisoners as convicts while the Irishmen regarded themselves as gentlemen and prisoners of war. Denison had to admit that the general public in Van Diemen's Land was in sympathy with the Irish prisoners. The public believed the Irishmen "were looked upon by the British Government more as persons whose presence in England was not desirable, than as men sentenced to death for an offense against Society of the deepest die." Denison thought the police magistrates who merely reprimanded the Irish prisoners for being truant were influenced by that opinion. He thought Dr. Casey, the physician who attended McManus and who failed to move the prisoner to a hospital where he could be put under constant surveillance, was influenced by that opinion. He thought the responsibility for all those groups developing such a mistaken notion was Grey's.[74]

*   *   *

The martyrdom of the three truants, McManus's legal battle, and his eventual escape helped to create an even larger sympathetic public opinion in Van Diemen's Land and on the mainland in support of the Irish state prisoners. Interest in the men had grown from a specific concern by the citizens of Van Diemen's Land that O'Brien was being mistreated to a general conviction in Van Diemen's Land and on the mainland that the state prisoners should be pardoned. As local support for the state prioners continued to grow, Denison's reputation suffered a decline.

Knight might not have had the victory he had hoped for in the Van Diemen's Land courts, but his actions must have helped unite public opinion in Van Diemen's Land and on the mainland behind McManus and against Denison. It would appear that the British ministers could not help but realize that the antitransportation forces were growing.

CHAPTER 6

A Quiet Year

O'Brien Teaches School

The last week of February 1851 had been of great importance to the state prisoners. McManus had been set free by a writ of habeas corpus, had been ordered back to a probation station, and had escaped. Meagher had been married, and O'Brien was about to leave New Norfolk in order to take a job.

When O'Brien accepted his ticket-of-leave, he decided to find employment of some kind. Mitchel wrote O'Brien informing him that he was planning to become a sheep farmer and urged O'Brien to join him in the venture,[1] but O'Brien refused Mitchel's offer. He had decided to develop a teaching service for local children, and he began to make his intentions known in an effort to attract students. With a teaching position, he hoped to live on his earnings and give the money that his family was regularly sending to him from Ireland to "those persons who have incurred liabilities on my account" as a result of the escape attempt. O'Brien believed that he would be able, in time, to pay off those debts.[2] O'Brien believed the debts amounted to approximately two hundred pounds, and on 10 January he asked his wife to send three fifty-pound drafts to him. On 27 January he wrote to Father William J. Dunne explaining that since he did not know what bills were still outstanding or the names of the creditors, he hoped Father Dunne and Mr. Reeves would gather the data and serve as a clearinghouse. O'Brien would forward the funds to them and they could arrange the necessary payments. O'Brien was optimistic. "I have no doubt that eventually all the liabilities will be satisfactorily provided for."[3]

In early January, O'Brien received a firm offer of a teaching position from a physician, Dr. Brock. Dr. Brock's wife had recently died, leaving two young boys in need of a tutor. When Brock made O'Brien the job offer, O'Brien asked if Superintendent Lapham's oldest boy, John, could also become a member of the class. Dr. Brock agreed, but unfortunately John developed tuberculosis, and, since the disease was contagious, it was impossible for the plan to be carried out.[4]

Martin did not approve of O'Brien's plan to teach school. In a letter to O'Doherty, Martin commented, "I fear he has made a rash and indiscreet *selection*." Martin thought the children were too young. He had heard the eldest was only ten and concluded O'Brien would "be merely a nursery governor." Martin had also heard that Dr. Brock was "a man of unpleasant temper." Martin had to acknowledge, however, that "the unpleasant circumstances of his new occupation will only add to his merit if he persevere in earning his bread by honest work."[5] O'Brien was prepared to do just that. He obtained the necessary permissions from the government officials in Hobart Town to change his place of residence, since Dr. Brock's home was in a different district, and prepared to leave New Norfolk on 20 February. Just before leaving, O'Brien arranged a meeting with O'Doherty at a point on the Snake River where their districts touched. The plan was to meet for tea between five and six o'clock in order to "talk over the malignant cunning & cruelty of our foes with as much charity as we can command."[6]

The night before O'Brien left New Norfolk he wrote to his wife expressing mixed emotions and some nervousness about starting a new career as a teacher, yet at the same time he acknowledged looking forward to the new experience, admitting that he was concerned whether he would be able to conform to the routine of the Brock family household.[7]

On 20 February, O'Brien left New Norfolk at 5:00 A.M. and rode to Bridgewater. There he boarded the Launceston coach and traveled to Ross. O'Brien was making his journey two days before Meagher was to be wed. When he left the coach at Ross, he was met by a group of Meagher's friends, among whom was Meagher's fiancée, Catherine Bennet. O'Brien had to admit, "She is in person and manners very pleasing" and "it is not unnatural that [Meagher] should have united to himself the first nice girl that fell in his way." But Catherine was obviously not someone who could be presented to society, and O'Brien knew that "in a worldy point of view the connexion cannot be considered advantageous for him." O'Brien recognized that Meagher loved Catherine and noted, "It is to be hoped that Love will compensate to him for the absence of all worldly advantages." He thought the young couple would get along very well at their new cottage secluded on the shores of Lake Sorell.[8]

Later on that same day, O'Brien proceeded to Campbell Town where he spent the night at a hotel that O'Brien believed could compete with the first-class hotels in England. No doubt it was Mrs. Kierney's. The next morning, he was greeted by Dr. Harrington, a local physician who conveyed him by carriage to his new home in Avoca. O'Brien marveled at the beauty of the scene, finding himself surrounded by wooded hills enclosing two valleys through which two rivers, the Esk and the St. Pauls, flowed and met near Avoca. In the distance rose Ben Lomond, part of the highest mountain range in Van Diemen's Land.[9]

*   *   *

Dr. Brock and his sons proved to be a hospitable family circle but, although O'Brien did get along with them and did enjoy the scenery, he was not engaged in a profession that gave him satisfaction and he could not help but dwell on the humiliating aspects of his situation. O'Brien had to admit his position was peculiar. He had spent thirty years cultivating his mind and acquiring experience "which ought to enable me to rule nations." Yet he was spending his time teaching two young boys the basic elements of language, which a pedagogue "whose aims never soared beyond the tuition of a village school" could do equally as well. He also recognized that his salary barely exceeded that being paid to his daughter's governess, while if he were in a position to practice law, he would probably make a very handsome salary. O'Brien was unhappy with his lot, but he did "not repine." He explained, "Pride has been through life one of my greatest failings and it is perhaps very desirable that my pride should be severely tried in the position which I now occupy."[10]

There was no doubt that his pride would be severely tried. O'Brien had accepted the teaching position in order to provide Dr. McCarthy with the money that was owing from the escape attempt. O'Brien believed the outstanding debt amounted to two hundred pounds and, according to his calculations, he would have to work at least a year before the debt would be satisfied. In June 1851, O'Brien learned that the debt actually totaled almost eight hundred pounds. Meagher had undertaken to pay the owners of the *Victoria* for their loss, which totaled five hundred and fifty pounds, but he had not informed O'Brien. When Meagher accepted the bill for five hundred and fifty pounds, he forwarded it to his father in Ireland, but the note of detailed explanation accompanying the bill did not arrive at the same time as the bill, and Thomas Meagher, Sr., noting that the bill had several days before payment was due, refused to honor it. When word of his father's refusal reached Meagher, he did not know what to do. The Van Diemen's Land bank, which held Meagher's note, agreed to wait ten days beyond the due date before acting and sent further word it would wait longer if necessary. Meagher hesitated to inform O'Brien of what had occurred, but Mitchel thought that the matter was urgent and, with Meagher's permission, wrote to O'Brien informing him of the additional liability. Once having learned the truth, O'Brien was prepared to act to help Meagher. O'Brien promptly wrote to John Regan, the gentleman who was handling the affair for Meagher, and began to make arrangements that he hoped would secure the money to pay for the *Victoria*. Meanwhile Meagher's father received his son's detailed letter of explanation, paid the bill, and wrote to his son to explain what had happened. "When your bill of £550 was presented to me, with only your note of advice pinned to it, I was at a loss to know what it was for, and in that state of doubt, I declined to accept the Bill—reserving to myself, however, the alternative of paying it when due, should I hear from you in the meantime." Meagher, Sr., admonished his son for his actions, writing, "The adventure in which you risked so much had been excessively improvident and fruitless."[11]

As soon as Mitchel learned that Meagher, Sr., had paid the bill, he informed O'Brien. Nevertheless, O'Brien announced his decision to assume the responsibility for the cost of the *Victoria*. O'Brien's personal expenses would be paid from the salary he earned for teaching the Brock children. The money coming to him from Ireland would pay the escape debts.[12] O'Brien had adopted a long-range plan to provide for the escape debts, and, if nothing unexpected happened, it would be a workable plan.

The Other State Prisoners

During the Australian fall of 1851, O'Donoghue, O'Doherty, and Mitchel were the three state prisoners who were the most active. On 31 March 1851 Patrick O'Donoghue completed his three-month sentence at the probation station. In early April, he was brought to Hobart Town where "with twenty other chained prisoners he was marched to the penitentiary." In Hobart Town, O'Donoghue's ticket-of-leave was renewed in reliance on his promise that he would not leave Van Diemen's Land, and he was ordered to leave Hobart Town within a week and take up residence in the district of Oatlands. O'Donoghue promptly sought out the men who had been publishing the *Irish Exile* during his absence with the hope of obtaining money on which to live in Oatlands. Unfortunately, the current editors had been unable to set aside money to give him "so that he had the *honour* of being the Owner of a Journal for three months, without deriving the slightest benefit from it." Forbidden to stay in Hobart Town and without any expectation of future earnings from the *Irish Exile*, O'Donoghue gave the order that his newspaper "should not appear after Saturday the 13th April." At the same time he concluded that it would be economically impossible for him to go to Oatlands, because he had no funds with which to support himself and because that district was a rural area where there would be scarcely any opportunity for employment. Consequently O'Donoghue applied for permission to reside in Richmond, where he could live as the guest of Father Dunne until he could find some way to support himself, but his request was denied. He then suggested to the officials that he might resign his ticket-of-leave, go into the Hobart Town Prisoners' Barracks and await assignment as a pass-holder servant, but Dr. Hampton denied his offer. O'Donoghue concluded that for officialdom "starvation, under colour of comparative liberty, is the object."[13]

As O'Donoghue was setting off for Oatlands with hopeless financial prospects before him, a committee in Melbourne issued a circular letter, dated 1 May, appealing for contributions on his behalf, and at Geelong 160 residents gathered on 19 May and made contributions for his support. The writers of the *Melbourne Argus* published an account of O'Donoghue's plight and noted the irony of the official situation: "How beautifully the conduct of Sir William Denison to Mr. O'Donoghue contrasts with his bountiful supply of 'Her Majesty's free pardons', to child murderers and highwaymen." O'Donoghue, who was referred to as "a gentleman and a scholar," could not get permission to live in an area where he could make a living while real criminals were getting tickets-of-leave and allowed to roam at will.[14]

Soon after O'Donoghue settled in Oatlands, he began to write a history of his harsh treatment in Van Diemen's Land. He hoped "to have it published in Dublin and London, for the benefit of his family, as well as in the Colonies and America." O'Donoghue's friend William Dowling believed that the book would have an enormous sale because "his three months' experience in the hell, called Port Arthur, will enable him to reveal secrets hitherto hidden to all, save the demons of that revolting region."[15] In addition to his literary activity, O'Donoghue displayed an interest in the Catholic Church, but evidently he continued to hope for a reassignment to an urban district where he could obtain a job. After several months in Oatlands, he applied for permission to live in Launceston and his request was granted.[16] No doubt he set off for Launceston glad for the chance to become self-supporting.

*　　　*　　　*

When Kevin O'Doherty was released from his term of probation, he returned to Hobart Town and took up his job with Dr. Crooke. He was not happy with his job since most of his time was spent in selling drugs, and he wrote, "Feeling no confident hope of any change for the better I am getting sick of it." By May 1851, O'Doherty had received word from Ireland about a favorable turn in his financial situation, and he saw that it was possible for him to resign his position and live independently. He planned to devote himself to study, but he also wished to engage in an occupation more congenial to his taste as well as to his intellect, one "which would . . . render . . . exile less dreary." He wanted to start a monthly literary magazine that would provide him some income from Australian sources, and he wanted Mitchel, Martin, Meagher, and O'Brien to join with him in the project. Mitchel mentioned the possibility that the views of the exiles might clash, but O'Doherty thought such friction would not be possible in a purely literary journal. As for the prospect of O'Donoghue's participation in the project, O'Doherty told O'Brien while O'Donoghue was in Hobart Town that O'Donoghue had "conducted himself in such a manner after his release from Port Arthur as I confess to render me perfectly indifferent to his fate."[17]

Nothing came of O'Doherty's plan to establish a literary magazine. O'Brien had resigned himself to teaching as an unavoidable means of supporting himself and enabling him to use the money sent from Ireland to pay the debts arising from the escape attempt. His teaching position took virtually all his time, and it was nearly impossible for him to do any serious and lengthy writing of his own.[18]

Mitchel no doubt also came to realize that he would not have the time to assist with writing a literary magazine, because his attention would by necessity be devoted to his family once his wife and children arrived in Van Diemen's Land. Although Mitchel had not received definite word of the expected arrival of his family from Ireland, he knew they were due and might arrive at any time, and he had gone so far as to obtain permission from the local authorities to go to Hobart Town to await their arrival. He planned to set out on his journey on 9 May.[19] On his arrival he faced a long wait during which he was able to visit with Kevin O'Doherty.

O'Doherty took the occasion of Mitchel's visit to take a day away from the hospital, and the two men set off for an excursion to Brown's River, a resort area where the people of Hobart Town spent the day breathing the "mean suburban air." When Mitchel and O'Doherty finally arrived at Brown's River, they "walked all day on the sands and cliffs of the bay shore, [and] dined at the hotel." It was on that trip that Mitchel learned of Kevin's continued love for Mary Anne. Mitchel marveled how "in the tangle of those silken tresses she has bound my poor friend's soul; round the solid hemisphere it has held him, and he drags a lengthening chain."[20] Mitchel must have been bound himself. He had not seen his wife for three years, and he was anxiously awaiting her arrival.

On 25 May, Mitchel received word that his wife would land at Launceston. He hurried there at once only to be thrown in jail by the local magistrate, W. Gunn, who refused to release him until he was certain Mitchel had the permission of the Hobart Town officials to be there. Mitchel was unconcerned about being jailed except that he realized his "wife might arrive that very day; and our first meeting, after nearly three years' separation, might be as our parting had been, in a British dungeon." Mitchel was released when the papers requested by Gunn arrived, and he remained in Launceston eagerly waiting the arrival of his wife and family. On 18 June, Mitchel received a letter from Kevin O'Doherty informing him that his family had arrived at Hobart Town. Mitchel promptly wrote to his wife and arranged for their meeting at Greenponds, which was "the point of the public coach road nearest to Bothwell." Mitchel must have set off for Greenponds by the night coach on the nineteenth, since on the twentieth he was reunited with his family. He wrote in his journal, "These things cannot be described."[21]

On the next day, 21 June, the Mitchel family set off through the woods to Bothwell where they took up residence at Mrs. Beech's hotel. Mitchel began almost at once to look for a farm where he could settle his family, and not long afterward they all settled at Nant Cottage, a two-hundred-acre farm three miles from the village. John Martin was invited to live with the Mitchels. Mitchel's penal status was changed by the Van Diemen's Land officials because of the arrival of his wife. On 26 June, Mitchel wrote to O'Brien about his new status, "I have received an official letter announcing to me that . . . I—not Martin—may for the future go into any district I please under the regulations in force for ordinary ticket-of-leave holders." Mitchel believed his wife's arrival had raised him to the "status & rank of a common swindler or burglar." Mitchel closed his letter with the news that his wife had brought a parcel for O'Brien from Lucy.[22]

Mitchel and Meagher now both had the family circle that they hoped would allow them to develop peace of mind. Only one state prisoner appeared to still be in serious difficulty, O'Donoghue.

American Interest and British Reaction to McManus's Escape

Just as O'Brien's struggle with Denison could not be contained within Van Diemen's Land, the struggle of the three truants could not be contained within Australia. Denison's dispatches to Grey, the letters from the state prisoners to their numerous friends in the British Isles, and copies of the local newspapers had arrived in the British Isles to once again reawaken public interest in the plight of the Irish revolutionaries. Denison's reputation, which had undergone an organized assault in Australia, was about to suffer a similar, if not so intense, assault in Great Britain. This time, however, there was a new dimension. McManus had escaped to America. While O'Brien had reawakened Irish-American support in New York, McManus initially reawakened Irish-American support in San Francisco. But McManus's arrival did more. It would, in time, set in motion the American national political machinery, which would extend its voice of sympathy to the exiles.

*   *   *

On 5 June 1851, the fugitive Terence Bellew McManus arrived safely in San Francisco in "capital health and spirits,"[23] where he received a warm and cordial welcome. At one reception, McManus was honored at a dinner attended by three hundred guests among whom were judges, senators, members of the House of Representatives, the collector of the United States customs, and various generals. The master of ceremonies was Charles J. Brenham, mayor of San Francisco. At that reception the first toast was to "Our guest, Terence Bellew McManus. Ireland gave him birth, England, a dungeon; America, a home, with a hundred thousand welcomes." The band then struck up the tune "Home, Sweet Home." McManus replied to the toast, saying "his heart was too full to express himself; he was a plain man and no orator." He took the opportunity, however, to make a few statements. He acknowledged, "He had failed in the project dearest to his heart, and he had paid the penalty; he had now another career open before him, beneath the flag—(seizing the American flag behind) and here, I swear allegiance to it, the allegiance of a true heart." The second toast was to "William Smith O'Brien and his companions in exile. Rebels to their government, Patriots to their country, Martyrs to liberty; they lost the day, but they have gained immortality." The musical accompaniment was "Erin is my home." After the toasts several speeches were given, "which were all happily and enthusiastically received." The dinner was finished about eleven, at which time the guests adjourned to a ball.[24]

Very soon after arriving in America, McManus wrote to Duffy in Ireland and told him of his successful escape, adding, "I am so embarrassed by the excess of kindness heaped on me since my arrival here, and the transition from slavery to liberty is so overpowering, that I cannot arrange my ideas to say more than bid the 'Old Land' have hope!"[25]

But the immediate concerns of Irish-America were not in extending hope to Ireland but rather in extending hope to the Irish state prisoners. McManus's arrival in the United States awakened a concern for the plight of those men. Committees began to be formed in some cities in the United States to petition the American government to press upon the British government the desirability of granting conditional pardons to the state prisoners. In addition, private citizens began to write their local representatives in Congress seeking congressional support for the release of the state prisoners. Those efforts were developing on the local level and would take several months before surfacing as a national concern.

McManus no doubt followed the development of the American petitions with interest, but he was more immediately concerned with earning a living. He decided to remain in California and was able to make a connection in a mercantile business.

Then suddenly a poignant memory of events in Van Diemen's Land was thrust upon him in the person of Captain Ellis of the *Victoria*. The Irish state prisoners had always believed Captain Ellis had informed the government officials at Hobart Town of O'Brien's intended escape and had allowed himself to serve as a tool of the government in setting a trap for O'Brien. After the failure of O'Brien's escape, Ellis had mysteriously disappeared for about a year. He was identified later at the port of Honolulu and had sailed for San Francisco only two days before McManus arrived in the Sandwich Islands on his flight to freedom. When McManus arrived in San Francisco, he determined in time to seek out Captain Ellis, but the events of his welcome had dominated his attention and Ellis had in the meantime disappeared again amid rumors that he had gone to the gold rush or possibly back to the Sandwich Islands. Then quite unexpectedly McManus learned that Captain Ellis was still in San Francisco, reportedly hiding on the *Caleo*, which was lying in the harbor. McManus reported what happened. He was standing in front of his store about five o'clock in the afternoon when a young man came up and inquired what McManus would do if he ever located Captain Ellis. McManus told the young man that he would welcome the opportunity of talking with Ellis in order "to get at the bottom of his treachery." In addition to discovering the whole truth of the incident, McManus wanted Ellis to refund the money that the "conspirators" had lost as a result of Ellis absconding with the *Victoria*. If those two conditions were met, McManus would be satisfied. With that information, the young man told McManus that Ellis was on board the *Caleo*. McManus summoned a few friends, and at 1:00 a.m. eight armed men boarded the *Caleo*, took Ellis prisoner, and proceeded by rowboat to a spot about two miles away, Mission Creek. McManus reported that at the moment they all reached the shore, he warned Captain Ellis "that he was his prisoner, and that any attempt to escape would meet with instant death." Ellis was then taken to a nearby hut, given refreshments, and charged with having committed "treachery." McManus served as the prosecutor, and the group of men with him served as the judges. Although Ellis admitted that he had stolen the *Victoria* and promised to repay the money that had been lost as result of his stealing the *Victoria*, he "would not be got to admit his treachery." The judges ruled that McManus had not presented adequate proof to convict Ellis of treachery, and a portion of the group conducted Ellis back to the *Caleo*.[26]

The following day, Captain Ellis went to the local Vigilance Committee, recounted his experience of the night before, and charged McManus's group with having fraudulently used the name of the Vigilance Committee at the time of his arrest. The Vigilance Committee promptly sent two members of the committee to McManus and respectfully requested him to appear in their committee room to answer Captain Ellis's charge. McManus went without delay. A friend recorded that McManus "stated openly that he was the man who headed the party, that he arrested him in his own name, and not that of the Vigilance Committee, and that whatever the results might be, he would take them on his own shoulders, and that he, and he alone, was responsible for the act." McManus turned to face Ellis and said to the group gathered, "That villain there first robbed and betrayed my friend, subjected him to a most dreadful imprisonment, and has now had the audacity to pollute those free shores with his presence."[27]

McManus explained how Ellis's betrayal had caused O'Brien untold suffering and great penury. His only regret was that Ellis was not found guilty by the men who tried him. McManus, however, did not believe it would be proper to serve as both prosecutor and judge, so he bowed to the decision of the jury. McManus pledged his "word of honour, as a gentleman," that neither he nor any one in his presence had used the name of the Vigilance Committee during the proceedings. McManus then left. The members of the Vigilance Committee told Ellis he had until evening to present proof before them "that the name of the Vigilance Committee had been used." That evening Ellis reappeared, but he was unable to present proof of his accusation. As Ellis left, "a body of teamsters, who had surrounded the Vigilance Committee room on the first report of the affair, beset him . . . , and gave him a pretty sound beating, giving him one or two severe cuts on the face."[28] That was the last any of the state prisoners heard of Ellis.

There was not much more heard from McManus. He never abandoned his hope that Ireland would some day free herself from England, but he was neither a political scientist nor a politician. He was actually a practical man interested in the world of business. Once having arrived in America he concentrated on making his way in that business world. He had had enough travel for a lifetime. He settled down.

*   *   *

By early May, Earl Grey realized the state prisoners would again cause him difficulties in Westminster. On 2 May the Colonial Office received Denison's dispatch describing the truancy of three of the Irish convicts and Denison's decision to revoke their tickets-of-leave and send them to probation stations. Grey also learned that O'Brien had accepted a ticket-of-leave. Grey supported Denison's actions regarding the truants and told Denison it was "absolutely necessary that the Regulations of Convict Discipline should be enforced with strictness and impartiality."[29]

Grey must have been pleased with the news that O'Brien had accepted the ticket-of-leave. He knew Sir Lucius O'Brien would be relieved. Sir Lucius had made a personal visit to the Colonial Office just a few weeks earlier expressing "anxiety" about his brother. Earl Grey wanted Sir Lucius to know about the recent events as soon as possible.[30]

The fact that O'Brien was not directly involved in the recent disputes between the state prisoners and Governor Denison politically weakened the opposition in Great Britain because it appeared that Sir Lucius would not be willing to antagonize the ministers on an issue that did not directly involve his brother. Once O'Brien had accepted the ticket-of-leave and was enjoying the fruits of comparative liberty, the members of O'Brien's family directed their efforts to obtaining a conditional pardon for him, realizing that if they were successful in obtaining such a pardon, similar pardons would likely be granted to the other state prisoners.

By the end of May, Earl Grey realized that the challenge of the truant state prisoners was far more serious than he had originally thought. The latest dispatch contained the information that McManus was seeking a writ of habeas corpus and that his attorney, Knight, was building a defense that challenged the transportation system. One of the officials in the Colonial Office noted, "A system of legal annoyance by the Irish convicts is not pleasant intelligence."[31] Grey realized the difficult position Denison was put in by not having the documentation he needed; namely, the certificates of conviction and complete copies of the Irish statutes on transportation. Grey had previously sent Knight's opinion on O'Brien's solitary confinement to Sir George Grey. At that time, neither minister had thought there was any rush to obtain a legal opinion. But now, with Knight entering the picture again, both men agreed it was time to consult the attorneys.[32]

The legal officers answered most of the questions with ease. They assured Earl Grey and Sir George Grey that there were Irish statutes on transportation. They were also able to assure the two ministers that Van Diemen's Land was designated as a penal colony by an order in council. The third question raised by Knight, whether the power of the lieutenant governor over transported felons was without restriction, was not so easy to answer. Could Denison place O'Brien in solitary confinement on his own authority? Could Denison revoke McManus's ticket-of-leave on his own authority and thus put him under confinement by day and by night in order to insure McManus's ordinary services? Earl Grey asked the legal officers to concentrate on that issue.[33]

On 11 June the opinion was given. The legal advisers stated that there were both English and Irish statutes that, in their opinion, assigned the services of a convict to the governor of Van Diemen's Land. The governor could, as a result of those statutes, "direct such Works to be performed and at such places and times as he may think proper & may prevent the Convict leaving his work; but we do not think that the Governor is empowered by these Statutes to imprison the Convict or to exercise any other control than may be necessary for securing his services."[34] In the latter proposition lay the practical problem, since there were no clear guidelines respecting the extent of the governor's power to enforce the government's right to the services of the convict. If a convict appealed to the courts of Van Diemen's Land alleging that he was being restrained and coerced in an illegal manner, it was up to the "discretion" of the judge as to whether the official means being employed were legal, and that determination affected the practical existence of the government's rights. As Herman Merivale explained to Earl Grey, "A Judge liking one view might justify almost any act of restraint & coercion as necessary to secure the services of the prisoner. Taking another view, a

Judge might declare a prisoner free from all coercion unless when his services were actually required by & being rendered to the Governor."[35]

The real meaning of the opinion was that public opinion in Van Diemen's Land as articulated by the judiciary could seriously limit the power of the governor in controlling the transported felons. It was indeed possible that both O'Brien's solitary confinement and McManus's confinement at the Cascades Probation Station could be declared "coercive" and the court could rule they should be freed from such restraints. After reading the opinion, both ministers urged the legal councillors to begin work on legislation that would clearly define the power of the governor and thus do away with the vagueness in the law that could result in the limitation of the governor's power. Shortly afterward Grey added another component to the new legislation. The assignment list replaced the certificate of conviction as legal proof of conviction. Grey also prepared to send Denison complete copies of all Irish statutes relating to transportation.[36]

*   *   *

Denison's reputation, which had come under assault in Australia, began to suffer a similar fate in the British Isles as the interrelated transportation–state prisoner issue was debated once again in Westminster and the press. On 6 May the question of the treatment that the truant state prisoners were receiving was raised in the Houses of Commons by Chisholm Anstey. Anstey concentrated on Denison's action of overturning the decision of the police magistrates, which he asserted revealed not only an ignorance of the law but also an arbitrary vengeful attitude toward the state prisoners. Anstey wanted Denison censored.[37]

For the ministry, Sir Benjamin Hawes replied that he could not conceive why Governor Denison should be censored. He stated that the governor had the power to withdraw the tickets-of-leave at his own discretion and had done so. For the moment the debate ended. Anstey tried on two other occasions to raise the issue but failed. At the moment Sir Lucius was not prepared to support Anstey, and without his direct involvement the issue was not really debated. Sir Lucius did take the opportunity to raise the question of Lapham's dismissal, stating that Governor Denison had been too "harsh" and had caused Lapham unjustifiably "great hardship."[38]

Duffy did what he could to support Anstey's move to censor Denison. He published a letter from O'Brien outlining what had transpired and complaining of the "malicious caprice" of Denison and Hampton, who had both done so much to aggravate the state prisoners.[39] Duffy also published an attack maintaining that Denison's official actions against the truants had been motivated by malice and even referred to Denison derisively as "a gaoler, a torturer, [and] a headsman." The *Nation* was joined in its assault of Denison by the editors of the *Daily News*. Those editors voiced their opinion that Denison's handling of the whole affair had placed him in disrepute.[40]

Nothing much came of the case of the three truants because McManus's suit for a writ of habeas corpus, his release, and his subsequent escape were all well covered in the press. In Ireland, McManus's escape was greeted with approval. Not only the *Nation* but also the *Freemans Journal*, the *Evening Herald*, the *Limerick Examiner*, and the *Sligo Champion* all published articles explaining that McManus's escape was honorable. The editors of the *Freemans Journal* wrote that both "*Conservative* Ireland and Democratic Ireland" joined together in acknowledging that McManus's honor was pure.[41]

A considerable number of Irishmen were so pleased with McManus's escape that they held a "public national soiree" at the Rotunda to commemorate it. The notice advertising the affair explained that after the speeches there would be a ball, and the sponsors also noted that "intoxicating drinks are to be excluded from the refreshments."[42]

There was no doubt that the martyrdom of the truants and McManus's escape extended the political base of the state prisoners. Both Ireland and America were ready for further action. The sympathy in both places had become national in scope. There was also no doubt that the British ministers were feeling the harassment of the antitransportation movement. Grey, in particular, was anxious to end transportation to Van Diemen's Land, but two problems, what to do with the convicts being sent there and how to get immigrants to move there in large enough numbers to solve the labor-supply problem, were still unanswered. In the winter of 1851, however, gold was discovered in Australia. How extensive the gold deposits were was initially unknown. But if they were extensive and able to draw massive numbers of immigrants, the labor problem might be solved.[43]

The Mitchels Visit O'Brien

Neither O'Brien nor his fellow exiles had any inkling of the magnitude of the legal problem that the McManus affair had created for the British ministry during the summer and fall of 1851. Had the Irish prisoners learned promptly of the deficiences of their legal status, it is doubtful if Meagher or O'Donoghue at least would have sought freedom through the legal avenues opened to them. Meagher and O'Donoghue had both been deeply impressed by McManus's escape and had determined to follow his example and escape with their honor intact. Both men knew they would have to resign their tickets-of-leave before leaving the island in order to accomplish that goal. There was a difference in the way each man laid his plans. Meagher displayed great care, caution, and patience in preparing for his escape, while O'Donoghue acted in great haste.

Meagher and his new bride gave no indication of any intention to escape. They had been married in February 1851 and had promptly set up housekeeping in apparent earnestness to remain where they were. Mitchel and Martin had visited the couple not long after their marriage, and Mitchel described Catherine Meagher as "fair and graceful" and their cottage, charmingly situated at the head of a quiet bay on Lake Sorell, as "nestl[ed] under the shelter of [an] untamable forest . . . with a ve-randa and a gum-tree jetty stretching into the water." Mitchel wrote of the interior of the house, "They have elegant little rooms, books, . . . why it is almost like *living*."[44]

Martin's observations of the life of the Meaghers were recorded dur-ing the summer of 1851, in a letter he wrote to O'Doherty. He was pleased to find Meagher "in great spirits, skipping about like a 4 year old & entertaining Mrs M. & the Hall girls who are staying there." Martin enjoyed staying in the cottage, sailing on the lake, and the company of Catherine, commenting, "She seems very good natured & I think she is quite a sensible girl." He hoped "they will do very well."[45]

The Meaghers' first year of married life was spent mainly at the cottage on the lake. They did make a trip to Bothwell to greet the arrival of Mitchel's wife and children from Ireland. Unfortunately, on the return trip Catherine suffered "a severe attack of rheumatism—the road . . . being excessively wet, and the weather very damp."[46] Meagher was anx-ious about his wife's health because her rheumatic condition was compli-cated by pregnancy. In a letter to O'Doherty, Meagher mentioned that there was "some misunderstanding" among the doctors about the general state of her health.[47]

To all appearances, therefore, Meagher would be the least likely of the state prisoners to chance an escape attempt. But McManus had set an example of what could be accomplished with good friends and a good plan. In addition, Meagher believed that the local officials were consid-ering repressive actions against him because of the uncomplimentary manner in which he had referred to some of them in articles he had sent back to Ireland. Those articles had been published, "and when [his] re-marks began to filter back to [Van Diemen's Land] the author's popularity with officialdom was not enhanced." Probably Meagher was most strongly influenced by his own active nature, stifled in the prime of his life.[48] His marriage to Catherine had evidently not solved his problem.

Meagher's general plan was to resign his ticket-of-leave and then make his escape with the aid of a group of loyal friends. The most loyal help was to come from John Connell of Sugar Loaf, a longtime friend of all the Irish exiles. On 15 August 1851 Meagher forwarded an Irish song-book to John Connell's wife. The book was a gift from John Martin to the Connell girls. In his letter to Mrs. Connell, Meagher wrote, "Tell John I have often and often been on the look-out for the *fire at the Tea Tree Creek*, but do not despair of seeing it yet." That message would be the signal that plans had been completed for his escape, and while Meagher would have to wait several long months before seeing the fire, he had determined to go only after all was ready.[49]

O'Donoghue was not as patient. He had been living in Launceston and decided that it was time for him to make an escape attempt. In September 1851 O'Donoghue resigned his ticket-of-leave and prepared to flee Van Diemen's Land, but the "arrangements miscarried" and he was arrested and placed in jail. A report was carried in the press that O'Donoghue was removed to the Hobart Town Prisoners' Barracks and dealt with as an ordinary prisoner of the crown. O'Doherty wrote O'Brien of O'Donoghue's abortive attempt. What surprised O'Doherty was the fact "that [O'Donoghue] was permitted to hold [a ticket-of-leave] so long." O'Doherty wrote, "He must either be mad or as great a *villain* as there is in V D L." And he added, "I cannot feel the least part for him."[50]

But O'Donoghue was not held in confinement very long. He was allowed to renew his ticket-of-leave on his promise not to escape. He continued to live in Launceston as the houseguest of the Reverend Thomas Butler.[51]

*　　　*　　　*

Of all the state prisoners, O'Brien was at that time leading the most secluded and quiet life. Avoca was in a remote part of Van Diemen's Land, with few people in the area and an insignificant number of visitors. O'Brien spent his time teaching school and reading and rereading both the local and foreign press as well as the mail from home.

The news O'Brien received from home was rather gloomy. He learned that his brother-in-law Charles Monsell had died. O'Brien had a real affection for Charles. But Charles was important for another reason. O'Brien knew that Charles had repeatedly asked William Gladstone for help in obtaining a pardon for him. Interestingly enough, Gladstone was one of the last persons to visit Charles before he died, since the two couples, the Monsells and the Gladstones, were both visiting in Naples when Charles took ill.[52] To what extent Charles's death would affect Gladstone's efforts to help O'Brien was unknown.

With the same mail from home, O'Brien received a letter from his mother, who was furious with him. She had just read his letter of complaint published in the *Nation* on 10 May describing his treatment at the hands of Denison and Hampton. She told her son quite plainly, "I do not like you to attribute bad motives to their actions as you have." She also told him that the way to be content is to consider "what we *deserve from the hand of God.*"[53]

O'Brien had certainly not received much consolation from those letters, but toward the Australian spring news from some of the other state prisoners helped to lift his spirits. By September, O'Brien was reading the newspaper accounts of McManus's welcome in San Francisco. He was fascinated by the contrast between how he was being treated in Van Diemen's Land and how McManus was being honored in San Francisco. O'Brien told his wife, "I confess honestly to you that I have received no little pleasure from finding that in America our cause and our motives have been appreciated." O'Brien was particularly pleased when he read of the reception attended by three hundred persons honoring McManus. He was flattered to learn that one of the toasts was to "the health of William Smith O'Brien and of his companions in Exile." He told Lucy, "This tribute to our motives and conduct has tended to soothe the pains of my captivity." O'Brien wished McManus success. "I sincerely trust that he will soon be able to make for himself an honourable independence by his industry[,] enterprise[,] and mercantile knowledge in a land where his antecedent sufferings will have commended him to the sympathy and regard of the population."[54]

O'Doherty also seemed to be doing well. It appears that O'Doherty had made another attempt to obtain permission to practice medicine in Van Diemen's Land, and on that occasion he was successful. O'Doherty received an offer of an appointment to the medical staff of St. Mary's Hospital in Hobart Town, an offer that he promptly accepted. O'Doherty eagerly began the work that would, for the first time since his arrival, provide professional satisfaction.[55]

But it was the news from John Mitchel that brought O'Brien particular pleasure. On 7 September, Mitchel wrote to O'Brien and told him that he and his wife were making plans to visit O'Brien in Avoca. Although they expected to make the visit sometime during September, the Mitchels did not set out on their journey until approximately 14 October. It had been three and a half years since the men had last seen one another, and Mitchel thought, "From Meagher's description, I fear we shall find him much altered."[56]

It took the Mitchels two days to make the journey. During the entire trip they kept running into candidates who were busy electioneering for seats on the Legislative Council. It was the first election to be held under the new Constitution Act. There was only one issue that mattered in the campaign; namely, whether or not the voters wanted to elect a pro- or antitransportation candidate to represent their district. At one stage of the journey the Mitchels found themselves traveling with a group of antitransportationists on their way to a rally to support a Mr. Kermode. Mitchel saw some of the placards advocating R. Q. Kermode's candidacy. He wrote, "An expression caught my eye that led me to look further—the sharp pen of the hermit of the lake pointed every sentence: in every line I recognized the 'fine touch of his claw.'"[57] Mitchel suddenly realized Meagher had joined the antitransportationists. Once again Meagher's energy had found an outlet. On this occasion, however, he had displayed the common sense not to publicly become involved.

On arriving in Avoca, the Mitchels checked into the local hotel and then sat down to breakfast. Within a few minutes, they saw a gentleman pass by the window of the restaurant whom they believed was O'Brien. It had been a long time since John Mitchel had last seen O'Brien, and during those final meetings in Ireland the two men "had been somewhat distant" in their relationship. The Mitchels assumed the gentleman was O'Brien, rose from their table, and went to the door to greet him. As Mitchel recorded, "Our greeting was silent, but warm and cordial." Mitchel believed O'Brien's health was failing. He noted that O'Brien did not stand erect as before, nor step in such a stately manner. O'Brien's hair had become "more grizzled," and his face reflected the "pain and passion" of the last few years. Mitchel did believe that O'Brien was "haunted by the ghosts of buried hopes." Yet for all the signs of aging, the lines of pain, the anxiety caused by disappointment, Mitchel believed O'Brien was still a giant of a personality. "He is a rare and noble sight to see: a man who cannot be crushed, bowed, or broken; who can stand firm on his own feet against all the tumult and tempest of this ruffianly world."[58]

O'Brien also admired Mitchel. O'Brien acknowledged that their political differences back in Ireland had caused him "anxiety" and that on one occasion a riot in Limerick in 1848 had almost cost him his life. Nevertheless he enjoyed meeting Mitchel again. O'Brien admired Mitchel's "sturdiness of . . . character." He believed Mitchel had suffered more than any of the other exiles, having undergone twenty-two months of solitary confinement. But most of all O'Brien admired Mitchel's consistency. "Mitchel has throughout the whole period of his captivity displayed a fortitude well worthy of the lofty tone of defiance which he displayed both before and during his trial." Both Mitchel and O'Brien also had a similar goal, an eventual return to Ireland.[59]

In addition to having undergone similar punishment, possessing a similarly defiant attitude, and having similar goals, the two men could analyze and discuss "the mistakes which [they] had committed whilst engaged in our noble though inglorious and unsuccessful effort to redeem [Ireland] from ruin and oppression [and] the circumstances calculated to generate despondency or consolation with respect to its future destiny."[60]

After breakfast, O'Brien and the Mitchels took a long walk. O'Brien recounted the events of the revolution of 1848. Mitchel recorded in his *Jail Journal* that O'Brien blamed the Catholic clergy for the collapse of the revolution, for the clergy refused to support the revolution and intimidated the men who were willing to join O'Brien with threats of eternal damnation. Mitchel also recorded, "On the whole, O'Brien accepts defeat—takes desertion or backwardness of the people, and the verdict of the Clonmell jury, such as it was, for a final pronouncement against armed resistance; and therefore regards the cause as lost utterly, and the history of Ireland, as a nation, closed and sealed forever."[61]

Mitchel's conclusions made a complex issue simple. During his trial for treason, O'Brien wrote an account of his motives for leading the revolution and the general reasons for its failure. O'Brien believed he and his fellow revolutionaries "were defeated not by the military preparations" of the British Army nor by "the system of espionage organised" by the Irish government. While he did think the Catholic hierarchy was mainly responsible for the failure of the revolution he also believed part of the responsibility had to be shared by those who had previously led him to believe they would answer a call to revolution. He noted, "Had even a portion of those who professed their readiness to fight taken the field . . . had any success been obtained which would have given confidence to those who were waiting for encouragement it is impossible to say what might not have been the results of our undertaking." But ultimately O'Brien had to acknowledge his responsibility for failing to be an effective leader. "I am compelled to charge myself with having totally miscalculated the energies of the Irish People—I cannot disavow my responsibility for this disastrous failure."[62]

Mitchel was wrong in his statement that O'Brien believed the revolution of 1848 to have been such a failure that there was no hope of Ireland ever attaining self-government. O'Brien did believe that until the Irish developed self-reliance and united in a common effort to obtain self-government there was no sense calling them to the barricades. He also believed it unlikely, in the foreseeable future, that the British government would halt the constitutional processes that allowed the redress of grievances by the use of physical force. As long as the constitution was operable O'Brien would not justify revolution. But he did believe self-government was still a viable issue within the constitutional process. O'Brien's long-range plan was to work to influence Irish public opinion. He planned to do everything he could to educate the Irish people to appreciate the benefits of self-government and to realize that the continued dominance of England worked to the detriment of Ireland. In 1843 O'Brien had become convinced that Ireland should govern itself. He continued to believe in that principle until his death.[63]

As to the validity of his trial O'Brien later referred to it as a "mockery." O'Brien preferred not to comment in detail about the verdict of the Clonmel jury, but he later stated that in his opinion it was practically impossible to obtain a fair trial in a political case in Ireland.[64]

Mitchel also commented at this time on O'Brien's attitude toward

Queen Victoria and on the question of a pardon. Mitchel believed that if the Irish were to be free they would have to root out all the English institutions in Ireland. The British monarchy was one of those institutions. Mitchel could not and would not recognize the power of the queen in Ireland. In contrast, O'Brien held the more traditional view that sovereignty in Ireland resided in the queen, Lords, and Commons of Ireland. O'Brien was prepared to accept the establishment of a republic if conditions required it.[65]

Mitchel could not understand why O'Brien, who actually recognized the right of Queen Victoria to reign in Ireland, would not beg pardon from her. He concluded that O'Brien did not beg pardon from Queen Victoria simply because he was too proud to do so.[66] O'Brien repeatedly stated that he did not beg pardon because he did not believe he was wrong. He did believe England was assaulting Ireland by its display of indifference. He did believe that the suspension of habeas corpus closed the door to constitutional redress. He did believe that it was not only the right but even the duty of every Irishman to stand up and protect himself and his country from destruction. He acknowledged that he had made a mistake in thinking the Irish would prefer death or emigration to revolution. If he was guilty of any crime it was imprudence. It was in starting a revolution without being aware that he was alone.[67]

As O'Brien and the Mitchels completed their walk and turned back toward the hotel, O'Brien, looking down the path, saw "[a] large black snake" directly in front of Jane Mitchel. She was about to take a step forward that would land her foot squarely on the back of the reptile. O'Brien quickly "pushed her back, and jumped forward to kill the snake with a staff." The snake escaped into "some dense tufts of iris," and after searching in vain for the reptile the party continued to the hotel.[68]

The Mitchels and O'Brien spent the morning of the sixteenth together. They walked up the valley of the St. Pauls. It was then time for O'Brien to start his fourteen-mile walk to the Brock home in order to give a lesson that evening. After they parted Mitchel noted, "We stood and watched him long, as he walked up the valley on his lonely way; and I think I have seen few sadder and few prouder sights." After visiting with O'Brien, Mitchel concluded that neither the queen nor the "Parliament, . . . pulpit, press, [or] people" of England knew anything about honor or dishonor. The visit was over, "We turned slowly away—I, with a profound curse, my wife with a tear or two, and came back to Avoca."[69]

As O'Brien walked home he thought of the visit that he had just had with the Mitchels. He had indeed enjoyed himself. The truth was that O'Brien liked Mitchel, and he knew that Mitchel's reunion with his family was bringing him great pleasure. O'Brien commented, "I fancy that I could be *almost* happy if I were surrounded, even in this colony by the same elements of happiness; but nothing has yet shaken my determination to abstain in whatever sacrifice to myself from placing my wife and children under the control of the brutes who govern the prisoner population of this colony."[70]

*   *   *

On the sixteenth, the Mitchels traveled to Campbell Town and rested at the hotel before continuing their journey. On the seventeenth, they took a spring cart and journeyed sixteen miles to their next destination, the home of two Irish immigrants, John Connell and his wife. When the Mitchels had first made their plans to visit O'Brien at Avoca, they had been invited to stop on their return trip at the Connells. Mr. and Mrs. Connell had emigrated from Cork thirty-two years before. When they first arrived in Van Diemen's Land, they had had a difficult struggle taming the forest and turning it into cornfields and pastures, but they had worked hard and had succeeded. In those early days the challenge of nature, however, was compounded by the danger of the wild convict bushrangers, felons who were beyond the actual control of the authorities. Mrs. Connell became well known for her bravery in overcoming an attack by some bushrangers and was awarded some land for assisting in their capture.[71] Mr. Connell's courage was to be tested in Meagher's forthcoming escape attempt. Meanwhile, the Mitchels and the Connells enjoyed a pleasant visit.

By the eighteenth, the Mitchels were ready to move on to their next destination, a visit with the Meaghers at Lake Sorell. Mr. Connell had arranged for horses to be brought to his place so that the Mitchels could travel directly to the lakes after they left Sugar Loaf. As the Mitchels were taking leave of their friends, the Connells presented them with a baby kangaroo to serve as a pet for the Mitchel children. The Connells' son rode with the Mitchels for several miles and then turned back after giving them directions for the rest of their journey. Most of the journey was uphill because Lake Sorell was on top of a mountain. After riding for some time Mitchel and his wife dismounted, and Mitchel commenced to lead the horses up a rather steep incline, "when we suddenly saw a man on the track above us; he had a gun in his hand, on his head a cabbage-tree hat, and at his feet an enormous dog." When the man saw the Mitchels he called out "Coo—ee," a call that the people in Van Diemen's Land used when they wanted to be heard at a distance. Mitchel answered with a "Coo—ee," and the man and the dog came toward them. It was Meagher and his dog, Brian. They had set out to greet the Mitchels. Brian had previously belonged to McManus but had taken up residence with Meagher after McManus's escape. The Mitchels and Meagher continued up the steep incline of the mountain. When they reached the top, there was stretched before them a huge lake. Mitchel marveled at the scene of a lake at the top of a mountain. It was "a sight to be seen only in [Van Diemen's Land], a land where not only the native productions of the country, but the very features of nature herself, seem formed on a pattern the reverse of every model, form, and law on which the structure of the rest of the globe is put together; a land where the mountain-tops are vast lakes, where the trees strip off bark instead of leaves, and where the cherry-stones grow on the outside of the cherries?" The three continued to Meagher's house, where they were greeted by Catherine Meagher, enjoyed a pleasant meal, and afterward took a sail on the lake. Meagher's boat flew the American flag. The Mitchels and Meagher mainly discussed Ireland, the Australian League, and the coming elections in Van Diemen's Land. The Mitchels spent the night at Meagher's "Sylvan Hermitage," and the next morning after taking one more sail they bade farewell to their friends and started down the mountain to their home.[72]

The descent down the mountain was slow but not difficult. By the time the Mitchels reached the plain of Bothwell the horses were moving like "lightning" through the level grass. As they crossed the River Clyde, which bordered their farm, Mitchel described the reunion with their family, "John Knox and all the children were walking in the field with the dogs; they see us from the moment we have forded the river; they run to meet us with welcoming outcry; and there is joy at Nant over the little kangaroo."[73]

*   *   *

It was not long after Mitchel's visit that O'Brien read the population statistics for Ireland of 1841 and 1851, a period that encompassed the famine. The results were startling. He recorded the information in his journal. O'Brien estimated Ireland's population in 1846 at 8.5 million. He concluded that if a natural increase had taken place the population by 1851 would have been 9 million. Instead, he estimated there had been a loss of 2 million. He believed that one of those millions emigrated to other countries. But he noted, "There remains one million for whose premature extinction the British government is to be held responsible." O'Brien was furious. He knew that if a million lives had been lost in a series of wars waged by a "barbarous conqueror" the conqueror would "justly deserve the execration of mankind throughout all ages." Or if a million persons were driven into exile by a "ruthless tyrant" the tyrant would "justly deserve to be visited with a doom similar to that which divine vengeance inflicted upon Pharaoh King of Egypt." Yet O'Brien knew that neither the English people nor their rulers felt any guilt at all for allowing the famine, "which they have permitted if they have not caused it," to continue year after year. He also knew that some of the rulers looked upon the famine in a favorable light since they considered

Ireland to be "overpeopled and hostile." O'Brien was not of the opinion expressed by many that the failure of the potato crop and the resulting famine were the work of God. He believed that Ireland produced more than enough food, other than potatoes, to feed the population. But the additional foodstuffs were "exported as a tribute to absent proprietors" and hence not available to the starving population. O'Brien was willing to admit that the additional foodstuffs might not have been sufficient to provide for all those who were in need, but England could have made "ample provision" by means of "a wise and benevolent system of administration" to alleviate the distress. O'Brien believed that the English had been willing in the past to spend vast sums of money to wage a war "to maintain some trivial point of honour—possibly to vindicate some unjustifiable aggression." Yet when Ireland was in need and facing "ruin and extinction the smallest pecuniary sacrifice is regarded as a waste of the national resources which cannot be reconciled with the most approved principles of modern political economy." Under those circumstances O'Brien did not believe it was possible for him to "regard with respect or affection the government of England!"[74]

As O'Brien spoke so bitterly against the English he had to admit his censure did not include all Englishmen. He knew there were many who had protested the policy of the government and many who had made great personal sacrifices to help Ireland during her period of trial. His charges of "tyranny" and "conquest," however, were ultimately against "England as a Nation," regardless of whether or not individuals within the nation took a different stand. O'Brien was "compelled to say that history does not present to my inquiries any records of national injustice so revolting as those which it displays in the treatment which my beloved country has sustained from England from the time of Henry II to that of Queen Victoria."[75]

O'Brien was now ready to discuss what he thought Queen Victoria's role had been in the famine. He did not place the personal responsibility for the policies carried out during the famine on Queen Victoria. He held "the ministry, the Parliament, and the public of Great Britain" responsible. Nevertheless, O'Brien concluded, "When I ponder upon the statistical return of the Irish population which lies before me I feel that I did my duty when I endeavoured at the risk of my life to avert the evils which have been inflicted upon my country during the most calamitous reign that *Ireland* has experienced since it became subject to the British Crown—when I read the figures I have quoted I am proud to be in exile."[76]

*   *   *

By the middle of November, O'Brien's health had begun to fail. The pains in his chest had returned. He decided to leave his teaching position with the Brock family and take up residence in another district that might prove more beneficial to his health. About his relationship with his employer, O'Brien wrote in his journal that he was pleased to be able to write that Dr. Brock and he had gotten along very well. In the nine months O'Brien had lived in the Brock home no "unkind" words had passed between them. O'Brien wanted it clearly understood that his decision to leave his teaching position was based on a desire to regain his health. On 18 November he wrote to the comptroller general announcing his intention of leaving Fingal. O'Brien wanted to live in Hobart Town or Launceston where he would be able to practice law, but the government officials refused his request, so he prepared to return to New Norfolk. The officials did grant him permission to spend two days in Hobart Town in order to purchase supplies before going on to New Norfolk.[77]

*   *   *

Eighteen fifty-one had been rather a quiet year for all the state prisoners. It was true that McManus had had a great deal of excitement during the first few months, but once he had reached America his life had become quite normal. O'Brien had spent the year in almost virtual seclusion, and Mitchel, Martin, and Meagher had begun to enjoy the pleasures of family living. O'Doherty had finally got his chance to practice medicine. O'Donoghue remained unsettled.

Yet in 1851 a number of changes occurred that would make the next few years exciting, if not chaotic. McManus's escape and the truancy of the three state prisoners had prepared the Irish and American publics to react positively to an organized effort to obtain pardons for the state prisoners. O'Donoghue and Meagher had determined to follow McManus to America.

Nor was the struggle between the antitransportationists and Denison calming down. Whichever side captured the majority of the seats in the new Legislative Council could clearly claim the victory. Yet it was likely that the minority members on the council would look for reasons to dispute that victory. It would then remain for the British ministry to analyze the situation once again and decide whether the promise announced by Governor Denison in July 1848, that transportation would cease to Van Diemen's Land, should be kept.

CHAPTER 7

New Hope

O'Brien and the Antitransportationists

On Monday, 15 December 1851, O'Brien bid farewell to Dr. Brock and his family and traveled to the nearby town of Avoca to catch the coach for Campbell Town. From Campbell Town he would travel to Hobart Town, where he planned to do some shopping before going on to make his new home in New Norfolk. In Avoca he had about a three-hour wait for the coach, which he spent "promenading the little village of Avoca in the midst of a hurricane of dust." He had to admit that his stay in the District of Fingal had proved to be disappointing.[1]

At Campbell Town, O'Brien was met by his friend Meagher. The two men spent the remainder of the day visiting with one another. O'Brien was pleased to find his friend "looking well and in good spirits." The next morning Meagher took O'Brien in his gig to Ross. The original plan called for O'Brien to board the day coach for Hobart Town after breakfasting with Meagher, but the coach was full. The next coach would not leave until the evening.[2]

Since O'Brien was forced to spend the day in Ross, he decided to pay a visit to the Connells. The Connells had never met O'Brien but had issued an invitation to him to visit them whenever he had an opportunity to do so. O'Brien marveled at the scene: "I found in a residence perched in a beautiful spot on a romantic hill two old persons of the peasant class surrounded by their pretty daughters who in manners were qualified to enter any society." The Connells greeted O'Brien so warmly that O'Brien wrote, "If I had been King of Ireland I could not have been received with more affectionate homage by these simple-hearted people."[3]

After leaving the Connells, O'Brien had no time to do anything except board the night coach for Hobart Town. During his two-day stay in Hobart Town, O'Brien was the houseguest of the Carters. He then went on to New Norfolk.[4]

O'Brien had pleasant memories of his previous stay in New Norfolk and looked forward to settling down there once again. His expectations were not disappointed. There was no doubt that New Norfolk was a beautiful area. In addition, O'Brien returned to Mr. Elwin's hotel, which had previously proved to be more than satisfactory. Finally, O'Brien looked forward to renewing the friendships he had formed with some of the families who lived in the vicinity. O'Brien's old friends extended him their hospitality. O'Brien was again the guest of Mr. Barker in his house affectionately named Rose Garland. He also accepted an invitation to spend Christmas at the home of Major and Mrs. Lloyd, named Bryn Estyn, where the Lloyds "exhibited towards [O'Brien] the most friendly feelings."[5]

Another family that befriended O'Brien was that of Capt. Michael Fenton. The captain, born in Ireland, had as a young man become a professional soldier and served in India. After his military service he decided to settle in Van Diemen's Land and by 1852 he owned eight thousand acres of land. Captain Fenton was active in the antitransportation movement and had been elected to the new Legislative Council.[6]

Since O'Brien was a close friend of Captain Fenton, he followed the assembling of the Legislative Council on 30 December 1851 that inaugurated a new system of government for Van Diemen's Land. For the first time, the citizens had been able to elect their representatives. The new council had sixteen members elected by the people, four members appointed by the government, and four members who were officials of the government. The sixteen elected members were all antitransportationists, and they awaited Denison's opening speech on 1 January 1852 to see what his position would be on the transportation issue. Denison did not mention the transportation issue at all but rather discussed the introduction of legislation that would establish Hobart Town and Launceston as municipalities. In addition, he discussed such problems as supplying Launceston with water, constructing and maintaining roads throughout the island, and establishing schools.[7]

The antitransportation members of the council regretted Denison's omission of the transportation question from his speech and in their reply to his address expressed that regret. Later, the council "adopted an address to the Queen, remonstrating on the influx of criminals." Denison promised he would forward the address, but he informed the members of the council that he felt it was his duty both to the queen and to the queen's "loyal and faithful subjects [of Van Diemen's Land] to express the deep sorrow I feel at the language of the resolutions contained in the address." That statement did not endear him to the antitransportationists since those councillors felt Denison had charged them with disloyalty and they considered the address to have been respectfully worded. Those councillors knew that similar resolutions had unanimously passed the legislative councils in New South Wales, Victoria, and South Australia and that the governors of those areas had either openly approved of the resolutions or remained silent.[8]

O'Brien had nothing but respect for the newly elected councillors. Although he initially believed the transportation system as practiced on Maria Island had some merit, by 1852 he recognized that public opinion in Van Diemen's Land opposed its continuance. O'Brien knew his belief in the benefits of self-government overrode his conviction that transportation was better than the penal system in England. He believed Van Diemen's Land had a real chance to establish a government truly responsive to the will of the people: "If the elected members of the Council prove themselves to be honest and faithful they have it in their power to carry out the principles of *self-government* under circumstances most favorable to their advantageous development."[9] O'Brien certainly wished them well.

*   *   *

O'Brien's life back in New Norfolk was not exciting, but it was comfortable. For the first time since he had arrived in Van Diemen's Land, O'Brien found with the Fentons a family circle in which he could feel himself an integral part. The Fentons were important to O'Brien for other reasons. O'Brien did not want to be involved in local politics, but he readily admitted, "Political studies can never cease to interest me."[10] Captain Fenton's position on the Legislative Council gave O'Brien a firsthand view of the antitransportation struggle. It also gave him an easy entrée into the "new establishment." O'Brien's new friends were moving up in the world.

Meagher Escapes

While O'Brien was settling down to a comfortable life in New Norfolk, Meagher was waiting to make his escape. John Connell finally sent word that all of the arrangements had been made. A few days before Christmas, Catherine Meagher left Lake Sorell ostensibly to visit her parents. With the planned escape only a few days off, Meagher no doubt wanted Catherine out of danger and with her parents while she was nearing the time for the birth of their child. He probably reasoned that if his escape attempt failed, she could best be cared for by her parents, and if his escape attempt succeeded, Catherine and the baby could join him in America once they were both strong enough to make the journey.[11] On 27 December 1851 Meagher wrote to Gavan Duffy, "In great haste I have sat down to tell you that I am determined to withdraw my *parole*,— throw up my 'ticket-of-leave' and afterwards attempt my escape." On 3 January 1852 Meagher sent a note to the local police magistrate, Thomas Mason, informing him that he was withdrawing his ticket-of-leave. He was giving Mason twenty-four hours' notice of the withdrawal. Meagher stated that he believed that after the passage of that time he was free from his promise not to escape.[12]

Upon receiving Meagher's letter, Mason sent two officers to Meagher's home to arrest him.[13] When they arrived they began to search the premises. Meagher recorded that he and several "conspirators" rode up on horseback to within several yards of the officers. Meagher identified himself, challenged the officers to arrest him, and announced he would do all in his power to escape. The officers made no move toward him. Meagher and his associates then turned and rode off to the seacoast where he was taken in a small boat to one of the islands in the Bass Strait to await the *Elizabeth Thompson*, a vessel that would take him to South America. From South America, Meagher would make his way to New York City.[14]

But Meagher's escape, while successful, had certain problems attached to it. The two officers who had been sent to arrest him maintained they never saw Meagher that evening. They returned to Campbell Town the next day and reported that Meagher had fled Van Diemen's Land before they arrived at his home.[15] If the statement of the officers was true, then Meagher's escape was dishonorable. The rules of the game required Meagher to withdraw his ticket-of-leave and hence his promise not to escape. He did that on 3 January. He had given twenty-four hours' notice of the withdrawal, which meant he was not free to escape until noon of 4 January. However, once the government sent officers to arrest him, the government had withdrawn the ticket-of-leave and Meagher was free of his promise not to escape. The crucial point was whether Meagher knew the officers were at his home to arrest him. Meagher maintained they had had a face-to-face confrontation. The officers maintained they had not seen him that evening.

*   *   *

The news of Meagher's escape appeared in the 10 January edition of the Van Diemen's Land newspapers. The editors of the *Hobart Town Guardian* described the escape in general terms and wished Meagher "every success and a continuation of freedom." The editors of the *Launceston Examiner* used the opportunity to suggest that the Legislative Council demand that the remaining Irish state prisoners be pardoned. They asked, "What interest has this community in the incarceration of such men."[16]

The progovernment newspaper, the *Hobart Town Advertiser*, expectedly did not express the same sentiments. The government position was that Meagher had broken his parole and had acted in a dishonorable manner. The editors of the *Sydney Morning Herald* agreed. They wrote, "Such a mixture of mean evasion and bullying balderdash we have not read since the time when this same worthy, and some of his compeers, were spouting their treasonable trash through the columns of the *Nation*." They concluded, "Erin would indeed have been a *Green* Isle if she had allowed the vanity of such Copper Captains as Meagher to lead her into rebellion."[17]

Lady Denison thought all the Irish rebels had a very "strange" idea of "honour," therefore it did not surprise her that Meagher ran off without going through the proper formalities. She hoped Meagher's escape would finally convince the government officials in London "that they made altogether a mistake in treating them like honourable men, as prisoners of war, rather than as convicted felons."[18]

The question of the propriety of Meagher's escape was debated among the state prisoners as well, both Mitchel and Martin being deeply disturbed with the manner of the escape. By the eighteenth, Martin unequivocally told O'Doherty, "It now appears too plainly to both Mitchel and myself that Meagher *was not free in honour to go*."[19] On the nineteenth, Mitchel wrote to O'Brien saying that he had investigated what had taken place at Meagher's the night of his escape but that the information he was given convinced him that the government reports were correct. "The fact is that Meagher did not await the arrest in his own house, did not show himself to the Constables at all, & neither was arrested, nor gave [the constables] an opportunity to arrest him." Mitchel asked O'Brien to "favour us with a line telling us your own opinion," stating that both he and Martin were contemplating writing Meagher "requesting him *to come back*." Mitchel knew, "This seems romantic & absurd: yet I do believe if your judgement on the whole matter coincides with ours, and he be made aware of that, he will come."[20]

O'Brien "wished . . . the circumstances under which" Meagher had escaped "had been different" since they did give "rise to an imputation that he had violated his parole." But O'Brien knew Meagher was "most sensitive" about his honor and believed Meagher would explain what took place to everyone's satisfaction, except those "prejudiced and inveterate enemies." O'Brien had obviously decided to wait for Meagher's account.[21]

Mitchel and Martin remained dissatisfied. They wrote Meagher telling him of their displeasure with the manner in which he had effected his escape. They asked him to return to Van Diemen's Land.[22]

The Petitions

During the fall, winter, and spring months of 1851–1852 the plight of the state prisoners resulted in an organized national effort by both Americans and Irishmen to obtain the release of the exiles by means of petitions. The effort began in America and was the result of McManus's successful escape and his references to the plight of the remaining state prisoners in Van Diemen's Land. Once the local and national political leaders in America realized the pardon issue could be turned to their political advantage, the plight of the exiles received a great deal of attention.

The American petition movement on behalf of the Irish state pris-

oners began in the fall of 1851. Meetings were held to draft those petitions. In Boston, over three thousand citizens gathered in Faneuil Hall
on 25 October to petition the United States president, Millard Fillmore,
to ask the British government to release the state prisoners. The petitioners reasoned that Ireland was in such a quiet state that the exiles
could be released without any danger to the British government. The
petitioners were careful to mention that their request was not intended
in any way to be an interference in the internal affairs of Great Britain.
It was merely an expression of sentiment for which there were many
precedents. The Massachusetts petitioners thought they had a rather
good chance of success, mainly because the secretary of state was Daniel
Webster, ex-senator from Massachusetts. The petitioners were aware
that, in past times, Webster had said "some hard things" about the Irish,
but now that they were so numerous and so well organized in state politics, they awaited his "special sunshine."[23]

Between 25 October and 17 January, widely supported petitions asking for the release of the state prisoners were also drawn up by groups of
citizens in Baltimore, Maryland; Bangor, Maine; and Washington, D.C.
Plans were made for the delegates from each of the cities to assemble in
Washington in late January.[24]

On the afternoon of 22 January, the delegates from those cities gathered in front of the National Hotel, formed a procession, and proceeded
to the White House for the meeting with the president. There were
approximately three to four hundred persons assembled, including Generals Lewis Cass and Sam Houston, Senators Stephen Douglas and James
Shields of Illinois, and Secretary of State Daniel Webster. After President Fillmore was introduced, Thomas Yates Walsh, a member of Congress from the state of Maryland, presented the petition, which had been
signed by over twenty thousand persons. Walsh hoped Fillmore would do
all in his power to obtain the release of the exiles, exhorting the president to "send forth from this temple of liberty the proud bird of America,
that, like the dove of old, it may sweep across the waste of waters, and
bear in its beak the olive branch of peace."[25]

President Fillmore replied that he understood the feelings of the
Irish-Americans regarding the plight of the Irish exiles. Fillmore was not
prepared, however, to make the plight of the state prisoners an official
concern of the United States government. He explained that there was
a well-understood principle "that one nation cannot claim a right to
interfere with the internal concerns of another." Fillmore was willing to
make "private and personal" overtures to the officials of the British government on their behalf and promised to do all that was possible to obtain their release. Fillmore assured the petitioners that if the Irish exiles
were released, America would offer them "safe asylum and full protection."[26]

At the conclusion of the meeting, the delegates formed a procession and returned to the National Hotel. The members of the delegation were disappointed with the remarks of the president and concluded that there would be no "strenuous" effort put forth by the government. Reluctantly, they had no alternative but to put their trust in the president and the secretary of state to carry out the "private and personal" efforts on behalf of the state prisoners.[27]

Actually, Webster and Fillmore had become actively involved in the plight of the state prisoners even before the meeting of 22 January 1852. On 26 December 1851, Daniel Webster wrote Abbott Lawrence, the American ambassador to Great Britain, requesting Lawrence to make every effort he could to obtain the release of the Irishmen. Webster explained that the United States government recognized it would be improper to become officially involved in such an internal matter of the British government. Webster then explained, "Taking into consideration, however, the many natives of Ireland now in this country, and the influence, more or less, which they exercise over the policy of the Government, by means of the elective franchise, it has occurred to me that you might, at a proper time, and in a proper manner, make such suggestions upon the subject, in the right quarter, as would not be offensive, and might both lead to the result desired, and give it just credit for bringing it about."[28]

Neither Fillmore nor Webster made public "their private and personal" efforts until February 1852.[29] Meanwhile, many leading members of the American Congress were urging the passage of a congressional resolution asking the British government to release the state prisoners. But once again the effort bogged down over the question of whether such a resolution could be construed to be an interference with the internal concerns of Great Britain.[30]

By the spring of 1852, it was apparent to the American friends of the state prisoners that neither the executive branch of the federal government nor the legislative branch was willing to become officially involved in obtaining pardons for the exiles. Only one avenue remained open, the "private and personal" attempts by the president and the secretary of state to obtain the release of the state prisoners. The friends of the exiles now awaited word from Abbott Lawrence, who was charged with carrying out those efforts.

*   *   *

The friends and supporters of the state prisoners soon had another chance to win freedom for the exiled Irishmen, but that opportunity arose in Ireland when, toward the end of February 1852, Lord John Russell's Whig government fell from power. It had been during the period of

Russell's ministry that the Irish revolution of 1848 had occurred and that the trial, conviction, and transportation of the Irish revolutionaries had taken place. As a consequence, it had always been thought by the state prisoners and their friends that pardons would not be granted by Russell's Whig government. The Whig defeat was widely considered to have opened new opportunities for the Irish exiles.

The new Tory ministry was formed by Lord Derby. As time passed, various appointed officials of the Russell government were replaced. In Ireland, Lord Eglinton was appointed the new lord lieutenant. Shortly after Lord Eglinton arrived in Ireland, some of the friends of the Irish state prisoners began to interpret statements made to them to mean that the new administration would be willing to entertain a petition for the pardon of the state prisoners.[31] The unofficial messages appeared to be borne out by political promises, "rumoured by the supporters" of a Tory candidate in connection with a special election at Enniskillen, "that the exiles would be set at large by his government." A favorable attitude toward the pardon was also reflected in pro-Derby newspapers, which "industriously circulated . . . this boon to the people of Ireland."[32]

The friends of the Irish state prisoners promptly obtained an appropriate committee room in Dublin, drew up a petition, and commenced on 23 April to solicit signatures from prominent Irish people. Those friends made plans for a deputation to present the petition to Lord Eglinton on 17 May. The petition activities were aided by O'Brien's brother Henry, who was able to obtain the signatures of some very important men in various parts of Ireland. Financial support came from some members of the O'Brien family and was applied to the cost of the committee room. Three friends of the family, Dr. Spratt, Mr. Haughton, and Sir Colman O'Loghlen, worked hard to get the appropriate petition ready.[33]

The petition, sometimes called the memorial, was signed by peers, bishops, baronettes, members of Parliament, local government officials, clergymen, professional gentlemen, and other individuals "comprising . . . the highest respectability and station." There were approximately ten thousand signatures altogether. More signatures could have been obtained "if it had been considered necessary." The signatures included the names of "men of all creeds and shades of politics [who] would be rejoiced to learn that the prayer of the memorial was granted." The memorial asked the queen to pardon "William Smith O'Brien and his companions in penal exile" reasoning, "The state of the country at this time would justify the exercise of the royal clemency."[34]

Some prominent Irish people possessing firm allegiance to the British monarch declined to sign the memorial because it asked for a mere pardon without any suggestion that the exiles regretted their illegal acts or were willing to promise that they would not repeat such acts again. In fact, the friends of the Irish state prisoners had purposely omitted any such conditions or promises because they knew that the men in exile would not accept a pardon that demanded their confession of guilt or some promise based on an assumption of guilt.[35]

Actually, by the time the petition was officially circulated on 23 April the government opposed the pardons. Initially the Derby government had been inclined to give a "favourable answer," but gradually "as the fact became manifest the [friends of the state prisoners] were acting without authority from [the prisoners] the feeling changed."[36] The queen had also decided that the state prisoners ought to acknowledge fault before she would grant a pardon.[37] The official attitude against the release of the state prisoners was known to only a few people. One of those knowledgeable individuals was the American ambassador to Great Britain, Abbott Lawrence. On 23 April, he wrote Daniel Webster the results of his attempts to obtain the release of the state prisoners.[38]

He, too, had taken advantage of the change of ministry in order to raise the issue of the pardon of the state prisoners. Initially he contacted the foreign secretary, Lord Malmesbury, but he learned that Malmesbury's brother was married to O'Brien's sister Katherine and "could not with propriety interfere in so delicate a matter." Lawrence next spoke with the Earl of Derby about the "private and personal" request that was being made by Secretary of State Webster and President Fillmore on behalf of the exiles. Ambassador Lawrence told the earl that he believed the release of the prisoners "would cause beneficial, international results" both in the United States and in Great Britain.[39]

Derby agreed that the request of Webster and Fillmore had to be treated as unofficial and private. He assured Ambassador Lawrence that he "was happy" to talk about the case with that understanding. But the Earl of Derby was firm in his position that the exiles would not be released. Derby stated that he believed the Irish prisoners had already received "very unusual indulgence" from the British government. He did not think the indulgence was ever appreciated by them, since they had never expressed satisfaction but rather "constantly complained of their treatment." He noted that some of them had even attempted to escape. Finally, he noted that none of the Irish prisoners had ever said he was sorry, or had ever said he would never lead another rebellion against England.[40]

As to the "beneficial, international results," Derby believed that if the Irish prisoners were released and took up residence in the United States it would create bad feelings between the two countries. He believed that the exiles would be received as martyrs. Lawrence told Webster that he believed Derby spoke for the cabinet and that there was nothing more to be done at the moment. But interestingly enough, Lawrence told Webster he believed the Irish prisoners would be pardoned "at no distant day."[41]

If the Tory leadership had any doubts about their decision not to release the state prisoners, those doubts were probably dispelled by 24 April. The day the memorial was first circulated was 23 April, and on the twenty-fourth the *Nation* published the first unofficial news of Meagher's escape. In Britain the manner in which Meagher carried out his escape became critical. If it was dishonorable, it cast a cloud over the integrity of the remaining state prisoners since in the public mind they were a cohesive unit. Duffy was aware of the problem and attempted to justify Meagher with a blanket statement: "Let the lie [that his escape was dishonorable] choke him who shall dare to utter it."[42]

The editors of the *London Times* were also aware of the problem and announced that Meagher of "the sword" had taken "French leave." They further announced their belief that Meagher's flight did not help the cause of the memorial on behalf of the "misguided men" still remaining in Van Diemen's Land.[43]

The Irish memorial was to be presented to the lord lieutenant on 17 May at the viceregal lodge. Practically everyone involved in the memorial thought the pardon was assured. Some might have thought that Meagher's escape displayed bad timing, but the confidence of the petitioners was basically unshaken. The lord mayor of Dublin led the deputation. After everyone had been introduced to Lord Eglinton, the lord mayor read the memorial. Lord Eglinton then read his reply.[44]

Lord Eglinton refused to forward the memorial to the queen. He referred to the "criminal conduct" of the Irish prisoners in leading Ireland into revolution. He also dwelt on the heinous nature of the crime. He laid the blame on their "vanity or enthusiasm." The rest of Eglinton's comments were similar to those expressed to Ambassador Lawrence by the Earl of Derby. The state prisoners had received "unusual indulgence" but had never expressed any appreciation for those indulgences, and Eglinton even mentioned the fact that McManus had taken advantage of his situation and had escaped. Eglinton then stated what he considered to be the worst fault of the prisoners. They had never expressed any contrition nor had they made any statement of loyalty to the queen. Lord Eglinton was firm in his answer to the deputation. He had no intention of recommending the memorial for the queen's "favourable consideration." Obviously, the Tory ministry had no intention of pardoning the state prisoners. After hearing those words, the deputation withdrew.[45]

Public opinion, as expressed in the Irish newspapers of the time, reflected surprise and shock, but it was coupled with an unspoken conviction that the public had somehow been tricked or duped. The Irish people had been led by the press and some unofficial Tory political representatives to believe that the petition had been from the start a mere formality to enable the Derby government to do what it wanted to do all along: namely, free the Irish state prisoners, obtain the allegiance of Ireland to its administration, and thereby assure the election of Irish Tory members in the forthcoming elections. Such trickery was considered to be vicious, and the editors of the *Munster News* commented, "His Excellency's toe-nails are felt for the first time through the fur of his Excellency's paws."[46]

Naturally Duffy published a violent article in the *Nation* attacking Lord Eglinton personally and the Tory government generally. He urged the Irish people to take their revenge at the polls.[47] But what was interesting in the response of the newspapers to Lord Eglinton's refusal of the memorial was the universal attitude of the Irish press, which reflected all shades of political opinion, that the Irish state prisoners were men of honor who had been punished long enough and who should be returned to Ireland where the state of the country was such that they could be received without any fear of future violent revolution. The press also expressed an understanding of what had driven those men to revolution; namely, the abject condition of the country during the famine years, not a desire for riches or fame. Finally, there was a public recognition that bloodshed had been prevented during the revolution due to the character of the leader, O'Brien, who recognized that the revolution was not taking hold at the grass-roots level and ended the affair before it spun out of control and led to untold suffering as a result of uncontrolled violence. O'Brien had been criticized for the manner in which he led the revolution of 1848, but credit was given to him for preventing a bloodbath.[48]

If the views expressed by the Irish press were truly reflections of views deeply embedded in Irish public opinion, then the state prisoners had gained strength in their attempt to obtain a pardon. Before they could obtain a pardon, however, the state prisoners needed to wait for a new minister to take office and the occurrence of an event that would make their pardon politically advantageous to the new ministry.

*   *   *

After the Eglinton affair was completed and feelings began to subside, Gavan Duffy could at least write with some satisfaction, "Thank God a second victim [Meagher] has escaped the brutal turnkeys of Van Diemen's Land."[49] Duffy's remark could not be interpreted to mean that he was about to abandon peaceful political means as a way of obtaining the release of the state prisoners. The friends of the state prisoners in Ireland were awaiting the next election and preparing to take their fight for the release of those men to the polls and demand that any candidate running for an Irish seat in the House of Commons pledge himself to work for the release of the exiles. There was a new idea being expressed, however; namely, that redress might only be obtainable by escape.[50] The advocates of the petition had been given their opportunity and failed. While peaceful means had not been totally abandoned, escape began to receive serious consideration.

The Aftermath of Meagher's Escape

On the morning of 27 May a young man "with a bronzed and ruddy countenance, having all the appearance, in his dress and movement, of a U.S. Naval Officer," appeared at the law offices of John Dillon and Richard O'Gorman in New York and inquired if either of the partners was available. O'Gorman, hearing the voice of inquiry, suddenly realized that it was Meagher. He promptly greeted his friend, and they "were locked instantly in each other's embraces." By that time, "Mr. Dillon turned round, wondering who this acquaintance of Mr. O'Gorman's could be." He at once "recognized his long-lost associate, and a similar greeting ensued."[51]

Meagher no doubt recounted to his friends how he had escaped from Van Diemen's Land with the help of John Connell, how he had sailed to Pernambuco, South America, aboard the *Elizabeth Thompson*, and how he had booked passage on the *Acorn*, an American ship plying the sugar trade between Pernambuco and New York. The *Acorn* had sailed for New York on 23 April 1852 and had arrived there on the evening of 26 May.[52]

Even as the friends were talking, the word of Meagher's arrival began to spread throughout the city. At first the news was treated by many as a "hoax." But when a public bulletin was published making Meagher's arrival official, "the tears that were shed—the hands that were clasped, and the joyous excitement that diffused itself through the city . . . must have abundantly rewarded him for every trouble he endured."[53] Dillon and O'Gorman took Meagher to Brooklyn where O'Gorman's father had a law office. While the men were visiting, "some companies of the 69th [Second Irish] Regiment, New York State Militia, had been rounded up and, accompanied by the Brooklyn Cornet Band, serenaded Meagher." A crowd reputed to contain seven thousand people gathered, and, together with the musical background, a few words from Meagher were in order. Meagher appeared and told the crowd that he was exceedingly tired from the long voyage and that, while he appreciated their welcome, "He could not account for their enthusiasm, as he had been in no battles in Ireland." On hearing those words his admirers were "sent . . . into a frenzy of delight." One gentleman in the neighborhood, however, was furious. He opened his window and played on his piano, as loudly as he could, "God Save the Queen."[54]

Meagher probably spent the twenty-eighth catching up on all the news. He was no doubt particularly anxious to learn what had become of the other leaders of the revolution of 1848 who had made it to safety in

America. Dillon and O'Gorman later gave O'Brien an account of the ex-leaders living in America, and it is probable that Meagher heard the same report when he arrived in New York City. Thomas d'Arcy McGee had built a successful career as a lecturer, but he had ceased to consider himself a Young Irelander and as a matter of fact repented his previous connection with the group. Michael Doheny had become so infuriated at McGee's new attitude that while walking with him one day he could not restrain himself from pushing McGee into an open cellar. Doheny's main activity was in American politics. He was an active organizer and hoped someday to be rewarded for his efforts by being named the American ambassador to either England or France. In the interim he practiced law. Thomas Devin Reilly wrote for the *Democratic Review*, which was the voice of the "Young America Party."[55]

Doheny, Reilly, O'Gorman, and Dillon were satisfied with living in America. O'Gorman marveled that a political system in the hands of "intellectual Rowdies" was able to produce "out of a chaos of corruption and even violence, order and wise Government."[56] They also had some adjustments to make in regards to the social and economic scene. While the American society treated all religions equally *"before the law; in Society* it [was] far otherwise," and the "inconveniences" were "neither few nor inconsiderable," for anyone "of strong Catholic convictions."[57]

Doheny and Reilly were still actively interested in seeing Ireland engage in another revolution. But O'Gorman and Dillon were discouraged with Irish affairs, and Dillon heard only two voices rising out of the Irish scene, one the voice of "rabid bigotry" and the other the voice of "servile adulation." The European scene did not please them either. Dillon stated, "If the Queen had only shown some magnanimity [toward O'Brien] I am not sure that she would have a more ardent well-wisher than myself." Dillon had come to that conclusion when he realized it was only in America and England "where a man dares to speak the truth."[58]

But the four ex-leaders were by and large fitting in well. O'Gorman thought the Americans were "a money making people . . . and [he] who . . . does not amass dollars is held in small esteem."[59] They were all held in at least some esteem, and they were prepared to help Meagher make his way in the new world.

During the next few days Meagher was able both to meet with some of his old friends and to be introduced to some of the leading Irish-Americans of New York City. B. S. Treanor, who had known Meagher in Ireland, traveled all the way from Boston to see him. Meagher also met for the first time Robert Emmet, the son of Thomas Addis Emmet. Robert Emmet had written to Meagher in jail shortly after the revolution and had asked for a picture of him. On meeting Meagher, Emmet commented, "Now that I see the original, I do not care so much for the likeness."[60] Meagher also went to visit John Mitchel's mother, who had taken up residence in Brooklyn. Meagher next traveled to nearby Glen Cove to rest and regain his strength.[61]

The newspapers were filled with laudatory comments about Meagher, and the *New York Herald* contrasted him with Kossuth. Soon enough Meagher began to run across the controversial reports about his escape, and those reports that had been published in the Australian and British press demanded his attention. While at Glen Cove, Meagher wrote a public letter in which he told his side of the story. He wanted it clearly understood "that I am not deficient in the honourable spirit which qualifies a stranger to become a citizen."[62]

Meagher thought that by his actions he had fulfilled all of the conditions necessary to maintain his honor and at the same time flee Van Diemen's Land. Yet the opinions persisted that his escape had not been honorable, and at one time Meagher was so concerned about the controversy that he professed a determination to return to Van Diemen's Land if the matter was not cleared up. John Dillon, Richard O'Gorman, William Mitchel, and T. Devin Reilly served on a panel formed to hear Meagher's account of the escape and render judgment. Their verdict was unanimous that Meagher had satisfactorily met his parole obligations, but, since they realized that they could be suspected of partiality, an independent tribunal of American gentlemen was convened, made up of Horace Greeley, Felix Ingoldsby, and the Honorable John McKeon, to study the case and to "put the matter beyond dispute." They ruled that due to the nature of the parole "the prisoner was not bound to place himself in the position in which he was before accepting it; that he was bound to give the authorities a fair and reasonable opportunity to capture him dead or alive and that that he had done."[63] On the basis of that tribunal's decision, Meagher considered himself justified in honor to remain in the United States and start a new life for himself. Many of Meagher's friends in New York wanted to help him get started in his new life by giving him a public reception. Meagher refused the offer. He explained that he did not think it was appropriate for him to take part in celebrations while Ireland remained in "subjection" and while his friends in Van Diemen's Land remained in "captivity."[64]

But Meagher was unable to stop the flow of congratulations, and he received numerous invitations to visit a great variety of cities such as Albany and Troy, New York; Boston, Massachusetts; Cincinnati, Ohio; Easton, Pennsylvania; Detroit, Michigan; Macon, Georgia; and Chicago, Illinois. States invited him as well, such as Maryland and Indiana.[65]

The *London Times* followed the reception Meagher was receiving in the United States and concluded that the enthusiastic welcomers were all Irish-Americans, commenting, "He appears to meet with little sympathy from the American people."[66] It is true that Meagher's warmest supporters were Irish-Americans, but he had a large following among the American population as well. Meagher had the type of personality most Americans like. He was not only young and handsome, but, except for his exile in Van Diemen's Land, he was also a winner. And even in exile he had found a wife and started a family. His father was not only rich, but also generous. In addition, Meagher had numerous friends all over the world who were truly concerned about his welfare. And last but not least, he had the abounding energy and eloquent tongue that counted for so much in the New World. The editors of the *London Times* were wrong. Meagher was genuinely well received in the United States and more than any of the other state prisoners was able to feel at home in America.

*   *   *

The arrival of both McManus and Meagher in the United States stimulated interest in the other state prisoners still in Van Diemen's Land. With the arrival of McManus, committees had been formed throughout the United States whose purpose was to exert pressure on the American government, which in turn would exert pressure on the British government, to release the state prisoners. The effort failed. In addition, the American advocates of petition watched the Irish efforts to obtain the release of the state prisoners by that same means also fail. With the arrival of Meagher, the Americans abandoned petitions as a means of redress. Instead, the Irish Directory began to lay plans to aid the remaining state prisoners to escape. Meagher helped the directory lay those plans.

O'Brien and the Petitions

Initial news of the American petitions did not arrive in Van Diemen's Land until February 1852. It pleased O'Brien to find friendly assistance so well in evidence although so far away. O'Brien believed that if the American petitions were presented to the British government, there was a fairly good chance they would be accepted. O'Brien was aware that Lord Palmerston had professed "sympathy for the unsuccessful patriots of other countries"and had denounced the exercise of cruelty against political prisoners.[67]

O'Brien also believed England's best and most lasting friend was America. He believed America was England's child and there were "natural yearnings of a child towards its parent . . . which spring from a common language, a common origin and a common interest." But O'Brien also thought the American society had among its recent immigrants a large number of Irish-Americans who were anti-English. He thought the English would use this opportunity to woo the anti-English Irish-Americans to their side, since the request for the pardons could "be granted without the slightest sacrifice on the part of the English nation," and hence the English government could solidify a pro-English American public opinion.[68]

As the possibility of pardon grew, O'Brien received a letter from his wife asking him to renounce politics forever. O'Brien was not prepared to make such a promise. He told Lucy, "I would much prefer that you would invite me to shoot myself for the good of my children rather than call upon me to abdicate all the attributes of manhood." He told Lucy, "To suppose that I could live amongst men in any part of the world and not interest myself about public affairs is to suppose that I could consent to degrade myself below the beasts of the field." O'Brien, however, was prepared to make some concessions. "If the British Government have good sense and good feeling sufficient to give an unconditional pardon to all the parties compromised by the affair of 1848—and to proclaim a general amnesty extending as well to the refugees as to the prisoners now in Exile I should probably feel myself morally bound to abstain during my life from seeking to overthrow British dominion in Ireland." O'Brien explained, "But this result would be produced on my mind by the nature of the act itself not by any trickling promises which could be made for the convenience of the moment and violated and evaded whenever circumstances suggested a change of conduct."[69]

O'Brien had set his course. If the pardon was granted without conditions and to the broad spectrum of individuals who had taken part in the affair at Ballingarry, he would not actively engage in a campaign advocating Irish self-government. He would, however, never abandon his right of free speech.

Then suddenly, in June 1852, O'Brien read in the press that Russell's government had fallen. The news was greeted by him with the "greatest satisfaction."[70] He must have known the American petitions would have an even better chance of being accepted once Russell had fallen from power. But while he waited for further news, events in Van Diemen's Land captured his attention.

Tragically, the son born to Thomas and Catherine Meagher in February 1852 had died on 8 June 1852 and been buried at Richmond. O'Brien extended his sympathy, as did all the exiles, and reported that he had heard "she is much afflicted."[71] About the same time, news came that Jane Mitchel had given birth to a baby girl. John Mitchel chose to call her the "Native Girl," but her real name was Isabel.[72]

The other news reaching O'Brien at this time was all rather good. The losses that had developed as a result of the failure of his escape attempt, and for which O'Brien considered himself morally obligated, were finally met. By the end of June 1852, O'Brien learned that Lapham had just been appointed police magistrate in Victoria and was to receive the handsome salary of four hundred pounds a year. O'Brien was pleased not only because an especially able man had been returned to a useful and appropriate position, but also because his mind had been "relieved from the anxiety with which it has been so long oppressed on account of [Lapham's] amiable family."[73]

In addition, the total cost of his escape attempt had been paid by an unknown source. O'Brien received word in July 1852, from a friend of his in Ireland, Anthony O'Flaherty, that Thomas Meagher, Sr., had been repaid the total amount that he had advanced toward the debt amassed from the escape attempt and that a similarly appropriate amount of money was being sent to O'Brien to take care of the remaining expenses. O'Brien was delighted. He told Dr. McCarthy what had happened, explaining that the £215.13.9 had come from America through a friend of his in Ireland. Dr. McCarthy was as delighted as O'Brien. Several weeks later McCarthy once again apologized for involving O'Brien in such a fiasco, explaining he was unaware O'Donoghue had "drunken habits" and was therefore totally unreliable in planning and executing such an undertaking.[74]

O'Brien had been anxious to solve those problems not only because they weighed heavily on his peace of mind but also because the letters he was receiving from Ireland led him to believe pardon was imminent. O'Brien wanted to be able to leave Van Diemen's Land the moment the pardon was announced and start a new life without having to look back to Van Diemen's Land and the responsibilities of Lapham and McCarthy. He would now be free to do so.

*   *   *

O'Brien followed the political scene in the British Isles and America carefully by means of the newspapers. He knew that the success or failure of the petitions for his release would be affected by the political events of the day. When he learned that Lord Derby and the Tory government had formed the new ministry, he was not displeased for either Ireland's sake or his own. For Ireland's sake O'Brien recounted the many useful Irish measures that Derby supported, such as Catholic emancipation and national education. O'Brien acknowledged that Lord Derby was responsible for coercion laws but realized that neither the Whigs nor the Tories had a monopoly on the idea of ruling Ireland by force. For his own sake, O'Brien believed he was not as disliked by the Tory party as he had been by the Whigs. In addition Derby's ministry contained both family connections and longtime friends.[75]

When he received word that the Canadians had made "an appeal to the Queen in our behalf" and that the Irish were also preparing a memorial he grew even more confident.[76] O'Brien had always hoped that he would eventually be pardoned. But that hope had been a dream. With the American, Irish, and Canadian petitions being presented to a British government that had in its midst individuals who were not unfriendly to O'Brien and whose party might find it advantageous to their attempts to retain power to grant the request of the petitioners, that dream appeared to be a reality. On 6 August 1852, the anniversary of O'Brien's capture and imprisonment, he commented on what this new hope meant to him:

> Often have I regretted that I was not shot at Ballingarry or executed at Clonmel. Death must be terrible indeed if it be not preferable to such a life as that which I have led ever since I left the shores of Ireland. Nor could I have died in a holier cause, speaking as of worldly affairs, than in that of my country. Of late however this longing for death recurs less frequently to my mind. I am glad that I have lived to witness the sympathy which has been displayed in America and in Ireland for the Irish Exiles. I am glad that I have lived long enough to find that our efforts in behalf of a suffering land have been appreciated.[77]

It was not until mid-September that word reached the exiles that Lord Eglinton had rejected the Irish petition. O'Brien noted his thoughts in his journal: "The splendid fabric—we will call it 'the Temple of Hope'. . . . has tumbled to pieces as suddenly as if it had been a house of cards erected by a child."[78]

O'Brien wrote a letter of acknowledgment to those who had signed and presented the memorial to Lord Eglinton. He sent the letter to Duffy and asked that it be published in the *Nation.* In this letter, O'Brien commented directly on Lord Eglinton's reasons for rejecting the memorial; namely, that the Irish state prisoners had not expressed gratitude for the way they had been treated after their conviction for high treason, contrition for leading Ireland into revolution, or loyalty to the queen.[79]

As far as gratitude was concerned, O'Brien could not understand why he should be grateful. He had been prepared to be punished for committing high treason through either execution or imprisonment in Ireland "during the pleasure of the Queen." He was not grateful that ex post facto legislation was passed sending him sixteen thousand miles into exile. Nor was he grateful for the treatment he had received since arriving in Van Diemen's Land. He considered that the treatment of all of the Irish state prisoners while in Van Diemen's Land could be characterized by two words, *dastard spite.*[80]

O'Brien further noted that he was not contrite. He admitted that the revolution of 1848 had been both "rash and inexpedient." He had "miscalculated the chances of success." He regretted the revolution, not because its consequences changed his life, but because he believed the revolution had been disastrous for Ireland. Nevertheless, he stated, "Until my sentiments of patriotic duty shall undergo such a change as I do not now contemplate, I never can be brought to express of it contrition as for a crime."[81]

If there was a crime and a criminal, according to O'Brien, the crime was the English government's mismanagement of Irish affairs, particularly during the famine, and the criminal was Lord John Russell and the Whig ministry. O'Brien wrote, "I am contented to rest the vindication of my design upon the revelations of the Census of 1851." O'Brien "conscientiously believe[d]" that the loss of 2 million from the Irish population "might have been altogether prevented by wise and beneficent government."[82]

Lord Eglinton had also reproached the state prisoners for not professing loyalty to the queen. O'Brien explained that while he "regarded the interference of the British Parliament in the affairs of Ireland as an usurpation, I was willing to acknowledge the Queen of Great Britain as both *de jure* and *de facto* Sovereign of Ireland." O'Brien admitted that if the revolution had succeeded, the Irish probably would have established a republic and the monarchical connection between England and Ireland would have been broken. But with him the break "would have been a matter of necessity, rather than of choice." O'Brien admitted he did admire the institutions of the American republic, but he did not believe that the only good form of government was the republic form.[83]

O'Brien wondered why he was being asked to make a new profession of loyalty. He wrote, "I conceive that allegiance is an obligation reciprocal with, and conditional upon, good government." If the queen wished to remain on the throne, professions of loyalty were unnecessary as long as "regard for the rights and welfare of [Ireland]" was a "paramount duty" of the monarch.[84]

O'Brien told the memorialists that he was disappointed he had not been granted a pardon as a result of their request. O'Brien also realized his letter to them could be considered by the Tory government to be insulting and hence would "retard" his chances of future pardon, but he had decided he could not "forego, for prudential consideration, the attributes of manhood."[85]

*   *   *

By October 1852, O'Brien knew that on the grass-roots level he had solid support in Van Diemen's Land, America, and Ireland. His friends in Van Diemen's Land were quickly rising to an ascendancy of established power. O'Brien knew that British ministries rose and fell, and he no doubt hoped Derby's ministry would soon fall and that his grass-roots support in Ireland would help elect a new ministry favorable to a pardon. While he wondered what had happened to the American resolutions on behalf of the state prisoners,[86] he was knowledgeable enough about the

British system to know that continued public support in Canada and America would help push the new British establishment toward granting pardons for the exiles. O'Brien was not aware that the American directory was planning on playing more than a minor role in his release.

CHAPTER 8

One More Year

Denison Versus O'Donoghue and the Antitransportationists

The state prisoners were disappointed with the failure of the Derby ministry to respond in a positive manner to the Irish petitions. But the disappointment did not result in apathy on their part but rather in re-newed action to obtain their release. The next twelve months were to be a very trying period for Governor Denison not only because the state prisoners would continue to challenge his authority, but also because the antitransportation leaders would continue their campaign to defame him and end transportation. During the Australian spring of 1852, the state prisoners and the leaders of the antitransportation movement once again found common cause. The incident, which began in a local dispute over the practice of transportation, eventually involved O'Donoghue.

*   *   *

In the Australian spring and summer of 1851 and fall and winter of 1852, an official of Denison's government, John D. Balfe, came repeat-edly to public attention in Van Diemen's Land. The official turned out to have been a former political associate of the exiles in Ireland. Several articles appeared in the *Launceston Examiner* accusing John Balfe of hav-ing been a spy for the English government during the Irish revolution of 1848.[1] It was not until years later that the accusation was proved to be true.[2] In 1852 all the exiles had were suspicions, but when Balfe arrived in Van Diemen's Land with land, a job, and a magistracy, the exiles concluded that Lord Clarendon had paid Balfe for services rendered dur-ing and after the revolution. Mitchel observed that Balfe was "a man . . . eminently qualified for an office of trust and emolument under the British Government."[3]

The antitransportation forces in Van Diemen's Land did not restrain themselves from criticizing Balfe when he used his literary talents to justify and support transportation. His protransportation writings ap-peared in the columns of the *Hobart Town Advertiser* under his own name. In addition, Balfe was suspected of writing, under the pen name *Dion*, a series of vindictive attacks on the antitransportation movement and its leaders. Balfe was denounced for his divisive activities in Ireland prior to the revolution of 1848 and for his protransportation articles in 1851 and 1852, which were similarly divisive.[4]

159

The intensity of the assaults on Balfe became so great that Balfe reacted by threatening to beat one of his "suspected" opponents over the head with a large stick. That approach failed because the suspected opponent took Balfe before a magistrate and had him bound over to keep the peace. Balfe then decided to use the courts to stop the attacks on his character. He sued another "suspected" opponent for libel but lost the case. Finally, he determined to defend himself by writing a detailed explanation of his activities in Ireland in the 1840s. His defense was published in the *Hobart Town Advertiser* and the *Launceston Examiner*. Balfe denied being an English agent. In setting out his denial, Balfe insulted two of the 1848 revolutionary Irish leaders. He inferred that Meagher's escape from Van Diemen's Land was dishonorable and that Gavan Duffy was a libeler.[5]

Two of the Irish exiles, Kevin O'Doherty and Patrick O'Donoghue, rose to defend Meagher and Duffy. In a letter to the editor of the *Launceston Examiner*, O'Doherty accused Balfe of "cowardly libel" in his references to Meagher. O'Donoghue went even further. He not only announced, "Gavan Duffy is no libeller," but he next committed the unpardonable sin. He commented on government: "I apprehend Sir William Denison himself does not approve of Mr Balfe's thunderbolts; and, as to Mr Hampton, if he does not keep his 'weather gauge', and watch the helm, the Macquarie-street convict hulk may be wrecked by the imprudence of his subaltern."[6]

O'Donoghue's article was published in the 14 August 1852 issue of the *Launceston Examiner*. By that time, Denison could tolerate no more. "Without any trial or explanation" Denison withdrew O'Donoghue's ticket-of-leave and ordered him to be taken to the Cascades Probation Station for six months' work on a chain gang. O'Donoghue was arrested as he was walking along the street, and he was taken immediately to the police office and from there sent to the Cascades station.[7]

There was mixed reaction to O'Donoghue's arrest on the part of the press. As a result, O'Brien rose to O'Donoghue's defense and in a letter to the *Hobart Town Guardian* wrote, "I do not hold myself responsible for the acts of Mr O'Donoghue, but I have not ceased to feel interest for a companion in misfortune." If O'Donoghue had been arrested for "vindicating the veracity" of Duffy, O'Brien could not "withhold from him the avowal of his sympathy."[8]

*   *   *

No sooner had Denison solved his problem with O'Donoghue than he was forced to face an unexpected and serious defeat from the Legislative Council. On 16 September 1852, the antitransportation councillors proposed a resolution asking the queen to rescind the order in council that made Van Diemen's Land a penal colony. Everyone expected the elected antitransportation councillors who were present to vote in favor of the resolution, which they did. But of Denison's eight government councillors, two voted with the antitransportation councillors and one left the room rather than vote against the measure.[9]

Denison was thunderstruck. He considered the government councillors who sided with the antitransportation forces a fifth column and "virtually dismissed" two of the officials, allowing them to take a "leave of absence on half-pay" until he could seek the advice of the colonial secretary regarding their dismissal. The third gentleman had taken office with the understanding that he could vote his conscience on the transportation issue. The only positive result that Denison could draw from the incident was, "I have seen who are my friends and in whom I can trust."[10] Denison did not consider the struggle with the antitransportation forces to be over.

When the Legislative Council formally presented the infamous antitransportation resolution to Denison to be forwarded to the queen, Denison appended protransportation comments to the resolution. The antitransportation members of the council were annoyed by Denison's unsolicited comments, and they were furious when they learned the fate of two of the fifth-column councillors. O'Brien noted that under the leadership of his friend Captain Fenton the Legislative Council had passed a resolution to the queen "that the executive authority of this Colony has ceased to possess the confidence of the Legislature" and that "if such an address were adopted in the British House of Commons the minister would as a matter of course either resign or dissolve Parliament."[11]

O'Brien was not alone in drawing such a conclusion. The editors of the *Melbourne Argus* expected Denison to resign and when he did not asked, "Why is the case different in the colony?" The editors of the *Launceston Examiner* gave their answer. Van Diemen's Land actually had an "autocrat" at the head of the government, and Denison, like Louis XIV, had proclaimed, "Moi, je suis l'Etat." The editors of the *Sydney Morning Herald* called the attention of their readers to the important question at hand, namely, "SHALL [Van Diemen's Land] BE FREED, or AUSTRALIA FELONIZED?"[12] As a result of this incident there could be no doubt that the consensus of public opinion in both Van Diemen's Land and the mainland opposed transportation and Denison. The two had been linked unequivocally together. The decisions, therefore, as to whether transportation would cease and Denison be recalled were now both in the hands of the British ministers.

In fact, the decision regarding transportation was about to be made by the British officials in London. When Derby's Tory government had taken office in 1852, its position on the continuance of transportation was not publicly known. But when Parliament opened on 11 November 1852, the policy of the Derby government was announced by means of the queen's speech; transportation to Van Diemen's Land was to cease "at no distant period."[13]

Actually, the new colonial secretary, Sir John Pakington, did not delay in making a decision about when transportation should be brought to an end. In mid-December, he addressed a dispatch to Governor Denison proclaiming the cessation of transportation, effective immediately. However, within a day or two after making the decision to end transportation, the Derby government lost a crucial vote in the House of Commons, leading to the dissolution of that government and the formation of Aberdeen's coalition government.[14] As a result, Pakington's proclamation ending transportation was not implemented, the Duke of Newcastle became the new colonial secretary, and both Newcastle and his government sought additional time to study the cessation of transportation.

*   *   *

The antitransportation citizens of Van Diemen's Land would not learn about the policy set forth in the queen's speech for several months, but their growing weariness with transportation continued, as did their growing weariness with Governor Denison. Toward the end of the year, John Balfe was in the news once again, and Denison did not profit from the coverage.

John Compton Gregson had filed a libel action against the *Hobart Town Advertiser*. Balfe evidently became enraged at Gregson for filing such a suit and accosted him, attempting to beat him over the head with a "metal ended riding whip." Gregson escaped the attack and filed charges against Balfe. Gregson won the suits against both his assailants, the *Advertiser* and Balfe.[15]

Public opinion was indignant about Denison's retention of Balfe in public office. The editors of the *Colonial Times* thought Denison would like to rid himself of Balfe but could not. "He cannot—he dare not—dismiss a man whom he has employed to revile the colonists, and encouraged in all the insolence of abuse."[16] There was no doubt that Balfe's continued retention in office had further damaged Denison's image with the public.

O'Donoghue Escapes

In early November, O'Donoghue once again appeared in the news. Although O'Donoghue had originally been sentenced to serve six months in the chain gangs at the Cascades Probation Station, Bishop

Willson had interceded for him and had obtained his release after only three months. While O'Donoghue was still at the Cascades Probation Station, he had been informed that he would be released before his sentence had been completed and would be granted a ticket-of-leave if he promised not to escape from Van Diemen's Land. On 2 November he put such a promise in writing.[17] On 6 November, O'Donoghue returned to Launceston from Port Arthur. Despite his pledge not to escape, he went to his "trusty friend," identified only as G. D., and asked for his advice as to whether or not he should attempt to escape. The two men reviewed O'Donoghue's treatment at the hands of Denison. As a result of the review both men concluded that O'Donoghue "stood before God and man absolved from the moral and honourable responsibility originally implied and understood by the 'parole' entered into by myself and the other state prisoners, and without further hesitation [O'Donoghue's] escape was fixed upon." Both men thought it would be easier for O'Donoghue to obtain passage for freedom on a ship sailing from Melbourne rather than from Van Diemen's Land, so G. D. set off for Melbourne to arrange such a passage.[18]

During the first week of December, G. D. sent word from Melbourne that all was ready for O'Donoghue's escape and that he should leave Van Diemen's Land without any delay and travel to Melbourne where a ship was waiting to take him to America. The message was delivered by another friend of O'Donoghue's identified only as Mr. O'N. of Sydney. That evening, O'Donoghue and O'N. met at the home of another friend, known only as Mr. G. There O'Donoghue changed into a sailor's jacket and together with Mr. O'N. "walked at a quick pace to the Y.[arra] Y.[arra] steamer," which was to take them to Melbourne the next morning. That night O'N. concealed O'Donoghue in his own berth, and at daybreak O'Donoghue was awakened and placed on the platform of the engine room, only to be removed at 7:00 A.M. to the furnace room and placed in a stove. O'Donoghue "just fitted into it like a monster pie in an oven . . . about to undergo the process of baking." At 8:00, O'N. unlocked the door and told O'Donoghue that, after consulting with Mr. S., one of the ship's officers also involved in the plot, the stove was deemed inadequate because O'Donoghue would probably suffocate.[19]

Just at that time, the police were sighted on the dock preparing to conduct the customary search of the steamer for escaped convicts. O'N. and Mr. S. decided that there was not enough time to find another hiding place and it would be best for O'Donoghue to leave the ship. O'Donoghue was appalled by the turn of events. "It was the 9th December; my friend [G.] D. has his arrangements made in Melbourne for my reception and shipment from thence; my own hopes were buoyed up to the highest pitch of excitement—and all thus unexpectedly frustrated."

Nevertheless, O'Donoghue acted quickly: "There was no time, however, to be lost as the police were prowling about; I bade poor O'N. good morning and stepped on the wharf." There was no doubt O'Donoghue was disappointed. "What gloom, despondence, and sorrow pressed upon me a little afterwards, as I beheld the vessel with her steam up, gliding down the Tamar!"[20]

The Y. Y. steamer did not return to Launceston until 17 December, but when it did arrive O'Donoghue was on the dock waiting. His expectations in meeting the boat were not disappointed because both G. D. and O'N. had returned to help him carry out his escape plans. The Y. Y. steamer would sail again for Melbourne on 20 December, and it was decided that O'Donoghue should board the steamer on the nineteenth preparatory to sailing the next day, "and live or die I should proceed in her."[21] This time O'Donoghue's escape plans succeeded. He arrived safely in Melbourne, was spirited to Sydney, and placed in hiding while passage was being arranged for his final departure from Australia.[22]

There was very little comment about O'Donoghue's escape in the newspapers. Initially, it was merely reported in the press that O'Donoghue had been "absent from his registered place of residence." Later a news item announced that O'Donoghue had "made his escape, but the means have not transpired."[23] Finally the editors of the *Argus* noted, "The press, if they know any thing about it, are silent as to whether he had made his escape from the Island." Those editors were not silent about how they felt. "It is to be hoped, however, that the next we hear from him will be by an American newspaper."[24] O'Donoghue remained in hiding in Sydney for several weeks.

By early February, O'Donoghue's friends had arranged for him to sail to Tahiti and hence to America.[25] Before leaving Australia, O'Donoghue wrote Mr. Hawksley, the editor of the *Hobart Town Advocate*. His letter was interesting because it demonstrated how few friends O'Donoghue had in Van Diemen's Land and how O'Donoghue viewed O'Brien. O'Donoghue recalled that from the moment he had started the *Irish Exile*, through his internment at Port Arthur, his assignments in Oatlands and Launceston, and his various additional periods of incarceration, Hawksley and his paper had publicly supported him. O'Donoghue told Hawksley his support was "so unexpected, so generous and fervent, [it] has sunk into my soul." That was why he had wanted to write a letter of appreciation to Hawksley as he prepared to leave the country.[26]

In this letter, O'Donoghue explained, at least partially, why he had come under such intense attack. O'Donoghue believed the slander aimed at him was really intended to harm O'Brien and the cause of Irish nationalism. O'Donoghue had to admit, "I never loved O'Brien much; but his great nobility in general, and those exalted virtues which he so eminently possesses force me to acknowledge his great qualities." Actually

O'Donoghue considered that one of the great moments of his life had been at Ballingarry watching O'Brien's "great soul superior to fear—but so meek and subservient to mercy, to the rights of man, to virtue!!" O'Donoghue considered O'Brien to be the greatest man he had ever known in either fact or fiction. He described what could have happened during the revolution. "He could have taken towns—sacked villages—cut magistrates' throats . . . and hanged bailiffs on every tree." Yet O'Brien refused to act in such a manner. O'Donoghue admitted, "I would have executed the task, but the great pure man would have nothing but a revolution without blood." O'Donoghue explained, "He was really the immortal O'Connell, with a little more ardour on account of years, he being so much younger—and the country in its last struggles." O'Donoghue thanked Hawksley for defending him against the slander of the Hobart Town officials. But he was also thanking Hawksley for defending O'Brien and the cause of Irish nationalism.[27]

O'Donoghue sailed for Tahiti aboard the *Oberon* on 8 February and landed there on 3 April. His first call was made to the American consul, Captain Kelly. "I stated to him the particular circumstances in which I was placed—satisfied him of my identity as one of the Irish rebels of 1848—and requested that he would afford me the protection of the American flag." The consul did so and advised O'Donoghue to remain incognito during his stay on the island since there was a British consul in residence there and to book accommodations on the next vessel sailing for America.[28] O'Donoghue followed the consul's advice.

On 30 April, O'Donoghue sailed from Tahiti for San Francisco aboard the American ship *Otranto*. Once at sea, O'Donoghue presented himself to the captain and explained his real identity. Captain Kendrick was a native American, but his grandfather had emigrated from Ireland and the captain's sympathies were Irish. O'Donoghue evidently liked Captain Kendrick, referring to him as "a genuine, true-hearted republican." No doubt Captain Kendrick had fond memories of O'Donoghue. On 23 June, Captain Kendrick delivered O'Donoghue onto "the free soil" of California, and for that act he received a purse of one thousand dollars from a group of Irishmen in San Francisco. When O'Donoghue stepped ashore in California from his long and hazardous journey, he had been traveling for 185 days. His trip was not over by any means, as he intended to continue to New York. Nevertheless, at that moment he had "a light heart and [was] in perfect health."[29]

The End of Transportation

During the first week of February 1853 the citizens of Van Diemen's Land finally learned that the Derby government had taken steps to end transportation and had announced the new policy at the opening of Parliament on 11 November 1852. It had taken three months for the news to reach Van Diemen's Land. The citizens of Van Diemen's Land were generally satisfied with the news, even though no definite date for the cessation of transportation had been announced. The Launceston correspondent of the *Melbourne Argus* was also satisfied: "The question . . . is settled and so is Sir William Denison."[30]

Interestingly enough, Denison was not upset. He did not believe there would be any sudden changes. He believed there would be plenty of time to make arrangements to obtain a new supply of labor. If anyone was going to be upset, Denison believed it would be the members of the antitransportation party, for the moment was coming when they would "begin to calculate what the cost of their hobby will be to them." In a dispatch written to the colonial secretary on 16 March 1853, Denison wrote, "It is hardly necessary for me to say that I do not in any way concur in the opinion that Transportation is 'the great evil which has exercised a disastrous influence upon the highest social interests of the Colony',—or that it is 'a moral Incubus which has rendered the very name of the Country infamous, as well as depressed the development of its fine resources.'"[31]

But even before Denison had penned his remarks, the order to end transportation "immediately" had already been given. The new government under Lord Aberdeen had decided to complete the policy begun by Derby. On 22 February, Aberdeen's colonial secretary, the Duke of Newcastle, forwarded the news to Governor Denison. Newcastle justified the cessation of transportation to Van Diemen's Land on the basis that "the majority of the inhabitants of the Colony itself, and almost the whole population of the neighbouring colonies" were opposed to it. In addition he stated, "The altered circumstances of Australia since the discovery of gold must wholly change the penal character of transportation."[32] In other words, because of the gold discovery adequate amounts of free labor would be available in Australia. The ministers recognized that neither the free citizens then living in Australia nor the free citizens being drawn to Australia as a result of the gold rush wished to associate with transported felons. The new British ministry under Aberdeen accepted those realities and acted to adjust the system to meet the changing times.

By 2 May, Governor Denison had in his hand the Duke of Newcastle's dispatch announcing the policy of the Aberdeen government to end transportation immediately. Denison published the dispatch in the *Hobart Town Gazette*.[33] Western Australia was designated as the dumping ground for the convicts who previously had been sent to Van Diemen's Land. In addition, the status of the probationers, pass holders, and ticket-of-leave holders in Van Diemen's Land was not disturbed. The penal stations and the police force necessary to oversee the felons at liberty in the society were to be phased out gradually. O'Brien's hope that the British would close down the penal system by granting conditional pardons to all the felons in Van Diemen's Land at the same time transportation was brought to a halt did not become the policy.

In a letter to his mother, Denison expressed his disappointment with Newcastle's decision to end transportation immediately, but he could not help but observe, "As this has been the great bone of contention between me and my Council, I trust that we may be able to get on better than we have hitherto done."[34] Denison's problems were not over. His first six-year term as governor of Van Diemen's Land had just ended, but the demands that he not be reappointed to a second term did not cease. In the controversies over the transportation question public confidence in Denison had been seriously impaired. The editors of the *Melbourne Argus* explained the situation, "It is impossible to separate the man from his measures." Those editors believed Denison had truly earned the title "the *Champion of Rascaldom*."[35]

Actually, the antitransportationists in Van Diemen's Land not only wanted to get rid of Denison, they also wanted to forget that their home had ever been a penal colony. On receiving word that transportation would cease immediately, the Legislative Council petitioned the queen to rename the island Tasmania. That request was granted in 1855.[36]

The Arrival of P. J. Smyth

During the months when O'Donoghue was planning and executing his escape from Van Diemen's Land and the British ministers were planning and executing the cessation of transportation to Van Diemen's Land, the attention of O'Brien, Martin, and O'Doherty was concentrated on Meagher and Mitchel.

Shortly after mid-November 1852, word began to circulate in Van Diemen's Land that Meagher had arrived in New York. O'Brien was delighted Meagher had made it to safety. He was pleased when he learned Meagher had received "invitations and addresses of congratulations" from all over the United States. He was flattered by Meagher's refusal to be honored at a public reception as long as Ireland was in "subjection" and his friends in Van Diemen's Land remained in "captivity."[37]

O'Brien thought Meagher would do well in America. He hoped Meagher would have the opportunity to obtain a seat in the American Congress, display his oratorical powers, and develop into a statesman. O'Brien did not want Meagher or any Irish-American to forget that he owed his primary allegiance to his new country, the United States. But he thought there was an opportunity for these new Americans to assist Ireland.[38]

He hoped the Irish-American population would stimulate friendly relations between Ireland and America. O'Brien believed America would be a great power in a relatively short period of time. As such a power, containing a large Irish-American population, trained and active in local militias, it was not impossible that the United States would move to a position of arbiter between England and Ireland "without involving [America] in any deviation from the course of her own Trans Atlantic policy." O'Brien believed English statesmen were responsive to the dictates of self-interest, and therefore with intelligent Irish-Americans such as Meagher in the American Congress O'Brien believed American, English, and Irish interests could all be served.[39]

But Meagher's arrival in America did more than set the stage for a possible American-Irish entente. It set the stage for O'Brien to once again consider the possibility of escape. In early January 1852 Mitchel made a trip to Hobart Town and went to see Kevin O'Doherty. He found O'Doherty in his laboratory at St. Mary's Hospital. Mitchel reported, "He opened his eyes wide when he saw me, drew me into a private room, and bid me guess *who* had come to Van Diemen's Land." Mitchel could not guess. O'Doherty finally announced that an old friend from Ireland, P. J. Smyth, was the mystery man. Mitchel inquired if Smyth had been transported. O'Doherty replied, "No, my boy: commissioned by the Irish Directory in New York to procure the escape of one or more of us, O'Brien especially—and with abundant means to secure a ship for San Francisco."[40]

Smyth, O'Doherty, and O'Brien had arranged a rendezvous for that very night. The meeting was to take place at a hotel in Bridgewater, Smyth coming from Launceston and O'Brien from New Norfolk. O'Doherty invited Mitchel to join them, saying, "There cannot be a doubt of success, . . . for at least one of us."[41]

Later that day, Mitchel and O'Doherty set off together for Bridgewater. As they neared the hotel, they met O'Brien. The coach from Launceston bearing Smyth was late, so the three exiles strolled in the hotel garden, "talking of the matter in hand." They recognized "the difficulty, and almost impossibility" of all four of them escaping at once. They also agreed that the exact manner in which each escaping exile would resign his ticket-of-leave before escaping would have special importance to the honor of their cause. O'Brien accepted as proper only one way of withdrawing a ticket-of-leave, and it was agreed that whoever made the escape attempt would follow that procedure. The prisoner intending to escape would formally withdraw his ticket-of-leave at the police office of his assigned district during regular business hours between ten and three, thus affording the authorities "full opportunity to take him into custody if they are able." It was also agreed that bribery was an acceptable expedient in the circumstances, "even to buying the police magistrates." Finally, they agreed "that any force of violence (O'Brien says, short of killing) will then be allowable if the rascals attempt to secure us within their offices."[42]

The conversation continued, but, after waiting in vain for several hours for the coach from Launceston, O'Brien and O'Doherty were compelled to start their return trips to their "registered lodgings" so as to arrive at the required time of 10:00 P.M. Before taking leave of one another, O'Brien and Mitchel scheduled a meeting for the next night at O'Brien's lodgings at New Norfolk, in case Smyth would arrive after O'Brien and O'Doherty had left. Mitchel arranged for lodging in the hotel. Only half an hour after O'Brien and O'Doherty had left, the Launceston coach arrived carrying P. J. Smyth. Mitchel and Smyth "spent the evening . . . in a private room" and, no doubt, talked of all that had transpired since 1848.[43]

The next evening Mitchel and Smyth met with O'Brien at his lodgings in New Norfolk. Mitchel recorded that Smyth had been instructed "to secure the escape of O'Brien and of me, or either of us." O'Brien was "pressed" by Smyth and Mitchel to make the attempt. They argued to O'Brien that his sentence was for life, while Mitchel's sentence was for only fourteen years. But O'Brien declined, and his reasons were recorded by Mitchel. O'Brien stated that he had already had a chance at making an escape. The effort had failed and the cost had been "defrayed by public money." Turning to Mitchel, O'Brien said, "*This* . . . is *your* chance." O'Brien, furthermore, believed Mitchel would feel more at home in America than he would. He continued, "It may be . . . that the British Government may find it, sometime or other, their best policy to set me free, without making submission to them: in that case, I return to Ireland: if I break away against their will, Ireland is barred against me forever." Mitchel wrote, "O'Brien, as his friends know, is immovable; therefore, we soon desisted from the vain attempt to shake his resolution: and I then declared that I would make the attempt, in the way he prescribed."[44]

Once the decision had been made about who was to make the attempt, Smyth was anxious to accomplish the work for which he had traveled so far. Smyth and Mitchel set out for Bothwell to examine the layout of the police office where Mitchel would formally withdraw his ticket-of-leave.[45] They then set off for Mitchel's home at Nant Cottage. Smyth had been "intimately acquainted" with the entire Mitchel family when they had lived in Dublin and during that period he had also been on friendly terms with John Martin. Therefore, Smyth's arrival at Nant Cottage caused a "stir." Smyth recounted how, in America, he had become an editor of a Pittsburgh newspaper, after which he went to work for the *New York Sun*. When he told of how he had become a supporter and an advocate of an American plan to build a railroad in Nicaragua, the Mitchels began calling Smyth *Nicaragua*. Smyth's connection with American newspapers was advantageous, for while he was in Van Diemen's Land he was supposedly serving as a correspondent for the *New York Tribune*.[46]

Smyth stayed with the Mitchels long enough to take part in the family counsels concerning the escape and then departed "to other parts of the island [and the mainland] to . . . make needful arrangements."[47]

The preparations being made for Mitchel's escape apparently began to convince O'Brien of the feasibility of making an honorable escape, in preference to waiting for a pardon. On 12 January 1853 he wrote to his wife, Lucy, "I think it right . . . to inform you that unless some change for the better takes place during the present year it is my firm intention to resign my ticket of leave & take the chance of an escape." He cautioned her, "Be careful therefore as to what you may write & carry to other friends a similar warning."[48]

O'Brien had decided to wait one more year before taking such action. He hoped for a pardon that would allow him to return to Ireland and his family. O'Brien placed great value on his capacity, and on that of his children, as descendants of Irish kings and thus members of the Irish aristocracy, to provide leadership for Ireland. In that connection a new worry began to take hold of him. It was not unthinkable that in his absence his children could have developed prejudices against the Irish people.

O'Brien believed both he and his children had a special relationship with the Irish people, and he stated his ideas quite clearly to Lucy: "Above all things I am anxious that my children should be taught to entertain towards the Irish people the kindest possible sentiments." O'Brien recognized that the Irish people had their faults. "No one knows their faults better than myself." He then made his point: "No one deplores them more but they are my people—they are the race to whom my children owe their duties of patriotic regard and it would deeply, very deeply grieve me, if I were to find that irritation, occasioned by ingratitude on their part, should cause you to instil anti national sentiments into the minds of our children."[49]

The members of the O'Brien family basically looked to England for leadership and for avenues of advancement. It was during this period that O'Brien learned his wife was actively searching for an English governess. In a letter to her he unequivocally stated his preference for an Irish governess, noting, "Surely you do not entertain that *accursed* spirit of anti Irish prejudice which has been the cause of half the miseries which *my race* endure!"[50] O'Brien was even more displeased when he learned of the proposed plan "to place Lucius in the Navy." O'Brien made it quite clear to Lucy that "it is not probable that during my life I can ever consent to this proposal." O'Brien considered himself still to be the head of the family. He told Lucy that when he was dead she would be free to do as she pleased regarding the future careers of the children, but not until then.[51]

When O'Brien had left Ireland, his eldest son, Edward, had been eleven years old. By 1852 Edward had become a young man. On 25

January, O'Brien received a letter from Edward that, in one respect, was the letter of a loving and respectful son. "We are all very well & happy, indeed I think that we would be quite so if only you were with us." Edward wanted his father home but he realized the reunion was still a long way off. Yet he wanted his father to understand that the children in their own way were doing their part to help their father in his hour of trial. "We hope that you may be [home] soon, but if not that we may prove such good children that we may comfort you in your affliction."[52] O'Brien was actually very proud of Edward. He thought the boy had a good mind and more importantly a sense of "propriety of feeling and warmth of affection which is very winning," yet there was a problem. In that same letter Edward commented that the priests had incited the people to commit acts of violence during the recent elections. O'Brien decided to write Lucy about his growing concern with certain attitudes that he believed were developing in the mind of his son Edward. "I begin to fear however that his mind will be prejudiced against his own country and its interests by some with whom he associates." O'Brien urged Lucy to prevent the development of any prejudice. "Let me entreat you not to allow his mind to be imbued with those senseless prejudices against the priests and religion of the Irish people which have been the cause of so much misery to Ireland." O'Brien opposed any narrowness of mind. "Bigotry of all kinds is in my judgment to be abhorred." O'Brien was planning to ask Catherine Meagher to carry that letter to his wife, Lucy.[53]

Catherine was sailing for Ireland, where she would join her father-in-law. They would then both proceed to America for a reunion with the younger Meagher. Catherine sailed for London on the *Wellington* on 5 February 1853. Fortunately, she found someone she knew to also be a passenger; namely, Bishop Willson.[54]

*   *   *

During the Australian summer of 1853, O'Brien not only learned that his Irish-American friends were still actively interested in obtaining his release, but he also learned that his Irish friends were just as active, if not so directly.

Charles Gavan Duffy had recently run for Parliament and had been elected. Duffy wrote to O'Brien just before leaving Ireland to take his seat in Westminster, telling him that one of his objectives while in Parliament would be to raise a party on both sides of the Irish Sea to work for O'Brien's liberation. Duffy revealed that the O'Brien family had opposed his idea of making a motion on the floor of Westminster calling for O'Brien's release; consequently, he told O'Brien that he would work on his behalf indirectly. Duffy wanted to assure O'Brien that he had not been forgotten. "Ireland has often been weak, cowardly, mean spirited, but she seldom forgets those who were martyrs for her sake."[55]

O'Brien wrote to Duffy to congratulate him on his political victory, stating that he "rejoice[d] . . . in the personal triumph." Referring to advantages to be obtained through Duffy for himself and his fellow exiles, O'Brien wrote that he deprecated any public motions in the House of Commons on behalf of the state prisoners.[56]

Mitchel Escapes

Smyth was delayed in finalizing his plans for Mitchel's escape for several months. But by June 1853 all was ready. The day set for the escape was 8 June, but the village of Bothwell was so "full of police" that Mitchel and Smyth decided to put the attempt off for twenty-four hours. James Mitchel, John's second-eldest son, was sent to Hobart Town to inform the bribed shipping agents of the delay and to ask them to postpone the departure of the ship in which Mitchel was to escape. Meanwhile, Smyth took care of the police. Mitchel noted, "By the prudent employment of some money, Nicaragua has made sure that there will not be more than the ordinary guard of constables present." He was satisfied: "As matters stand, we are certain to meet not only the police magistrate himself, but also the police clerk, a respectable man, not purchasable by money, and at least two constables, neither of whom has been bribed, and both of whom will, probably, under the eye of the magistrate, attempt to do their 'duty.'"[57]

On 9 June all was ready. As Mitchel and Smyth set out for the police office in Bothwell for Mitchel to withdraw his ticket-of-leave, they met James Mitchel on his return from Hobart Town. James carried a note from the shipping agents to his father informing him that the ship had sailed. The agents maintained that "it was impossible to detain her any longer without exciting suspicion." The agents sent word urging Mitchel either to give up the attempt or to postpone it. But Mitchel had no intention of doing either, even though "there was no arrangement for escaping out of the island at all."[58] The two men continued on their way. After resigning his ticket-of-leave, Mitchel would have to hide until Smyth could arrange passage for him out of the island.

Mitchel described what happened. He walked into the courtroom where Magistrate Davis had his office and presented Davis with a copy of a note that he had just dispatched to Governor Denison resigning his ticket-of-leave. Davis read the note but remained speechless and motionless. Mitchel explained, "You observe, sir, that my parole is at an end from this moment; and I came here to be taken into custody pursuant to that note." Davis remained speechless and motionless, that is, until Mitchel bid him "Good Morning" and started for the door. At that point Davis called to Mitchel to remain where he was and to the constables to restrain him, but none of the constables made any attempt to prevent his departure. Smyth and Mitchel walked out of the building, mounted their horses, and rode off.[59]

*   *   *

News of Mitchel's escape spread quickly. On 9 June, Mitchel wrote from his hiding place to the *Hobart Town Courier* describing what had happened. Remembering the controversy about Meagher's escape, Mitchel wanted it clearly understood that he had returned his ticket-of-leave at the district constable's office during working hours and was accordingly free in honor to make his escape. There was little editorial comment. The press did not know, of course, whether Mitchel had made good his escape.[60] The most commonly believed story was that reported by the Melbourne correspondent of the *Dublin Nation*; namely, that after Mitchel had turned in his ticket-of-leave he had quickly hurried to the seacoast with two trusty friends, "where a boat awaited [him], and the patriot was soon pacing the deck of an American vessel, which at once put to sea, and has not since been heard of."[61] The government officials in Hobart Town did not appear to be overly concerned. They "gazetted [Mitchel] as an absconder and a reward of £2 'or such lesser sum as may be determined upon by the convicting magistrate' is offered for his apprehension."[62]

Mitchel actually did not leave Van Diemen's Land until 20 July. For approximately seven weeks he moved around the island receiving shelter and assistance from a large number of individuals who were previously totally unknown to him. Most of the individuals who helped Mitchel were of Irish descent and were sympathetic with his plan to leave the area. But at least one of the individuals who helped him did so because he opposed Governor Denison and believed any enemy of Denison's was a friend of his.[63]

Smyth was not only arranging for Mitchel's departure, he was also arranging for the departure of Mitchel's wife and children. Smyth booked passage for the entire Mitchel family on the *Emma*. John Mitchel's accommodations were, by necessity, booked under a fictitious name. When the time came to leave, Jane Mitchel and the children boarded first. Mitchel came on board minutes before the *Emma* set sail and, although he could see his wife and children at the far end of the deck, no words of greeting passed between them. The *Emma*'s destination was Melbourne, and, once they landed, Smyth immediately set out to get the entire Mitchel family accommodations on the next boat to San Francisco.[64]

Smyth was anxious to get Mitchel out of Australia as soon as possible. A vessel, the *Orkney Lass*, was sailing on 2 August, first for the Sandwich Islands and then for San Francisco, but there was only room for one person. Mitchel's family and friends urged him to book those accommodations with the understanding that Smyth would remain with Mitchel's wife and children, obtain passage on the first vessel to San Francisco that could accommodate them all, and then rendezvous with John Mitchel in San Francisco. Mitchel sailed on the *Orkney Lass* on 2 August. As Mitchel sailed out of the harbor he watched "the sun . . . setting beyond the blue mountains; and the coast of New South Wales, a hazy line upon the purple sea . . . fading into a dream." He noted, "Whether I ever was truly in Australia at all, or whether in the body or out of the body—I cannot tell; but I have had bad dreams."[65]

*					*					*

Smyth booked the rest of the Mitchels on the *Julia Ann*, which was scheduled to sail on 17 August. While Smyth waited, he wrote two interesting letters. The first letter was to O'Brien and concerned the possibility of O'Brien's escaping from Van Diemen's Land. Smyth was not interested in helping Martin and O'Doherty escape; he agreed with O'Doherty's analysis that both O'Doherty and Martin would be pardoned before their sentences were up. But in addition Smyth did not feel that Martin would be a wise companion for O'Brien, if an escape attempt was made. Smyth recognized Martin's "excellent qualities." But he also recognized that Martin's personality had a "spirit of contradiction" about it, "a desire to do the thing which his friends advise him *not* to do." Smyth did not want the extra burden of Martin's personality involved in helping O'Brien escape. He urged O'Brien not to "hastily decide upon taking any decisive course in conjunction with Martin."[66]

Smyth also recounted the important factors in Mitchel's escape. To begin, Mitchel was at large seven weeks between the time he turned in his ticket-of-leave and the time he left Van Diemen's Land. During those seven weeks, Mitchel received the aid of over twenty persons, some of whom were friends, and some of whom were total strangers. Smyth was convinced that Mitchel's seven-week period of being at large truly demonstrated the fact that the respectable citizenry of Van Diemen's Land was in total sympathy with the plight of the state prisoners. He believed O'Brien would receive similar help if he attempted an escape. Smyth also believed Mitchel's escape had been accomplished according to all the rules agreed to when the escape was initially planned. Mitchel's honor had remained unblemished. Smyth knew O'Brien would only attempt an escape that was absolutely honorable.[67]

Smyth also knew that O'Brien was considering the possibility of resigning his ticket-of-leave and returning to the exact state of confinement in which he was when he accepted a ticket-of-leave. O'Brien was thinking of returning to a probation station as a way of calling the attention of the Irish people to his continued exile. He hoped Irish public opinion would unite and obtain his release and his return to Ireland. If that effort failed O'Brien would attempt an escape that could be viewed in no other way than honorable. Smyth advised O'Brien not to resign his ticket-of-leave and thus allow himself to be returned to a probation station. He informed O'Brien that such action would be viewed by the public as too quixotic and would lead in the end to the collapse of the support O'Brien currently had from the public. In addition Smyth told O'Brien that he was not certain an escape was possible under those circumstances. He urged O'Brien to remain where he was and to seriously consider escape under the same conditions as those under which Mitchel had escaped. He hoped O'Brien would inform his friends in America of his decision and, if it were in the affirmative, Smyth looked forward to returning to Australia to lend his efforts to the enterprise.[68]

Smyth's second letter was a very captivating letter to O'Doherty. Smyth had been busy during his stay in Van Diemen's Land, making arrangements for Mitchel's escape, but he had also found time to fall in love. Smyth had evidently proposed marriage to the young lady, Jennie Regan, and had awaited an answer in Sydney. On 17 August, as he was about to set sail on the *Julia Ann* for San Francisco, he had not received a reply to his proposal. Before sailing he wrote to O'Doherty and asked his friend to give an enclosed message to his sweetheart, Jennie. He wanted Jennie to know that if she decided to marry him, she should send a letter addressed to him to the law office of Dillon and O'Gorman in New York City. He would then return to Australia to marry her. But regardless of Jennie's answer, Smyth announced his intention of returning to Van Diemen's Land to help O'Brien escape. Smyth urged O'Doherty, "With regard to yourself, . . . Keep quiet." He sent the same advice to Martin. Smyth stated, "O'Brien's case is the one which should now command all our sympathies."[69]

*   *   *

On 25 August, the *Orkney Lass* made a stop at Tahiti to unload cargo. Mitchel waited patiently for the ship to sail again. By 13 September, the *Orkney Lass* was ready to leave Tahiti, but on the same day the American ship, *Julia Ann*, was sighted outside the reefs. Mitchell watched the *Julia Ann* through the watch glass. He saw a boat put off from the side of the ship and head for shore. "Anxiously I watched the boat; and while it was still a mile off I recognized one of my own boys sitting in the bow, and Nicaragua beside him." Mitchel was delighted, "They have come for me." Mitchel joined his family and Smyth on the

Julia Ann. As he boarded the American ship, he "took off [his] hat in homage to the Stars and Stripes."[70]

The British Isles

Just as the ultimate decision as to whether transportation would cease could only be made by the British ministers in London, it was in the jurisdiction of those same ministers to decide whether or not the state prisoners should be pardoned. Those ministers had decided to end transportation because it was more to their advantage to end it than to continue it. Public opinion in Australia wanted it to end, and the discovery of gold solved the immigrant problem. In addition, war loomed on the horizon with Russia, and the British ministry wanted a united and loyal empire ready, if need be, to assist in the struggle.

Similar reasoning would, no doubt, affect the decision of the ministers regarding pardons for the state prisoners. Was the granting of the pardons more to the advantage or disadvantage of the British ministers? Was Irish public opinion really behind such pardons? Would the pardons unite Ireland behind English leadership if war became a reality? Could the 1848 revolutionaries be returned to Ireland without fear of political unrest? In what location would O'Brien be of the greatest value to the British ministers, in Van Diemen's Land, America, or Ireland?

* * *

The swing of public opinion regarding the pardons was of the greatest importance between March 1853 and February 1854. Once again, it was the *Times* and the *Nation* that led the way in attempting to form public opinion either for or against the pardon. The *Times* used O'Brien's reply to the memorialists who had petitioned Lord Eglinton for a pardon to support the position of keeping O'Brien in Van Diemen's Land. The *Nation* used the anti-O'Brien article of the *Times* to work toward obtaining O'Brien's release from Van Diemen's Land.

On 29 March, the *London Times* published O'Brien's letter to the Irish memorialists. But, in addition, it published an editorial ridiculing O'Brien, his letter, and his views in general. Once again the *Times* referred to O'Brien as the "misguided man" who led the country "upon the farcical course" of revolution. He was "not in a sound state of mind." He was delinquent. The editors of the *Times* agreed with Lord Eglinton's decision. Until O'Brien and his companions were contrite for their actions in trying to take Ireland into revolution, grateful for the indulgence granted to them after their conviction, and ready to express loyalty to the queen, they should not be pardoned. But most of all the editors of the *Times* wanted O'Brien and their readers to understand that the time

O'Brien took to reply to the memorialists was a waste of effort since the British government had succeeded in burying him alive. The transportation order had carried him into oblivion. "There are not a hundred people in Ireland, and not three in England, whose thoughts [O'Brien] ever crosses for a moment."[71]

On 9 April, there was a reply to the *Times* in an article published in the *Nation*. The editor of the *Nation* was not prepared to write a lengthy reply. He felt that would be a waste of words, because, "The same brutal malignity which induced the *Times* to coin the 'cabbage garden' lie in '48, animates it still, and it can never forgive SMITH O'BRIEN for having flung himself gallantly into a struggle for the liberty of his country." But the editor attempted to identify the reason behind the *Times*'s constant harassment of O'Brien. The editor believed that the *Times* was particularly mad at O'Brien because they felt he had deserted his class. "If he, a Protestant Irishman gentleman of noble lineage and ample fortune, had walked through life as a place-hunter in England, deaf to the claims of his country and the miseries of his countrymen, the *Times* would have made a 'WELLINGTON' Irishman of him, as it did lately of a wretched deserter from the cause of Ireland." The reply went on, "It is because he was true to his native land and his own manhood, and because he redeemed his order from the reproach of being barren of Irish patriots, that even in his dreary penal exile he is made the object of vilification and hatred by those who grow prosperous and fat on the miseries of Ireland." In addition, the editor could not refrain from speaking to the *Times*'s statement that O'Brien was a forgotten man. "The *Times* has made many a man think of [O'Brien] and [the exiles], and it has given the question of their liberation a prominence and importance it never dreamed of." The editor had recently learned that Queen Victoria was planning her second visit to Ireland during the next few months. He wanted the *Times* to understand that when Victoria visited Ireland, more Irish would be thinking about O'Brien "on that day than of the English Queen and her gaudy train; Ladies-in-waiting, Gold-sticks, Bearer of the Smelling Salts, Guardians of the pocket handkerchief, august babies, and all."[72]

*　　*　　*

Unknown to practically everyone was the fact that Lord Palmerston was one of the individuals who had been thinking about O'Brien. During the summer of 1853, the O'Brien family must have received O'Brien's letter announcing his intention to wait one more year for a pardon and then escape to America if none came. There was never a doubt that O'Brien's family wanted O'Brien to return to Ireland. From the moment he was transported they had done whatever they could to obtain a pardon for him. A new effort began in August 1853 when a friend of the O'Brien family, Sir D. Norreys, visited with Lord Palmerston on the subject of O'Brien's pardon. While Norreys had to admit to O'Brien that "nothing favourable has resulted from our conversation," he was able to tell O'Brien there was hope. On a personal level, Palmerston told Norreys he "would be glad to oblige" O'Brien and felt "neither personal nor political hostility" toward him. Palmerston had no hesitation admitting that he was aware O'Brien had "many sincere friends" in the Parliament and that their support had placed him "in a far better position" than when the session began.[73]

Norreys learned that the possibility of a pardon for O'Brien had already been discussed by Palmerston and Sir George Grey. Both ministers decided a pardon was "*not expedient; at present.*" Both ministers "consider[ed] it a subject which might fairly be revised in a short time and that in the meantime circumstances may have occurred which might lead to a more favourable answer to a similar application."[74]

Norreys then described to O'Brien the final moments of the interview. As he got up to leave he turned back to Palmerston and summed up his thoughts. "Well then I think I may tell Mr O'Brien that he had better have patience, and not take any step hastily which would be likely to separate him from this country—that his course is to remain quiet for the moment." Palmerston agreed that Norreys's summation was correct.[75]

O'Brien's chances for a pardon had substantially improved since the Eglinton refusal. A new ministry was in power. Public opinion in Ireland was sympathetic to a pardon. A growing number of parliamentarians favored a pardon. An ambitious political leader, Lord Palmerston, was looking for additional friends who would help him rise to further heights. Transportation had ceased to Van Diemen's Land. But one last ingredient for the O'Brien pardon was still missing, an event that would force English public opinion to accept the idea of pardon. The event was on the horizon. Great Britain was moving toward war with Russia.

*   *   *

Queen Victoria made her second visit to Ireland during the summer of 1853. The announced purpose of the trip was to provide the royal family with an opportunity to visit the Dublin exhibition. The prince consort had been the main force in developing the plans for the Great Exhibition in London in 1851, so it was only natural that the royal family would take an interest in a similar exhibition set in Dublin. It was not unlikely, however, that the queen was visiting Ireland in an attempt to bind the two countries more closely together, especially with the probability of war growing every day.

The *Nation* did not look forward to the queen's visit and advised its readers to "shun" the whole affair.[76] But the civic authorities and many of the business people decided that the best course of action was to do their utmost to make the queen's visit a grand affair and began fitting the gas lamps along the major streets with devices in the form of "crowns, stars, and the initials of Her Majesty and the Prince Consort."[77]

The queen landed in Ireland on 29 August. When she arrived in Dublin, she was met by the lord mayor and the members of the corporation of Dublin who delivered "up the keys of the city, as a gage of their fealty," and a procession then formed to escort the royal couple and several of their children to the viceregal lodge where they were staying.[78]

In the afternoon the royal family visited the exhibition for an hour, during which they concentrated their attention on the picture gallery and on meeting William Dargan, the gentleman who had financed the exhibition. In the evening, the main streets, public buildings, and leading hotels were "brilliantly illuminated." Crowds filled the avenues. The *Times* reported, "Pleasure was expressed in every face, and all seemed to think, . . . that 'the good time coming' had at last 'come' for Ireland."[79]

Between 29 August and 3 September, the queen and the royal family spent most of their time at the Dublin exhibition. Crowds lined the streets between the viceregal lodge and the exhibition building in order to catch a glimpse of the queen. How extensive or enthusiastic those crowds were depended on one's political point of view. The editors of the *Times* described Victoria's reception as a great success. The editors of the *Nation* reported that the queen's visit "has been a flat failure."[80]

Queen Victoria had visited Ireland twice in four years. It was no doubt hoped by the British ministers in London that those visits, regardless of what the *Nation* had said, had evoked loyal feelings on the part of the Irish both to the royal family and to the British nation. Only time would tell.

During the queen's visit to Ireland, there had been no petitions presented on behalf of the state prisoners. By mid-September, new petitions began to be drawn up throughout Ireland. The new effort began in Cork, spread quickly to Waterford, and was picked up throughout the country.[81] At the same time, the Irish press also began to openly discuss the possibility of war.

A reporter for the *Nation* encouraged those petitions, for he thought England was in a conciliatory mood, possibly because she was moving toward war. The editors of the *Tuam Herald* maintained that a pardon for O'Brien would unite Ireland behind the queen. Such a move would be greeted with thanks by every Irishman regardless of his "creed or political complexion." The *Wexford Guardian* pointed out the dangers of not granting a pardon. Those writers maintained that if the queen did not pardon O'Brien after such a long and vigorous exile, the Irish people would conclude the queen was vindictive "and place the prerogative of the crown in the odious predicament of an unrelenting tyrant."[82]

There was no doubt Great Britain was on the brink of war. There was also no doubt that the petitions asking for a pardon for O'Brien would be read with interest by the British ministry under such a potential outside threat.

*   *   *

Between the fall of 1852 and the fall of 1853, the struggle for public opinion had been extremely intense on both the transportation issue and the state-prisoner-pardon issue. Denison had not fared well in the transportation struggle. He had never made a real effort to influence the citizens of Van Diemen's Land that transportation had merit. He concentrated his persuasive efforts on those individuals who held power. He placed his main protransportation arguments in his dispatches to the colonial secretary. He trusted eight appointed representatives on the Legislative Council to continue the fight with the local political establishment. He relied on the progovernment newspaper, the *Hobart Town Advertiser*, and his protransportation literary expert, John Balfe, to carry the official line to the general public. Those sources of support, however, vanished during 1853. Three of his eight appointed officials on the Legislative Council as well as the colonial secretary in London changed sides, due to the rising pressure from the citizenry in Van Diemen's Land, who had seized control of the Legislative Council and joined with the antitransportation forces of the Australian League. Both the *Hobart Town Advertiser* and John Balfe discredited not only themselves but Denison as well by their libelous and violent conduct.

Denison's problem was that he was still learning. He had not concentrated enough attention on the importance of public opinion. In his first post as governor he had not yet developed the ability to build, manipulate, and, if need be, listen to and react to public opinion. On the other hand, O'Brien was keenly aware of the importance of public opinion, and his attention to building a sympathetic public opinion was beginning to bear fruit. But, like his fellow state prisoners O'Donoghue and Mitchel, O'Brien was beginning to tire of waiting for public opinion and the force of events to push the British ministers into acting on his behalf. It was that very fact that caused O'Brien's family to step up their efforts to obtain his release and no doubt caused the British ministers to watch the swing of public opinion concerning O'Brien in Ireland, England, and America more carefully than they had before. It appears there was no real doubt on the part of the O'Brien family or the British ministry as to what should be done. O'Brien's family wanted him home. So did the British ministry. O'Brien was valued by them both. There is no record that the British ministers cared if the other state prisoners made their escape to America. But those same ministers knew they had a valuable political prisoner in O'Brien. His family connections, his princely heri-

tage, and the demands of the Irish public for his release made him valuable. From Norreys's account of his meeting with Palmerston, it appears
that the ministers were willing to pardon O'Brien. But it also appears the
ministers wanted to get the greatest value from their prize. They were
smart enough to know that English public opinion had to swing with
Irish public opinion before the pardon could be granted. Palmerston's
remarks to Norreys implied, at least, that "circumstance" might lead to
a pardon. The Crimean War would probably be that circumstance, since
with the threat of an outside attack the English public would look much
more favorably on a pardon for O'Brien. In August and September 1853,
the British ministers were still observing the scene and were not quite
ready to act.

CHAPTER 9

The Pardon

The State Prisoners in Tasmania and America

By the fall of 1853, there were more state prisoners in America than in Tasmania, as Van Diemen's Land had been renamed, even though the change did not become official until 26 November 1855. O'Brien, O'Doherty, and Martin remained in Tasmania, hoping to be allowed to return to Ireland, while McManus, O'Donoghue, Meagher, and Mitchel were all leading rather active lives in America.

The Australian winter and spring of 1853 was a quiet time for the three exiles who still remained in Tasmania. Of the three, Martin was the most active. With the departure of the Mitchels went Martin's home, companions, and principal means of financial support. Almost immediately after the Mitchels left, Martin sought out new living accommodations. By 10 August he was preparing to move to the District of Brighton and take up residence at the Broad Marsh Inn. Martin needed money. By early September, he had to borrow twelve pounds from O'Brien. He was anxious to get a job, but he did not find work until the end of October, when he obtained a teaching position in the home of Mr. and Mrs. Jackson. Martin was not overjoyed with his new job, but he was making the best of it. He told O'Doherty, "I begin to get reconciled to my situation, and to convince myself that it is *pride* that irritated and almost disgusted me at first." Martin hated the lack of privacy that resulted from living with the Jacksons, but he acknowledged that the various members of the family could not be kinder to him. Martin found a friend, Father Caldwell, with whom he spent the evening hours, and on weekends he visited the Connells.[1]

O'Doherty did not have financial troubles, but he decided he wanted a change of scene and a different kind of challenge. By early September he was planning to move to the Huon District and set up a private medical practice.[2]

In mid-October, O'Brien was making plans for an extended visit to Hobart Town. O'Brien was not certain how long he would stay, but he planned to return to New Norfolk and Mr. Elwin's hotel.[3] During those closing months of 1853, O'Brien's correspondence mainly centered on recent problems within the O'Brien family circle and the growing friendship that was developing between O'Brien and the Fenton family of New Norfolk.

O'Brien was particularly concerned about his eldest son, Edward. He had recognized early in his exile that Edward's role in the O'Brien family circle was an important one. If he died, Edward would have to take his place as the protector of the younger children in the family. In addition, while O'Brien was in exile, the responsibility of watching out for the younger children rested not only with Lucy but with Edward as well. O'Brien appreciated deeply the generous attention Edward gave to his younger brothers and sisters. In earlier letters to Edward, O'Brien expressed his fear that the two younger children, Charlotte and Donough, would have no memory of a father, therefore he asked Edward to stay at home as long as possible and thus give the younger children the attention that O'Brien could not give them.

O'Brien recognized that the time would come when Edward would have to leave the family circle in order to complete his education. He therefore had expressed his wish that when that time came, Edward should attend Trinity College, Dublin, work hard, distinguish himself, and finally travel abroad for about a year in order to perfect his knowledge of foreign languages.[4]

Both Lucy and Edward agreed with O'Brien regarding Edward's role in relation to the other children. However, conflict developed when Edward began to plan for his university education. On 6 November 1853 Edward made the most important request of his young life to his father. He wanted to attend an English university that would offer him a course of study he preferred, namely, the classics, and the kind of society with which he wished to associate. Edward considered the Dublin university system to be unattractive since it was based on the cram system. Nor did he care for the society found at Trinity College. Edward finished his letter of request by saying, "This is the first time that I have asked you to consider *my* choice in any matter, and I hope it will not be the first unsuccessful request."[5]

O'Brien was opposed to Edward's request. He wrote Lucy telling her he was indignant toward her and the members of his family for encouraging Edward in his plan to attend an English university. O'Brien also gave Lucy the reasons he opposed Edward's request. O'Brien believed that by the time Edward came of age, if he attended an English university, he would be as anti-Irish as his instructors wanted him to be. If Edward disregarded O'Brien's wishes, then the boy had to clearly understand that his actions were "*against my wishes, not under sanction of my conscience.*" O'Brien also informed Lucy that he was motivated in his stand by his attachment to Ireland, "nor can I consent to waive my own strong opinion in favour of the institutions of Ireland."[6]

Neither Lucy nor Edward had any intention of disregarding O'Brien's wishes. Lucy had no hesitation in informing O'Brien that he was "unreasonable" in his "indignation against us all" for encouraging

Edward in the idea of attending an English university. She believed the tutorial system that was practiced at both Cambridge and Oxford was a better system. She recognized that while Edward had a firm grasp of math and would have no difficulty passing an examination on that subject, she did not believe that everyone "possessed equal ability to study all subjects." It was on that basis that she believed Edward would be better off attending an English university where guidance would be available in those subjects in which the young man needed assistance. Lucy closed her letter by saying, "Of one thing I wish you to be assured, that is, *your word will be his law.* He will therefore enter Dublin University next October and will I know do what he can to distinguish himself and gratify you." Lucy told O'Brien that Edward would "act according to [his] duty— even if [his] will [was] not complied with."[7]

Although the conflict O'Brien had encountered with his wife and eldest son was real, he was still held in the highest esteem by the members of his family. His sisters, Grace, Anne, and Katherine, were regular correspondents offering him sympathy, prayers, advice covering a variety of subjects such as remedies for O'Brien's poor eyesight, and informationon the new planting at Dromoland. His mother attempted to bolster his spirits by advising him to think positively and consider how other men whose careers were in the army and navy were separated for long periods of time from their families. O'Brien's mother also thought highly of Lucy and admired the way she was raising the children. She thought her comments regarding Lucy would please him.[8] O'Brien's children wrote to him consistently. His daughter Lucy was the best correspondent, informing her father that they now had a dog who was so devoted to them that he never left their side. She described walnut hunts, nightly readings by Mama, kettle-holder-making projects, and parties where they all played charades. Lucius's letters contained comments on hunting and scholarly readings, such as the *History of France* by Mrs. Markhauss. Willie, who was deaf, was pleased to report he was perfectly capable of amusing himself when he was alone and making others happy when he was in their company. Robert informed his father that he was reading *Leila* and noted, "I will send you some violets in this letter."[9] But it remained for O'Brien's baby, Charles Murrough, to describe the love that Lucy O'Brien gave her children while her husband was in exile as well as to describe the longing that the children had for their father. Charles reported, "I am growing rather tall from the hugging I get every morning when I always go into Mama's bed." He further reported that "she talks to me & reads me stories." Charles than expressed the hope of the children: "I hope the Queen will let you go because I want to see you and I want to tell you many things."[10]

At this same time O'Brien's correspondence also reflected his continued friendship with the Fenton family of New Norfolk. O'Brien told

Lucy that his "visits to this amiable family have been of frequent occurrence during the last twelve months." O'Brien looked upon their home as his home. O'Brien left no detailed record of the family entertainment at the Fentons, but he did make a collection of their poetry and sent copies of the Fenton family's poetry for the O'Brien family to enjoy.[11]

*　　　*　　　*

The *Julia Ann* arrived in San Francisco on 9 October 1853. The Mitchels and Smyth remained in California for three weeks before proceeding to New York. During those three weeks they were the "guests of the city," the principal guests at a public feast, and the house guests of Terence Bellew McManus at his ranch in San Jose. When McManus had first arrived in California he had had a difficult time getting started, since he lacked capital. After a few months he concluded, "It is really as hard to get on in business here as any place in the World." However, he expected in time to become "tolerably comfortable."[12] By October 1853, his tolerable comfort was reflected in his new ranch. The Mitchels and Smyth visited with McManus for a week. Mitchel recorded in his journal that they "cantered through the oak-openings at the base of the coast-range, and penetrated the Santa Cruz gap, amongst wooded mountains, where our senses were regaled with the fragrance of pine woods—unfelt for five years." McManus and Mitchel enjoyed this time together. They spent the entire time "talking of scenes new and old." In that environment Jane Mitchel "recovered from the effects of her long Pacific voyage." At the end of the week, the Mitchels and Smyth bade farewell to McManus. On 1 November they left for New York City via Nicaragua.[13]

*　　　*　　　*

Thomas Meagher, no doubt, was delighted when he learned Mitchel had escaped and was on his way to New York. Since his arrival in the United States, he had been active on the lecture circuit. During the summer of 1853, Meagher had been joined by his wife, Catherine, and his father, Thomas Meagher, Sr.[14] By the end of November, the Meagher family like most of the other Irish-American families in New York City was awaiting the arrival of John Mitchel.

On 29 November, the Mitchels and P. J. Smyth arrived on board the *Prometheus* at their final destination, New York City. As the ship came up the river, Mitchel's brother, William, and Mitchel's old friend, Thomas Meagher, boarded the *Prometheus* in order to give the travelers an early welcome. On landing Mitchel went immediately to visit his mother.[15]

At his mother's home, old and new friends began to call in order to tender their congratulations. Many of those friends such as Mr. and Mrs. John Dillon and Michael Doheny stayed for tea. At 10:00 P.M., Mitchel could hear music being played outside. The first tune he could clearly make out was "Garryowen." Mitchel wrote, "My friends all smile; they know this city; and they presently tell me that I must get up and prepare to receive the greetings of my friends."[16]

Mitchel spoke to each of the groups that appeared. P. J. Smyth was also called on to speak on that occasion. He demonstrated his concern for those exiles still in Tasmania: "Of our friends in Van Diemen's Land— I have to assure you of their continued good health, and I pray God the time is not far distant ere they will be with you ready to renew the glorious struggle for Irish liberty."[17]

Mitchel truly appreciated the warm welcome he had received. He was astounded to discover that the "welcoming" processions continued for several days after his arrival. He commented, "This sort of thing went on for three or four nights; there seemed no end to the societies, clubs, companies, that made it a point to come and welcome me to their hospitable land."[18]

During the period of the "festivities" and the initial weeks of settling down, Mitchel was also pursuing two other interests; namely, the plight of the remaining Irish exiles in Tasmania and the founding of a newspaper. Mitchel initially gave his attention to doing all he could to help the three Irish exiles who were still in Tasmania. P. J. Smyth had a similar interest. Both men took part in the meetings with the members of the Irish Directory where escape plans were discussed. The most immediate problem was financial. On his first trip to Tasmania, Smyth did not have sufficient funds to pay all the necessary bills. When he left Hobart Town he was already in debt by three hundred pounds. When Smyth made his presentation to the Irish Directory in New York asking them to empower him to go back to Tasmania and help O'Brien escape, he asked for one thousand pounds "clear." That sum did not include his travel and living expenses or the three hundred pounds necessary to pay off his previous debts. Additional monies were requested for those purposes. The directory agreed, and once again Smyth set off for Tasmania. This time Smyth first sailed to England. Mitchel noted that Smyth intended "to go out openly to Australia, making no secret of his object."[19] No doubt, Smyth hoped that by going "openly" to Australia to rescue O'Brien he would motivate the British government to grant O'Brien a pardon. Most people recognized that Great Britain was moving toward war with Russia. Under those circumstances, additional troops would be needed to augment the British army. Vast numbers of Irish citizens had petitioned for the release of the state prisoners. If the request of the Irish citizens was granted, it was not illogical that the Irish people would be cooperative in a war venture.

While the directory was making plans to sponsor Smyth's return to Australia to help O'Brien escape, Mitchel was making plans to establish a newspaper that he decided to call the *Citizen*. Under his leadership, Mitchel hoped the *Citizen* would "direct [Irish-American] sympathies at least aright, and perhaps prepare the way for some noble enterprise in Ireland, if this [English-Russian] . . . war should open a way for it."[20]

Meagher was originally going to join Mitchel in the enterprise, but he had already committed himself to a lecture tour in California. Meagher had not only been offered free transportation to San Francisco but as the *New York Herald* reported he had every hope that when he returned to New York in the spring "his pockets [would be] full of gold."[21] Meagher's trip to California not only postponed his involvement in the *Citizen* but it also postponed his having a normal family life with Catherine. She was expecting another child and was unable to undertake the rigors of the California lecture circuit. Her father-in-law was preparing to return to Ireland, and it was decided that Catherine should return to Ireland with him where she could await the birth of her child in comfort and security. Once that decision was made, Meagher left for California via Nicaragua.[22]

With or without Meagher, Mitchel was prepared to proceed with the *Citizen*. The first issue appeared on 7 January 1854. During the early months of 1854, Mitchel's main policy was to expose "the odious designs of England" in the East in the hope of obtaining sympathy for the Russians.[23] Finally Mitchel decided the time had come for him to do something to bring Ireland and Russia together. Mitchel went to Washington, D.C., met with the Russian ambassador, Baron Stockl, and suggested that Ireland might ally with Russia in the forthcoming war against England. Nothing came of Mitchel's suggestion.[24]

From that point on Mitchel turned the attention of the *Citizen* to American topics such as the Know-Nothings and slavery. Interestingly enough, he became the opponent of the Know-Nothings and the proponent of slavery. For those of his readers who were interested in Irish history he published his *Jail Journal*, which dealt with the Irish revolution of 1848 and the period of his exile.[25] Like most other subjects that Mitchel dealt with, the contents of the *Jail Journal* were exceedingly controversial. The peace and tranquillity that had reigned since the failure of the revolution of 1848 were at an end. Mitchel had returned to the public arena.

* * *

On 1 October 1853 word reached the British Isles of Mitchel's escape. Unlike O'Donoghue's successful escape, which received rather little publicity, not only did Mitchel's escape and triumphant arrival in

San Francisco and New York receive complete coverage in the press, but also editorial judgments relating to his escape and welcome in America were rendered at periodic intervals by both the *Times* and the *Nation* over the next eight months.

The editors of the *London Times* had no hesitation in making known their editorial view regarding Mitchel's escape and his triumphant arrival in America. On 3 October 1853 those editors initially reported to their readers the fact that Mitchel had escaped. They concluded, "Who would have thought of the doughty editor of the *United Irishman*—the incarnation and moving spirit of the treason of 1848—breaking gaol like the veriest pickpocket that ever came under the judicial notice of the Recorder of Dublin?" As to the welcoming ceremonies that the citizens of New York gave Mitchel, the editors warned all Americans that Mitchel was a violent man, prone to using extreme measures in order to obtain his goals, and that it would not be long before Mitchel would show his real character. According to the *Times*, it would not be long before American leaders would wish that Mitchel would go some place else to live.[26]

Duffy of the *Nation* hesitated to make his editorial comment. Mitchel was not one of Gavan Duffy's favorite persons. For the moment, he merely reported the details of the escape. The animosity between the two men was not evident.

Just as the *Times* was lambasting Mitchel and the *Nation* was giving ample coverage to the details of Mitchel's escape, the announcement was made that O'Brien had escaped. Duffy had no hesitation in making an editorial comment on that occasion. He wrote, "It is the happiest news we ever read." Duffy also announced that if the report was true he would sail to America "to clasp the hand of O'Brien, a free man."[27]

The *Times* was more cautious in reporting O'Brien's escape. It waited to discover whether or not the rumor was true. Within ten days of the initial report it announced, "Such as have any real regard for the honour and good faith of Mr Smith O'Brien will scarcely be displeased to learn that he had not imitated the example of his late fellow prisoners, and that the reports of his flight are totally destitute of foundation."[28] The *Times* appeared to have mellowed regarding O'Brien during this period.

*   *   *

There was one other event that occurred toward the end of January 1854 that was of interest to the Irish exiles and those who followed their activities. Yet very little comment was made by either the exiles or the press regarding the event. Unexpectedly, Patrick Denis O'Donoghue died. Since his arrival in America, it appears that O'Donoghue made the newspapers only once prior to his death. That was on the occasion of a birthday celebration held by the citizens of Boston to honor Meagher. O'Donoghue had attended the affair and while attempting to speak found himself being silenced by the acting chairman, B. S. Treanor. Shortly afterward the lights went out and a fight ensued. The quarrel continued during the next day. Treanor reacted by challenging O'Donoghue to a duel. O'Donoghue reacted by accepting the challenge. Their friends had them both jailed until their tempers cooled.[29]

O'Donoghue's next appearance in the press was his death notice. He died on 22 January 1854 while residing in Brooklyn, New York. The editors of the *Nation* announced, "The immediate cause of his demise was diarrhea; but his constitution had been previously impaired and his nervous system was considerably shattered." O'Donoghue had anxiously been awaiting the arrival of his family from Ireland when he was taken ill. As his illness grew more serious, the arrival of his family took on a greater importance. Mr. Henry, O'Donoghue's landlord, heard that the ship on which O'Donoghue's family had traveled from Dublin "arrived on Saturday afternoon [21 January] at quarantine ground, Staten Island." On Sunday morning, 22 January, "Henry . . . attempted to board the vessel," but the bay was too rough. O'Donoghue was aware his family had made the journey safely, he thanked God and announced, "I will now die easy and contented." Shortly after, he breathed his last. His relatives had arrived too late. "Their feelings of woe and desolation can be more easily imagined than described."[30]

In the *Citizen*, Mitchel placed the responsibility for O'Donoghue's premature death on the "liberal . . . statesmen of England." Mitchel co-operated with a committee seeking funds for O'Donoghue's wife and child. He published the appeal of the committee, which acknowledged O'Donoghue was "not great or gifted" but that he had "courage and de-votion to a desperate cause." The committee concluded, "If he had faults, let them lie with him."[31]

Mitchel was not listed among those who attended the funeral, and at O'Donoghue's inquest, his landlady, Mrs. Henry, attacked Mitchel, Meagher, and Smyth. She considered them to be a "money-making pack" who "were not true to one another." At the time of his death, O'Donoghue's total wealth was a draft for one hundred and fifty dollars.[32]

Palmerston Announces the Pardon

By the beginning of 1854, the British ministers had decided to par-don O'Brien. It would appear that O'Brien was more valuable to the ministry in Ireland than in Tasmania or America. In fact, the Tasmani-ans did not want him. Transportation had ceased, and conditional pardons were being given out to many of the convicts holding tickets-of-leave. The Tasmanians had already spoken in favor of pardons for the Irish revolutionaries. They had no interest in the continued incarceration of those men.

The Americans were willing to receive O'Brien. The fact was that four of the prisoners had already escaped to America and received warm welcomes. At the moment P. J. Smyth was openly returning to Australia to aid O'Brien's escape. It was evident that as long as O'Brien held a ticket-of-leave it would be almost impossible to stop him from escaping, if he decided to do so. Since the Eglinton affair, there had always been some thought that the presence of O'Brien in America would be dangerous for the peace of Ireland, as well as for British-American relations.

The Irish wanted him home. The Irish had repeatedly petitioned for his pardon. Ireland was quiet. The country was still attempting to restore itself from the devastation of the famine. The Repeal Association had collapsed, and no comparable organization had replaced it. There was no danger that O'Brien could set off another revolution. The British could also see a positive benefit to be gained from returning O'Brien to Ireland. The possibility of war with Russia was growing more certain every day, and the British ministers needed the united and loyal support of the Irish. It was logical to assume that the Irish would give that support as a sign of their appreciation for O'Brien's release.

In addition, it was quite probable that both Lord Aberdeen and Lord Palmerston could see ways in which the pardon would benefit them directly. Members of the O'Brien family as well as close personal friends were in the ministry and asking for the pardon. No doubt Aberdeen wanted and needed their support. In addition Palmerston had personal ambitions. Both men knew they would profit from the grateful response of O'Brien's politically powerful family and friends.

The fact was that the British ministers had more to gain by pardoning O'Brien now then they ever had had before. The editors of the *Launceston Examiner* had always maintained that the state prisoners were sent to Van Diemen's Land to live temporarily in retirement but would eventually be pardoned. O'Brien basically agreed with that statement, but he believed the British would only bring him out of exile if they were pressured into doing so. That was why he struggled so fiercely to prevent gentlemanly oblivion and why he encouraged sympathetic support. By the winter of 1854 O'Brien had a solid base of support. The antitransportation leaders in Van Diemen's Land, the Canadian legislators, the state prisoners in America, the Irish-Americans and the American politicians, Gavan Duffy and the Irish people, as well as O'Brien's family and close personal friends contributed to building an advantageous position for O'Brien that tipped the scale in his favor. The impending war in the

Crimea was the event that made him especially important. In February 1854 the moment for his release had come.

During the winter of 1854, members of the British ministry worked on the details of a pardon for O'Brien without giving the public any reason to suspect that they were doing so. From the first days following the convictions of the Irish state prisoners, there had always been rumors that they would be pardoned, so in early February 1854 when the *Liverpool Courier* reported that O'Brien would be pardoned it appeared merely to be publishing another of many such rumors. Expectedly, the *Nation* reprinted the article "with hesitation and anxiety."[33]

O'Brien's friend Isaac Butt, who was a member of Parliament, expressed his intention in mid-February to formally ask the ministry whether or not the most recent rumor had any factual basis. Butt's formal inquiry was scheduled for late February. On 21 February 1854, James Buchanan, the American ambassador to Great Britain, had an interview with the home secretary, Lord Clarendon, regarding "the propriety of emancipating Smith O'Brien from his condemnation and banishment to the Australian Island."[34] The results of the interview were not made public. When Parliament convened on 22 February, Butt was late in arriving. The inquiry went forward and the question regarding the release of O'Brien was asked by another friend, F. B. Beamish. Viscount Palmerston answered that the matter had been considered by the members of the government. "The facts appear to be, that while some of those persons who were transported with Mr Smith O'Brien have thought fit to break their parole, and have escaped from the place of their destination, Mr Smith O'Brien himself, whatever might have been his faults and guilt, has acted like a gentleman, and has not taken advantage of opportunities for escape of which, if he had been a less honourable man, he might have availed himself." Palmerston then announced, "It is, therefore, the intention of Her Majesty's Government to advise the Crown to extend to Mr Smith O'Brien the means of placing himself in the same situation, by an act of clemency on the part of the Crown, in which those other persons have placed themselves by a violation of the pledges which they had given."[35]

Later on that same evening Isaac Butt arrived at Westminster. After being informed by his friends that Palmerston had promised to grant O'Brien a pardon, Butt made an additional request accompanied by an astute observation. He asked that John Martin and Kevin O'Doherty be granted a similar pardon. Butt connected the pardons to the impending war: "After the compliments which had recently been paid to Irish loyalty, and the readiness with which Irishmen had come forward to assist the country now that there was a prospect of war, it would be a grateful act of mercy, of which the government might well avail themselves."[36]

Word of the promised pardon reached the O'Brien ancestral estate, Dromoland, on Friday, 24 February. The *Nation* reported that "two immense bonfires were lighted at Dromoland Gate." Several houses in the immediate area were illuminated, and in one portraits of the exiles were displayed in the windows. The nearby village of Clare was totally illuminated, and the village of Ennis was partly lighted in celebration. While the citizens of nearby Newmarket did not have bonfires or illuminations, it was reported that the inhabitants were "overjoyed . . . when they learned the glad tidings of the release of Mr William Smith O'Brien from penal bondage."[37] Amid the jubilation, the O'Brien family wrote a letter to their exiled kinsman, congratulating him and giving him some explanation of what had happened. O'Brien's sister Grace, who was responsible for most of the news, wrote,

> With what joy did we read that Palmerston declared in the House that you were to be let go where you pleased out of Her Majesty's dominions. It is what our hearts have so long desired and there seemed just no hope. All seemed sinking down so.—Only that we knew among private friends an effort was in the making. William Monsell with his kindness and enthusiasm always working the point and arranging it in a manner that would make it acceptable to you. Mr Gladstone [a] personal friend of Harriet's and her dear husband Charles, while Sidney Herbert with a good feeling towards you on the part of the Duke of Newcastle made his feelings thus, if the present ministry did not do something it would never be done. Oh if you knew what overwhelming joy it brought . . . at the thought we might clasp you in our arms. . . . We all take it for granted that this is but the first step.—Home with us all.—Well pleased with how it was received in the House.—And you may be sure there is no lack of bonfires in and about this part of the world. I never knew Mama before having any zeal for bonfires but poor thing she was quite overcome and on the farm they had a grand one. Gave out porter."

O'Brien's sister Harriet wrote, "The thought of you as a free man makes my heart feel light." She said that while O'Brien's brother Lucius was not in good health, and had even been forced to abandon his position on temperance and have an occasional drink for medicinal purposes, he appeared to be regaining his health, and with the news of O'Brien's pardon Harriet believed that "he will be able to dance an Irish jig on your arrival even though as Kate says you will find three sisters grown old." Harriet also informed O'Brien that his wife, Lucy, was not with them at Dromoland when the news of the pardons came to them, as she had been called back to Cahirmoyle respecting some domestic problem. Harriet attributed much of the credit for the pardon to her brother-in-law, William Monsell, "a true friend in the matter asking always about you—just as you would have liked." She in turn attributed Monsell's hard work to the urgings of her late husband, Charles, and assured O'Brien that "he never had a truer friend than her Charles." Harriet allowed herself to imagine how she would feel at their reunion: "Alone: I shall be alone. I shall none the less feel that dear Charles is beside me." Harriet concluded by assuring her brother that there was a "general feeling of respect for you—shown by all parties."

O'Brien's mother offered her "congratulations—on the happy prospect so unexpectedly opened." She was overjoyed with the news, "I do indeed trust it will open a new era in your life and [the lives of] your wife and children." She hoped the "blessings of God" would descend on them all. Lucius wrote, "I am rejoiced to be at home just at this moment to witness and join in the general joy." Grace wrote a final admonition, "Come back as quickly as you can and come as near as is possible. I hope my next holiday will be taken to pay you a visit but when can we see you and how will you come? We want to know so much and we have to wait so long."[38]

On 25 February the *Nation* published an editorial concerning Palmerston's recent statement in Westminster. "Never did happier news come across the channel. Never, never." Those editors believed, "When centuries have passed away, when the loud-sounding titles of the generation are buried in almanacs or lost in Lethe, we profoundly believe SMITH O'BRIEN will be a name in Ireland to typify the highest patriotism and honour, as his great ancestor still typifies national courage after eight hundred years."[39]

By early March the government had still not made any statement as to whether or not Martin and O'Doherty would receive similar pardons. It remained for a newspaper, the *Observer*, to announce that Martin and O'Doherty would "probably" also be pardoned. The editors also made it clear that the only condition attached to the pardons was that the men could not return "within her Majesty's dominions."[40]

Once the decision was made, Palmerston officially announced that several other individuals who were then serving sentences as transported felons in Tasmania were also to receive pardons. In addition to Martin and O'Doherty, pardons were to be granted to three English Chartists, Frost, Williams, and Jones, who had been convicted of high treason in 1839 for taking part in the Newport riots. It had been noted that the conduct of those convict Chartists "had been most exemplary, and had been so represented by the Governor of Van Diemen's Land."[41]

After those announcements, the *Times* gave its editorial opinion of the pardoning of the Irish state prisoners. Those editors believed Ireland was ready for such a pardon. It had become "prosperous and contented" by not following the advice of the agitators. Those editors assumed O'Brien "must now be painfully aware of the fallacy of his views." But whether or not O'Brien was aware of his mistaken notions he was "entitled to the respect of his countrymen and of his opponents, as far as his personal character is concerned. No man has given more terrible proofs of sincerity, and we are fully disposed to admit that the manner in which he has conducted himself during his exile, and his respect for his plighted word, fully entitle him to favourable consideration. Others will respect the man who has respected himself."[42]

The Public Arena

In the winter of 1854, even before the news of the pardons of O'Brien, Martin, and O'Doherty had reached Tasmania, the public in Great Britain and America learned for the first time of the controversies that had long divided Mitchel and Duffy. Mitchel had decided to publish his *Jail Journal* in the *Citizen* in serial form. As copies of the *Citizen* arrived in Ireland, Duffy published the installments of Mitchel's *Journal* in the *Nation*. Duffy must have suspected that the *Jail Journal* contained passages critical of his actions during the crucial months of 1848. Nevertheless he published the installments as they arrived in Ireland. It was not long before critical passages did appear. Mitchel criticized Duffy for appearing during his five trials in 1848–1849 to be opposed to violence and for allowing a memorial to be presented at the close of the fifth trial begging for his release. Duffy was prepared for the criticism and declared he had remained silent for five and a half years regarding his opinion of John Mitchel because Mitchel had been in jail. Now Duffy explained, "There is no longer any impediment," Mitchel was a "free man."[43]

On 13 April 1854 Duffy answered the charges made by Mitchel by means of a public letter published in the *Nation*. He saw nothing wrong with the statements made at his trial depicting him as a man opposed to violence. As to the memorial presented on his behalf, he had no control over its contents. Duffy then charged Mitchel with being an "ingrate," a "slanderer," and a "hypocrite."[44]

All of Duffy's previous charges were minor compared with the final charge. Duffy now made his editorial comment regarding Mitchel's escape, namely, that Mitchel had not escaped Tasmania with honor. Duffy maintained that Mitchel's friends in America "hang their heads in shame" over the dishonorable act.[45]

On that same day, 13 April, Duffy wrote his friend Thomas Meagher a private letter asking him to stand by him and "separate himself publicly from the slanders of Mr Mitchel." On 25 April Duffy wrote a public letter to Thomas Meagher that was published in the *Nation* on 29 April and entitled "The Principles and Policy of the Irish Race." It had been reported in Ireland that Meagher had been making speeches advocating the exclusion of priests from Irish politics and the adoption by the Irish people of the deistic philosophy of Giuseppe Mazzini. Duffy asked Meagher to repudiate those charges. He reminded Meagher of their final conversation before Meagher was sent into exile, when Meagher stated, "If Ireland is to have a new birth, she must next time be baptised in the Old Holy Well." Duffy informed Meagher that that policy had been adopted by the new Young Ireland party and recognized as "memorable among wise men for its truth."[46]

Unfortunately, it was not long after Duffy had written his public letter to Meagher, which for all intents and purposes meant the end of a long and valued friendship, that the death of Meagher's twenty-two-year-old wife, Catherine, was announced. Several weeks before, Catherine had given birth to a son, who was named Thomas Francis. Then suddenly on 9 May 1854 she died.[47] The *Nation* made the announcement "with feelings of profound sorrow."[48]

*   *   *

By the end of May, John Mitchel's reply to Gavan Duffy's letter of 13 April had arrived in Ireland. It appeared in the 27 May edition of the *Nation*. Naturally, Mitchel denied being an ingrate, a slanderer, and a hypocrite. He refused to even discuss the charge that his escape from Tasmania had been dishonorable. But seven of Mitchel's friends answered for him. Three of those individuals were John Dillon, Richard O'Gorman, and Terence McManus. All seven stated unequivocally that John Mitchel's escape had been honorable. Mitchel commented that he had made the only reply possible "to the venomous slayer of this dead dog."[49]

Meagher reacted to Duffy's private and public letters to him by means of a short note explaining that he did not wish to correspond with Duffy on any subject until Duffy retracted his charge that Mitchel had escaped from Tasmania in a dishonorable manner.[50] Duffy commented in the *Nation* that even though he realized Meagher's response was written during a period of severe emotional upset, due to the recent death of Catherine, and even though he was truly fond of Meagher, he did not believe he could retract his statement that Mitchel's escape was dishonorable. He explained, "I might . . . as . . . [well] retract the Apostles' Creed." Duffy considered Mitchel's escape to have been a farce since Duffy had heard that the arresting officer was bribed not to take Mitchel into custody. As to Meagher's refusal to discuss the anticlerical and deistic statements attributed to him, Duffy concluded that Meagher's role as an Irish leader was at an end.[51]

The press in both America and the British Isles had been following the battle of words taking place between Duffy and Mitchel and ultimately between Duffy and Meagher. The *Irish American* had nothing but regret about the whole incident. It remained for the *New York Truth Teller* to discuss the importance of the war between Duffy and Mitchel. Those

editors believed that while both Duffy and Mitchel had the right to criticize each other, they had both gone too far in their remarks. "There are
limits to the weapons used in discussion, and we believe that both have
trespassed too far on the forbidden regions of personality." The editors
lamented the fact that in the future the two men would never be able to
cooperate with one another.[52]

Actually, Mitchel, Meagher, and Duffy all suffered from a quarrel in
which too much had been said. Mitchel had cast a cloud of suspicion
over Duffy's actions during and after the revolution of 1848. But just as
Duffy's career had been clouded, so had Mitchel's and Meagher's. Both
men still had loyal followers in Ireland, but Mitchel's outspoken advocacy of slavery had not been well received by the majority of the Irish
people. Meagher's reported statements on the impropriety of the clergy
becoming involved in political affairs and his seeming adherence to
deism were not well received either. Many Irishmen believed that if
Mitchel or Meagher wanted a public career it would be best for them to
remain in America. Duffy would shortly begin to think about immigrat-
ing to Australia.

*   *   *

Years before, when Mitchel had arrived in Tasmania and met the
other state prisoners at the lakes, he had marveled at the cooperative,
friendly relationships that existed between the men. But even then he
was aware that once they returned to the public arena arguments and
differences would probably develop.

Mitchel had been right. The state prisoners were only human. As
they returned to an active life their different attitudes toward solving the
Irish problem reasserted themselves and the controversies between the
men that had existed before the revolution of 1848 returned. As debate
developed, two important questions surfaced. The first question was
whether debate could take place without personal involvement and vin-
dictiveness. Mitchel and Duffy had failed that part of the test. The second question was whether the positions taken by each leader made him
more or less of an Irish leader. It appears that both Meagher and Mitchel
were losing ground in that regard.

The Exiles Leave Tasmania

The distance between the British Isles and Tasmania delayed the
news of the pardons, which had been announced on 22 February, and
the declaration of war, which had been made on 28 March. During the
Australian fall of 1854, O'Brien, Martin, and O'Doherty were unaware
of either event. Martin continued to stay with the Jackson family and to

serve as the tutor to their children. O'Doherty's medical practice in the Huon District had proved to be a disappointment. O'Brien attempted to urge O'Doherty to exert greater effort, writing, "Try again! is the motto of the brave man and I have no doubt that by perservering in your efforts you will eventually attain the object of your hopes."[53]

By that time O'Brien had, no doubt, received Norreys's letter containing the information that Palmerston was not quite ready to ask the queen to extend a pardon to him. But through it all O'Doherty continued to believe that a pardon would be coming very shortly for them all. O'Brien commented to O'Doherty, "I cannot say that I entertain any such expectations as that which you cherish with respect to the probability of our release but I shall strive to bear with fortitude the continued prolongation of exile." He could not help but say, "How happy should I be if like you I could hope to return home in four years."[54]

During April, O'Brien found it necessary to move. Mr. Elwin had decided to give up the hotel business and had sold his establishment. O'Brien applied for and received permission to reside in Hobart Town, but after examining the accommodations available to him there he decided to accept an offer from a Mr. Espy who lived in the district of Richmond. Espy had a cottage, in which O'Brien occupied two rooms. O'Brien was also attracted to the Richmond district because his dear friend Father Dunne resided there.[55]

Then, unexpectedly, unofficial word was received in the Australian colonies in mid-May that the state prisoners had been pardoned. On the mainland, the editors of the *Sydney Morning Herald*, the *Sydney Empire*, and the *Melbourne Argus* all made the same general editorial comment. They believed the pardon was a result of the request of the Irish people and had nothing to do with the actions of the state prisoners. The editors of the *Argus* were truly astounded at the rationale that Palmerston had given for granting the pardons; namely, that since four of the Irish prisoners had broken their word and escaped, O'Brien should be pardoned for not acting in such a dishonorable manner. The editors commented, "If this reasoning be worth anything, it will apply with equal force to the case of every individual who has been sent to Van Diemen's Land to expiate his political sins." Those editors were pleased to learn that the English Chartists, Frost, Williams, and Jones, as well as the Irish prisoners, Martin and O'Doherty, had received similar pardons. They concluded that the British ministry appeared to have arrived at the just decision as an afterthought.[56] In Tasmania the editors of the *Hobart Town Courier* were similarly concerned.[57]

P. J. Smyth arrived in Melbourne shortly ahead of the news of the pardon and waited patiently in Melbourne for such news. If it had not come within a reasonable period of time, he would have attempted to proceed to carry out the instructions of the Irish Directory; namely, to aid O'Brien and, if possible, the remaining state prisoners to escape. On 16 May 1854 Smyth wrote O'Brien a letter containing the "glorious" news that a report of the pardon had appeared in the Melbourne papers. Smyth also announced that the pardon extended to Martin and O'Doherty. After congratulating O'Brien, Smyth announced he would be coming to Tasmania shortly.[58] Smyth wanted to make the departure of the state prisoners from Australia a celebrated event. He delayed his departure to Tasmania in order to initiate plans for such a celebration in Melbourne. At that point Smyth had £1,650 in his possession, money given to him by the American Irish Directory to help O'Brien escape. In making plans to celebrate the departure of the exiles from Australia, he made himself responsible for debts that were eventually satisfied out of at least part of the escape-fund money. Such a decision eventually came to haunt him, but at the moment Smyth had no premonition of difficulties. Smyth began to plan the festivities by contacting friends of his in Melbourne whom he believed would help him honor the exiles before their departure. Once Smyth had started the Melbourne celebration committee on the right path, he moved on to Hobart Town to establish a similar committee.[59] Meanwhile, a committee had already been formed for that purpose in Launceston. On 23 May the Launceston committee wrote O'Brien inviting him to attend a celebration for the purpose of demonstrating "Irish feeling." While the committee wished to honor O'Brien, they hoped to avoid "any Political colouring."[60]

On 26 May, O'Brien sent word to the Launceston committee that he appreciated their offer. Once the pardon was confirmed, O'Brien was exceedingly anxious to leave Tasmania as soon as possible. But he could not bring himself to turn his "back upon the friends who in the North have evinced so much kindly feeling towards us." He therefore resolved to go to Launceston for the celebration.[61] As the Hobart Town and Melbourne celebration committees contacted him he accepted their invitations as well. Finally, a group of his friends in New Norfolk expressed their wish that O'Brien dine with them prior to his departure.

The official pronouncements regarding the declaration of war and the pardons for the state prisoners did not arrive until 26 June. Denison took the war news very calmly, commenting, "We exhausted our fears in anticipations, and have none left for the reality."[62] The information regarding the pardons was published in the *Government Gazette* on 27 June, and the actual pardons were forwarded to the state prisoners "without note or comment." The pardons had no conditions attached to them other than the stipulation that the men could not return to the British Isles. There was no need to make an application or sign any forms or apologize. Lady Denison did comment on the news of the pardons for the state prisoners and the Chartists, "These [Chartists] deserve it as far as they can do by good conduct during their imprisonment: this can hardly be said for Smith O'Brien and Co."[63]

On 28 June, O'Brien wrote his wife informing her that he had received his pardon on the day before. O'Brien told Lucy it had been unnecessary to make any application in order to receive the pardon. He also told her that he had "resolved not to say or write or do any thing which could be interpreted as a confession on my part that I consider myself a 'criminal' in regard to the transaction of 1848." O'Brien had been ready to face the consequences of a pardon requiring a confession. "I had made up my mind that not withstanding the demonstration made in the House of Commons I should be left to die in V D L *alone*." O'Brien told Lucy his spirits were excellent, "though I am unable to tell you which is the next spot in the world from which I shall write you, still less when we shall meet." O'Brien closed his letter "with affectionate love to all friends who are entitled to such love."[64]

It was on 28 June that O'Brien actively began to make plans to leave Tasmania. On that date also Sir George Grey wrote Denison informing him that he too was to leave Tasmania. Denison was to become the governor of New South Wales. Denison did not receive Grey's letter for many weeks, but when he did receive it he was pleased. In a letter to the Duke of Newcastle, Denison admitted he was probably going into an area where there would be a prejudice against him. Yet he believed he had always advocated measures that had merit and if he continued to follow such a policy he would be able to get along in New South Wales.[65]

Lady Denison was delighted with the news. Her husband was quite young to receive such a post. In addition, the promotion made their removal from Tasmania especially sweet since such an appointment was a "triumph."[66]

*   *   *

When it was time for O'Brien to leave Tasmania he was entertained first at New Norfolk, then at Hobart Town, and, finally, at Launceston.[67] On all three occasions the assembled groups were chaired by leaders in the community who were friends of the state prisoners. Captain Fenton chaired the celebration at New Norfolk, W. Carter the one at Hobart Town, and Mr. Dry the one at Launceston. Captain Fenton was a member of the Legislative Council, Carter had recently been elected mayor of Hobart Town, and Dry was the speaker of the Legislative Council. All three groups presented O'Brien with an address signed by citizens attesting to the purity of his motives in leading Ireland into revolution and evincing admiration for the fortitude that he had displayed while in exile. O'Brien made remarks at each celebration thanking those assembled for being there and expressing appreciation to the Irish people for participating in his sorrows and working strenuously for his release. He also explained he was sustained in exile "only by consciousness that my sufferings have been incurred in an endeavour faithfully to discharge the duty which I owed to the land of my fathers."[68] Martin and O'Doherty were present at the Hobart Town and Launceston celebrations and also made a few remarks.

By 7 July, the festivities in Tasmania were over, but the Hobart Town correspondent of the *Melbourne Argus* was disappointed in what he had observed. The writer admitted that O'Brien, Martin, and O'Doherty were honorable men and did justifiably deserve congratulations on the announcement of their pardons. Yet he noted that the queen was getting very little credit for granting the pardons and that none of the pardoned state prisoners expressed regret at having engaged in revolution in 1848. He wondered if another opportunity for revolution presented itself whether or not the men would "play the same game over again," as they did "at the commencement of their insane political career." He concluded that the three pardoned state prisoners would probably never again engage in revolutionary activity. He believed, "Clemency will work more good than the harshest restrictions that power could devise; but yet some little acknowledgement of favors received would not have been amiss."[69]

John Martin had not taken a major speaking part in the Tasmanian ceremonies; therefore, he did not have an opportunity to express his feelings about his period of exile. Just before leaving the island, however, he wrote a letter expressive of those feelings that he hoped would be published in the press. His hopes were fulfilled, and Martin's letter received wide publication throughout Australia. Martin thanked the citizenry of Tasmania for its "hospitable and friendly attention." He hoped, "May famine and famine plagues, and pauperism, and all the horrors that have desolated my country, keep far away from this lovely land, and may peace and prosperity dwell here forever!" He thought the Tasmanians had a government that they could "obey and respect." He envied them. "Would to God there were in my unhappy country a government to which I might be a loyal subject!" Martin make it clear that he was not sorry for having engaged in revolution in 1848. He considered his actions to be those of a patriot. With a final thanks to "the kindly brown woods of Tasmania, which have often almost charmed my melancholy away," Martin bade farewell.[70]

*　　　*　　　*

Meanwhile, the preparations on the mainland to honor the exiles were proceeding rapidly. Groups in Sydney, Geelong, and Bendigo all

wanted to honor the exiles on their departure. The Melbourne committee solved the problem by extending an invitation to those groups to join
them in honoring the exiles, since by then it had become obvious that
time did not allow the exiles to partake in more than one celebration
once they got to the mainland.[71]

The chairman of the Melbourne committee, Mr. O'Shanassy, also
announced that the committee had received nine hundred pounds by
means of subscriptions to honor the exiles. The committee "unanimously
agreed that a gold vase of not less than 100 ozs. at £ 7 per ounce of fine
gold should be manufactured by Mr Hackett, . . . the same to be presented to Smith O'Brien."[72]

When Sir William Denison heard the news of the plans for the
Melbourne reception honoring O'Brien, he told his mother, "A set of
rabid Irishmen are preparing an address to him, and are striving to make
his release a sort of triumph." Denison then told his mother that he had
written to the governor of Victoria, Sir Charles Hothan, "pointing out
the inconsistency of a set of people who make it penal to a man holding
a conditional pardon to appear in Victoria, asking a man holding such a
pardon as this to come over and be fêted; and I have asked him to release
all the unfortunates who have, by the above law, been sentenced to hard
labour in irons."[73]

On 22 July 1854, at 4:00 P.M., the final celebration honoring the
Irish exiles took place at the Criterion Hotel, Melbourne. O'Brien,
O'Doherty, and Martin had gathered together to receive the honors. The
festivities began in the concert room of the hotel, which was filled with
over a hundred persons. Deputations were present from Melbourne, Geelong, and Bendigo. Several individuals had come from Sydney. At the
appropriate time, O'Brien, O'Doherty, and Martin were ushered into the
concert room and led to a platform at the front of the room. "They were
received with several salvos of vocal and manual artillery, and had much
difficulty in even reaching the platform." The address that was presented
contained the signatures of hundreds of the inhabitants of Melbourne
and hundreds from Geelong, including "a large portion of the Corporation of Melbourne, and the entire Corporation of Geelong."[74]

The Melbourne address was similar in content to those presented to
the exiles in Tasmania. O'Brien's reply was also similar. Only in the Melbourne address O'Brien discussed the nature of the pardon that had been
given to him. He mentioned that his pardon did not allow him to return
to Ireland, the country which "from time immemorial [was] the home of
[his] fathers," the country that he desired "should be the home of [his]
children." O'Brien stated that as much as he wanted to return to Ireland,
he would not solicit the government to extend to him a free pardon. He
had refrained from solicitation while in Tasmania and he would continue
to do so. O'Brien also spoke at length about his involvement in the

revolution of 1848. He considered his role in the revolution to be one of a patriot, not a criminal. He continued to hold the same point of view in 1854 that he had in 1848; namely, that the revolution was justified, Ireland was fighting for her survival. O'Brien also spoke at length about the state prisoners who had previously escaped. He stated that Mitchel's and McManus's escapes were without doubt perfectly honorable. Meagher had not consulted him regarding his escape attempt, but he knew Meagher well enough to state that the young man "would never have escaped in any way that he did not deem honourable."[75]

Both Martin and O'Doherty spoke at the Melbourne celebration. They each had received two hundred sovereigns to help defray the expenses of their journey to the European continent. Martin's speech was short, O'Doherty spoke longer. O'Doherty took the opportunity afforded him not only to thank those present for the financial gift but also to explain why he did not consider his involvement in the revolution of 1848 to have been criminal. He explained that he had been a medical student at the time of the famine. He had witnessed for months on end the sight of starving and diseased Irishmen who were "piled together in the fever sheds, happily unconscious, in their wild delirium, of the horrors of their condition." He had concluded that the policy of the British government was "heartless" and the "interests and lives of these people was the least item of consideration." O'Doherty thus explained how, when the revolution came in 1848, he had been prepared to risk all, asking, "Is it wonderful that . . . I should have raised my voice in favour of deposing this government, that thereby the people might save themselves."[76]

In addition to the speeches in the concert room, those gathered took part in a sumptuous banquet served in the dining room. While they dined there were more speeches, toasts, cheers, and general conviviality. "Shortly after nine o'clock the guests of the evening took their departure amid loud cheer."[77]

On the same day as the Melbourne celebration, the *Launceston Examiner* published a farewell article to O'Brien. The editors knew they would miss O'Brien. They explained that O'Brien's presence among the members of the community gave them all a sense of inspiration. The community beheld "in him the accomplished gentleman—the man of unspotted honour, pure and devoted patriotism." But the editors knew O'Brien was anxious to leave. They could only wish him well. "Wherever he goes, we shall not fail to cherish a sincere desire that he may regain that position and influence for good which he magnanimously sacrificed at what he believed to be the shrine of his country's welfare." Those editors believed O'Brien had "charmed" many of the residents of Tasmania.[78] There was no doubt that he had.

*   *   *

After the final celebration in Melbourne, the exiles bade each other farewell. O'Doherty and P. J. Smyth decided to delay their departure. The two young men planned to try their luck in the goldfields. O'Brien and Martin were anxious to leave. On 26 July 1854 William Smith O'Brien and John Martin sailed out of the harbor at Melbourne on board the *Norma*.[79] The exile was almost over.

*   *   *

The editors of both the *Citizen* and the *Nation* followed the speeches made by O'Brien before leaving Australia. Mitchel was proud of the way O'Brien continued to justify Ireland's right to revolt in 1848 and O'Brien's own right as a patriotic Irishman to take part in the revolution. Mitchel was delighted with O'Brien's statement that Mitchel had made an escape from Tasmania with his honor intact. Mitchel noted, "It is only what we had a right to expect from Smith O'Brien; and whatever any man has a right to expect from Smith O'Brien that he is sure to get." Mitchel valued O'Brien's qualities highly, for as long as there was an O'Brien, "manhood is not yet extinct upon the earth." Mitchel warned his readers, "The days are coming upon us when 'a Man will be more precious than gold—even a Man than the golden wedge of Ophir.' "[80]

The *Nation* struck a similar note. The editor admitted that O'Brien had failed "in the hour of trial to elicit that quick cordial, electric response" from the people that is a necessary component for most Irish leaders. He acknowledged "that O'Brien's character was pitched too high for wide popular sympathy." He knew he had "the loftiest . . . aim of all the patriots of [the] day, . . . an antique purity of principle, [a] chivalrous honour, [a] large philanthropy, and [had made] magnanimous sacrifices for Ireland." But he also knew that, prior to 1848, all those qualities had failed to obtain for O'Brien the leadership position he deserved. He had to admit, however, that during the period of exile "a clearer insight of O'Brien's rare and reticent nature has grown up in the popular mind." As the people watched "during the dreary years of gloomy agony which blanched the noble head [the English] could not bow," O'Brien's leadership qualities had come home to the Irish people, and "the opinion that is slow of growth is sure as well as sound."

> Not as the sport of their enthusiasm or the creature of their passions, will the Irish people receive Wm. O'Brien from exile, but as a true and tried father and friend. He has conquered the right—and it will be accorded him ungrudgingly—so rarely yielded to public men, of shaping his future course by the light of his experience and his conscience—unchal-

lenged by party or faction. Wherever his path lie, it will be hedged in by this veneration, and cheered by the confiding and grateful affection of the whole Irish race.[81]

Smith O'Brien had gone into exile as the leader of a small group of Irish intellectuals who had tried and failed to separate Ireland from England by means of revolution. His leadership was rejected in Ireland, he suffered ridicule in England, and in 1849 he was practically unknown in either the United States, Canada, or Australia. In 1854 he left Tasmania as a world renowned figure, honored and respected in Australia, the United States, Canada, Ireland, and, to a certain extent, England. The Irish were prepared to welcome him as a father figure and to give him a permanent leadership position.

The Exile Ends

The three state prisoners who had been granted conditional pardons could not yet return home to Ireland. All three decided they would eventually make their way to the European continent in order to be as close to their families and friends in Ireland as possible. The assumption was that the conditional pardons were a necessary step toward obtaining full pardons and that it was only a matter of time before they would be allowed to return home.

There was no doubt that Martin would arrive on the Continent ahead of O'Brien and O'Doherty, since O'Brien planned a stopover in India and O'Doherty was delaying his departure from Australia in order to try his luck in the goldfields. Martin and O'Brien had started the journey together. They parted company at Ceylon. Martin continued by sea to the port of Aden. He traveled by open carriage on a desert road between Suez and Cairo. His next stops were Alexandria, Malta, Marseilles, and he finally arrived in Paris at the end of October.[82]

Martin's years as an exile had not resulted in a reformation. Only a few days after his arrival in Paris, he wrote his friends the Connells thanking them for their many kindnesses to him, describing his journey to Paris, and concluding with a political observation regarding the relationship between England and Ireland: "When the Irish drive [the English] out of power in Ireland, then [the English] will respect us & perceive the force of our argument; and never till then."[83]

O'Brien parted from Martin at Ceylon in order to travel to Madras and visit his brother-in-law, Major Gabbitt, who was serving with the British army in India. After leaving Madras, O'Brien traveled to Malta. He booked first-class accommodations on the *Candia*, which took him to Gibralter. It was reported that he "entered into familiar conversation with those on board on every topic except politics." It was also reported that "he looked careworn." The *Candia* was bound for England, but O'Brien was forbidden under the terms of his pardon to visit the United Kingdom. Therefore, he left the *Candia* at Gibralter. By the end of November he was in Paris.[84]

By the end of the year, O'Brien was in Brussels. He had no really pressing duties, so his time was spent on a book that he had begun while residing in Tasmania entitled *Principles of Government*.[85] He also continued his extensive correspondence with his numerous friends.

One of the first letters O'Brien wrote on arriving in Brussels was to Gavan Duffy. It was a letter of thanks. "I do not know to what extent my liberation from Tasmania is due to you, but whether your efforts tended to advance or to retard my release I feel equally indebted for the persevering zeal with which you have striven during a period of five years to keep in the recollection of our countrymen that the Irish exiles were suffering at the Antipodes for their devotion to Ireland."[86]

Duffy had meanwhile written O'Brien, "I believe I will never again in life have a thrill of such joy as when I heard you were about to be liberated." Duffy then returned to the question of a full pardon and informed O'Brien that Palmerston's personal ambitions would give the Irish their chance. "Lord Palmerston is labouring to make a personal party who will help him to the Premiership and out of this disposition I hope will come your unqualified and unconditional return." Duffy was also ready at this time to explain to O'Brien why he had been compelled to battle with John Mitchel. "[Mitchel] sat down as deliberately to assail my character, as the allies sit down before Sevastopol." Duffy finally told O'Brien that disappointment with the Irish political scene and broken health were motivating him to consider migrating to Australia. He was interested in learning the nature of the climate and any information regarding the society and the position of the Irish population in that society. Duffy was not planning an immediate departure, but he was beginning to seriously consider such a move. He explained his disillusionment with Irish politics. In the last general election forty to fifty men had announced that they would vote as an Irish party independent of both the Whigs and the Tories, in other words, they would vote according to the needs of Ireland, not according to the needs of the Whigs or the Tories. Each of those men agreed not to accept a place in Aberdeen's government, for that would necessarily mean voting with the government and hence the loss of an independent position. By 1854, Duffy noted, only twelve members of the Irish party had remained faithful to their pledge not to accept such a place.[87]

O'Brien appreciated Duffy's efforts to obtain a full pardon for him and told him so, but he hoped Duffy would remember that there were others involved, commenting, "All the Irish political offenders [are]

equally with William Smith O'Brien entitled to such a [pardon]."
O'Brien hoped that when his friends took his case to Palmerston they
would keep that principle in mind.[88]

O'Brien next explained to Duffy why he considered Mitchel's escape
honorable. Mitchel had done all that was required; namely, inform the
government he was going. "Our parole was exacted not in order to confer
advantage upon us but as a *security* to the Government."[89]

O'Brien received one other interesting letter of congratulations during this time that somewhat complemented Duffy's letter. Richard
O'Gorman wrote his congratulations from New York City welcoming
O'Brien "back to liberty." O'Gorman told O'Brien that for years the object nearest his heart was to hear of O'Brien's release. "You bore it all
through like a man." O'Gorman then went on, "You accepted the severe
punishment, that was the consequence of our failure, with calm dignity,
without useless clamour or complaint—in every incident of your release,
you sustained your high character—you carried it through the hardest
ordeal without a hurt; and now, there is no man that ever knew you,
that will not hold his head the higher and be stronger and better for the
example you have given of courage, fortitude and honour."[90]

O'Gorman, like Duffy, also commented on John Mitchel. O'Gorman
did not believe Mitchel had singled Duffy out to do battle. O'Gorman
believed Mitchel warred against practically everyone "with a vigour and
impartiality that is astounding." O'Gorman did not think Mitchel's wars
were without merit. "Regarding him in the light of a moral hurricane, he
is likely to blow away cants and absurdities and do some good."
O'Gorman also reported that Meagher was currently in the West giving
a series of popular lectures, while he and Dillon had settled down in New
York as lawyers.[91]

*   *   *

As Christmas approached, John Martin wrote O'Doherty's sweetheart, Mary Anne Kelly, to wish her a Merry Christmas. Kevin
O'Doherty had planned to visit Mary Anne as soon as he returned from
Australia even though the conditions attached to his pardon forbade a
return to the British Isles. Martin thought Kevin might be with Mary
Anne when he wrote his Christmas letter to her, and he extended his
Christmas wish to Kevin as well. Martin did not give many details of his
life in France except to say his relatives from Ireland had visited him and
he had several close Irish-French friends in Paris. Martin considered
France to be as foreign as Tasmania, but he preferred France, stating, "I
am from under the British flag & from under convict regulations, and I
am near my kindred and my friends in Ireland."[92]

As the year turned, P. J. Smyth and O'Doherty had returned from the goldfields and were preparing to leave Australia. O'Doherty set sail for Europe shortly after the first of the year. P. J. Smyth married Jane Anne Regan on 8 February 1855 at St. Joseph's Church in Hobart Town. Bishop Willson had returned to Tasmania and performed the ceremony. The young couple set out for the United States on 15 August 1855. Neither of the young men had struck it rich at the goldfields, and Smyth had discovered that the Irish Directory disapproved of the use of any of the escape-fund money for purposes other than that for which it had been designated. Smyth had used at least a part of the escape-fund money to assist in financing the festivities that were accorded the state prisoners on leaving Australia, and it appears that he used some of it for living expenses. He hoped to "settle to the full with the Directory" before he died.[93]

Meanwhile, Duffy continued his efforts to obtain a full pardon for the Irish exiles. On 2 April 1855 Duffy informed O'Brien of his latest activities. Duffy had a friend by the name of Edmund Roche who as a result of his long support of the Whig party had just been made a peer. Duffy asked Roche if he would ascertain from Palmerston whether a memorial signed by members of all parties in the House of Commons asking for a full pardon for O'Brien would be favorably received.[94]

Roche complied with Duffy's request and returned with Palmerston's reply. Palmerston announced that he was upset over the fact that O'Brien had "made a violent speech in Melbourne" before departing from the Australian colonies. Palmerston added that there were some friends of O'Brien's who truly had his interest at heart and believed it would be better if O'Brien did not return to Ireland. Nevertheless Palmerston sent word to Duffy that a memorial for a full pardon signed by members of Parliament would be "favourably listened to." Duffy acted immediately. By the time he wrote O'Brien in April, he already had one hundred signatures, and a large majority of those were English.[95]

Norreys and Butt played a major role in the attempt to obtain O'Brien's release. On 14 May they led a small delegation to Lord Palmerston on O'Brien's behalf. Butt read the memorial to Lord Palmerston, which by that time contained 140 signatures. Palmerston accepted the memorial but told the delegation he would have to consult with the members of his cabinet before making a response. While the members of the deputation waited for Palmerston's answer, Norreys received a letter signifying the support of a pardon for O'Brien by both the English and Irish members of the Conservative party. Norreys quickly forwarded the information to Palmerston. Norreys told Palmerston that he thought the O'Brien memorial was truly remarkable not only because the men who signed it represented "every shade of political opinion" but also because "I do believe that there never has been a Memorial presented to a government to which there were so many signatures attached representing the *really* sincere and earnest opinions and wishes of the subscribers to it than that which has been presented to your Lordship in favour of Mr Smith O'Brien."[96]

The efforts of the friends of O'Brien, however, came to no avail, for Palmerston decided to refuse to consider granting O'Brien a pardon at that time. The *Citizen* called Palmerston's refusal "a mockery, a delusion, a snare." It was stated that Palmerston was holding out O'Brien's pardon as a lure to induce Irishmen to volunteer into the ranks "of a perishing army in Crimea." One other explanation was given; namely, the cabinet did not want to grant O'Brien a pardon unless he promised never to engage in revolution. Regardless of the reasoning behind the refusal, it was reported that there was still hope, the door was not shut.[97]

*　　*　　*

By the summer of 1855, O'Doherty had arrived in Europe. O'Doherty evidently spent several weeks in Ireland during this period of time, Mitchel thought, "clandestinely," in order to pick up an inheritance resulting from the death of an uncle, and probably to see Mary Anne. He then returned to France. In August, O'Doherty wrote O'Brien and discussed his wedding plans. Shortly after writing O'Brien, O'Doherty crossed over to London and on 23 August 1855 he and Mary Anne were married by Cardinal Wiseman in his church at Moorfields.[98] The couple then went to Paris where O'Doherty began to study surgery at the Hospital Pitie.

By the end of November 1855 the O'Dohertys decided to register their marriage officially with the British government. Mary Anne was pregnant. On 30 November 1855 they paid a call at the British consul's office in Paris and took out a marriage certificate. They were accompanied by John Martin and Kevin's brother George, who served as witnesses.[99]

*　　*　　*

During the early months of 1856, the memorial asking for a full pardon for O'Brien and his associates was revived. The Crimean War was nearing an end, and O'Brien's friends believed that on such an occasion pardons were often granted to political prisoners.

On 13 March the *London Times* editorially supported the pardon. It did so because it believed Ireland was at perfect peace with England and because it did not think the revolution of 1848 was even a respectable riot. Once again the ridicule heaped on the revolution was repeated. Referring to the affair at Ballingarry, the editors wrote, "There was a paltry riot in a cabbage-garden—the country entirely refused its adhesion to the Smith O'Brien dynasty—not even a pig was injured; the bubble burst, and the foolish persons who had amused themselves with playing at treason found themselves within the grasp of the constables, and in due course lodged in gaol." The editors of the *Times* continued. They supported the pardon because O'Brien had behaved during his period of exile as "a gentleman and a man of honour." But more than anything else, they supported it because public opinion wanted O'Brien "restored to his country and his friends." The support of the *Times* afforded the memorialists "considerable confidence in the result."[100] Palmerston, however, was in no hurry to give his answer.

The announcement was finally made on 9 May, in response to a question raised by Thomas Slingsby Duncombe as to whether, "a full and free pardon [would be granted] to Messrs. Frost, Williams, Jones, Smith O'Brien, and other political prisoners, whose conduct during exile has been without reproach." Palmerston had no hesitation to reply that the queen was "determined to take advantage of the return of peace, and of the unexampled loyalty which prevailed from one end of her dominions to the other," by granting full pardon "towards all persons under the sentence for political offences, with the exception of those unhappy men who had broken all the ties of honour and fled from their place of banishment." Such an amnesty would cover William Smith O'Brien, John Martin, and Kevin O'Doherty.[101]

O'Doherty and Mary Anne crossed over to Ireland almost immediately. They were both anxious to return to Ireland. Mary Anne was about to give birth to the first of their eventual eight children. O'Doherty had, in the course of his year-and-a-half stay in Paris, spent a year studying surgery and six months studying anatomy. He was not only anxious but ready to take his examinations in order to obtain the right to practice medicine in Ireland.[102]

Martin was also in Paris when he heard the news, and he too set out immediately to visit his family in Ireland. He only remained in Ireland for a short time. Martin "had resolved that so long as England ruled Ireland, and that against the will of the Irish people, so long would he remain absent from the country; as his efforts towards removing the foreign tyranny had been of no avail."[103]

It took O'Brien a little longer to get back to Ireland, since he was visiting in Greece when he received the news. His homecoming took place in July.[104]

No doubt the bonfires of Cullen lit up the sky.

The exile was over.

*   *   *

O'Brien's decision to wait one more year before making an escape attempt had been an important one. Whether or not he would have actually made such an attempt is unknown. But he did wait, and he did receive the pardon. O'Brien had survived the exile as a man of honor and looked forward to being reunited not only with his family but also with Ireland. O'Brien was aware he was returning to Ireland as a recognized leader who would give advice to the Irish people and who would be afforded the courtesy of a listening audience. O'Brien probably realized his new role would be almost as difficult as his years in exile. But he would, at least, be back on Irish soil.

The truth was that the exiles who had escaped to America were not particularly successful at maintaining their positions as Irish leaders. All of them were affected by the American scene, and the "Americanization" they were undergoing made them less appealing as leaders to large numbers of the Irish people. The American exiles would find it increasingly difficult to straddle the ocean.

CHAPTER 10

The Finale

The Other State Prisoners

By 1856, the state prisoners had left the "Tasmanian" period of their lives behind them. O'Brien, Martin, and O'Doherty had returned to Ireland with the official permission of the government and were reunited with their families and friends. McManus, Meagher, and Mitchel could not help but realize that the chance of their eventual return was growing slighter every day.

Yet even though the state prisoners were separated geographically, there was still a unity among them. They were the acknowledged leaders of the 1848 revolution and together had experienced the pains of exile in Tasmania. In addition they were still united in the same beliefs that had carried them into revolution and into exile. None of them ever apologized for his involvement in the 1848 revolution. They all continued to believe they had performed their patriotic duty. They all continued to believe in the truth of the Young Ireland motto, "Ireland for the Irish."

The exiles spent the remaining years of their lives in an almost predictable manner. In America, McManus concentrated on business activities, Meagher on finding an outlet for his energies, and Mitchel on struggling in the public arena. In Ireland, O'Doherty concentrated on medicine, Martin on Irish reform, and O'Brien on molding Irish public opinion. In addition to those particular concerns, the broad base of their lives had been shaped by a belief in Irish nationalism, and in one way or the other for the remaining years of their lives they continued to affect and/or be affected by that belief.

*   *   *

McManus had remained in California. There had been "a move to secure an amnesty for him," but he announced that even if it was granted he would not return to Ireland, "if I cannot go without the consent of a foreign ruler." Then suddenly on 15 January 1861 he died. He had not achieved the financial success he had hoped would be his. Although he was not a Fenian, the members of that organization decided to take charge of returning McManus's body to Ireland for burial. The body was brought across the country to New York where a funeral mass was said at

St. Patrick's Cathedral. John Joseph Hughes, archbishop of New York, gave the sermon, "upholding the right of an oppressed people to struggle for their liberation." McManus's body was then sent by the steamer *Glasgow* to Ireland.[1] When O'Brien realized what was happening, he wrote a letter to the *Nation* lauding McManus as a "patriot" and a "martyr." He urged the Irish to "exhibit calmness, dignity, and self-control whilst they manifest the fervency of their patriotism by offering an affectionate homage to the remains of the latest victim of English misgovernment."[2] But one of the leaders of the Catholic Church in Ireland, Bishop Cullen, opposed honoring any revolutionary. When McManus's body arrived in Ireland he refused to allow a funeral mass to be said. During the 1848 revolution, Bishop Cullen had been in Italy and had witnessed the violence of the Carbonari. The Fenians concluded the bishop had never gotten over his revolutionary experience and had "Carbonari on the brain." But regardless of the bishop's strong feeling, the Irish people decided to turn out for McManus's funeral. The crowd of mourners stretched for miles behind the casket on the route to McManus's final resting place at Glasnevin Cemetery.[3]

Public opinion was so obviously in favor of McManus and the nationalistic ideals for which he stood that the leaders of the Fenian organization in America and its counterpart in Ireland, the Irish Republican Brotherhood, began to believe they had a chance to free Ireland from England by means of a revolution. From that point on the Fenians began to actively prepare for their revolution, which came several years later. Interestingly enough the leader of the Fenian organization in America was John O'Mahony. The leader of the Irish Republican Brotherhood in Ireland was James Stephens. Both O'Mahony and Stephens had fought in the Irish revolution of 1848. Stephens had been the young man who had exchanged caps with O'Brien after the collapse of the revolution in order to assist O'Brien's escape. But it was Stephens who got away, and he had joined O'Mahony in France. While in France, the men roomed together and studied secret societies, awaiting the day when another opportunity would come to revolt against English rule.[4]

*   *   *

Meagher was more of a success in America than McManus. Initially he pursued a career as a lecturer. It was not long, however, before he realized that his lecturing could not sustain him forever, so he studied law and, in 1855, was admitted to the New York bar. While waiting for his law business to build up, he continued his lecturing. Meagher noticed one young woman who came to hear him speak. Her name was Elizabeth Townshend, and her father, Peter Townshend, was a wealthy Fifth Avenue merchant. Meagher began to court Elizabeth, but her father refused to give his consent to their marriage. Meagher and Elizabeth were determined to marry, and on 14 November 1855 Archbishop Hughes performed the wedding ceremony at his home. At that point Townshend accepted what had been done.

In addition to being a lecturer and a lawyer, in 1856 Meagher in cooperation with some friends founded a newspaper, the *Irish News*. During the American Civil War, Meagher joined the Union army. He eventually led the Irish Brigade. In a speech given in Boston, Meagher urged all Irish-Americans to join the Northern army. He recalled what fine soldiers the Irish made and their wide experience as soldiers fighting all over the world. He noted how the German-Americans had united behind Lincoln and the Northern cause. He urged his fellow Irish-Americans to unite with him behind the same cause. Meagher did not succeed in his efforts to recruit all Irish-Americans into the Northern army. Many Irish immigrants had settled in the South and had formed new loyalties there. At the end of the Civil War, Meagher was named acting governor of the Montana Territory. Shortly afterward while traveling on the Missouri River he drowned. The date was 1 July 1867.[5]

* * *

Sometime during the winter of 1854–1855, John Mitchel gave up the *Citizen* and when the spring came relocated his family in the "shady valleys of East Tennessee." Mitchel wrote during this period a book entitled *The Last Conquest of Ireland*. In it he criticized O'Brien's handling of the 1848 revolution. O'Brien calmly wrote Mitchel stating he was persuaded that Mitchel did not wish "to misrepresent" him. He then reminded Mitchel that Mitchel was not present at the rising at Ballingarry, while O'Brien was, and that Mitchel had been "misinformed" about O'Brien's actions.[6]

Between 1860 and 1862, Mitchel lived in France. During that period, Mitchel believed France and England were moving toward war with one another. In the event a French-English war broke out he hoped to obtain French aid for Ireland and thus aid Ireland to break its connection with England. By 1862, Mitchel had returned to America. He did not go to the North, however, but to the South where he edited a newspaper, the *Enquirer*, which was the semiofficial organ of the president of the Confederacy, Jefferson Davis. At the end of the American Civil War, Mitchel initially went to New York where he became the editor of the *Daily News*, but on 14 June 1865 he was arrested and confined in Fort Monroe. On his release he traveled once again to France and then returned to the United States to edit another newspaper, the *Irish Citizen*, which was democratic in its tone.[7]

Mitchel had never received a pardon from the British government, yet he returned to Ireland for a short visit in 1872. In 1875, the citizens of Tipperary elected him to Parliament. At that point, the Conservative party leader, Benjamin Disraeli, openly attacked him. He announced that Mitchel's election to Parliament was invalid since Mitchel was a convicted felon. The Parliament agreed with Disraeli and refused to seat Mitchel. A new election was held, and once again Mitchel was elected. Mitchel declared he did not believe Irish representatives should sit in Westminster and, therefore, he had no intention of going to London. He died shortly afterward on 20 March 1875.[8]

*   *   *

O'Doherty practiced medicine in Dublin from 1857 until 1860. By that time, O'Doherty and Mary Anne had decided that for the good of their children they should emigrate. O'Doherty had liked Australia, so, in 1860, the O'Doherty family left Ireland and after surveying the Australian scene settled in Brisbane. O'Doherty practiced medicine there. He was also involved in politics. He was elected to the Queensland Legislative Assembly and in 1877 "nominated by the Governor of Queensland to be a member of the Legislative Council." In 1882, he was appointed surgeon major of the Queensland Volunteer Force. In 1885, he was invited by the Irish National party to return to Ireland and run for Parliament. He did so and was elected to Parliament from North Meath. O'Doherty did not remain in Ireland long, possibly because he was out of touch with home politics. In 1888, he and his family returned to Brisbane. Unfortunately, he was unable to recover his rather extensive medical practice. He was, however, able to support himself and his family as a result of obtaining two appointments. The first appointment was to the post of secretary to the board of health and the second was to that of quarantine officer. Those posts brought him an income of £250 a year. O'Doherty's vision began to fail, and during his last years he suffered from blindness. He died on 15 July 1905. After his death his wife was supported by a fund raised by the Irish people. Mary Anne died on 21 May 1910, and a monument paid for by public subscription marks the resting place of the O'Dohertys.[9]

*   *   *

Martin continued to live in Paris since he had resolved not to live permanently in Ireland as long as England ruled Ireland. That resolution collapsed in 1858 when a catastrophe struck his family. Martin had received word that his sister-in-law "was dangerously ill." He quickly crossed over to Ireland only to discover that his sister-in-law was dead and his brother Robert was also dying. Within a week's time, Robert had died. By their deaths, Martin had become responsible for raising their seven children, the eldest of whom was ten years old.[10] Under these circumstances, Martin remained in Ireland.

Martin visited with his old friend John Mitchel in 1859, when Mitchel was in France. The visit lasted a month. It was the first meeting they had had in six years, "so they talked and smoked as of old."[11] Martin believed, as Mitchel did, that there was a possibility of war between England and France. Like Mitchel, he favored the idea of the French giving aid to the Irish in an effort to break the hold England had on Ireland. Both men had no fears of direct French aid to Ireland in the event an Irish war of independence broke out and welcomed the idea of French troops landing in Ireland to give what assistance they could. Their views, however, conflicted with those of O'Brien, who opposed the idea of direct French aid and had written a series of letters to the newspapers giving his reasons. Martin wrote, "I don't agree with [O'Brien]. He and I have some private correspondence upon it, and the more we write the further we seem to get asunder." Martin did not care for the disagreement that had developed. "It is very sad to me, for there is nobody with whom I would rather agree to co-operate than with O'Brien."[12] O'Brien probably felt the same way. But friendship would not stop O'Brien from speaking his mind, nor would such disagreement lead to personal bad feelings since O'Brien advocated "unlimited toleration in regard of opinion with respect to politics and religion." He explained, "I never quarrelled—I never will quarrel with any man for avowing honest convictions different from those which impress my own mind."[13]

In 1864, Martin became active in politics again, establishing the "National League," whose purpose was to obtain legislative independence for Ireland. In 1867, he took part in a funeral procession and made a speech honoring the "Manchester Martyrs." He was prosecuted for making such a speech but was not convicted. Soon after his release he married Henrietta, the sister of John Mitchel. In 1871, he was elected to Parliament for the district of Meath and continued to make speeches maintaining that the Irish people were bound only by the queen, Lords, and Commons of Ireland. Martin was supported by funds that he received as a result of being the honorary secretary of the Home Rule League. Martin's friendship and loyalty to John Mitchel never faltered. He defended Mitchel against Disraeli's charge that he had broken his parole when he escaped from Tasmania. Finally, although Martin was not well when Mitchel died, he insisted on attending the funeral. As a result he caught bronchitis and died on 29 March 1875.[14]

O'Brien and the "Popular Hope"

When O'Brien returned to Ireland in July 1856, there were no demonstrations on his behalf. Before a fortnight was out, however, O'Brien was asked to run for Parliament as the candidate from Tipperary.[15] The editors of the *Times* opposed the idea of O'Brien returning to Westminster. They hoped he would become "usefully employed as a country gentleman." Then, "when years have gone by, and he has by a steady discharge of the duties of his station given evidence to his fellow-subjects that he has broken with his past history, he may again acquire weight in counsel; but he has yet to earn a character for solid judgement."[16] O'Brien was unconcerned with the reasoning displayed in the *Times*. He had decided for other reasons not to enter Parliament, and on 18 July 1856 he formally refused the offer. He explained that being a member of Parliament would necessitate being separated from his family several months out of every year. "I am not prepared, under present circumstances, to make this sacrifice of the duties and pleasures of domestic life." But O'Brien had other reasons for refusing the offer. "Perhaps I should feel some compunction in thus refusing to re-enter the House of Commons, if I could persuade myself that in that sphere I could be useful to my country; but in 1843, after having attended Parliament with continuous assiduity during twelve years, I arrived at the conclusion that my time would have been much more usefully occupied if I had remained in Ireland, and everything that has occurred since that period has confirmed rather than weakened this conviction."[17]

O'Brien's refusal to run for Parliament did not mean he had abandoned politics. He announced his intention to keep a "vigilant watch" over legislation affecting Ireland, and he believed his long experience on the political scene would be useful. He informed anyone who was interested, "I shall not hesitate to offer such suggestions as the occasion may require."[18] O'Brien believed freedom of expression was the right of all Irish citizens. It was a right he had never abdicated and never planned to abdicate. There were no conditions attached to his pardon forbidding him to speak out. He would not have accepted a pardon if there had been any such conditions. This was an issue that O'Brien considered to be of paramount importance, stating, "I have the satisfaction of thinking that by me, at least, the national standard of free expression has never been lowered—nor will it ever be lowered."[19]

The editors of the *Times* were pleased to learn that O'Brien had no intention of returning to Parliament, even though his reasons were different from theirs, but they clearly opposed any speeches or statements from O'Brien on public issues. They advised O'Brien to remain silent, believing as they did that "all speech other than a few formal phrases of friendship and goodwill must needs be a mistake." Yet it was during this time that the editors of the *Times* paid tribute to O'Brien for being an admirable adversary. Such a tribute appeared only once. The editors acknowledged that whatever "errors" were made, O'Brien "acted with remarkable dignity"; however "evil the times," O'Brien "acted with perfect simplicity and good faith"; and however "selfish" his coconspirators were, O'Brien "believed in the righteousness and justice of the cause." The editors had to admit, "The very height of his imprudence may be taken, in one sense, as the test of his sincerity." They explained, "His coadjutors would have contented themselves with talking and writing treason; with him rebellion was not a thing to be talked about, but a thing to be done." Such a man was obviously of unsound intellect to attempt to fight the power of the British Empire. Yet fight them he did and for that struggle the editors of the *Times* finally acknowledged his role as an admirable opponent. "His friends may admit that he acted like a fool; his enemies cannot say of him that he was a knave. This is no mean praise of any one of the heroes who have figured in the chronicles of Irish agitation."[20]

By the end of September, various groups of Irishmen were urging O'Brien to appear before them in celebration of his return to Ireland. O'Brien agreed to meet with a group from his home area, Cahirmoyle, and in mid-September 1856 ten thousand men, women, and children gathered to welcome him home and urge him to reassume the position of leader that his heritage, love of truth, and past sufferings merited for him. O'Brien was pleased with the gathering and used the opportunity to state his position on several important matters. He spoke about his role as a revolutionary leader, the propriety of the revolution of 1848, and what he considered to have been its chance for success. O'Brien stated clearly that he "never maintained nor do I now maintain that it is the duty of Irish patriots to seek separation from England by forcible means." Yet O'Brien was still not prepared to apologize for his role as the leader of the revolution, and after describing the desperate condition of the country he stated, "Under all probable circumstances when in 1848 this country was reduced by misgovernment to a condition more abject than any that it had known, even in the worst period of its disastrous history, and when we were deprived of all constitutional methods of re-dress by the suspension of the Habeas Corpus Act, I thought, and I still think, that resistance was justifiable." O'Brien also thought the revolu-tion had had a chance of success. "I thought then, and I still think, that if we had been supported by the Irish nation in the struggle which we commenced, we should have been able to secure for Ireland within a few months, or perhaps a few weeks, the inestimable blessing of self-govern-ment." Yet O'Brien knew his opinions were out of style and stated that if the Irish people were happy with the British Parliament and no longer interested in obtaining a local legislature he would be "compelled to ac-quiesce in that preference." He knew that all those who had assembled agreed on one point, "We all love Ireland."[21]

O'Brien lived with his family at their home, Cahirmoyle. Unfortu-nately for O'Brien, his family life on his return from exile was not with-out problems. Most of the older members of the O'Brien family, including O'Brien's wife, Lucy, had always found it difficult to understand why O'Brien had become a revolutionary. On his return from exile, O'Brien discovered that several of his children could not understand his revolutionary activity either, while one of his children, his daughter Lucy, refused to engage in political discussions of any kind. In addition, it was difficult for several of the children to adjust to a father who had, during his period of exile, become only a dim memory, while several of his children could have no real memory of him at all. Finally, O'Brien was a disappointed man, and that disappointment must have affected the relationship between himself and his children. But regardless of what frictions were present, peace reigned because Lucy O'Brien was able to effectively serve as a mediator. The love and respect that Lucy and O'Brien had for one another had endured through the period of the exile.[22]

By the end of 1856, O'Brien had settled down to a relatively peaceful domestic life. At that point he was ready to once again assume a leadership role in Irish affairs by speaking and writing on those matters he deemed important. O'Brien thought there were several major areas of concern. He hoped the Irish would stop "boasting" about how they were willing to die for their country's freedom since they had turned their backs on such an opportunity in 1848. He hoped all Irishmen would work together to end "the scandalous and barefaced system of corruption" that went on in Parliament by which the Irish members were exchanging their votes for favors. He hoped a "sound national feeling" could be engendered by both Catholics and Protestants "based upon the sentiment of *self*-reliance." He hoped that when the Irish had attained "an attitude of purity, strength, and unity" they would be able to take advantage of all contingencies that would advance "the interests of Ireland," from minor matters, such as establishing "steam communication with America," to matters of major importance, such as "the restoration of the legislative independence of this country."[23]

O'Brien's first letter to the Irish people was written on 22 December 1856. It dealt with the continuation of an increase to the income tax that had been voted years before to supply the revenue necessary to finance the Crimean War. The war had ended, and with its end a demand was being made for a downward revision of the tax. O'Brien joined his voice with those who wished a reduction in taxes.[24]

O'Brien asked, "The question now at issue is whether the British Government ought or ought not to be encouraged by the continuance of this tax to subject the resources of Ireland to exhaustion, in order to maintain a war establishment for the promotion of objects in which Ireland has no, imaginable concern." O'Brien noted that during the Irish famine, the British Parliament had advanced a loan of 8 million pounds for relief. Yet the loan was accompanied with "insulting language" and statements foretelling the exhaustion of English resources in an effort to provide an act of "unparalleled generosity." O'Brien found that in 1855 "an addition of £30,000,000 was made to the ordinary war estimates of the united kingdom with scarcely a murmur of dissension, and Ireland has been subjected to an increase of taxation which would have been much more than sufficient to provide an interest upon loans that would have been adequate not only to preserve the lives of the myriads who died of actual starvation, but also to render the occurrence of the famine an era of unprecedented improvement."[25]

O'Brien urged his Irish readers to instruct their representatives to Westminster to vote against the continuation of the war income tax, "or at least to demand that it shall be applied to objects beneficial to Ireland."[26]

The editors of the *Times* commented, "There are tales of men who have slept for years to awake in a world which had forgotten them, and to talk in a style which had long departed." Those editors identified O'Brien as one of those sleepers. Those writers deplored O'Brien's references to "Irish interests," noting, "Englishmen and Irishmen have no separate interest, and wish to have none."[27] Therein was the kernel of the struggle. O'Brien clearly recognized it, and so did the editors of the *Times*. Between 1856 and the time of his death in 1864, O'Brien addressed numerous letters to the Irish people through the columns of the *Nation*. Those letters all dealt with Irish interests, separate and distinct from English interests.

O'Brien did believe England and Ireland were separate countries. He told his readers he had come to that conclusion during his early days in politics when he was trying to work for the betterment of Ireland through Westminster. Looking back on that period he wrote, "I found that, whether from difference of race or from difference of religion, there was an entire alienation of feeling from this country in the minds of the English people—that, in point of fact, Ireland and England are essentially two different countries."[28] During the period of the famine O'Brien reported that he had heard English politicians put those feelings into words. They "exulted in the destruction of the Irish race" that was taking place, reasoning, "The Irish are a bad race—they are hostile to us; 'they are' (to use the memorable words of Lord Lyndhurst), '*aliens in blood, aliens in language, aliens in religion*'—the sooner we get rid of them the better." O'Brien believed, "The majority of the British people, and of British statesmen . . . wish that Ireland should be deserted by its Roman Catholic inhabitants, in order that it might be re-peopled by what is called *the great Anglo-Saxon race*, and that many of the measures adopted at the time of the famine were designed to produce an approximation to this eventual result."[29]

O'Brien studied the relationship that had existed between England and Ireland for a period of seven hundred years. He maintained, "There is no impartial historian who does not admit that the relations which have subsisted between the English government and Ireland, have been, during nearly seven centuries, those of an oppressor towards the oppressed." Since the time of the "unprovoked invasion in 1172, the British government has been known to the natives of Ireland . . . only by a continuous series of rapine, confiscation, and religious persecution."[30]

O'Brien admitted that it was painful to him to have to say such things about the English nation since he acknowledged that there were "many excellent, humane, and generous" Englishmen. Yet nations like individuals had to be judged by their acts, and after studying those acts O'Brien concluded, "All the dealings of the English nation, with the people of Ireland, during a period of nearly seven hundred years, appear to have been governed by a spirit of the most intense selfishness."[31]

No one had any doubt as to what O'Brien wanted from the Irish people. His exile had effected no change in the political position he had adopted in 1843 when he joined the Repeal Association. He was still a Young Irelander. "I am an Irish nationalist who wishes to see Ireland governed by Irishmen for the benefit of Irishmen." He wrote, "I am prepared to maintain that this country ought to be *self-governed*—whether it be self-governed in connection with England or as an independent power, is a question upon which I am not disposed to raise any controversy." O'Brien wanted the Irish people to once again engage in a struggle with the English for self-government. He was convinced "Ireland would prosper more under a domestic than under a foreign Government."[32]

Just as in 1848, O'Brien preferred sovereignty to be in the queen, Lords, and Commons of Ireland. He was, however, still prepared to accept the idea of independence and hence witness the end of the monarchy. But during his exile he had come to see another opportunity that would satisfy his dream for Irish self-government; namely, the development of dominion status, by which the local legislature would have the right to control internal affairs and the British government would have the right to control external affairs.[33]

O'Brien maintained that the struggle for self-government could be carried on successfully by peaceful means. He believed conditions in Great Britain were such that "nothing but the exercise of public virtue is now required to give [the Irish] command, . . . over the destinies of their own country." He wrote, "I avow myself to be one of those who think that if the people of Ireland were animated by a truly patriotic spirit, this country would be able to [obtain and] maintain its independence."[34]

O'Brien also let it be known that he had not abandoned his belief that there had been "occasions" in "past times" when "force of arms" was "fully justified in seeking to obtain . . . the independence of [Ireland]." He did not believe it was "expedient at all times to incur the hazards of rebellion in an attempt to secure the national independence of Ireland."

He did believe the current era was one where such a force of arms could not be fully justified.[35] But O'Brien was not prepared to abandon the principle, adopted in 1846 at the time of the secession, that a nation like an individual did have the right to defend itself from attack by the use of physical force. He still recognized the right of revolution.

O'Brien knew he was virtually alone in asking the Irish people to once again resurrect the move for self-government. Actually he was appalled at the lack of interest in the subject. But O'Brien believed the day would come when that interest would be revived because he believed it was "the will of Providence" that Ireland would someday govern herself. If the revival came during his lifetime, O'Brien wanted the Irish people to know that he was prepared to reenter the political arena and "act in whatever manner might be most conducive to that end."[36]

Meanwhile, O'Brien had decided he would "remain a passive, but not indifferent, spectator of events." In that role, O'Brien suggested the Irish develop a "secondary system of policy" sanctioned by "public opinion" that would serve to help the Irish nation obtain better legislation from Westminster. O'Brien urged the Irish to establish an independent Irish party.[37]

Such an idea was not new. O'Connell had used bloc voting in the 1830s and 1840s. In 1843, when O'Brien had joined the Repeal Association he had begun to articulate the idea "that the Irish Nation ought to abstain from connecting itself with any English party whatsoever." O'Brien urged the Irish people to once again adopt such a policy. He reasoned that with a united bloc of independent Irish votes in Westminster the Irish members could begin to work with whichever party was willing to pass good legislation for Ireland. O'Brien hoped such measures as true equality for Irish Catholics could be obtained, as well as judiciously planned public-works projects, a tax to discourage absentee landlordism, and legislation giving tenants their equitable rights. Instead O'Brien noted that coercion acts and arms bills were being passed by Westminster for Ireland, and, although the Irish population had decreased since 1843 by one-fourth, the police force had been doubled. O'Brien wanted his Irish readers to understand that a great deal of the blame for the lack of good Irish legislation had to be placed at the feet of the current Irish members of Parliament who were busy serving as patronage brokers for themselves, the members of their families, their friends, and their constituents. Once a parliamentarian took patronage from the ministry in power he lost his independence, hence Ireland lost its opportunity for good legislation. Old Ireland and Young Ireland had taken different sides on this issue in 1846. O'Connell had thought there was merit in advancing Irishmen into the ranks of government even if the individuals were lost to the party. O'Brien did not think patronage was good for either Ireland or the smooth workings of the British governmental system. He advocated a system of public examination as a means of obtaining the best civil servants.[38]

O'Brien understood why the Irish members of Parliament were so ready to bargain their votes in exchange for patronage. Ireland had only 105 representatives in Westminster, and those representatives, even if united, were not strong enough to pass the kind of legislation that most Irishmen recognized was needed. In such a situation many parliamentarians decided that forfeiting one's independence was all right. But O'Brien reasoned that if those representatives could unite and maintain their independence they would not only be models of virtue for the Irish people but they could also cooperate with other groups in Westminster who advocated reform. O'Brien was particularly interested in seeing reforms adopted such as the extension of the franchise to practically all adult males, a redistribution of parliamentary seats based on population, the use of the secret ballot, and more frequent elections. O'Brien also favored a plan by which election costs would be absorbed by the public in order to allow men who had ability but did not possess riches to run for public office. With the passage of such reforms Ireland's representatives to Westminster would increase to 150, or one-fourth of the total number of parliamentarians in Westminster. In addition those representatives would be more reflective of the actual will of the Irish people as a result of the extension of the franchise, the use of the secret ballot, and the more frequent opportunity to select a new candidate to Westminster or reaffirm support for the old one.[39] Such a united independent group of Irish representatives could realistically exert enough pressure and influence to obtain good Irish legislation in Westminster, for they would not only be a force within Parliament but they would also carry with them the force of a united Irish nation, a force that O'Brien believed had to be acknowledged.

O'Brien "prefer[red] that the Irish representatives should meet in Dublin rather than in London, if they were sufficiently numerous to form even the committee of a national council," but he knew that idea was not acceptable. He therefore suggested a secondary policy. He urged the Irish to adopt an idea suggested during the repeal agitation of the 1840s and known as the Irish council. He wanted the Irish to select approximately two to three hundred of the ablest Irishmen "from each corporation, . . . from each body of town Commissioners . . . together with other persons who enjoy in a pre-eminent degree the confidence of the Irish people, [and that the group] should meet in permanent session in Dublin, to deliberate upon the special interests of Ireland, and also upon all questions in regard of which the interposition of Irish opinion could promote the general interests of mankind." O'Brien thought such a body "would exercise . . . influence over the deliberations of Parliament" because it would reflect the national will.[40] If an Irish council was established and did develop along the lines anticipated by O'Brien, it would not be as difficult to move toward repeal.

O'Brien was well aware that there was another group of Irishmen also urging the Irish to obtain self-government; namely, the Fenians. O'Brien urged the Irish people not to join that organization. He opposed the Fenians mainly because they were a secret society. He believed such secrets "become known almost immediately to the government, and furnish a pretext for invasions upon public liberty." In addition, he thought that if a man wanted to serve as a leader of his fellow countrymen it was best to "let him stand forth to the scrutiny of daylight." Experience had taught him that "the leaders of secret societies generally keep out of danger themselves; whilst they allow those whom they inveigle, to be sacrificed for having acted upon their perilous suggestions." O'Brien was proud of having done his *"Patriotic Duty"* of standing up for the right of Irish self-government even though it had resulted in his being convicted of *"High Treason."* Finally, he opposed secret societies because they dissipated the efforts of the Irish people to obtain self-government by splitting the people into two separate and distinct groups, those who were working openly and through recognized organizations, and those who were working secretly and through organizations that acted surreptitiously. Such secret organizations would more likely have to rely on outside foreign assistance in order to obtain the physical force necessary to free Ireland from England. But foreign assistance had its price, and O'Brien feared the cause of Irish self-government would suffer.[41]

O'Brien and the Fenians both looked back to the eighteenth century for guidance. The Fenians looked to Wolfe Tone, the United Irishmen as a secret society, and the revolution of 1798, which had been assisted by French troops. O'Brien looked to Henry Grattan, the Volunteers as an open organization, and the revolution of 1782 assisted by Irish troops and the votes of College Green and Westminster. As far as O'Brien was concerned, the divisiveness of Wolfe Tone's plan, which had relied on a secret society and foreign aid, led not to self-government but to union. The divisiveness of the Fenians would have similar disastrous results for the Irish people. O'Brien's reccurring message to the Irish people was not to divide, but to unite; to rely not on others, but on themselves. He hoped the Irish could learn how to speak with one voice and demand self-government. He was not opposed to the physical force of a weapon being added to the moral force of the national will, if the constitutional conditions warranted it.

Two other subjects continually appeared in O'Brien's various missives to the Irish people. One was the disdain that O'Brien had for the internal struggles of Irishman against Irishman. He particularly deplored the struggle of Catholics and Protestants. He believed such divisiveness did nothing but help England continue to deny Ireland's claim to self-government. He urged all his countrymen to forget their arguments and work together for the betterment of Ireland. The second was O'Brien's great pride in being Irish. He recalled the ordeal of his trial for high treason and the fact that he was forced to stand in the dock for ten successive days for periods of seven, eight, and nine hours a day, with the courtroom carefully filled only with curiosity seekers totally unsympathetic to him and the revolution. He believed it was his "old Irish pride" that saw him through the ordeal.[42]

But the most interesting statement on his pride, both in being an O'Brien and in being Irish, was written on 21 September 1862. His brother Lucius had recently obtained the title Baron of Inchiquin. It was customary for the brothers and sisters of a newly appointed baron to apply for the use of the title *honorable*. O'Brien refused to make any such application. He explained that his progenitor who had lived during the "reign of Henry VIII accepted English titles in lieu of the royal honours which belonged to his family, submitted to a derogation of dignity by accepting such titles." O'Brien was proud that he was a member of "one of the oldest and most distinguished families in Europe." He acknowledged that some members of his family, "in different ages, disgraced themselves by assisting to establish a foreign dominion in this country, yet, upon the whole, the O'Briens have participated, to at least as large an extent as any other race, in all the proceedings which have conferred renown upon the Irish nation." Belonging to a family that had served as monarch of Ireland for centuries, a family that deserved the respect it received from home and abroad, O'Brien could "not consider [himself] elevated in rank by acquirement of the highest title that the Queen of England could bestow." O'Brien felt it was, therefore, unnecessary "for me to add that I do not covet the lowest of the appendages which belong to the English nobility."[43]

*   *   *

In 1859 O'Brien visited America, and on his return he presented two lectures on his American experience at the hall of the Mechanics Institute, Dublin. The proceeds from his lectures went for the benefit of that society.[44]

In 1861 he traveled to France and had a pleasant visit with John Mitchel. O'Brien still kept a journal and left a record of his visit with Mitchel. Mitchel was living outside of Paris in a town called Choisy-le-Roi. Once again Mitchel was surrounded by his family and friends, and, although it was impossible for O'Brien and Mitchel to visit one another without experiencing a certain amount of sadness, the two men had the warmest regard for one another and both enjoyed the visit. O'Brien's friendship with Mitchel was interesting. O'Brien wrote, "There are few politicians in the world from whose opinions I dissent so widely as from those of John Mitchel." The two men had "but one opinion in common—that is a desire that Irishmen should govern Ireland." Yet, regardless of how they differed politically, their friendship was firm. Even O'Brien noted how strange it was that a man of Mitchel's fierce political beliefs could be so loved by his family and close friends. While they visited, O'Brien learned that Mitchel was in difficulties not only in England and Ireland but in America as well. Mitchel had sided with the Confederacy, and it was possible that two of his sons might find themselves in action against the Irish Brigade of the North led by Tom Meagher. O'Brien and Mitchel also discussed their differences over the question of French aid to Ireland in the event France and England became embroiled in a war.[45]

Mitchel and Martin advocated French aid while O'Brien believed "that Irishmen should undertake and accomplish the liberation of their country by their own energy applied unceasingly but prudently in vindication of the rights of Ireland."[46] O'Brien urged the Irish to form volunteer units similar to those developed during the American Revolution. The Volunteers of the eighteenth century were originally formed to repel the French, had they chosen to invade the British Isles,[47] but ultimately the Volunteers intimidated College Green and Westminster into granting Ireland a free parliament. O'Brien hoped the Volunteers of the nineteenth century would help foster a national spirit.

O'Brien was realistic enough to understand that his plan to create volunteer units to repel the French invaders had only the slightest chance of being adopted. He realized that Mitchel's plan, which was endorsed by a large number of Irishmen, was indeed a possibility.[48] If such events developed and a French army landed in the British Isles, O'Brien hoped Mitchel would arrange for the landing to take place in England rather than Ireland. He reasoned, "A war between France and England would be a national war on both sides and an invasion of England would be conducted on the principles of regular warfare whereas an invasion of Ireland by a French force would probably superinduce a civil war of the most disastrous kind." O'Brien concluded, "The strongest argument in support of my views is perhaps to be found in the reflection that a patriotic Englishman would earnestly desire that Ireland, rather than England, should be chosen as the battlefield on which the strife would be conducted most advantageously for England."[49]

O'Brien also visited Hungary at this time and wrote a letter that was published in the *Nation* describing his journey. He expressed his sympathy for the Hungarian nationalists and supported their claim for self-government. He also made a special plea to the Irish people to exhibit sympathy for a Hungarian nationalist, Count Teleki, who had only recently been arrested and sent as a prisoner to Vienna. O'Brien hoped

Emperor Francis Joseph might release the count as a result of an Irish appeal to his "generosity." Whether O'Brien's attempt to stir up Irish sympathy for Count Teleki affected the emperor was unknown, but the count was released and "restored . . . to his liberty."[50]

By 1862, O'Brien was ready to comment on the American Civil War. In making those comments O'Brien found himself in opposition to Tom Meagher. He explained he was "prepared to break a lance with [Meagher] in argument." Meagher had thrown all his energies behind the Union cause. O'Brien believed the war would be so devastating that neither side could possibly attain its stated goals.[51]

O'Brien opposed slavery. He had earlier written, "No abstract argument—no evidences of kindly treatment derived from actual observation—could ever induce me to believe that slavery is in itself an institution to be desired." O'Brien maintained that he had "never heard any satisfactory answer . . . to the question—'Would you wish to be a slave yourself?'"[52] O'Brien considered the days of slavery to be numbered whether the South won the war or the North and the South split from one another as a result of negotiation. If the North won the war, he believed the South would have to be subjugated by means of a military occupation. The result would be that the republican institutions of the North would be severely damaged. O'Brien urged mediation between the North and the South before additional American lives were lost or before England and France entered the war. If the day ever came when England did enter the war, O'Brien recommended that the Irish people refuse to supply either men or money that could be used to hurt any American. O'Brien believed the Irish nation owed a debt of gratitude to all Americans for receiving the Irish during the period of the famine. O'Brien did not fear that the dissolution of the Union would result in ruin to either the North or the South. He had many friends in leadership positions in both the North and the South, and he offered to serve as a mediator if negotiations toward ending the conflict began.[53]

In 1863 O'Brien traveled to Poland. On 1 July 1863 he delivered a lecture on his Polish experience at the Rotunda in Dublin. O'Brien spoke favorably of Thaddeus Kosciusko and his supporters in their struggle against Russian tyranny. The proceeds of the lecture went to the Polish relief fund.[54]

O'Brien's letters to the Irish people and his public appearances clearly demonstrated that he had a following in Ireland. He periodically was urged to become active in politics. John Francis Maguire expressed his wish that O'Brien lead a national party. He reasoned, "Unless we have a man of your weight with us, leadership is out of the question, & division is certain." J. E. Pigott told O'Brien, "You have the ear of the country." He spoke of O'Brien's strength. "You *can* do individually 'as a unit', all the good that it would be possible for you to do in the country."[55] O'Brien refused all overtures.

While O'Brien knew he had a following, he also knew the Irish were not prepared to stand with him in his demand for an independent domestic legislature. In addition, he was aware that there were moments when his particular advice had resulted in the loss of the support of those who were basically sympathetic to him. When he openly opposed French aid he felt so alienated that he wrote, "I . . . now find myself in a state of political *isolation*."[56] He stated the problem clearly. "I am myself at present one of the most unpopular politicians in Ireland, because I implore my fellow countrymen not to place their hopes of salvation upon the caprice of a foreign despot, or upon the embrace of a selfish step-sister, but to found their aspirations for national prosperity and national greatness upon the manly vigour and self-reliance of the Irish nation."[57]

The editors of the *Nation* informed O'Brien that he had not been abandoned. They admitted that his views "on some important points" were not shared by "a large mass of his fellow-countrymen," but that did not mean they had "ceased to regard him with respect and affection," nor that he had lost his popularity.[58]

In a few short sentences they analyzed why O'Brien could never really fall from favor with the Irish people. Those editors noted how O'Brien had "won the respect of his countrymen not so much by the great powers of intellect, by great influence, by his identification with great projects of popular interest, as by his stern consistency, his honour, without a stain, and his public reputation, without the shadow of reproach." They reminded their readers that O'Brien had at the start of his political life "sufficient influence to advance his claims to place and profit . . . but he took his stand amongst the people." By doing so, "he gave up many a reality for a popular hope, and to that hope he has remained faithful to this hour." Such a man was appreciated by the Irish people, and, although differences were bound to occur, such a man would never cease to be a respected leader.[59]

The *Nation* was right. O'Brien's role as a respected leader would always be recognized. But no one recognized as clearly as O'Brien that he had failed to become "the leader." The people had not followed him to the barricades at Ballingarry. They had not followed his recent urgings to resurrect the demand for self-government. They had not followed his advice to shun the notion of French aid. Many had not followed his advice to avoid associating with the Fenians.

He knew he was out of step with the times. But that realization still did not keep him from feeling "deeply disheartened" by the Irish scene, especially because there was "a total absence of self-reliance, and a consequent prostration of our national dignity." He knew he did not have the outgoing, warm, vibrant personality that "the leader" was expected to have. O'Brien recognized those failings and wrote, "I . . . deeply deplore my inability to realize my aspirations for the good of mankind." But O'Brien also recognized his strengths. He was stubborn, courageous, and absolutely convinced he was right in his demand for Irish self-government. He determined to continue speaking out, explaining to the Irish people, "I have desired to *serve* rather than to please you." He had accepted the fact that he was not first in their hearts, but he felt they recognized his worth. He could not have helped but know that, for the most part, his continued stand for the "popular hope" of self-government was also the people's stand.[60]

O'Brien also came under particular criticism from some of his fellow Irishmen for his interest and involvement in affairs outside Ireland. Many of his countrymen considered his statements on Hungary and Poland to be absurd. O'Brien was challenged mainly because it appeared as if he was putting himself on a level with Kosciusko and Kossuth. The editors of the *Nation* once again came to his defense. They thought the problem centered around the definition of patriotism. "If it mean the will to do, the will to dare, and the courage to lose all and everything for [his country]," then O'Brien was a patriot on the level of Kosciusko and Kossuth. However, the writers had to agree, "If patriotism be a thing of clime or locality, then, indeed, his defamers are right in their purposes." Under those circumstances, O'Brien "must always be considered, until the end of the chapter—only a rebel at Cork."[61]

More than anyone else, O'Brien knew that his period of active political leadership had passed. That was why he had concentrated on addressing letters to the Irish people, not to leading political organizations, outlining Irish national interests. O'Brien was also active in cultural and agricultural projects. He was a member of the Gaelic Literary and Antiquarian Society, and he made a gift of a silver cup in an effort to encourage the growing of flax. He also donated to the Royal Dublin Society a gold medal that had been given to him by a group of admirers in California. The medal was to be presented to the winner of the annual art competition.[62]

With all of his activities, O'Brien was as content as possible, that is, until the death of his wife, Lucy, on 13 June 1861. O'Brien was truly affected by his wife's death. He not only suffered the loss of a loved one, but with the disappearance of Lucy's services as the family mediator, O'Brien's relationship with his children changed drastically. The initial change centered around a financial problem. Just prior to the revolution of 1848, and then after its failure, when O'Brien was in prison, he had divested himself of his property, for if he had been convicted of committing treason, it would have been possible for the state to seize whatever he owned. In divesting himself of his property he had lost title to the estates. At that point, the property passed to several trustees who looked after the property for Lucy and the O'Brien children. Once Lucy died, O'Brien attempted to get his name back on the property, but the trustees refused to recognize such a transaction. O'Brien next drew up a new settlement that would allow the property to be transferred to his eldest son, Edward. O'Brien would receive a yearly cash settlement. O'Brien then took the new settlement to court for approval. The trustees did not plead against this settlement, and the court ruled in favor of it.[63]

From that point until his death, O'Brien considered himself a visitor at Cahirmoyle. In 1864, while traveling in Anglesey, Wales, on a visit to his sister, O'Brien was taken ill. He died on 18 June 1864.[64]

On 18 June the *London Times* published O'Brien's death notice. On the twentieth, those editors wrote, "His name has been so long familiar to the readers of newspapers, his career has been so remarkable, and he gave the Government of his country so much trouble in his time, that a brief review of his life and adventures will be read with some interest, not only throughout the United Kingdom but abroad and in the colonies, and wherever Irishmen are found." The editors then wrote a lengthy article tracing the general history of the O'Brien family and the specific history of William Smith O'Brien. They noted that since his return to Ireland, "with few exceptions, he kept himself aloof from politics, but his political opinions were still unchanged, his hostility to the British Government unmitigated, and he never could see anything wrong in the course he had adopted except the miscalculation of means to accomplish the end." They wrote, "Personally Mr Smith O'Brien was regarded by all parties as one of the most truthful, honourable, and kind-hearted of men." But the editors concluded, "His talents were respectable, but most of his errors and misfortunes arose from the exorbitant vanity by which they were overrated."[65]

The *Nation* announced his death by writing, "The Kingly blood—derived from ancestors who bore sway before the present dynasties of Europe were heard of, pulses through his veins no more." In Dublin a "hastily convened" public meeting was held in the lecture room of the Mechanics Institute "to express the feelings of the working men who sympathized with the deceased in his political sentiments, and to make arrangements for a great demonstration on the arrival of the remains in Dublin." It was reported that the lecture room was filled and hundreds more had attempted to attend but were turned away since there was insufficient room. Other groups such as the Trades of Dublin, the Irish National League, the Polish Committee, and the Brotherhood of St. Patrick held similar meetings. The smallest meeting was held at the home of John Dillon, who had returned to Ireland and was currently an alderman for the city of Dublin. That meeting was attended by personal friends of O'Brien. The lord mayor of Dublin was present and informed those in attendance that when he had initially learned of O'Brien's death he had gone to members of the O'Brien family and expressed his desire to aid in giving O'Brien a public funeral. The lord mayor then presented a letter from one of O'Brien's sons "who, in the name of the family, deprecated in the most earnest manner any demonstration of the kind contemplated." The son stated that "he wished the remains of the lamented father to be conveyed in the quietest manner possible from Kingstown to their last resting place." Those gentlemen attending the meeting at Dillon's house "at once deferred to the wishes thus expressed," and all the plans for a public funeral ceased.[66] However, plans of an informal nature began to take shape. O'Brien's body was coming by steamer from Bangor, Wales, to Dublin. After landing at the North Wall, the body would have to proceed through Dublin to the railroad station at Kingsbridge terminus, where it would then be taken by train to its final internment in Rathronan Churchyard near his home, Cahirmoyle.

Many Irishmen who had nationalistic sympathies or who admired O'Brien as a man of honor decided to walk behind the hearse as it proceeded through the streets of Dublin from the wharf to the railroad station.[67] The police became alarmed and took the necessary precautions. One of those responsible, Mr. Turner, reported to his superior, "All the arrangements have been made for the occasion you refer to—the Police will be in sufficient force along the whole line, (from the North Wall to the Kingsbridge Station), to meet any emergency but they will not appear, unless, their interference should be necessary."[68]

O'Brien's body was being brought into Dublin sometime during the early morning hours of 23 June. At 3:00 A.M. two river steamers set out from the North Wall "having on board a number of persons, whose enthusiasm enabled them to brave the discomforts of a wet, chilly morning, and proceeded into the bay to meet the *Cambria*, which conveyed the body." The steamers carried three hundred persons, some of whom were members of the St. Peter and St. James bands who planned to play appropriate music on sighting the *Cambria*. The steamers had not been out long when they sighted the *Cambria* flying a flag at half-mast. Those gentlemen on the steamers took off their hats and the band played "Adeste Fideles." By 4:00 A.M. the *Cambria* was at her moorings at the North Wall. The river steamers had also returned and continued to play appropriate music. The dock was filled with people of all ranks. It was only a short time before the coffin was taken off the *Cambria*. "The coffin was of oak, with a large cross on the lid and a nameplate bearing the deceased's name and age." A reporter for the *London Times* noted, "A hearse was in waiting, into which those in charge attempted to bear [the coffin], but a loud shout of remonstrance arose from the assembled crowd, a rush was made towards it, and the honour of first aiding in carrying it was furiously contested." The family obviously did not put up a struggle since the *Times* further commented, "Those in charge did not think fit to offer any very strenuous opposition to the crowd, and it was elevated on the shoulders of six men."[69]

A procession formed in front of and behind the coffin amounting to between two and three thousand men. Many of those men wore crepe around their arms tied with a green or a white ribbon. Several carriages took part in the procession. The lord mayor of Dublin appeared in a state carriage, while John Martin, P. J. Smyth, and John Dillon had private carriages. Two of O'Brien's sons, a son-in-law, and another relative were also in the procession. The other relative referred to in the press reports was possibly O'Brien's daughter Charlotte, who had gone to nurse her father during his last illness and was now returning to Ireland. Men, women, and children lined the streets and watched from their windows. The *Nation* reported that twenty thousand persons watched the proceedings, while the *London Times* put the figure at two thousand, "among whom there could not be seen more than a dozen persons of respectable exterior."[70]

The *Nation* reported that when the procession passed the spot where Robert Emmet was executed all the men in attendance removed their hats and the "pace slackened." At 6:00 A.M. the procession reached the railroad terminus, the crowd swarmed onto the platform, and as the coffin was moved across the platform to the waiting train, "hundreds scrambled to touch it." Once again the men took off their hats and the band played "Adeste Fideles." The train departed at 7:00 A.M.[71]

The editors of the *Nation* were pleased with the numbers and the decorum of those who attended O'Brien's funeral. "It showed that a strong national feeling is still alive in Ireland, and scarcely less important—by the orderly and reverent manner in which it was conducted, it proved that Irishmen are not the mercurial and turbulent people whom our Saxon neighbours describe us to be."[72]

O'Brien's body was taken to Cahirmoyle. Once again a funeral procession was formed to take O'Brien to his final resting place at Rathronan Churchyard. The procession "comprised a large number of the gentry of the country, about 20 Catholic clergymen, and over 200 of the tenantry of the O'Brien estate, principally mounted, and wearing scarfs and hatbands." Two of O'Brien's brothers-in-law, the Reverend J. and the Reverend R. Gabbit, read the service. The *Times* noted, "There was not the slightest indication of any political feeling in connexion with the proceedings, which were characterized by the greatest order and solemnity."[73]

But O'Brien's nationalistic friends were not quite finished honoring the leader of the 1848 revolution. A committee was formed for the purpose of collecting money to erect a monument to William Smith O'Brien. By 17 December 1864 this committee had collected £480.11.2. By 22 April 1865 the sum amounted to £683.1.9. The money was used to construct a statue of O'Brien that was unveiled on 26 December 1870.[74] It stands today in O'Connell Street.

*   *   *

William Smith O'Brien was a remarkable man. In his early forties he came to the conclusion that the only way for Ireland to survive and

eventually to prosper was for her to sever her legislative connection with
Great Britain. If in severing that legislative connection the tie with the
monarch happened to be broken and a republic established, O'Brien was
willing to accept that radical political change. By coming to that conclusion, he destroyed his professional career as a parliamentarian and seriously damaged all his personal family connections. By coming to that
conclusion, he greatly advanced the cause of Irish nationalism, for
O'Brien was the leader who represented the hope of many nineteenth-
century Irishmen for a free Ireland. He was a remarkable man because he
never compromised nor dishonored that hope. Brian Boru performed the
easy task. He died a victor and thus remained a hero. William Smith
O'Brien performed the impossible task. He lost a battle and became a
hero.

Conclusion

Historians have long interested themselves in studying wars and revolutions. In recent years greater attention has been paid to the aftermath of war and revolution mainly because with the rise of nationalism whole peoples are involved in the winning and the losing. There is no guarantee that the winner of a war or revolution will win the peace. The stage is set for the winner to reap the rewards of victory, but victory is complex. In the modern society victory involves not merely an opportunity for such factors as economic advancement but also an opportunity for a conversion of the defeated peoples to the ideals of the victor.

William Smith O'Brien was not a modern man when he fought the revolution of 1848. But he was quite in tune with the modern era when he went into exile. He and his companions were conscious of the struggle over the ideals that had set them on the course of revolution. They never abandoned those ideals. They never apologized for taking Ireland into revolution.

O'Brien, in particular, sensed that with the failure of the revolution the main principle that O'Connell, the Repeal Association, and the revolutionaries of 1848 advocated, Irish self-government, was in jeopardy. Ultimately he believed Providence would grant the Irish the right to govern themselves. But the timing of that deliverance could be speeded up or slowed down by the action of Irish leaders.

Between 1848 and the creation of the Independent Irish party under the leadership of Isaac Butt, Ireland had a paucity of political leaders who were willing to work within the system for Irish self-government. Part of that lack of leadership was Daniel O'Connell's fault since he did not prepare the younger men to assume the reins of power. Part of the lack of leadership was O'Brien's fault since with the failure of the revolution of 1848 disappeared a large number of young Irish leaders. Yet O'Brien did what he could to fill the void. The battle was not easy.

The British ministers displayed real expertise by transporting the state prisoners to a penal colony sixteen thousand miles from the British Isles where they hoped their gentlemanly treatment would result in oblivion for the prisoners. When the oblivion unexpectedly ended, the ministers merely changed their tactics. They fought off the assaults of the friends of the state prisoners in Westminster and ignored the petitions and private pleas on their behalf made by a growing number of individuals. They successfully kept the most important of the revolutionaries, O'Brien, in exile until it was most advantageous for British policy to grant him a pardon. When they granted the pardon those ministers did appear as if they were responding to the wish of both Irish and English public opinion as well as to the requests from Australia and America. Those ministers probably were affected by those requests. With the approach of the Crimean War the time had come to unite the British Isles and claim the friendship and support of Australia and America. If the pardons would help attain that goal the ministers had no hesitance to act. The ministers would probably have preferred that the state prisoners apologize for their revolutionary activity, declare their loyalty to the monarch, and promise to never again lead Ireland into revolution. But pragmatically the ministers were satisfied. All things considered, the British government handled the state-prisoner issue rather well.

The editors of the *London Times* were also difficult adversaries. They set out to ruin O'Brien and by and large they succeeded. Between 1848 and 1864 the *Times* continued its campaign of ridicule against O'Brien. Periodically the editors acknowledged that he was a worthy foe, but those acknowledgments generally came at periods when it was important to move English public opinion to a more conciliatory position regarding the pardon issue. But in some ways the length of the campaign and the consistency of the editorial position during those years of assault did reflect O'Brien's power. The *Times* protested too long and too vigorously that O'Brien was unworthy of attention.

Governor Denison should have been as serious an adversary as the British ministers and the editors of the *London Times*, but he was not. It would have to be admitted that Denison was in an almost impossible situation. He was to continue to keep Van Diemen's Land as a receptacle for convicts while the antitransportation movement grew stronger every day. He was to treat the Irish prisoners as gentlemen while he was to control twenty-nine thousand convicts by administering a penal system in a fair and equitable manner. His main problem was that he was inexperienced. Regarding the transportation question he blended his person too closely with the transportation system. When it went Denison had to go as well. Regarding the state prisoners he made two serious misjudgments. Denison considered the Irish prisoners to be nothing but convicts and their supporters in Australia to be made up solely of Australian-Irish. The truth was that the state prisoners were not convicts in either the minds of the British ministry or the minds of the Australian people. In addition the state prisoners had the support of both the Australian-Irish and the antitransportation citizenry. Denison's treatment of the state prisoners as convicts caused his reputation to decline and theirs to rise, and hence helped their cause. Denison's removal and promotion to the post of governor of New South Wales displayed the common sense of the British ministers who gave him credit for accomplishing what they needed; namely, keeping Van Diemen's Land a penal colony until they could solve the transportation problem, as well as keeping O'Brien in exile until they were ready to pardon him. But Denison did not make either task easy.

O'Brien and his companions were aided by the support of public opinion in Australia and America. But it would have to be admitted that both those groups initially rose to support the state prisoners in an effort to forward their own interests. The antitransportationists in Australia recognized that Denison was the common foe and used the martyrdom of O'Brien and the three truants, McManus's legal contest, and O'Brien's reputation as a man of honor to defame Denison and turn public opinion against transportation. That policy, however, did help the state prisoners because it did result in the building of a sympathetic public opinion favorable to their pardon. The American politicians used the state-prisoner-pardon issue in order to insure their election. The growth of the influence of Irish-American voters was being felt in the American political scene on both the local and national levels. On the local level, the exiles who escaped to America could receive warm welcomes without any fear of repercussions from the British or commitment to Irish revolution. On the national level the personal and private efforts of the president and the secretary of state to obtain the release of the Irish revolutionaries could also be pursued without similar risk or commitment. Most Irish-Americans were in the process of becoming American-Irish, and, while they did want the release of all of the exiles and would have welcomed their arrival in America, they probably did agree with the attitudes of the American political leaders. They wanted neither risk nor commitment. If the American-Irish wanted anything from the American political leaders other than the release of the exiles, it was a recognition by those leaders that the American-Irish voters counted and their political power had to be acknowledged. Meanwhile the exiles benefited by the sympathy extended to them by the Australians and the Americans.

O'Brien's family, Irish public opinion, and English public opinion eventually all displayed attitudes favorable to a pardon, but in different degrees, for different reasons, and at different times. O'Brien's family and the English people opposed the revolution. The Irish people failed to support it. All three understood why the British government wanted to send the revolutionaries into gentlemanly oblivion. From the beginning O'Brien's family wanted him home. He was after all a part of their circle and deeply loved by all of them. Initially the Irish people were confused about the revolution of 1848. O'Brien's revolutionary leadership did not inspire them. In addition he had fallen victim to the ridicule of the *Times*. He had no grass-roots organization to serve in his defense. But the Irish people did not want O'Brien and his companions mistreated. And as word of O'Brien's solitary confinement reached Ireland and as the *Nation* newspaper dedicated itself to obtaining a pardon for O'Brien, the move began that grew over a period of years to be a national demand for his release. The Irish people did want O'Brien home. He was a descendant of Irish kings. He was an honorable gentleman. And he was one of their leaders. English public opinion resented O'Brien's involvement in the revolution of 1848. It found repeal to be incomprehensible and could not understand how a member of the aristocracy could not only advocate repeal but also use violence to obtain such a goal. The explanation that O'Brien was insane took deep root in English public opinion. It was quite likely that English public opinion acquiesed in the O'Brien pardon not for O'Brien's sake but for the sake of the Irish people who wanted his return. There was no doubt that Irish good will was needed as Great Britain approached the Crimean War.

O'Brien's companions in exile assisted him in the struggle. But they were not merely revolutionaries, they were human beings with all the strengths and frailties that implies. In exile they sought love and affection from family relationships, companionship from among themselves and their new friends, and meaningful work activities in order to restore a sense of usefulness to their lives. They also learned to be well aware of Denison's power over them. They quarreled with one another. At least one of them drank too much, while another reflected the snobbery of one class over another. Yet they consistently maintained the principles that had made them revolutionaries. None of them apologized for the role they had played in the 1848 revolution, begged for pardon, expressed gratitude for their treatment, swore fidelity to the queen, or promised never to engage in another revolutionary effort. They were men who knew why they had become revolutionaries and saw no change in the Irish situation that would cause them to abandon their principles.

The key figure in the story was, of course, O'Brien. His power and position were the reason the British ministry devised the scheme of gentlemanly oblivion. His refusal of the ticket-of-leave reawakened Irish public opinion on his behalf and created a sympathetic American public opinion. His gentlemanly bearing and decision to fight against solitary confinement opened the door to an alliance with the antitransportationists in Australia. His martyrdom made Denison and Grey look bad. His leadership of his six companions made them look good. O'Brien's strength was that he had devised a workable plan for his period of exile and he was stubborn enough not to deviate from it. O'Brien concentrated his efforts while in exile on demonstrating to the Irish people that he was not defeated. In addition he consciously worked at making the period of the exile as short as possible. When he returned to Ireland he spoke as clearly and as often as he could in favor of self-government. He battled with words. He reasoned. He taught. He pleaded. He cajoled. He threatened. But he persisted. He was the voice of the popular hope. And a great many of his thoughts were in the mainstream of what many Irishmen held to be true, and as time passed even more Irishmen held them to be true. His analysis of the Irish scene was not far off the mark. The English did not, after all was said and done, win the peace. O'Brien had lost the revolution, but he did everything he could to save the aftermath. O'Brien was a man descended from Irish kings who was affected by that relationship. He was a man whose reputation was severely damaged by the *London Times*, but whose courage and sense of history helped keep the principle of Irish self-government a viable policy.

Notes

Chapter 1: Revolution, Conviction, and Transportation

1. A general background for the period can be found in Kevin B. Nowlan, *The Politics of Repeal*; Sir Charles Gavan Duffy, *Four Years of Irish History*; Denis Gwynn, "Smith O'Brien and the Secession"; William Smith O'Brien, "Motives which induced Smith O'Brien to take up arms against the British Government," MS 464, William Smith O'Brien Papers (hereafter cited as O'Brien, "Motives"); *Times* (London), 20 June 1864.

2. Great Britain, *Hansard Parliamentary Debates*, 3d series, 97:1203–7 (hereafter cited as *Hansard*).

3. Duffy, *Four Years of Irish History*, p. 719.

4. *Hansard*, 98:33, 20–34, 37–39, 537.

5. Alfred Webb, *Memoir of John Mitchel*, pp. 1–10; *Nation* (Dublin), 22 November 1845, p. 88, and 6 November 1847, p. 904; Mitchel was born on 3 November 1815, *Dictionary of National Biography*, edited by Sir Leslie Stephen and Sir Sidney Lee, 13:505 (hereafter cited as *DNB*).

6. *Times* (London), 20 June 1864.

7. Ibid., 27 December 1853, 20 June 1864.

8. *United Irishman* quoted in Duffy, *Four Years of Irish History*, p. 551.

9. John Mitchel to O'Brien, 6 October 1852, MS 444/2813, O'Brien Papers.

10. Thomas Francis Meagher, *Speeches on the Legislative Independence of Ireland*, pp. 269–70; Webb, *Memoir of John Mitchel*, pp. 1–10.

11. J. H. Cullen, *Young Ireland in Exile*, pp. 101–3; Martin was born on 8 September 1812, *DNB*, 12:1170.

12. Duffy, *Four Years of Irish History*, pp. 612, 613.

13. P. A. Sillard, *The Life and Letters of John Martin*, pp. 106–23, 144.

14. Duffy, *Four Years of Irish History*, pp. 613, 737–38; John Kiernan, *The Irish Exiles in Australia*, pp. 121, 132; O'Doherty was born on 7 September 1823, see *DNB*, 2d supp., 3:40–41. Cullen, *Young Ireland in Exile*, p. 131. Mary Anne Kelly was also known as Mary Eva, Mary, or Eva.

15. Duffy, *Four Years of Irish History*, pp. 700–755.

16. Nowlan, *Politics of Repeal*, p. 212; *Hansard*, vol. 100, pp. 693–713, 755.

17. Nowlan, *Politics of Repeal*, p. 213, taken from the *Nation* (Dublin), 29 July 1848; O'Brien, "Motives," p. 63.

18. *Times* (London), 20 June 1864; O'Brien, "Motives," pp. 11–13; *Nation* (Dublin), 6 November 1858, p. 148; Notes of Dr. Brendan O'Brien to B. Touhill, Dublin, Ireland, 15 July 1976; O'Brien was born on 17 October 1803, see *DNB*, 14:777.

19. O'Brien, "Motives," pp. 17–19, 21.

20. Ibid., pp. 21–23.

21. Nowlan, *Politics of Repeal*, pp. 111–15.

22. O'Brien, "Motives," p. 59; *Times* (London), 20 June 1864.

23. Daniel O'Connell to the Very Rev. Dr. Costello, V.G.P.P., London, 16 May 1839, in Daniel O'Connell, *Correspondence of Daniel O'Connell*, 2:183–84; John Mitchel, *Jail Journal*, p. 7.

24. O'Brien, "Motives," p. 25.

25. Ibid., pp. 29–41.

26. *Nation* (Dublin), 6 November 1858, p. 149.

27. O'Brien, "Motives," pp. 65, 67, 69, 71.

28. Duffy, *Four Years of Irish History*, pp. 693–95.

29. Ibid., p. 642.

30. Ibid., pp. 643–84.

31. Ibid., pp. 690 n, 684–90; *Times* (London), 10 August 1848, p. 6.

32. *Nation* (Dublin), 2 August 1856, p. 777.

33. *Times* (London), 8 August 1848, p. 4.

34. Ibid., pp. 4–5.

35. *Punch* quoted in *Times* (London), 10 August 1848, p. 6.

36. *Times* (London), 10 August 1848, p. 6.

37. John Locke to O'Brien, 5 May 1849, MS 443/2541; J. C. Anstey to O'Brien, 4 April 1850, MS 444/2711;

Mrs. O'Brien (mother) to O'Brien, 7 May 1850, MS 444/2726, O'Brien Papers.

38. *Nation* (Dublin), 6 November 1858, p. 148.

39. Duffy, *Four Years of Irish History*, p. 759; Richard O'Gorman to O'Brien, 24 May 1849, Brussels, Belgium, MS 443/2547, O'Brien Papers; Nowlan, *Politics of Repeal*, p. 216.

40. Earl Grey to Sir William Denison, 5 June 1849, Colonial Office, 408/32–9874, London Public Record Office (hereafter cited as PRO). On 26 November 1855, Van Diemen's Land was officially renamed Tasmania.

41. Ibid.

42. O'Brien to the House of Commons, 6 June 1849, MS 443/2559, O'Brien Papers.

43. O'Brien to Archdeacon Marriot, 16 November 1849, MS 443/2575, O'Brien Papers.

44. O'Brien to the House of Commons, 6 June 1849, MS 443/2559; O'Brien to the Sheriff of Dublin, 5 June 1849, MS 443/2548; O'Brien to Sir Colman O'Loghlen, 5 June 1849, MS 443/2550; O'Loghlen to Mr. Redington, n.d., MS 443/2555, O'Brien Papers.

45. O'Brien to Speaker of the House of Commons, 6 June 1849, MS 443/2551, O'Brien Papers.

46. *Hansard*, 106:158–62.

47. O'Farrell to O'Brien, 21 June 1849, MS 443/2556, O'Brien Papers; *Hansard*, 106:389–449, 823–30.

48. McManus to Mrs. Potter, 15 June 1849, in Kiernan, *Exiles in Australia*, p. 105; John Martin, The Diary of John Martin, 28 June 1849, MS D. 560, p. 14, Belfast Public Record Office, Northern Ireland (hereafter cited as BPRO); Grey to Denison, 27 June 1849, CO 408/32–9874, PRO.

49. The Diary of John Martin, 16 October 1849, pp. 96–98, BPRO.

50. *Hansard*, 111:1231–33; Redington to Lucy O'Brien, 19 June 1849, MS 443/2554, O'Brien Papers.

51. O'Brien, "Motives," pp. 103, 105.

52. *Times* (London), 8 October 1850, p. 8.

53. Sir William Denison, *Varieties of Vice-Regal Life*, 1: 134, 135–36.

54. Meagher to Martin and O'Doherty, 31 October 1849, in Kiernan, *Exiles in Australia*, pp. 61–62; William Smith O'Brien, Journal of William Smith O'Brien,

1:1, 9 July 1849, MS 3923, O'Brien Papers (hereafter cited as O'Brien, Journal).

55. Memorandum of W. S. O'Brien, 6 June 1849, MS 443/2552, O'Brien Papers; O'Brien, "Motives," p. 97.

56. Duffy, *Four Years of Irish History*, pp. 7–10; Meagher was born on 3 August 1823, see *DNB*, 13:194; Mitchel, *Jail Journal*, p. 7.

57. Gwynn, "Smith O'Brien and the Secession," pp. 139–40; O'Brien, "Motives," p. 63.

58. Mitchel, *Jail Journal*, p. 443; McManus was born "about 1823," see *DNB*, 12:673.

59. *Nation* (New York), 26 January 1850, p. 2, and 24 November 1849, p. 4; in October 1849 O'Donoghue was listed as forty-one years of age, Official Records of Prisoners, MS 13,610, O'Brien Papers.

60. Meagher to Martin and O'Doherty, 31 October 1849, in Kiernan, *Exiles in Australia*, pp. 61–62; *Freeman's Journal* quoted in *Times* (London), 11 July 1849, p. 8; *Nation* (New York), 4 August 1849, p. 2; O'Brien, Journal, 1:1–3, 9 July 1849.

61. O'Brien, Journal, 1:5, 9 July 1849.

62. Meagher to his Family, 3 September 1849, *Nation* (New York), 26 January 1850, p. 2; William Smith O'Brien, Journal of William Smith O'Brien, 30 August 1849, Private Collection of Dr. and Mrs. Brendan O'Brien (hereafter cited as O'Brien, Journal, PC).

63. O'Brien, Journal, 1:5, 9 July 1849; Thomas F. Meagher, *Meagher of the Sword*, p. 237.

64. Mitchel, *Jail Journal*, pp. 1–2, 53, 95–96, 141.

65. O'Brien, Journal, 1:7–8, 10 July 1849.

66. Ibid., pp. 11, 12.

67. Ibid., p. 13.

68. Ibid., p. 14.

69. O'Brien, Journal, PC, 27 August, 8 September 1849; Meagher, *Meagher of the Sword*, pp. 235, 237; O'Donoghue's Diary to his Family, 31 August 1848, *Nation* (New York), 26 January 1850, p. 2.

70. McManus to a friend in Limerick, 12 September 1849, *Times* (London), 15 December 1849, p. 5; O'Donoghue to Patrick Carmola, 9 September 1849, *Nation* (New York), 12 January 1850, p. 3; Meagher to his Family, 3 September 1849, *Nation* (New York), 26 January 1850, p. 2; O'Brien, Journal, 1:32–33, 24 July 1849; O'Donoghue's Diary to his Family, 2 Au-

gust 1849, *Nation* (New York), 26 January 1850, p. 2.

71. *Times* (London) quoted in supplement to the *South Australian Register* (Adelaide), 7 November 1849; *Nation* (New York), 15 September 1849, p. 2.

72. Inhabitants of the Town of Six Mile Bridge to the Queen, 30 July 1849, MS 443/2562, O'Brien Papers; *Times* (London), 2 August 1849, p. 5; *South Australian Register*, 15 December 1849, p. 414.

73. O'Brien, Journal, PC, 11, 12 September 1849; *Nation* (New York), 26 January 1850, p. 3, and 25 May 1850, p. 2.

74. O'Brien, Journal, PC, 11, 12 September 1849.

75. O'Brien to Mr. Gabbitt, 7 March 1850, MS 443/2662, O'Brien Papers; *Nation* (New York), 26 January 1850, p. 3, and 25 May 1850, p. 2; Mitchel, *Jail Journal*, 19 September 1849, p. 175.

76. O'Brien, Journal, PC, 8, 12 September 1849; O'Brien, Journal, 1:69, 20 October 1849; *Nation* (New York), 26 January 1850, p. 3, and 25 May 1850, p. 2.

77. *Cork Examiner* quoted in *Times* (London), 7 December 1849, p. 5.

78. O'Brien, Journal, PC, 13 September 1849.

79. Meagher, *Meagher of the Sword*, p. 235.

80. O'Brien, Journal, 1:73, 23 October 1849, 1:74–75, 25 October 1849.

81. Meagher to his Family, 3 September 1849, *Nation* (New York), 26 January 1850, p. 2.

82. *Nation* (New York), 26 January 1850, p. 3.

83. O'Brien, Journal, 1:58–59, 7 August 1849; 1:87–90, 24 August 1849.

84. Ibid., 1:79, 28 October 1849.

85. Meagher, *Meagher of the Sword*, pp. 239–40.

Chapter 2: Van Diemen's Land

1. *World Guide*, p. 402; Sir William Denison, *Varieties of Vice-Regal Life*, pp. 12–15.

2. Gregson Opinion, MS 443/2648, William Smith O'Brien Papers.

3. Ibid.

4. Ibid.

5. Ibid.

6. Ibid.

7. William Smith O'Brien, Journal of William Smith O'Brien, 2:13, 18 November 1850, MS 3923, O'Brien Papers (hereafter cited as O'Brien, Journal).

8. Ibid., p. 14.

9. John Mitchel, *Jail Journal*, p. 225.

10. John West, *History of Tasmania*, 2:313, 314, 315, 318–20.

11. Ibid., 2:313, 314 (footnote taken from the *Examiner*, 1846), 315, 318–20.

12. Ibid., 2:130, 202.

13. Denison to Mrs. Denison (mother), 7 March 1847, in Denison, *Varieties*, pp. 32–33.

14. West, *Tasmania*, 2:225, 226.

15. O'Brien, Journal, 6:39, 2 June 1852.

16. West, *Tasmania*, 1:271, 276, 278, 280–83, 2:306, 334–35.

17. Ibid., 1:272, 284–86; James Fenton, *A History of Tasmania*, 1:185–87, 193–97, 198–99.

18. West, *Tasmania*, 1:272–73, 286, 289–90, 318; Fenton, *Tasmania*, 1:180–84, 242–44, 265–66; Denison to Grey, 14 June 1851, in Denison, *Varieties*, pp. 158–60.

19. O'Brien, Journal, 1:78, 28 October 1849; Meagher to his friends in Dublin, 1 December 1849, *Nation* (New York), 25 May 1850, p. 2.

20. *Courier* quoted in *Melbourne Argus*, 15 November 1849; *Launceston Examiner*, 3 November 1849.

21. 29 October 1849, in Denison, *Varieties*, p. 131.

22. Meagher to his friends in Dublin, 1 December 1849, *Nation* (New York), 25 May 1850, p. 2; Meagher to Gavan Duffy, Campbell Town, February 1850, in Thomas F. Meagher, *Meagher of the Sword*, p. 242.

23. O'Brien, Journal, 1:79, 29 October 1849.

24. Ibid., 1:80.

25. Ibid.

26. Ibid.

27. Ibid.

28. Meagher to Duffy, in Meagher, *Meagher of the Sword*, pp. 244–45.

29. 30 October 1849, in Denison, *Varieties*, pp. 132, 133.

30. O'Brien, Journal, 1:80–81, 29 October 1849; Meagher to Duffy, in Meagher, *Meagher of the Sword*, p. 246.

31. Meagher to Duffy, in Meagher, *Meagher of the Sword*, p. 245.

32. O'Brien to Lucy O'Brien, 29 October 1849, MS 8653/25, O'Brien Papers.

33. *Nation* (Dublin), 2 August 1856, p. 777; O'Brien to T. Chisholm Anstey, 22 November 1849, MS 443/2582, O'Brien Papers; 2 November 1849, in Denison, *Varieties*, p. 134; O'Brien to Kitty, 2 May

1850, MS 444/2687, and O'Brien to I. H. Bindon, Esq., 5 June 1850, MS 444/2694, O'Brien Papers.

34. *Nation* (Dublin), 5 January 1850, p. 2; O'Brien, Journal, 2:46, 20 March 1850.

35. Meagher to Duffy, in Meagher, *Meagher of the Sword*, p. 247; 2 November 1849, in Denison, *Varieties*, p. 134.

36. Ibid.; Official Records, MS 13,610, O'Brien Papers.

37. 30 October 1849, in Denison, *Varieties*, p. 134.

38. Meagher to Duffy, in Meagher, *Meagher of the Sword*, pp. 247–50; J. H. Cullen, *Young Ireland in Exile*, pp. 73–74.

39. Meagher to Duffy, in Meagher, *Meagher of the Sword*, pp. 250–52; Meagher to O'Brien, 16 December 1849, MS 443/2591A, and 29 November 1849, MS 443/2584, O'Brien Papers.

40. Meagher to O'Brien, 16 December 1849, MS 443/2591A, O'Brien Papers; Meagher to Duffy, in Meagher, *Meagher of the Sword*, p. 254.

41. Meagher to O'Brien, February 1850, MS 443/2649, O'Brien Papers.

42. Meagher to Dunne, 10 January 1850, in Cullen, *Young Ireland in Exile*, pp. 70–71.

43. Cullen, *Young Ireland in Exile*, pp. 125, 126, 128; O'Doherty to O'Brien, 27 May 1850, MS 444/2691, O'Brien Papers; O'Brien to O'Doherty, 27 December 1849, in John Kiernan, *The Irish Exiles in Australia*, p. 67; Meagher to Duffy, in Meagher, *Meagher of the Sword*, p. 256.

44. Meagher to Duffy, in Meagher, *Meagher of the Sword*, pp. 256–57.

45. Martin to O'Doherty, November 1849, in Kiernan, *Exiles in Australia*, pp. 62, 63.

46. Meagher to Duffy, in Meagher, *Meagher of the Sword*, pp. 254–55.

47. Meagher to Dunne, 12 December 1849, 10 January 1850, in Cullen, *Young Ireland in Exile*, pp. 69–72; Meagher to O'Doherty, in Kiernan, *Exiles in Australia*, p. 79.

48. Kiernan, *Exiles in Australia*, p. 52; Cullen, *Young Ireland in Exile*, p. 70.

49. Kiernan, *Exiles in Australia*, p. 52; *Launceston Examiner*, 11 January 1851, p. 28; Denison to Grey, 11 December 1849, Colonial Office, 280/249–2759, London Public Record Office (hereafter cited as PRO).

50. McManus to O'Doherty, 24 November 1849, MS 10,522, John Martin Papers.

51. Martin to O'Doherty, 29 November 1849, in Kiernan, *Exiles in Australia*, p. 64; Cullen, *Young Ireland in Exile*, p. 94.

52. McManus to O'Doherty, 24 November 1849, MS 10,522, Martin Papers; McManus to O'Brien, 4 November 1850, MS 444/2760, O'Brien to McManus, 28 January 1850, MS 443/2629, O'Brien Papers.

53. O'Donoghue to O'Doherty, 9 November 1849, in Kiernan, *Exiles in Australia*, pp. 66–69; Cullen, *Young Ireland in Exile*, pp. 114–15.

54. O'Donoghue to O'Doherty, 9 November 1849, in Kiernan, *Exiles in Australia*, pp. 66–69.

55. Ibid., pp. 66–69.

56. Meagher to Duffy, in Meagher, *Meagher of the Sword*, pp. 258–59.

57. Kiernan, *Exiles in Australia*, p. 65.

58. 6 December 1849, in Denison, *Varieties*, p. 135.

59. O'Brien, Journal, 2:1–3, 31 October–6 November 1849.

60. Ibid., p. 3.

61. 2 November 1849, in Denison, *Varieties*, p. 134.

62. O'Brien, Journal, 2:3, 31 October–6 November 1849.

63. Nairn to Lapham, 29 October 1849, CO 280/249–2759, PRO.

64. O'Brien, Journal, 2:4–5, 31 October–6 November 1849.

65. Ibid., 2:4, 6; *The South Australian Register*, 12 December 1849, p. 410.

66. 30 October 1849, in Denison, *Varieties* p. 132; Fenton, *Tasmania*, 1:213.

67. Nairn to Lapham, 6 November 1849, CO 280/249–2759, PRO.

68. Ibid.; O'Brien, Journal, 2:7–8, 8, 13 November 1849.

69. Denison to Grey, 11 December 1849, CO 280/249–2759, PRO.

70. Nairn to Lapham, 13 November 1849, CO 280/249–2759, PRO.

71. O'Brien to Archdeacon Marriot, 16 November 1849, MS 443/2575, Archdeacon Marriot to O'Brien, 3 December 1849, MS 443/2581, Reeves to O'Brien, 1 November 1849, MS 443/2579, O'Brien to Reeves, 26 November 1849, MS 443/2580, O'Brien Papers.

72. O'Brien to T. Chisholm Anstey, 22 November 1849, MS 443/2582, O'Brien Papers.

73. O'Brien to Sir Lucius O'Brien, 6 December 1849, MS 443/2567, O'Brien to Charles and Harriet Monsell, 20 December 1849, MS 443/2595, O'Brien to Wil-

liam Monsell, 20 December 1849, MS 443/2594, O'Brien Papers.

74. *The South Australian Register*, 12 December 1849, p. 410; *Guardian* quoted in *Melbourne Argus*, 14 December 1849.

75. O'Brien, Journal, 2:26, 15 December 1849.

76. 11 January 1850, in Denison, *Varieties*, pp. 135–36.

77. T. Chisholm Anstey to O'Brien, 14 April 1850, MS 444/2711, O'Brien Papers.

78. Donough O'Brien, *History of the O'Briens*, pp. 223–24; Personal notes Brendan O'Brien, as well as conversations.

79. O'Brien to Kitty, 2 May 1850, MS 444/2687, O'Brien to I. H. Bindon, Esq., 5 June 1850, MS 444/2694, O'Brien Papers.

80. O'Brien, Journal, 2:26–27, 25 December 1849.

81. O'Brien to Ellen O'Brien, 1 January 1850, MS 443/2605, O'Brien Papers.

82. O'Brien, Journal, 2:28–29, 4 January 1850.

83. Ibid., 2:29, 10 January 1850.

84. Ibid., 3:25, 8 September 1850.

85. Ibid., 2:29–30, 10 January 1850.

86. Denison to Grey, 23 January 1850, CO 280/255–5546, PRO; O'Brien to Robert Pitcairn, 7 January 1850, MS 443/2610 and 2613, Pitcairn to O'Brien, 22 January 1850, MS 443/2633, O'Brien Papers.

87. Pitcairn to O'Brien, 19 February 1850, MS 443/2646, Gregson Opinion, MS 443/2648, O'Brien Papers.

88. Pitcairn to O'Brien, 26 February 1850, MS 443/2656, Knight Opinion, MS 443/2647, O'Brien Papers.

89. O'Brien, Journal, 2:43, 8 March 1850.

90. O'Brien to Rev. Robert Gabbitt, 7 March 1850, MS 443/2662, O'Brien to T. Chisholm Anstey, 8 March 1850, MS 443/2663, O'Brien Papers.

Chapter 3: Old Policy and New Plans

1. *Melbourne Argus*, 14 December 1849; *South Australian Register*, 18 January 1850, p. 63; *Hobart Town Gazette* quoted in the *Nation* (Dublin), 8 June 1850.

2. Denison to Grey, 6 December 1849, Colonial Office 280/249–2757, London Public Record Office (hereafter cited as PRO).

3. Ibid., 11 December 1849, CO 280/249–2759, PRO.

4. Ibid.

5. Ibid., 13 December 1849, CO 280/249–2761; 24 December 1849, CO 280/249–2816; 11 December 1849, CO 280/249–2759, PRO.

6. Ibid., 23 January 1850, CO 280/250–5546, PRO.

7. Ibid., 29 January 1850, CO 280/255–5550, PRO.

8. Ibid., 17 April 1850, CO 280/258–7883, PRO.

9. Ibid., 6 December 1849, CO 280/249–2757; 11 December 1849, CO 280/249–2759; 13 December 1849, CO 280/249–2761; 24 December 1849, CO 280/249–2816; 27 December 1849, CO 280/249–2817; 28 December 1849, CO 280/249–2818; 10 January 1850, CO 280/255–2996; 12 January 1850, CO 280/255–2998, PRO.

10. Grey to Denison, 29 April 1850, CO 280/249–2757, 2759, PRO.

11. Denison to Grey, 23 January 1850, CO 280/255–5546; 29 January 1850, CO 280/255–5550; 12 February 1850, CO 280/259–4709; Grey to Denison, 12 July 1850, CO 280/255–5550 (105), PRO.

12. Denison to Grey, 17 April 1850; notation by Merivale, 24 September 1850, CO 280/258–7883, PRO.

13. Ibid., notation by Merivale, 24 September 1850, CO 280/258–7883, PRO.

14. Denison to Grey, 17 April 1850, notation by Grey, 28 September 1850, and note to H. Waddington, 14 October 1850, CO 280/258–7883, PRO.

15. Notation contained in List of Dispatches on the Political Prisoners from Ireland waiting to be answered and now forwarded for Directions, 22 April 1850, CO 280/249–2759, PRO.

16. T. Chisholm Anstey to O'Brien, 14 April 1850, MS 444/2711, William Smith O'Brien Papers.

17. Lucius O'Brien to Willy, May 1850; Lucius O'Brien to Government Officials, 6 May 1850; and Hawes to Sir Lucius O'Brien, 11 May 1850, MS 8655/8, O'Brien Papers.

18. Lucius O'Brien to O'Brien, 1 May 1850, MS 444/2743; Anne Martineau to O'Brien, 6 May 1850, MS 444/2723; Mrs. O'Brien to O'Brien, 7 May 1850, MS 444/2726; Katherine Harris to O'Brien, 23 July 1850, MS 8656/11, O'Brien Papers.

19. *Nation* (Dublin) quoted in *Times* (London), 22 April 1850, p. 5; *Nation* (Dublin), 20 April 1850, p. 536.

20. *Limerick Chronicle* quoted in *Times* (London), 14 June 1850, p. 6; *Evening*

Packet quoted in *Nation* (Dublin), 29 June 1850, p. 652; *Galway Vindicator, Sligo Champion,* and *Cork Examiner* quoted in *Nation* (Dublin), 22 June 1850, p. 676.

21. *Nation* (Dublin), 29 June 1850, pp. 689, 693, 696; 6 July 1850, pp. 707, 709, 713, 717; 13 July 1850, p. 728; 20 July 1850, p. 744; 3 August 1850, p. 780; *New York Tribune* quoted in *Nation* (Dublin), 12 October 1850, pp. 102–3; Memorandum, 6 July 1850, pp. 707–9, 713, MS 444/2697, O'Brien Papers.

22. *New York Tribune* quoted in *Nation* (Dublin), 12 October 1850, pp. 102–3.

23. *Times* (London), 22 April 1850, p. 5.

24. Ibid., 8 October 1850, p. 8.

25. Great Britain, *Hansard Parliamentary Debates,* 3d series, 111:1231.

26. Ibid., 111:1231–33.

27. Ibid., 111:1233–34, 112:151–53.

28. Ibid., 112:786–95.

29. Ibid. At least two individuals did lose their lives.

30. Duffy to Meagher, 13 September 1850, in John Kiernan, *The Irish Exiles in Australia,* p. 94.

31. James Fenton, *A History of Tasmania,* 1:225–28; John West, *History of Tasmania,* 1:274–75.

32. *Courier* quoted in *Launceston Examiner,* 23 February 1850, p. 125.

33. Ibid.

34. Meagher to O'Doherty, in Kiernan, *Exiles in Australia,* p. 79.

35. O'Doherty to O'Brien, 27 May 1850, MS 444/2691, O'Brien Papers.

36. John Mitchel, *Jail Journal,* pp. 108–10, 114–15, 116–17, 138–39, 149–50, 176.

37. Ibid., pp. 172–74, 175–79, 204, 217–18, 225.

38. Ibid., pp. 224–26.

39. Denison to Grey, 2 May 1850, CO 280/259–7900, PRO.

40. *Sydney Morning Herald,* 25 July 1850.

41. *Launceston Examiner,* 10 April 1850, p. 227.

42. West, *Tasmania,* 1:296–305; Fenton, *Tasmania,* 1:197–99.

43. Henry Dowling to his brother in Dublin, in *Nation* (Dublin), quoted in *Times* (London), 30 September 1850, p. 5.

44. Kiernan, *Exiles in Australia,* p. 105; Mitchel, *Jail Journal,* p. 236.

45. Mitchel, *Jail Journal,* p. 228; Martin to Mary Anne Kelly, 6 June 1850, in Kiernan, *Exiles in Australia,* p. 86.

46. Mitchel, *Jail Journal,* p. 230.

47. Martin to Meagher, 11 April 1850, in Kiernan, *Exiles in Australia,* p. 80.

48. Mitchel, *Jail Journal,* pp. 232–34.

49. Ibid., p. 235.

50. Ibid.

51. Kiernan, *Exiles in Australia,* p. 55.

52. Mitchel, *Jail Journal,* pp. 235–37.

53. Ibid., pp. 237–38.

54. Ibid., p. 227.

55. *Sydney Morning Herald,* 2 April 1850.

56. *South Australian Register,* 30 May 1850, p. 517.

57. J. H. Cullen, *Young Ireland in Exile,* pp. 118–19.

58. William Smith O'Brien, Journal of William Smith O'Brien, 4:2–3, 20 December 1850, O'Brien Papers; *Melbourne Argus,* 21 June 1850; Cullen, *Young Ireland in Exile,* pp. 94–95.

59. John Martin to Mary Anne Kelly, 6 June 1850, in Kiernan, *Exiles in Australia,* p. 86; P. A. Sillard, *The Life and Letters of John Martin,* pp. 150–51.

60. Mitchel, *Jail Journal,* pp. 245, 246.

61. John Martin to Mary Anne Kelly, 6 June 1850, in Kiernan, *Exiles in Australia,* pp. 86, 98.

62. Ibid., p. 86; Nairn to O'Doherty, 15 August 1850, in Kiernan, *Exiles in Australia,* pp. 123, 168; Cullen, *Young Ireland in Exile,* p. 125; O'Doherty to O'Brien, 27 May 1850, MS 444/2691, O'Brien Papers.

63. Bishop Willson to O'Doherty, August 1850, in Kiernan, *Exiles in Australia,* pp. 123–24.

64. Ibid., 29 August 1850, pp. 124–25.

65. Bishop Willson to O'Doherty, 12 November 1850, MS 10,522, John Martin Papers; Kiernan, *Exiles in Australia,* p. 126.

Chapter 4: The Ticket-of-Leave

1. William Smith O'Brien, Journal of William Smith O'Brien, 2:45, 13 March 1850, William Smith O'Brien Papers (hereafter cited as O'Brien, Journal).

2. McCarthy to O'Brien, 9 October 1852, MS 445/2838, McCarthy to O'Brien, 21 September 1852, MS 445/2837, O'Brien Papers; O'Brien, Journal, 3:19, 14 August 1850, and 3:54, 17 November 1850; Denison to Grey, 30 September 1850, Colonial Office 280/263–442, London Public Record Office (hereafter cited as PRO).

3. J. H. Cullen, *Young Ireland in Exile,* p. 16; O'Brien, Journal, 2:4, 31 October–6

November 1849. The chief conspirator was not Dr. MacNamara but Dr. Mc-Carthy.

4. O'Brien, Journal, 3:21, 14 August 1850.

5. Ibid., 2:46–47, 20 March 1850, and 3:21–22, 14, 20 August 1850.

6. O'Brien to Lucy O'Brien, 15 January 1851, MS 8653; "Proceedings in relation to the Estate of William Smith O'Brien," Memorandum, Dublin, 6 January 1862, O'Brien Papers.

7. McCarthy to O'Brien, 21 September 1852, MS 445/2837, O'Brien Papers; Cullen, *Young Ireland in Exile*, p. 16.

8. Cullen, *Young Ireland in Exile*, p. 16.

9. O'Brien, Journal, 3:19–21, 14 August 1850.

10. Ibid.

11. Hampton to Lapham, n.d., MS 444/2803, O'Brien Papers.

12. Denison to Mrs. Denison, 28 August 1850, in Sir William Denison, *Varieties of Vice-Regal Life*, p. 144.

13. Ibid., pp. 144–45.

14. *Launceston Examiner* quoted in *South Australian Register*, 3 September 1850, p. 222; *Melbourne Argus*, 21 August 1850.

15. *Colonial Times* quoted in *Launceston Examiner*, 17 August 1850, p. 526; *Launceston Examiner*, 17 August 1850, p. 523; *Irish Exile* quoted in *Nation* (Dublin), 18 January 1851, p. 329; *Hobart Town Advertiser* quoted in *Melbourne Argus*, 26 August 1850.

16. *Irish Exile* quoted in *Nation* (Dublin), 18 January 1851, p. 329.

17. James Fenton, *A History of Tasmania*, 1:215.

18. ———to Duffy, 30 September 1850, in *Nation* (Dublin), 25 January 1851, pp. 344–45; Cullen, *Young Ireland in Exile*, p. 17; *Nation* (Dublin), 9 August 1851, p. 793; *Irish Exile* quoted in *Nation* (Dublin), 18 January 1851, p. 329.

19. Denison to Grey, 30 September 1850, CO 280/263-442, PRO; Denison to Mrs. Denison, 28 August 1850, in Denison, *Varieties*, p. 144; *Nation* (Dublin), 18 January 1851, p. 325; *Melbourne Argus*, 12, 21 September 1850; *South Australian Register*, 20 September 1850, p. 282, and 25 September 1850, p. 300.

20. O'Brien, Journal, 3:22, 20 August 1850; T. Chisholm Anstey to O'Brien, 14 April 1850, MS 444/2711, O'Brien Papers.

21. O'Brien to Anstey, 20 August 1850, MS 444/2712, O'Brien Papers.

22. Ibid.

23. Ibid.

24. O'Brien, Journal, 3:23, 24 August 1850.

25. John West, *History of Tasmania*, 2:243.

26. Ibid.

27. Ibid., 2:243–44.

28. Ibid., p. 244.

29. Ibid., quoting evidence from Arthur and Murdoch.

30. O'Brien, Journal, 3:23, 24 August 1850.

31. Ibid.; *Hobart Town Courier* quoted in *Times* (London), 30 July 1850.

32. O'Brien, Journal, 3:23, 24 August 1850.

33. Nairn to O'Brien, 23 August 1850, in O'Brien, Journal, 3:23–24, 24 August 1850.

34. O'Brien, Journal, 3:24, 24 August 1850.

35. Ibid., 3:25, 8 September 1850.

36. Ibid., 3:25–26, 8 September 1850, and 3:26–27, 11 September 1850; O'Brien to Comptroller General, 9 September 1850, MS 444/2721; O'Brien to Bishop of Tasmania, 11 September 1850, MS 444/2724, O'Brien Papers.

37. Bishop Nixon to O'Brien, 14 September 1850, MS 444/2728, O'Brien Papers; O'Brien, Journal, 3:28, 18 September 1850.

38. Denison to Mrs. Denison, 28 August 1850 and September, in Denison, *Varieties*, p. 145.

39. O'Brien to Lucius O'Brien, 2 October 1850, MS 444/2740, O'Brien Papers; O'Brien, Journal, 3:29, 20 September 1850.

40. O'Brien, Journal, 3:25–26, 8 September 1850; O'Brien to Comptroller General, 21 September 1850, in O'Brien, Journal, 3:29, 21 September 1850; O'Brien, Journal, 3:29, 2 October 1850.

41. O'Brien, Journal, 3:40, 25 October 1850; 3:41–42, 28 October 1850; 3:48–49, 6 November 1850; 3:36–37, 16 October 1850.

42. O'Donoghue to O'Brien, 24 September 1850, MS 444/2733, O'Brien to O'Donoghue, 30 September 1850, MS 444/2735, O'Brien Papers.

43. O'Brien to O'Donoghue, 5 October 1850, MS 444/2741, O'Donoghue to O'Brien, 7 October 1850, MS 444/2742, O'Brien Papers.

44. *Colonial Times* quoted in *Melbourne Argus*, 1 October 1850.

45. *Britannia* quoted in *Launceston Examiner*, 12 October 1850, p. 657.

46. *Launceston Examiner*, 16 October 1850, p. 663, and 26 October 1850, pp. 687, 689.

47. Ibid., 2 November 1850, p. 703.

48. McManus to O'Brien, 4 November 1850, MS 444/2760, Mitchel to O'Brien, 6 November 1850, MS 444/2762, Martin to O'Brien, 7 November 1850, MS 444/2763, O'Brien Papers.

49. Mrs. O'Brien to O'Brien, 7 May 1850, MS 444/2726, O'Brien Papers.

50. Anne Martineau to O'Brien, 6 May 1850, MS 444/2723, O'Brien Papers.

51. Katherine Harris to O'Brien, 23 July 1850, MS 8656/11, O'Brien Papers.

52. O'Brien to Lucy O'Brien, 14 November 1850, MS 8653/26, O'Brien Papers.

53. Lucius O'Brien to O'Brien, 1 May 1850, MS 444/2743, O'Brien Papers.

54. *South Australian Register*, 3 December 1850, p. 534; *Hobart Town Chronicle* quoted in *South Australian Register*, 23 November 1850, p. 502; O'Donoghue to O'Brien, 5 November 1850, MS 444/2761, O'Brien Papers; O'Brien, Journal, 3:47–48, 6 November 1850.

55. Reeves to O'Brien, 8 November 1850, MS 444/2765, O'Brien Papers; *Nation* (Dublin), 22 March 1851, p. 472; O'Brien, Journal, 3:49, 9 November 1850.

56. O'Donoghue to O'Brien, 8 November 1850, MS 444/2764, O'Brien Papers.

57. O'Brien to Lucy O'Brien, 14 November 1850, 8653/26, O'Brien Papers.

58. O'Brien, Journal, 3:49, 9 November 1850; O'Brien to Reeves, 9 November 1850, in *Nation* (Dublin), 22 March 1851, p. 472.

59. Reeves to O'Brien, 12 November 1850, MS 444/2772, O'Brien Papers; Denison to Mrs. Denison, 17 December 1850, in Denison, *Varieties*, p. 146; Nairn to O'Brien, 12 November 1850, MS 444/2774, and November 1850, MS 444/2773, O'Brien Papers.

60. O'Brien to Lapham, 13 November 1850, MS 444/2777, O'Brien to Comptroller General, 13 November 1850, MS 444/2775, Nairn to O'Brien, 19 November 1850, MS 444/2781, O'Brien Papers.

61. O'Brien, Journal, 3:2, 25 April, 1 May 1850, and 3:24–25, 5 September 1850; Nairn to O'Brien, 18 November 1850, MS 444/2780, O'Brien Papers.

62. O'Brien, Journal, 3:52, 17 November 1850.

63. Ibid., 3:53.

64. Ibid., 3:52–53.

65. Denison to Mrs. Denison, 2 April 1847, in Denison, *Varieties*, p. 39; O'Brien, Journal, 3:52, 17 November 1850.

66. West, *Tasmania*, 2:245–47.

67. Denison to Mrs. Denison, 2 April 1847, in Denison, *Varieties*, pp. 39–40; O'Brien, Journal, 3:52, 17 November 1850.

68. Ibid., 3:53–54.

Chapter 5: The Three Truants

1. William Smith O'Brien, Journal of William Smith O'Brien, 4:1, 22 November 1850, William Smith O'Brien Papers (hereafter cited as O'Brien, Journal).

2. Ibid.; *South Australian Register*, 10 December 1850, p. 559; *Melbourne Argus*, 29 November 1850; *Irish Exile* quoted in *Nation* (Dublin), 29 March 1851, pp. 488–89; Denison to Mrs. Denison, 17 December 1850, in Sir William Denison, *Varieties of Vice-Regal Life*, p. 146.

3. O'Brien, Journal, 4:1, 22 November 1850, 1:77–78, 27 October 1849; O'Brien to Father Norbert Woolfrey, 14 January 1851, in J. H. Cullen, *Young Ireland in Exile*, p. 21.

4. O'Brien, Journal, 4:1, 22 November 1850, 4(cont.):1, 7 December 1850.

5. O'Brien to Dunne, 28 November 1850, in Cullen, *Young Ireland in Exile*, pp. 19–20.

6. O'Brien, Journal, 4(cont.):8–9, 8 February 1851; 4:2–3, 2 January 1852; 4:12, 28 February 1852.

7. *Melbourne Argus*, 6 January 1851; Denison to Grey, 28 February 1852, Colonial Office 280/289–6356, London Public Record Office (hereafter cited as PRO); O'Brien, Journal, 4(cont.):3, 20 December 1850.

8. *Hobart Town Guardian* quoted in *Nation* (Dublin), 10 May 1851, p. 582; O'Brien to Duffy, 15 February 1851, MS 2642/3486, O'Brien Papers.

9. O'Brien to Duffy, 15 February 1851, MS 2642/3486, O'Brien Papers.

10. *Nation* (Dublin), 5 July 1851, p. 714; Meagher to Colman O'Loghlen, 27 August 1851, MS 3900, Thomas F. Meagher Papers.

11. Denison to Grey, 28 February 1852, Extract from the Record Book, Police Office, Launceston, 18 December 1850, CO 280/289–6356, PRO; O'Brien, Journal, 4(cont.):3, 1 January 1851.

12. Denison to Grey, 28 February 1852, Extract from the Record Book, Police Office, New Norfolk, 19, 20 December 1850, CO 280/289–6356, PRO; O'Brien, Journal, 4(cont.):2, 20 December 1850.

13. O'Brien, Journal, 4(cont.):2, 20 December 1850.

14. Cullen, *Young Ireland in Exile*, p. 120; Denison to Grey, 28 February 1852, Extract from the Record Book, Police Office, New Norfolk, 23 December 1850, CO 280/289–6356, PRO.

15. Denison to Grey, 14 January 1851, CO 280/273–3745, PRO.

16. Grey to Denison, 12 July 1850, CO 280/255–5550 (105), PRO.

17. O'Donoghue to Meagher, New Year's Day 1851, in *Nation* (Dublin), 5 July 1851, p. 714.

18. Denison to Grey, 28 February 1852, Nairn to McManus, 24 December 1850, Nairn to O'Doherty, 24 December 1850, Nairn to O'Donoghue, 24 December 1850, Nairn to the Chief Police Magistrate, 24 December 1850, CO 280/289–6356, PRO.

19. O'Donoghue to Meagher, New Year's Day 1851, in *Nation* (Dublin), 5 July 1851, p. 714; Cullen, *Young Ireland in Exile*, pp. 95, 96; McManus to Meagher, 30 December 1850, in Cullen, *Young Ireland in Exile*, p. 96.

20. O'Donoghue to Meagher, New Year's Day, 4 January 1851, in *Nation* (Dublin), 5 July 1851, p. 714.

21. Ibid.

22. Ibid.

23. Ibid.

24. O'Brien to Lucy O'Brien, 25 December 1850, MS 8653/26, O'Brien to Duffy, 15 February 1851, MS 2642/3486, O'Brien Papers.

25. Meagher to O'Brien, Christmas 1850, MS 444/2779, O'Brien Papers.

26. Cullen, *Young Ireland in Exile*, pp. 76–77.

27. Martin to O'Doherty, 27 January 1851, in John Kiernan, *The Irish Exiles in Australia*, p. 95.

28. Meagher to O'Doherty, postmarked 2 January 1851, in Kiernan, *Exiles in Australia*, pp. 97–98.

29. McManus to Meagher, 30 December 1850, in Cullen, *Young Ireland in Exile*, p. 96.

30. O'Doherty to Meagher, in Cullen, *Young Ireland in Exile*, pp. 130–31; O'Donoghue to Meagher, New Year's Day 1851, in *Nation* (Dublin), 5 July 1851, p. 714.

31. Cullen, *Young Ireland in Exile*, pp. 120–21.

32. McManus to O'Brien, 29 January 1851, MS 444/2789, O'Brien Papers.

33. Ibid.

34. Denison to Grey, 14 January 1851, CO 280/273–6069, PRO.

35. Ibid.

36. Ibid.

37. *Launceston Examiner*, 28 December 1850, p. 838.

38. Ibid., 4 January 1851, pp. 11–12, and 11 January 1851, p. 28.

39. *Melbourne Argus*, 14 February 1851; *Sydney Morning Herald*, 13 January 1851.

40. John West, *History of Tasmania*, 1:298–318.

41. *Melbourne Argus*, 14 February 1851.

42. *Maitland Mercury* quoted in *Launceston Examiner*, 15 March 1851, p. 176.

43. Father Hugh Magorian to ———, 8 March 1851, in *Nation* (Dublin), 19 July 1851, p. 745.

44. Denison to Grey, 22 March 1851, Sworn Affidavit by Adye Douglas before Commissioner Soms of the Supreme Court of Van Diemen's Land, Launceston, 29 January 1851, CO 280/275–7124, PRO.

45. *Colonial Times* quoted in *Melbourne Argus*, 7 February 1851.

46. McManus to O'Doherty, 30 January 1851, in Kiernan, *Exiles in Australia*, pp. 108–9.

47. Denison to Grey, 22 March 1851, Attorney General to Denison, 25 February 1851, CO 280/275–7124, PRO.

48. *Melbourne Argus*, 19 February 1851.

49. Denison to Grey, 22 March 1851, Attorney General to Denison, 25 February 1851, CO 280/275–7124, PRO.

50. Denison to Grey, 8 February 1851, CO 280/274–4286, PRO.

51. *Irish Exile* quoted in Kiernan, *Exiles in Australia*, p. 109.

52. Denison to Grey, 22 March 1851, Copy Return to Writ of Habeas Corpus, 14 February 1851, R. Ballantine, CO 280/275–7124, PRO.

53. *Melbourne Argus*, 28 February 1851.

54. Denison to Grey, 14 January 1851, CO 280/273–3745, 22 March 1851, CO 280/275–7124, PRO.

55. *Melbourne Argus*, 28 February 1851.

56. Denison to Grey, 22 March 1851, Substance of the Judgment of the Supreme Court delivered by The Chief Justice in the case of Terence Bellew McManus on Friday, 21 February 1851, CO 280/275–7124, PRO.

57. *South Australian Register*, 19 March 1851; *Irish Exile* quoted in Kiernan, *Exiles in Australia*, p. 109; *Launceston Examiner*, 26 February 1851, p. 135.

58. Denison to Grey, 22 March 1851, Attorney General to Denison, 25 February 1851, CO 280/275–7124, PRO.

59. Denison to Grey, 28 February 1851, CO 280/274–5299, and 18 April 1851, CO 280/276–8638, PRO.

60. 27 February 1851, in Denison, *Varieties*, p. 152.

61. Denis Gwynn, "Thomas Francis Meagher," speech, p. 36; Cullen, *Young Ireland in Exile*, pp. 77, 97.

62. *Cornwall Chronicle* quoted in *Melbourne Argus*, 20 March 1851.

63. *South Australian Register*, 19 March 1851, p. 266; *Launceston Examiner* quoted in *Melbourne Argus*, 13 March 1851; Denison to Grey, 28 February 1851, CO 280/274–5299, PRO.

64. Denison to Grey, 22 March 1851, Hampton to Denison, Memorandum, 8 March 1851, Dr. Casey to Dr. Dawson, 3 March 1851, CO 280/275–7124, PRO.

65. Denison to Grey, 22 March 1851, Medical Certificate, 27 February 1851, Launceston, C. Gavin Casey, Col. Surgeon and Grant, Surgeon, CO 280/275–7124, PRO.

66. Denison to Grey, 22 March 1851, Denison to Hampton, 28 February 1851, CO 280/275–7124, PRO.

67. Denison to Grey, 22 March 1851, Medical Certificate, 28 February 1851, C. Gavin Casey and Grant, CO 280/275–7124, PRO.

68. Denison to Grey, 22 March 1851, C. Gavin Casey and Grant to Dr. Dawson, 4 March 1851, CO 280/275–7124, PRO.

69. Ibid.; *Courier* quoted in *Melbourne Argus*, 19 March 1851.

70. Cullen, *Young Ireland in Exile*, pp. 97–98; Kiernan, *Exiles in Australia*, p. 110.

71. *Launceston Examiner*, 26 March 1851, p. 200; *Hobart Town Advertiser* quoted in *South Australian Register*, 26 March 1851.

72. *Cornwall Chronicle* quoted in *Melbourne Argus*, 20 March 1851; *Launceston Examiner*, 5 March 1851, p. 151; McCarthy to the *Hobart Town Advertiser*, in *Nation* (Dublin), 19 July 1851, p. 746.

73. *Melbourne Argus*, 19 March 1851; Cullen, *Young Ireland in Exile*, p. 122.

74. Denison to Grey, 22 March 1851, Hampton to Denison, Memorandum, 10 March 1851, Dr. C. Gavin Casey to Dr. Dawson, 3 March 1851, CO 280/275–7124, PRO.

Chapter 6: A Quiet Year

1. Mitchel to O'Brien, 21 October 1850, MS 444/2754, William Smith O'Brien Papers.

2. William Smith O'Brien, Journal of William Smith O'Brien, 4(cont.):1–2, 7 December 1850, O'Brien Papers (hereafter cited as O'Brien, Journal).

3. O'Brien to Lucy O'Brien, 10 January 1851, MS 8653/27, O'Brien Papers; O'Brien to Dunne, 27 January 1851, in J. H. Cullen, *Young Ireland in Exile*, pp. 21–22.

4. O'Brien, Journal, 4(cont.):6, 30 January 1851; 5:15–16, 24 February 1851; 5:20, 20 March 1851.

5. Martin to O'Doherty, 27 January 1851, in John Kiernan, *The Irish Exiles in Australia*, p. 96.

6. O'Brien to Comptroller General, 14 January 1851, MS 444/2782, Nairn to O'Brien, 17 January 1851, MS 444/2783, O'Brien to Mason, 1 February 1851, MS 444/2787, O'Brien to O'Doherty, 25 January 1851, MS 10,515/3, O'Brien Papers.

7. O'Brien to Lucy O'Brien, 19 February 1851, MS 8653/27, O'Brien Papers.

8. O'Brien, Journal, 5:12–13, 24 February 1851.

9. Ibid., pp. 13–14.

10. Ibid., p. 19, 10 March 1851.

11. Meagher to O'Doherty, 5, 18 June 1851, in Kiernan, *Exiles in Australia*, pp. 99–100; Mitchel to O'Doherty, May 1851, MS 3226/67–69, Rev. William Hickey Papers.

12. Mitchel to O'Brien, 26 June 1851, MS 444/2792, O'Brien Papers; Meagher to Sir Colman O'Loghlen, 27 August 1851, MS 3900/1, Thomas F. Meagher Papers; O'Brien to Dunne, 26 October 1851, MS 10,515/1, O'Brien Papers.

13. Cullen, *Young Ireland in Exile*, p. 122; *Melbourne Argus*, 6 May 1851.

14. *Melbourne Argus*, 6, 21 May 1851.

15. *Nation* (Dublin), 12 June 1852, p. 653.

16. Cullen, *Young Ireland in Exile*, pp. 122–23.

17. O'Doherty to O'Brien, 30 May 1851, MS 444/2804, O'Brien Papers.

18. O'Brien to Dunne, 26 October 1851, MS 10,515/1, O'Brien Papers.

19. John Mitchel, *Jail Journal*, pp. 249–50.

20. Ibid., pp. 251–55.

21. Ibid., pp. 255–59.

22. Ibid., pp. 259, 260; Martin to O'Doherty, 17 November 1851, MS 10,522, John Martin Papers; Mitchel to O'Brien, 26 June 1851, MS 444/2792, O'Brien Papers.

23. *Times* (London), 31 July 1851.

24. *Sydney Morning Herald,* 21 August 1851.

25. McManus to Duffy, 14 June 1851, in Cullen, *Young Ireland in Exile,* p. 99.

26. *New York Truth Teller* quoted in *Nation* (Dublin), 21 February 1852, p. 396.

27. Ibid.

28. Ibid.

29. Denison to Grey, 14 January 1851, Colonial Office 280/273–3745, Grey to Denison, 30 May 1851, CO 280/273–3745, London Public Record Office (hereafter cited as PRO).

30. Denison to Grey, 14 January 1851, Notation: Mr. Elliot, Mr. Hawes, Earl Grey, CO 280/273–3745, PRO.

31. Denison to Grey, 8 February 1851, Notation: Colonial Office official, CO 280/274–4286, PRO.

32. Waddington to Merivale, 27 May 1851, Notation: G[rey], [May] 31, [1851], CO 280/284–4668, PRO.

33. Merivale to Grey, Notation: Grey, June 1851, and Waddington to George Moulle, 4 June 1851, CO 280/284–4668, PRO.

34. A. E. Cockburn and W. P. Wood (attorney and solicitor general) to Waddington, 11 June 1851, CO 280/284–4668, PRO.

35. Merivale to Grey, 18 June 1851, CO 280/284–4668, PRO.

36. Ibid.; Waddington to Merivale, 4 December 1851, Grey to Merivale, 9 December 1851, Merivale to Waddington, 22 December 1851, and Note of Merivale to Grey, CO 280/284–10152, Grey to Denison, 28 November 1851, CO 280/275–9260, PRO.

37. Great Britain, *Hansard Parliamentary Debates,* 3d series, 116:588–89 (hereafter cited as *Hansard*).

38. Ibid., 116:589–90, 640–41; 117:634–41, 1067.

39. O'Brien to Duffy, 4 January 1851, in *Nation* (Dublin), 10 May 1851, pp. 584–85.

40. *Nation* (Dublin), 10 May 1851, p. 584; *Daily News* quoted in *Launceston Examiner,* 4 October 1851, p. 654.

41. *Nation* (Dublin), 5 July 1851, p. 704; 19 July 1851, p. 745; 2 August 1851, p. 775; *Times* (London), 29 August 1851; *Freemans Journal, Limerick Examiner, Sligo Champion,* and *Evening Herald* quoted in the *Nation* (Dublin), 2 August 1851, p. 775.

42. *Times* (London), 29 August 1851.

43. O'Brien, Journal, 5:35–36, 31 May 1851.

44. John Mitchel to John Gray, St. Patrick's Day 1851, in *Nation* (Dublin), 19 July 1851, p. 746.

45. Martin to O'Doherty, Summer 1851, in Kiernan, *Exiles in Australia,* p. 98.

46. Meagher to Mrs. Connell, 15 August 1851, in Cullen, *Young Ireland in Exile,* p. 81.

47. Meagher to O'Doherty, 31 July 1851, in Kiernan, *Exiles in Australia,* p. 101.

48. Robert G. Athearn, *Thomas Francis Meagher: An Irish Revolutionary in America,* p. 23; Cullen, *Young Ireland in Exile,* pp. 78–80.

49. Meagher to Mrs. Connell, 15 August 1851, in Cullen, *Young Ireland in Exile,* pp. 81–82.

50. Cullen, *Young Ireland in Exile,* p. 123; *Colonist* quoted in *Sydney Morning Herald,* 29 September 1851; O'Doherty to O'Brien, n.d., MS 444/2800, O'Brien Papers.

51. Cullen, *Young Ireland in Exile,* p. 123.

52. O'Brien to Lucy, 17 August 1851, MS 8653/27, O'Brien Papers; T. T. Carter, *Harriet Monsell, A Memoir,* p. 7.

53. Mrs. O'Brien to O'Brien, 16 May 1851, MS 8656/1, O'Brien Papers.

54. O'Brien, Journal, 5(cont.):9, 6 September 1851.

55. Kiernan, *Exiles in Australia,* p. 128.

56. Mitchel to O'Brien, 7 September 1851, MS 444/2794, O'Brien Papers; Mitchel, *Jail Journal,* pp. 260, 262–66.

57. Mitchel, *Jail Journal,* pp. 264–66, 275.

58. Ibid., pp. 266–67.

59. O'Brien, Journal, 5(cont.):17–18, 20 October 1851.

60. Ibid., p. 17.

61. Mitchel, *Jail Journal,* p. 267.

62. William Smith O'Brien, "Motives which induced William Smith O'Brien to take up arms against the British Government," pp. 83, 85, 87, MS 464, O'Brien Papers (hereafter cited as O'Brien, "Motives").

63. *Nation* (Dublin), 21 March 1857, p. 474; 20 March 1858, p. 457; 29 May

1858, p. 618; 23 February 1861, p. 412; 14 March 1857, p. 457; 3 April 1858, p. 489; 30 October 1858, p. 137; 6 November 1858, p. 148; 9 July 1859, p. 711; 8 June 1861, p. 645; 24 May 1862, pp. 617–18.

64. Ibid., 6 November 1858, p. 148; 1 May 1858, pp. 556–57.

65. Mitchel, *Jail Journal*, pp. 267–68; Mitchel to O'Brien, 6 October 1852, MS 444/2813, O'Brien Papers; O'Brien, "Motives," pp. 21, 99.

66. Mitchel, *Jail Journal*, pp. 267–68.

67. Smith O'Brien "To the Nobility, Clergy, Members of Parliament, Corporate Bodies, and Gentlemen who have Memorialed in favour of the Irish State Prisoners now Living in Penal Exile in Van Diemen's Land," 14 September 1852, in *Nation* (Dublin), 26 March 1852, pp. 472–73; *Nation* (Dublin), 6 November 1858, pp. 148–49.

68. Mitchel, *Jail Journal*, p. 269.

69. Ibid., pp. 269–70.

70. O'Brien, Journal, 5(cont.): 17–18, 20 October 1851.

71. Mitchel, *Jail Journal*, pp. 271–72; Mrs. Connell to John Martin, 19 August 1851, in Cullen, *Young Ireland in Exile*, pp. 104–5.

72. Mitchel, *Jail Journal*, pp. 272–77.

73. Ibid., p. 278.

74. O'Brien, Journal, 5(cont.): 18–20, 11 November 1851.

75. Ibid., 5:20.

76. Ibid.

77. Ibid., 5:22, 21 November 1851; 5:23, 29 November 1851, O'Brien to Comptroller General, 18 November 1851; 5:23–24, Nairn to O'Brien, 21 November 1851.

Chapter 7: New Hope

1. William Smith O'Brien, Journal of William Smith O'Brien, 6:1, 2 January 1852, William Smith O'Brien Papers (hereafter cited as O'Brien, Journal).

2. Ibid., 6:1–2.

3. Ibid., 6:2.

4. Ibid.

5. Ibid., 6:2–3; 6:33–34, 12 May 1852; 6:12, 28 February 1852.

6. Ibid., 6:4–5, 15 January 1852; James Fenton, *A History of Tasmania*, pp. 227–28.

7. Fenton, *Tasmania*, pp. 227–28, 236–37.

8. Ibid., pp. 238–39; John West, *History of Tasmania*, 1:316–17.

9. O'Brien, Journal, 2:11–15, 18 November 1849; 5(cont.):20–21, 15 November 1851.

10. Ibid., 5(cont.):20.

11. Testimony of John Wilson, passholder in the service of Mr. Meagher, Police Office, Campbell Town, 7 January 1852, Denison to Grey, 27 April 1852, Colonial Office 280/291–9012, London Public Record Office (hereafter cited as PRO); Mrs. Meagher to Julia ——, 11 January 1852, in J. H. Cullen, *Young Ireland in Exile*, pp. 84–85; Robert G. Athearn, *Thomas Francis Meagher: An Irish Revolutionary in America*, p. 24, based on *New York Herald*.

12. Meagher to Duffy, 27 December 1851, in *Nation* (Dublin), 22 May 1852, p. 601; Meagher to Police Magistrate Thomas Mason, 3 January 1852, Denison to Grey, 27 April 1852, CO 280/291–9012, PRO.

13. Sworn statement by Henry Joseph Dureen, Police Office, Campbell Town, 7 January 1852, Denison to Earl Grey, 27 April 1852, CO 280/291–9012, PRO.

14. *Nation* (Dublin), 3 July 1852, p. 698; Thomas Francis Meagher, "Six Weeks in the South Pacific," *Irish News* (New York), 9 April, 14, 21 May 1859; Athearn, *Meagher*, pp. 24–26; *Launceston Examiner*, 14 February 1852, pp. 114–15.

15. Sworn statement by Henry Joseph Dureen, Police Office, Campbell Town, 7 January 1852, Denison to Grey, 27 April 1852, CO 280/291–9012, PRO.

16. *Hobart Town Guardian* quoted in *Nation* (Dublin), 22 May 1852, p. 597; *Launceston Examiner*, 10 January 1852, p. 21.

17. *Hobart Town Guardian* quoted in *Nation* (Dublin), 22 May 1852, p. 597; Denison to Grey, 27 April 1852, CO 280/291–9012, PRO; *Sydney Morning Herald*, 2 March 1852.

18. 10 January 1852, in Sir William Denison, *Varieties of Vice-Regal Life*, pp. 181–82.

19. Martin to O'Doherty, 18 January 1852, MS 10,522, John Martin Papers.

20. Mitchel to O'Brien, 19 January 1852, MS 444/2808, O'Brien Papers.

21. O'Brien, Journal, 6:6, 30 January 1852.

22. O'Doherty to O'Brien, 1852, MS 444/2799, O'Brien Papers.

23. *Nation* (Dublin), 22 November 1851, p. 181.

24. Ibid., 21 February 1852, p. 396.

25. Ibid.

26. Ibid.

27. Ibid.

28. Daniel Webster to Abbott Lawrence, Washington, D.C., 26 December 1851, Harvard University, Houghton Library, Dartmouth College's edition of the Daniel Webster Papers, 035582–035583, in the Manuscript Division, Library of Congress, Washington, D.C.

29. President Fillmore to William H. Romeyn, Esq., 2 February 1852, in *Nation* (Dublin), 28 February 1852, p. 411.

30. *The Congressional Globe*, U.S. Senate, vol. 24, pt. 1, p. 11, 2 December 1851; pp. 407–9, 28 January 1852; p. 418, 29 January 1852; pp. 525–31, 11 February 1852.

31. *Nation* (Dublin), 22 May 1852, p. 601; *Evening Mail* quoted in *Sydney Morning Herald*, 6 October 1852; Henry O'Brien to O'Brien, 26 May 1852, MS 444/2818, O'Brien Papers.

32. *Galway Vindicator* and *Tipperary Free Press* quoted in *Nation* (Dublin), 22 May 1852, p. 597.

33. *Evening Mail* quoted in *Sydney Morning Herald*, 6 October 1852; Henry O'Brien to O'Brien, 26 May 1852, MS 444/2818, O'Brien Papers.

34. *Nation* (Dublin), 22 May 1852, p. 597.

35. Henry O'Brien to O'Brien, 26 May 1852, MS 444/2818, O'Brien Papers.

36. Ibid.

37. Harriet Monsell to O'Brien, 29 May 1852, MS 8656/12, O'Brien Papers.

38. Abbott Lawrence to Daniel Webster, Legation of the United States, London, 23 April 1852, 036597–036604, Webster Papers. Original letter in the Daniel Webster Papers, Manuscript Division, Library of Congress.

39. Ibid.

40. Ibid.

41. Ibid.

42. *Nation* (Dublin), 24 April 1852, p. 536.

43. *Times* (London), 26 April 1852.

44. *Nation* (Dublin), 22 May 1852, p. 597.

45. Ibid.

46. *Munster News* quoted in *Nation* (Dublin), 22 May 1852, p. 597.

47. *Nation* (Dublin), 22 May 1852, p. 601.

48. *Munster News, Limerick Examiner,* *Freeman's Journal, Sun, Cork Examiner, Tipperary Free Press, Galway Vindicator, Newry Examiner* quoted in *Nation* (Dublin), 22 May 1852, p. 597.

49. *Nation* (Dublin), 22 May 1852, p. 601.

50. *Cork Examiner* quoted in *Nation* (Dublin), 22 May 1852, p. 597.

51. *Irish American* quoted in *Nation* (Dublin), 19 June 1852, p. 659.

52. Athearn, *Meagher*, pp. 24–27.

53. *Irish American* quoted in *Nation* (Dublin), 19 June 1852, p. 659.

54. Athearn, *Meagher*, p. 28, based on *New York Herald* and *Irish American*.

55. O'Gorman to O'Brien, 12 December 1852, MS 445/2842, John Dillon to O'Brien, 12 December 1852, MS 445/2841, O'Brien Papers.

56. O'Gorman to O'Brien, 12 December 1852, MS 445/2842, O'Brien Papers.

57. Dillon to O'Brien, 12 December 1852, MS 445/2841, O'Brien Papers.

58. Ibid.

59. O'Gorman to O'Brien, 12 December 1852, MS 445/2842, O'Brien Papers.

60. *Irish American* quoted in *Nation* (Dublin), 19 June 1852, p. 659.

61. Athearn, *Meagher*, p. 29, based on *New York Herald*; note that Mrs. Mitchel was the mother of John Mitchel.

62. *New York Herald* quoted in *Nation* (Dublin), 19 June 1852, p. 659; Meagher to ———, Glen Cove, 5 June 1852, in *Nation* (Dublin), 26 June 1852, p. 685.

63. Statement of P. J. Smyth Re: The Escape of T. F. Meagher, 8 March 1884, MS 8216/2, P. J. Smyth Papers.

64. *Nation* (Dublin), 26 June 1852, p. 682.

65. Ibid.; Athearn, *Meagher*, pp. 29–31, based on *Irish American* and *New York Herald*.

66. *Times* (London), 14 June 1852.

67. O'Brien, Journal, 6:11, 12 February 1852.

68. Ibid., 6:50, 28 June 1852.

69. O'Brien to Lucy O'Brien, 2 May 1852, MS 8653/29, O'Brien Papers.

70. O'Brien, Journal, 6:41, 12 June 1852.

71. Cullen, *Young Ireland in Exile*, p. 85; O'Brien, Journal, 6:47, 15 June 1852. The child's name was Henry Emmet Fitzgerald O'Meagher. Meagher used the name O'Meagher while he lived in Van Diemen's Land.

72. Martin to O'Doherty, incorrectly

dated 26 September 1851 (no doubt it was 26 September 1852), in John Kiernan, *The Irish Exiles in Australia*, pp. 112, 128.

73. O'Brien, Journal, 6:48, 28 June 1852.

74. O'Flaherty to O'Brien, 16 February 1852, MS 444/2810, O'Brien to McCarthy, 5 July 1852, MS 445/2830, McCarthy to O'Brien, 6 July 1852, MS 445/2832, and 21 September 1852, MS 445/2837, O'Brien Papers.

75. O'Brien, Journal, 6:50–55, 28 June 1852.

76. Ibid., 6:65–66, 6 August 1852.

77. Ibid.

78. Ibid., 6(cont.):4–5, 20 September 1852.

79. *Nation* (Dublin), 26 March 1852, pp. 472–73.

80. Ibid.

81. Ibid.

82. Ibid.

83. Ibid.

84. Ibid.

85. O'Brien to O'Doherty, 2 October 1852, MS 10,515/3, O'Brien Papers.

86. Ibid.

Chapter 8: One More Year

1. Virginius to the Editor, 5 September 1851, in *Launceston Examiner*, 13 September 1851, pp. 592–93; Erin-Go-Bragh to the Editor, 6 October 1851, in *Launceston Examiner*, 11 October 1851, p. 669.

2. Kevin B. Nowlan, *The Politics of Repeal*, p. 210.

3. John Mitchel, *Jail Journal*, pp. 433–34.

4. Virginius to the Editor, 5 September 1851, in *Launceston Examiner*, 13 September 1851, pp. 592–93; Erin-Go-Bragh to the Editor, 6 October 1851, in *Launceston Examiner*, 11 October 1851, p. 669.

5. Erin-Go-Bragh to the Editor, 6 October 1851, in *Launceston Examiner*, 11 October 1851, p. 669; *Launceston Examiner*, 7 April 1852, p. 243; J. D. Balfe to the Editor of the *Hobart Town Advertiser*, in *Launceston Examiner*, 14 April 1852, p. 260; J. D. Balfe to the Editor, 30 April 1852, in *Launceston Examiner*, 5 May 1852, pp. 312–13.

6. Kevin I. O'Doherty to *Hobart Town Advertiser*, in *Launceston Examiner*, 8 May 1852, p. 321; O'Donoghue to the Editor, 5 August 1852, in *Launceston Examiner*, 14 August 1852, p. 553.

7. J. H. Cullen, *Young Ireland in Exile*, p. 123; *Sydney Advocate* quoted in the *Na-*

tion (Dublin), 22 January 1853, p. 326.

8. *Sydney Advocate* quoted in *Nation* (Dublin), 22 January 1853, p. 326; O'Brien to the Editor of the *Hobart Town Guardian*, 23 August 1852, in *Nation* (Dublin), 22 January 1853, p. 326.

9. William Smith O'Brien, Journal of William Smith O'Brien, 6(cont.):11–12, 26 October 1852, William Smith O'Brien Papers (hereafter cited as O'Brien, Journal).

10. James Fenton, *A History of Tasmania*, 1:241; Denison to Mrs. Denison, 13 October 1852, in Sir William Denison, *Varieties of Vice-Regal Life*, p. 197.

11. O'Brien, Journal, 6(cont.):12, 26 October 1852. Van Diemen's Land had representative government, not responsible government.

12. *Melbourne Argus*, 14 October 1852; *Launceston Examiner*, 25 September 1852, pp. 651–52; *Sydney Morning Herald*, 10 July 1852.

13. *Sydney Morning Herald*, 16 April 1853.

14. Fenton, *Tasmania*, 1:245; *Melbourne Argus*, 7 May 1853.

15. *Sydney Morning Herald*, 1 January 1853; *Melbourne Argus*, 2 February 1853.

16. *Colonial Times* quoted in *Melbourne Argus*, 12 February 1853.

17. Denison to Sir J. S. Pakington, 23 March 1853, Colonial Office 280/305–7876, London Public Record Office (hereafter cited as PRO).

18. *Launceston Examiner*, 29 October 1853, p. 50.

19. Ibid.

20. Ibid.

21. Ibid.

22. Ibid.

23. *Melbourne Argus*, 14 January 1853; *Sydney Morning Herald*, Supplement, 12 February 1853.

24. *Melbourne Argus*, 18 January 1853.

25. *Launceston Examiner*, 29 October 1853, p. 50.

26. O'Donoghue to Hawksley, 3 February 1853, *People's Advocate*, quoted in *Nation* (Dublin), 9 July 1853, pp. 715–16.

27. Ibid.

28. *Launceston Examiner*, 29 September 1853, p. 50.

29. Ibid.; Cullen, *Young Ireland in Exile*, p. 124.

30. *Melbourne Argus*, 12 February 1853.

31. Denison to Mrs. Denison, 28 February 1853, in Denison, *Varieties*, p. 210; Denison to Sir J. S. Pakington, 16 March

1853, CO 280/305–7870, PRO.

32. *South Australian Register*, 15 June 1853, p. 625.

33. Fenton, *Tasmania*, 1:245.

34. Denison to Mrs. Denison, 2 May 1853, in Denison, *Varieties*, p. 211.

35. *Sydney Morning Herald*, 1 January 1853; *Colonial Times* quoted in *Melbourne Argus*, 9 March, 8 June 1853; *Melbourne Argus*, 8 February 1853.

36. Fenton, *Tasmania*, 1:251–52; *South Australian Register*, 30 July 1853, p. 104.

37. *Launceston Examiner*, 13 November 1852, p. 763; O'Brien, Journal, 6(cont.):18, 17 November 1852.

38. O'Brien, Journal, 6:18–20, 17 November 1852.

39. Ibid., pp. 20–21.

40. Mitchel, *Jail Journal*, p. 300.

41. Ibid.

42. Ibid., pp. 300–301.

43. Ibid., pp. 301–2.

44. Ibid., p. 302.

45. Ibid., pp. 302–3.

46. Ibid., pp. 303–4, 310.

47. Ibid., pp. 303–4.

48. O'Brien to Lucy O'Brien, 12 January 1853, MS 8653/29, O'Brien Papers.

49. O'Brien to Lucy O'Brien, 19 September 1852, MS 8653/28, O'Brien Papers.

50. O'Brien to Lucy O'Brien, 6 June 1853, MS 8653/29, O'Brien Papers.

51. O'Brien to Lucy O'Brien, 1 June 1853, MS 8653/29, O'Brien Papers.

52. Edward O'Brien to O'Brien, 8 August 1852, MS 8656, O'Brien Papers.

53. O'Brien to Lucy O'Brien, 29 January 1853, MS 8653/29, O'Brien Papers.

54. Cullen, *Young Ireland in Exile*, pp. 85–86; Robert G. Athearn, *Thomas Francis Meagher: An Irish Revolutionary in America*, p. 42.

55. Duffy to O'Brien, 7 November 1852, MS 5758/108, Charles Gavan Duffy Papers.

56. O'Brien to Duffy, 22 November 1852, MS 2642/3488, O'Brien Papers.

57. Mitchel, *Jail Journal*, p. 309.

58. Ibid.

59. Ibid., pp. 310–11.

60. *Hobart Town Courier* quoted in *Nation* (Dublin), 29 October 1853, p. 115; *Melbourne Argus*, 18 June 1853.

61. Melbourne correspondent of *Nation* (Dublin) to Duffy, 1 July 1853, *Times* (London), 3 October 1853.

62. *South Australian Register*, 30 June 1853, p. 677.

63. Mitchel, *Jail Journal*, pp. 309–38, 451–53.

64. Ibid., pp. 337–38.

65. Ibid., pp. 340, 342.

66. P. J. Smyth to O'Brien, 5 August 1853, MS 445/2846, O'Brien Papers.

67. Ibid.

68. Ibid.

69. P. J. Smyth to O'Doherty, 17 August 1853, in Kiernan, *Exiles in Australia*, pp. 119–20.

70. Mitchel, *Jail Journal*, pp. 343–44, 349.

71. *Times* (London), 29 March 1853.

72. *Nation* (Dublin), 9 April 1853, pp. 504–5.

73. Sir C. D. Norreys to O'Brien, 7 August 1853, MS 445/2847, O'Brien Papers.

74. Ibid.

75. Ibid.

76. *Nation* (Dublin), quoted in *Times* (London), 29 August 1853, p. 5.

77. *Times* (London), 29 August 1853, p. 5.

78. Ibid., 31 August 1853, p. 7.

79. Ibid.

80. Ibid., 5 September 1853, p. 7; *Nation* (Dublin) quoted in *Times* (London), 5 September 1853, p. 8.

81. *Nation* (Dublin), 24 September 1853, p. 46; 10 September 1853, p. 8.

82. Ibid., 10 September 1853, p. 8; *Tuam Herald* and *Wexford Guardian* quoted in *Nation* (Dublin), 24 September 1853, p. 46.

Chapter 9: The Pardon

1. Martin to O'Doherty, 10 August 1853, MS 10,522, John Martin Papers; Martin to O'Brien, 5 September 1853, MS 445/2848, William Smith O'Brien Papers; Martin to O'Doherty, 30 November 1853, in John Kiernan, *The Irish Exiles in Australia*, pp. 129–30.

2. Martin to O'Brien, 5 September 1853, MS 445/2848, O'Brien Papers.

3. O'Brien to Martin, 16 October 1853, MS 8653, O'Brien Papers.

4. O'Brien to Edward O'Brien, n.d., MS 444/2704, O'Brien to Lucy O'Brien, 27 June 1853, MS 8653/28, O'Brien Papers.

5. Edward O'Brien to O'Brien, 6 November 1853, MS 8656, O'Brien Papers.

6. O'Brien to Lucy O'Brien, 17 April 1854, MS 8653/39, O'Brien Papers.

7. Lucy O'Brien to O'Brien, 1854, MS 8654, O'Brien Papers.

8. Grace O'Brien to O'Brien, 20 July 1852, MS 8656/9, Anne Martineau to O'Brien, 31 August 1852, MS 8656/4, and 24 December 1851, MS 8656, Katherine Harris to O'Brien, 2 March 1852, MS 8656/11, Mrs. O'Brien to O'Brien, 31 January 1852, MS 8656/4, O'Brien Papers.

9. Lucy Josephine O'Brien to O'Brien, 3 January, 26 July, 16 October 1852, and 14 April 1853, MS 8656/10, Lucius Henry O'Brien to O'Brien, 3 February 1852, MS 8656, O'Brien to Willy O'Brien, 6 July 1852, 2 September 1853, MS 8655/7, Robert D. O'Brien to O'Brien, 14 February 1852, MS 8656, O'Brien Papers.

10. Charles Murrough O'Brien to O'Brien, Friday, MS 8656, O'Brien Papers.

11. William Smith O'Brien, Journal of William Smith O'Brien, 6(cont.):37, 14 February 1853, O'Brien Papers (hereafter cited as O'Brien, Journal).

12. John Mitchel, *Jail Journal*, pp. 349, 350; *Times* (London), 14 December 1853; McManus to O'Brien, February 1853, MS 445/2844, O'Brien Papers.

13. Mitchel, *Jail Journal*, p. 350.

14. Denis Gwynn, "Thomas Francis Meagher," speech, p. 42; *Sydney Morning Herald*, 16 May 1853.

15. *New York Tribune* quoted in *Times* (London), 13 December 1853; Mitchel, *Jail Journal*, pp. 362–63.

16. Mitchel, *Jail Journal*, p. 367.

17. *New York Tribune* quoted in *Times* (London), 13 December 1853.

18. Mitchel, *Jail Journal*, p. 368.

19. P. J. Smyth to O'Doherty, 28 February 1856, in Kiernan, *Exiles in Australia*, pp. 181–82; Mitchel, *Jail Journal*, p. 371.

20. Mitchel, *Jail Journal*, p. 376.

21. Ibid., pp. 375–76; Robert G. Athearn, *Thomas Francis Meagher: An Irish Revolutionary in America*, p. 42, based on *New York Herald*, 4 December 1853.

22. Athearn, *Meagher*, p. 42, based on *New York Herald*, 10 February 1854.

23. Mitchel, *Jail Journal*, pp. 375, 377.

24. Ibid., pp. 378–79.

25. Ibid., pp. 379–87; *Nation* (Dublin), 4 February 1854, p. 347.

26. *Times* (London), 3 October, 27 December 1853, p. 6.

27. *Nation* (Dublin), 17 December 1853, p. 233.

28. *Times* (London), 30 December 1853.

29. Athearn, *Meagher*, pp. 40–41, taken from *New York Herald*, 6 August 1853.

30. *Nation* (Dublin), 18 February 1854, p. 380.

31. *Citizen* (New York), 28 January 1854, p. 53, and 18 February 1854, p. 103.

32. Athearn, *Meagher*, p. 46, taken from *New York Herald*, 1 February 1854; *Citizen* (New York), 2 February 1854, p. 79.

33. *Liverpool Courier* quoted in *Nation* (Dublin), 18 February 1854, p. 376.

34. *Nation* (Dublin), 25 February 1854, p. 387; *Ledger* quoted in *Nation* (Dublin), 15 April 1854, p. 504.

35. Great Britain, *Hansard Parliamentary Debates*, 3d series, 130:1112–13 (hereafter cited as *Hansard*).

36. *Nation* (Dublin), 25 February 1854, p. 387.

37. Ibid., 4 March 1854, p. 407.

38. Grace O'Brien to O'Brien, 26 February 1854, MS 445/2867, O'Brien Papers.

39. *Nation* (Dublin), 25 February 1854, p. 392.

40. *Observer* quoted in *Nation* (Dublin), 4 March 1854, p. 407.

41. *Nation* (Dublin), 11 March 1854, p. 419.

42. *Times* (London), 8 March 1854.

43. *Nation* (Dublin), 25 March 1854, pp. 456, 460, and 4 February 1854, p. 347; Mitchel, *Jail Journal*, pp. 428–30.

44. *Nation* (Dublin), 15 April 1854, supp.

45. Ibid.

46. Ibid., 10 June 1854, p. 633, and 29 April 1854, pp. 537–38.

47. Athearn, *Meagher*, p. 47.

48. *Nation* (Dublin), 13 May 1854, p. 568.

49. Ibid., 27 May 1854, p. 604.

50. Ibid., 10 June 1854, p. 633.

51. Ibid.

52. *Irish American* and *New York Truth Teller* quoted in *Nation* (Dublin), 27 May 1854, p. 604.

53. O'Brien to O'Doherty, 29 April 1854, in Kiernan, *Exiles in Australia*, pp. 130–31.

54. Ibid.

55. O'Brien to Lucy O'Brien, 17 April 1854, MS 2642, O'Brien Papers.

56. *Sydney Empire* quoted in *Nation* (Dublin), 12 August 1854, p. 771; *Sydney Morning Herald*, 19 May 1854; *Melbourne Argus*, 16 May 1854, p. 2.

57. *Courier* quoted in *Citizen* (New York), 11 November 1854, p. 700.

58. P. J. Smyth to O'Brien, 16 May

1854, MS 445/2869, O'Brien Papers.

59. P. J. Smyth to O'Doherty, 28 February 1856, in Kiernan, *Exiles in Australia*, pp. 181–83; *Melbourne Argus* quoted in *Nation* (Dublin), 12 August 1854, p. 771.

60. Launceston Committee to O'Brien, 23 May 1854, MS 445/2871, O'Brien Papers.

61. *Limerick Chronicle* quoted in *Times* (London), 6 October 1854; O'Brien to Martin, 29 June 1854, MS 3226/107, Rev. William Hickey Papers.

62. Denison to Mrs. Denison, 26, 27 June 1854, in Sir William Denison, *Varieties of Vice-Regal Life*, pp. 247–49.

63. O'Brien to Palmerston, 8 December 1856, MS 445/2936; O'Brien to Lucy O'Brien, 28 June 1854, MS 8653/30, O'Brien Papers; 27 June 1854, in Denison, *Varieties*, p. 248.

64. O'Brien to Lucy O'Brien, 28 June 1854, MS 8653/30, O'Brien Papers.

65. Denison to the Duke of Newcastle, 13 September 1854, in Denison, *Varieties*, pp. 254–55.

66. 12 September 1854, in Denison, *Varieties*, pp. 256–57.

67. *Courier* quoted in *Melbourne Argus*, 10 July 1854, and in *Nation* (Dublin), 21 October 1851, pp. 86–87; *Launceston Examiner*, 11 July 1854, p. 2.

68. *Launceston Examiner*, 11 July 1854, p. 2.

69. *Melbourne Argus*, 18 July 1854.

70. Martin to ———, 12 July 1854, in *Nation* (Dublin), 28 October 1854, p. 107.

71. O'Brien to Lucy O'Brien, 12 July 1854, MS 8653/30, O'Brien Papers; *Melbourne Argus*, 15 July 1854.

72. *Melbourne Argus*, 15 July 1854. The vase is currently on display in the National Museum of Ireland.

73. Denison to Mrs. Denison, 27 June 1854, in Denison, *Varieties*, p. 248.

74. *Citizen* (New York), 4 November 1854, pp. 694–95.

75. Ibid.

76. Ibid.

77. Ibid.

78. *Launceston Examiner*, 22 July 1854, p. 2.

79. Mitchel, *Jail Journal*, p. 400.

80. *Citizen* (New York), 4 November 1854, p. 696.

81. *Nation* (Dublin), 12 August 1854, p. 776.

82. John Martin to Mrs. Williams, 3 January 1855, in P. L. Brown, ed., *Clyde Company Papers*, 6:230–34; P. A. Sillard, *The Life and Letters of John Martin*, p. 156.

83. Martin to the Connells, 5 December 1854, MS 3224, Thomas Francis Meagher Papers.

84. Sillard, *Life of John Martin*, p. 156; O'Brien to Lucy O'Brien, 28 June 1854, MS 8653/30, O'Brien Papers; *Times* (London), 4 November 1854; W. S. O'Brien to the editors of *Galignani's Messenger*, 23 November 1855, in *Times* (London), 27 November 1854.

85. *Dictionary of National Biography*, edited by Sir Leslie Stephen and Sir Sidney Lee, 14:781.

86. O'Brien to Duffy, n.d., MS 2642/3489, O'Brien Papers.

87. Duffy to O'Brien, 2 December 1854, MS 445/2877, O'Brien Papers. Duffy did immigrate to Australia. In 1871 he became prime minister of Victoria and in 1873 he was knighted by Queen Victoria. Mitchel, *Jail Journal*, p. 438.

88. O'Brien to Duffy, n.d., MS 5757/419, Charles Gavan Duffy Papers.

89. Ibid.

90. O'Gorman to O'Brien, 5 November 1854, MS 445/2874, O'Brien Papers.

91. Ibid.

92. Martin to Mary Anne, 22 December 1854, in Kiernan, *Exiles in Australia*, pp. 170–71.

93. John O'Shanassy to O'Brien, January 1855, MS 445/2880, O'Brien Papers; John Mitchel to Mrs. Williams, 24 July 1855 in Brown, ed., *Clyde Company Papers*, 6:275–81; Dunne to O'Brien, 13 September 1855, MS 445/2885, O'Brien Papers; Kiernan, *Exiles in Australia*, p. 131; P. J. Smyth to O'Doherty, 28 February 1856, in Kiernan, *Exiles in Australia*, pp. 181–83.

94. Duffy to O'Brien, 2 April 1855, MS 445/2855, O'Brien Papers.

95. Ibid.

96. "Newspaper cutting in favour of memorial & Mr Smith O'Brien's release"; John Brady to Sir C.D.O.J. Norreys, 25 May 1855, and Norreys to Palmerston, 26 May 1855, HMC, GC/NO/627–Broadlands MS 12889, Palmerston Papers.

97. *Citizen*, 8 September 1855, pp. 567–69; 7 July 1855, p. 425.

98. John Mitchel to Mrs. Williams, 24 July 1855, in Brown, ed., *Clyde Company Papers*, 6:275–81; O'Doherty to O'Brien, 2 August 1855, MS 445/2886, O'Brien Papers; J. H. Cullen, *Young Ireland in Exile*,

p. 132; Kiernan, *Exiles in Australia*, p. 132.

99. Kiernan, *Exiles in Australia*, p. 132.

100. *Times* (London), 13 March 1856, p. 8; John Francis Maguire to the Editor, 9 May 1856, in *Times* (London), 10 May 1856, p. 12.

101. *Hansard*, 142:262–64; O'Brien to Palmerston, 8 December 1856, MS 445/2936, O'Brien Papers.

102. The O'Dohertys' first child was born on 26 May 1856; in October 1856, O'Doherty took his primary examination to qualify for a medical license and in June 1857 he took and passed his finals. See Kiernan, *Exiles in Australia*, p. 132.

103. Sillard, *Life of John Martin*, pp. 156–57.

104. O'Brien to Palmerston, 8 December 1856, MS 445/2936, O'Brien Papers; O'Brien to Rev. P. Hickey, 18 July 1856, in *Nation* (Dublin), 26 July 1856.

Chapter 10: The Finale

1. Desmond Ryan, *The Fenian Chief*, pp. 170–71; *Dictionary of National Biography*, edited by Sir Leslie Stephen and Sir Sidney Lee, 12:673 (hereafter cited as *DNB*); William D'Arcy, *The Fenian Movement in the United States: 1858–1886*, p. 19, quoting *Boston Pilot*.

2. *Nation* (Dublin), 12 October 1861, p. 107.

3. D'Arcy, *Fenian Movement*, p. 19.

4. Ryan, *The Fenian Chief*, pp. 22–34, 43–49, 170–79.

5. Denis Gwynn, "Thomas Francis Meagher," speech, p. 43; *DNB*, 13:195; *Nation* (Dublin), 26 October 1861, pp. 132–34; John Mitchel, *Jail Journal*, p. 444.

6. Mitchel, *Jail Journal*, pp. 405–6; P. L. Brown, ed., *Clyde Company Papers*, 6:275; O'Brien to Mitchel, 4 October 1858, in *Nation* (Dublin), 20 November 1858, p. 189.

7. *DNB*, 13:506; Mitchel, *Jail Journal*, p. 406; William Smith O'Brien, Journal of William Smith O'Brien, 1861, Private Collection of Mr. and Mrs. Brendan O'Brien (hereafter cited as O'Brien, Journal, PC).

8. *DNB*, 13:506–7.

9. John Kiernan, *The Irish Exiles in Australia*, pp. 132–34; *DNB*, supp. 3, p. 40.

10. Martin to Miss Connell, 15 December 1858, MS 3224, Thomas Francis Meagher Papers.

11. P. A. Sillard, *The Life and Letters of John Martin*, p. 157.

12. Martin to Miss Thompson, December 1860, in Sillard, *Life of John Martin*, p. 160.

13. *Nation* (Dublin), 6 November 1858, p. 148.

14. *DNB*, 12:1171.

15. *Nation* (Dublin), 4 January 1862, p. 299.

16. *Times* (London), 2 August 1856, p. 8.

17. *Nation* (Dublin), 26 July 1856.

18. Ibid.

19. Ibid., 6 November 1858, p. 148.

20. *Times* (London), 19 September 1856, p. 6, and 2 August 1856, p. 8.

21. *Nation* (Dublin), 20 September 1856, p. 54.

22. Stephen Gwynn, *Charlotte Grace O'Brien*, p. 28; Ryan, *The Fenian Chief*, pp. 67–73; comments by Dr. Brendan O'Brien and the Reverend Aubrey Gwynn, descendants of William Smith O'Brien.

23. *Nation* (Dublin), 8 December 1860, pp. 236–37.

24. *Times* (London), 29 December 1856, p. 9.

25. Ibid.

26. Ibid.

27. Ibid.

28. *Nation* (Dublin), 6 November 1858, pp. 148–49.

29. Ibid., 4 January 1862, p. 299.

30. Ibid.

31. Ibid., 17 April 1858, p. 522.

32. Ibid., 9 July 1859, p. 711; 6 November 1858, p. 148; 14 March 1857, p. 458.

33. Ibid., 8 June 1861, p. 645; 6 November 1858, pp. 148–49.

34. Ibid., 21 March 1857, p. 474; 20 March 1858, p. 457.

35. Ibid.

36. Ibid., 21 March 1857, p. 474; 30 October 1858, p. 137; 3 October 1857, p. 76.

37. Ibid., 3 October 1857, p. 76; 20 March 1858, p. 457; 14 March 1857, pp. 457–58; 3 April 1858, p. 489.

38. Ibid., 14 March 1857, pp. 457–58; 22 October 1859, p. 118; 15 May 1858, pp. 585–86.

39. Ibid., 17 April 1858, pp. 521–22; 15 May 1858, pp. 585–86.

40. Ibid., 23 February 1861, p. 412; 3 April 1858, p. 489.

41. Ibid., 30 October 1858, p. 137; 4 January 1862, pp. 299–300; 23 February 1861, p. 412.

42. Ibid., 30 March 1861, p. 494; 1

September 1860, p. 843; 6 November 1858, p. 148.

43. Ibid., 27 September 1862, p. 73.

44. Ibid., 26 November 1859, pp. 197–99; 3 December 1859, pp. 213–15.

45. O'Brien, Journal, PC, 1861.

46. Ibid.

47. *Nation* (Dublin), 1 September 1860, p. 843.

48. Ibid., 8 December 1860, pp. 236–37.

49. O'Brien, Journal, PC, 1861.

50. *Nation* (Dublin), 12 August 1861, p. 101; 12 January 1861, p. 313.

51. Ibid., 26 October 1861, pp. 139–40.

52. Ibid., 26 November 1859, p. 199.

53. Ibid., 26 October 1861, pp. 139–40; 4 January 1862, pp. 299–300.

54. *DNB*, 14:781.

55. John Francis Maguire to O'Brien, 2 September 1857, MS 445/2977, J. E. Pigott to O'Brien, 18 August 1857, MS 445/2976, William Smith O'Brien Papers.

56. *Nation* (Dublin), 13 April 1861, p. 525.

57. *Cork Examiner* quoted in *Nation* (Dublin), 6 April 1861, p. 510.

58. *Nation* (Dublin), 6 April 1861, p. 510.

59. Ibid., 12 January 1861, p. 313.

60. Ibid., 13 April 1861, p. 525; 22 February 1862, p. 407; 29 May 1858, pp. 617–18; 12 January 1861, p. 313.

61. Ibid., 12 January 1861, p. 313.

62. Ibid., 25 June 1864, pp. 696–97; private notes of Brendan O'Brien.

63. *Times* (London), 20 June 1864, p. 5; *Nation* (Dublin), 15 February 1862, p. 393, and 22 February 1862, p. 407; *DNB*, 14:781; private notes of Brendan O'Brien.

64. Private notes of Brendan O'Brien; *DNB*, 14:781; *Nation* (Dublin), 22 February 1862, p. 407.

65. *Times* (London), 18 June 1864, p. 14; 20 June 1864, p. 5.

66. *Nation* (Dublin), 25 June 1864, pp. 693–97.

67. *Times* (London), 24 June 1864, p. 12.

68. Turner to Sir Thomas, 22 June 1864, MS 7698, Thomas Aiskew Larcon Papers.

69. *Nation* (Dublin), 25 June 1864, pp. 693–95; *Times* (London), 24 June 1864, p. 12.

70. Ibid.; comments of Brendan O'Brien.

71. *Nation* (Dublin), 25 June 1864, pp. 693–95.

72. Ibid.

73. *Times* (London), 27 June 1864, p. 6.

74. Notation on Committee formed to collect money for a statue to O'Brien, MS 7698, Larcon Papers.

Bibliography

Books

Athearn, Robert G. *Thomas Francis Meagher: An Irish Revolutionary in America*. Boulder: University of Colorado Press, 1949.
Brown, P. L., ed. *Clyde Company Papers*. Vol. 6. London: Oxford University Press, 1968.
Carter, Reverend T. T. *Harriet Monsell, A Memoir*. London: J. Masters & Co., 1884.
Cullen, J. H. *Young Ireland in Exile*. Dublin: Talbot Press, 1929.
D'Arcy, William. *The Fenian Movement in the United States: 1858–1886*. Washington, D.C.: The Catholic University of America Press, 1947.
Denison, Sir William. *Varieties of Vice-Regal Life*. Vol. 1. London: Longmans, Green, and Co., 1870.
Duffy, Charles Gavan. *Four Years of Irish History*. New York: Cassell, Petter, Galpin & Co., 1882.
Fenton, James. *A History of Tasmania*. Vol. 1. Hobart, Tasmania: J. Walch and Sons, 1884.
Gwynn, Stephen. *Charlotte Grace O'Brien*. Dublin: Maunsel and Co., Ltd., 1909.
Kiernan, John. *The Irish Exiles in Australia*. Dublin: Clonmore and Reynolds, 1954.
Meagher, Thomas F. *Meagher of the Sword*. Edited by Arthur Griffith. Dublin: Gill, 1916.
———. *Speeches on the Legislative Independence of Ireland*. New York: Redfield, 1853.
Mitchel, John. *Jail Journal*. Dublin: M. H. Gill & Son, Ltd., 1913.
Nowlan, Kevin B. *The Politics of Repeal*. London: Routledge & Kegan Paul, 1965.
O'Brien, Donough. *The History of the O'Briens*. London: B. T. Batsford, 1949.
O'Connell, Daniel. *Correspondence of Daniel O'Connell*. Vol. 2. Edited by William John Fitzpatrick. London: John Murray, 1888.
Ryan, Desmond. *The Fenian Chief*. Coral Gables: University of Miami Press, 1967.
Sillard, P. A. *The Life and Letters of John Martin*. 2d ed. Dublin: James Duffy and Co., 1901.
Webb, Alfred. *Memoir of John Mitchel*. Dublin: Printed by the A———Y G———L, 1849.
West, John. *History of Tasmania*. Vols. 1–2. Launceston, Tasmania: Henry Dowling, 1852.

Dictionaries and Guides

Dictionary of National Biography. Edited by Sir Leslie Stephen and Sir Sidney Lee. Vols. 12, 13, 14. London: Oxford University Press, 1917. Reprinted 1949–1950.
Dictionary of National Biography. Edited by Sir Sidney Lee. 2d supp. Vol. 3. London: Smith, Elder & Co., 1912.
World Guide. New York: Rand McNally & Co., 1953.

Documents

Great Britain. Colonial Office Records. London. London Public Record Office. Correspondence to and from the Lieutenant Governor of Van Diemen's Land and the Colonial Secretary in London, 1849–1854. CO 280/249, 250, 255, 258, 259, 263, 264, 273, 274, 275, 276, 284, 289, 291, 300, 305, 408/32.

Great Britain. *Hansard Parliamentary Debates*. 3d series. Vols. 97 (1848), 98 (1848), 106 (1849), 111 (1850), 117 (1851), 130 (1854), 142 (1856).
United States. *The Congressional Globe*. U.S. Senate. Vol. 24 (1852).

Manuscript Sources

Belfast. Public Record Office of Northern Ireland

Diary of John Martin. MS D. 560.

Dublin. National Library of Ireland

Charles Gavan Duffy Papers. MS 5757–MS 5758.
Rev. William Hickey Papers. MS 3226.
Thomas Aiskew Larcon Papers. Fenian Miscellaneous 2. MS 7698.
John Martin Papers. MS 10, 522.
Thomas F. Meagher Papers. MS 3900, MS 3224.
William Smith O'Brien Papers. MS 443, MS 444, MS 445, MS 2642, MS 8653, MS 8654, MS 8655, MS 8656, MS 10,515.
———. Journal of William Smith O'Brien. Parts 1–6. MS 3923.
———. "Motives which induced Smith O'Brien to take up arms against the British Government." 1848. MS 464.
———. Proceedings in relation to the Estate of William Smith O'Brien. 1862.
———. Official Records of Prisoners. MS 13,610.
P. J. Smyth Papers. Statement of P. J. Smyth re the escape of T. F. Meagher. MS 8216.
Young Ireland Papers. Letters to and from the Young Irelanders. MS 3226.

Dublin. Private Collection of Dr. and Mrs. Brendan O'Brien

William Smith O'Brien Papers and Journals.

London. British Museum

Palmerston Papers. GC/NO/627–Broadlands MS 12889.

Washington, D.C. Library of Congress. Manuscripts Division

Daniel Webster Papers. MS 036597–036604, MS 035582–035583.

Newspapers

Argus (Melbourne), 1849–1854.
Citizen (New York), 1854–1855.
Irish News (New York), 1859.
Launceston Examiner (Launceston), 1849–1854. CO 284/18–23, London Public Record Office.
Morning Herald (Sydney), 1850–1854.
Nation (Dublin), 1843–1864.
Nation (New York), 1849–1850.
South Australian Register (Adelaide), 1849–1853.
Times (London), 1848–1864.

Speeches and Articles

Gwynn, Denis. "Smith O'Brien and the Secession." *Studies* 36. Dublin, 1947.
———. "Thomas Francis Meagher." Speech delivered at University College, Cork, National University of Ireland, 17 July 1961.

Index